GW01035706

THE
GENTLEMAN'S
Recreation

THE
GENTLEMAN'S
Recreation

by
NICHOLAS COX

With a new introduction
by
JAMES WENTWORTH DAY

EP PUBLISHING LIMITED
1973

ISBN 0 85409 897 6

Please address all enquiries to EP Publishing Limited
(address as above)

Printed in Great Britain by
The Scolar Press Limited, Menston, Yorkshire

INTRODUCTION

by JAMES WENTWORTH DAY

former Acting Editor to "The Field", Editor of
"The Illustrated Sporting & Dramatic News", and
Author of "The Modern Fowler", "The Modern Shooter",
"Sporting Adventure", "King George V As A Sportsman",
"The Dog Lover's Pocket Book", "The Angler's Pocket Book", etc.

Nicholas Cox ranks high in the noble gallery of British sporting writers. He comes not far short of Dame Juliana Berners and Turberville. He is far above the ruck of such 18th and 19th century Grub Street scribblers as Pierce Egan and his like who collected snippets of sporting gossip and frequently inaccurate "instructions" and then chucked the lot into volumes with impressive titles and lick-spittle dedications to noblemen.

Cox, it is true, collected much of his information from other people but reading it one feels instinctively that he went to the right men, men who knew their stuff. In short, Cox, an Oxfordshire man, probably of the lesser country gentry was, we may assume, brought up to country life and rural sports. They were in his blood. He was a man of the land with that natural philosophy, love of beauty, of nature and of animals, which is part of the make-up of the true sportsman.

Reading him you feel that here was a man who spoke what he truly felt when he said; "Hunting neither remits the Minde to Sloath nor Softness nor (if it be used with moderation) hardens it to inhumanity; but rather inclines men to good Acquaintance and generous Society." That sums up the benefits of hunting to mind and body. It emphasises that the true sportsman is not inhumane, nor a sadist.

Not even the most rabid anti-sport crank could quarrel with our author of 1677 when he wrote this; "It is no small advantage to be enured to bear Hunger, Thirst and Weariness from ones Childhood; to take up a timely habit of quitting ones Bed early, and loving to sit well and safe upon an horse."

Those simple precepts mean all the difference between the softness of the townsman of today who never gets his feet wet, never walks if he can go on wheels, breathes centrally heated thrice-breathed air and would fall off a horse if he sat on it, and the countryman brought up to the sports of the field, particularly hunting. The first is usually middle-aged at forty, has a coronary at fifty and is an old man thereafter, whereas the countryman, even today, is still fit at seventy and more.

Thus, the precepts, and, to a large extent, the advice of Nicholas Cox are not merely pleasant antique reading to us in this Age of Urban Ugliness, The Era of Permissive Decay, but they make sense.

Much of what he has to say about hunting, and particularly falconry, now becoming increasingly popular, is applicable today.

The shooting man no longer fires his gun to frighten wildfowl into the nets he has already staked out on nearby Fens and rivers. Nor does he set springes for snipe and plover as Fenmen did in my youth in Cambridgeshire. Few of us, except for a few antique-minded cranks of whom I am one, still use muzzle-loading fowling pieces five or six feet long, but for my own part I am now fired by Mr. Cox with the desire to make a canvas stalking horse and see what sort of luck it will bring against the wild geese which pull up our spring wheat, and the mallard and wigeon which sit out all day on flooded cattle marshes.

It is not so very long in years since that fine old Essex wildfowler "Admiral" Bill Wyatt of Mersea Island used a cow as a stalking horse when he set out to poach hares on Old Hall marshes. On one occasion he fired straight under the cow's belly at a sitting hare. He got the hare. The cow was airborne for an instant second. All four legs left the earth and, as William remarked, "She'd have won the National that day."

His natural enemy, Bill Fell, the marsh keeper, turned the tables a few weeks later by also using a cow as a stalking horse to approach, identify and apprehend a bunch of cheerful web-footed poachers from Mersea. What Nicholas advocated in 1677 was perfectly applicable in 1935, and is so today.

In my boyhood days East Anglian poachers and bird-catchers, who caught small song-birds for the now-illegal trade in them, which flourished in the East End of London and country pubs, used bird-lime, with which they smeared the roosting places of the birds. Once the bird alighted it stuck fast. Bird lime was sold ready-made in pots by ironmongers, back-street gun-makers and others. Nicholas Cox gives you the full recipe at length and even tells you how to take wood pigeons, magpies, crows, rooks and kites thereby.

Kites today are rare and protected, but pigeons increase and crows and magpies are a menace. All three are un-protected.

I am intrigued when Cox tells us that a heron will do more mischief in one week than an otter will do in three months. He quotes a man who shot a heron and found seventeen carp in its belly. They must have been very small carplets. Another man found that his tame heron would eat fifty small roach and dace in a day. These grim figures do not destroy one's love for the heron, that magnificent medieval survivor which gives dignity to the stream and windblown beauty to the sky.

His instructions for the care of hawks, including hair-raising cures for their diseases, should be read to be believed. None-the-less, not all of them are to be dismissed as antique flights of fancy. In Cox's day hawking was the sport of kings and noblemen, with a thousand years or so of history behind it. Cox could not afford to be inaccurate in such an age.

His list of "Terms of Art in Faulconry" are fascinating and to a large extent still in use today. That applies also to the several pages of "Hunters Terms", which cover everything from the names of deer at all ages, their "lodgings", "dis-lodging", noises at rutting times, terms for copulation, ditto for "Footing and Treading", otherwise footmarks, together with the terms for the noises of hounds, the names of hounds and beagles, most of which spring splendidly to the tongue, and the notes of the horn.

The book is packed with practical information, much of which still endures in practice today. It is equally full of fanciful beliefs and hair-raising veterinary advice which would give any good vet nightmares for a week. If, for example, your spaniel is bitten by a fox, Nicholas Cox solemnly advises you to; "anoint it with Oyl wherein Earth-worms and Rue have been boiled together. If by a mad Dog, let him lap twice or thrice of the broth of Germander, and eat the Germander too boiled.

"Others bore the Skin of his Neck through with a hot-Iron just betwixt his Ears, so as the fire may touch both sides of the Hole made: after that, plucking up the Skin of the Dog's Shoulders and Flanks backwards, thrust it through with a hot-Iron in like manner: by giving the Venom this vent, it is a ready way to cure him.

"To help a Spaniel that hath lost his sense of Smelling.

"Spaniels, sometimes, by reason of too much rest and grease, or some other accident, do lose their sense of Smelling, so as they cannot spring or retrive a Fowl after their usual manner: To recover it again, take Agarick two drams, Sal Gemma one scruple; beath these into powder, and incorporate them with Oxymel, making a Pill as big as a Nut, cover it with Butter, and give it the Dog by fair means or foul. This will bring him into a quick scent, as I have oftentimes proved it." Fair means or foul, mark you!

All this and far more is of the richness of this book. It has survived near three centuries as a sporting work of worth. It has been constantly quoted and seldom faulted. We must remember that when Cox's beliefs, practices and "veterinary hints" seem ludicrous to us, they were accepted values and practices of his day.

Who are we to criticise when, within the foreseeable future our present greedy, mindless destruction of wild life by toxic sprays, our impoverishment of the soil by artificial manures, our pollution of the air and oceans, our squandering of natural resources and our suicidal tampering with atom power, may have destroyed the world in which we live? We are not so clever that we can afford to jeer at the past.

The publishers are to be congratulated on their masterly re-print of this classic work. Heaven knows that the few surviving copies of 1677 are scarce enough. I have been offered only two copies in fifty years of book collecting. When the copy from which this re-print is made, was mislaid for months, the publishers could find only one other in existence. That was in the London Library, which does not permit reproductions of its treasures. Fortunately the former copy was found when hope for it had almost been given up. So now Nicholas Cox, gentleman and sportsman of Tudor England, the England where the wolf and wild boar still lingered, the wild cat and marten were common pests, and kites swooped on every farmyard, is brought to life again.

You may hunt with him in wild forests of great oaks and bracken glades. You may wade through the marshes and fens which covered half eastern England, where the wings of wildfowl were like thunder in the dawn and the skies were blackened. You may set springes for snipe and go bat-fowling—as I did with villagers in boyhood—or cast off your hawk in the bright challenge of dawn. Sound your horn in brazen triumph when hounds have "bit and shaked the dead Wolf, let the Huntsman then open his Belly straight along, and taking out his Bowels, let him throw in Bread, Cheese and other Scraps, and so let the Dogs feed therein."

If you are an angler you will be interested to know of the "variety of discourse concerning the being of an Eel, whether they breed by some Generation or Corruption as Worms or by certain glutinous Dew-drops, which falling in May and June on the Banks of some Ponds and Rivers, are by the heat of the sun turned into Eels."

If you don't believe that, you can at least set up your home-made "Stocks of Angling Tools in winter." It will cost you much less than going to the impeccable Mr. Hardy. But God forbid that, when you set out fishing in the dawn, you should ever come across that revolting fish of which Cox says; "The Sargus is a Fish so lascivious (as Du-Bartas expresseth it rarely well) that when he cannot finde change of Mates enough in the Sea, he will get ashore and Cuckol a Goat.

"Goes courting She-Goats on the grasse Shore,
Horning their Husbands that had Horns before."

This, one feels, is no British fish at all, but some lecherous Latin monster, fit- only to be fished for by the lower and greasier type of film producer at the Cannes Film Festival. Nicholas had strayed a little in his field of enquiries, one feels.

To offset this shuddering fish you can reduce your more precious dry-fly fishing friends to frenzy by pointing out gently that Cox, like Izaak Walton, when describing the methods of catching trout and the baits to be used, puts the worm first, the minnow second and the fly last. Any Test or Itchen pundit will come at this in a head-and-tail rise.

And you can enjoy it all from an armchair—without getting your feet wet.

AUGUST, 1973

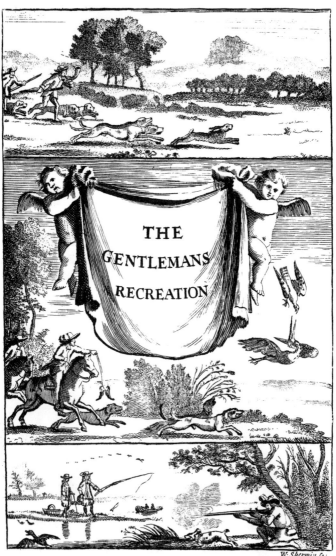

THE
GENTLEMANS
RECREATION

W. Sherwin fe:

THE
GENTLEMAN'S
Recreation :

In Four Parts,

Viz.

HUNTING, } { FOWLING,
HAWKING, } { FISHING.

Wherein thefe Generous Exercifes are largely treated of, and the Terms of Art for *Hunting* and *Hawking* more amply enlarged than heretofore.

Whereto is prefixt a large Sculpture, giving eafie Directions for blowing the Horn, and other Sculptures inferted proper to each Recreation.

With an 𝔄𝔟𝔰𝔱𝔯𝔞𝔠𝔱 at the end of each 𝔖𝔲𝔟𝔧𝔢𝔠𝔱 of fuch 𝔏𝔞𝔴𝔰 as relate to the fame.

Collected at firft from Antient and Modern Authors, and now in this Second Edition Corrected and very much Enlarged by feveral eminent and skilful Perfons, Lovers of thefe Sports.

LONDON:
Printed by *J. C.* for *N. C.* and are to be fold by *Tho: Fabian* at the Bible in *Paul's Church-yard,* the Corner-Shop next *Cheap-fide,* 1 6 7 7.

To the Right Honourable

JAMES

Lord NORREYES

Baron of *Rycot*,

His Majesties Lord-Lieutenant

OF

OXFORD-SHIRE.

IF to admire Worth and Honour were a Crime, it would highly concern me to beg your Lordfhips pardon for the prefumption of this Addrefs. For that's the Caufe, this the Effect. It is true, the obſcurity of my Condition, and remoteneſs of my Situation, have plac'd me out of the reach of your LordſhipsKnowledge; yet your Lordſhips Fame Ecchoing out of *Oxford-ſhire* through all the very Corners of the Kingdom, could hardly eſcape my Ears,were I not particularly entitled to the ſame County, which hath given me thereby the greater opportunity both to know, and admire the greatneſs of your Generoſity, the Magnificence of your Living, and Prudence of your Go-

Governing, accompanied
with all other qualifications and endowments re-
quiſite to render any perſon both Great and Good:
As alſo, that though your
Lordſhip is a great impro-
ver of your own natural
parts by your elaborate ſtu-
dies, and of others Know-
ledge by your Edifying
Converſation; yet to ob-
viate Idleneſs, and to anti-
dote Sickneſs, as alſo the
better to enapt your active
Body to ſuit your Loyal
Minde for Martial employ-
ments, ſhould the concerns
of your King and Country
call you forth into the Field,

your

your Lordſhip is a moſt indefatigable uſer of all active
Sports and Recreations, and
conſequently become the
great Oracle and Maſter
of them all, and all their
Artful Terms. Under what
other Wing then could this
little Treatiſe on thoſe Subjects ſo properly creep for
Shelter and Protection ?
Under no other certainly,
without ſome kinde of in-
juſtice to your Lordſhip, and
real injury to the Work it
ſelf. Be pleaſed therefore
a little to unbend your
thoughts (I humbly be-
ſeech your Lordſhip) from
your more ſerious Studies,
al-

allowing your eyes to run over thefe few Leaves, and either vouchfafe to correct their Errours, (if any have efcaped thofe judicious Sports-men who have been pleafed to be my Guides in perufing this Work, and purging it from many Errors and Miftakes of the former Edition) or ftamp them with the unqueftionable authority of your Lordfhip's Approbation. This will oblige all true Lovers of the fame generous Recreations to become greedy purchafers of thefe Rules, both to improve their Knowledge, and reduce their Language

A 3   to

to the same significant terms, to the great satisfaction of the Buyers, and the benefit of Proprietor and Seller, who humbly craves leave to lay himself at your Lord-ships Feet, in the quality of

(May it please your Lordship)

Your Lordship's

most devoted humble Servant,

Nicholas Cox.

ADVERTISEMENT.

Courteous Reader,

THe words *Bind* and *Canceleer* are inserted amongst the Terms of Art in *Faul-
sonry* (by accident) without their Expla-
nations; and therefore thou art desired to
take notice of them in this place. Also be
pleased to read an *Intermewer* (the Second
year of a *Hawks* Age) instead of *Interview*.
Some other small Faults have escaped the Press,
the which thou art desired to excuse.

 Binding is Tiring, or when a *Hawk* Seizeth.

 Canceleer is when a high-flown *Hawk* in her
stooping turneth two or three times upon the
Wing to recover self before she Seizeth.

Post-

POSTSCRIPT.

TO *shun Ingratitude*, I *must not omit mentioning* Mr. Michael Marsh *Horner*, *living at* Holborn-Bridge , *who teaches to blow the Horn*, *and as a Master who teaches the Notes* (*it is not onely mine*, *but the vogue of all who know him*) *is inferiour to none of that Function.*

Books to be fold by *Tho. Fabian.*

The

THE
GENTLEMAN'S
Recreation :
O R,
A TREATISE
Giving the beſt Directions for
HUNTING,
A N D
KILLING all manner of CHASES
uſed in *ENGLAND.*

With the Terms of Art belonging thereunto.

A L S O,

A ſhort account of ſome peculiar Beaſts
not uſually hunted in *England.*

Firſt Collected from Antient and Modern
Authors; and now very much Corrected and Enlarged by many Worthy and experienced Artiſts
of this Recreation.

With an Abſtract of ſuch Statute-Laws
as relate to Foreſts and Hunting.

The Firſt P A R T.

L O N D O N, Printed by *J. C.* for *N. G.*

OF

HUNTING.

The Introduction.

*H*Unting is a Game and Recreation commendable not onely for *Kings*, Princes, and the Nobility, but likewise for private Gentlemen : And as it is a Noble and Healthy Paftime, so it is a thing which hath been highly prized in all Ages.

Befides, *Hunting* trains up Youth to the ufe of manly Exercifes in their riper Age, being encouraged thereto by the pleafure they take in hunting the *Stately Stag*, the *Generous Buck*, the *Wilde Boar*, the *Cunning Otter*, the *Crafty Fox*, and the *Fearful Hare*; alfo the catching of Vermin by Engines, as the *Fitchet*, the *Fulimart*, the *Ferret*, the *Polecat*, the *Moldwarp*, and the like. Exercife herein preferveth Health, and increafeth Strength and Activity. Others inflame the hot Spirits of young men with roving Ambition, love of War, and feeds of Anger : But the Exercife of Hunting neither remits the Minde to Sloth nor Softnefs,

nor

nor (if it be ufed with moderation) hardens it to
inhumanity ; but rather inclines men to good Acquaintance, and generous Society.　It is no fmall
advantage to be enured to hear Hunger, Thirft, and
Wearinefs from ones Childhood ; to take up a timely habit of quitting ones Bed early, and loving to
fit well and fafe upon an Horfe.　What innocent and
natural delights are they, when he feeth the day breaking forth thofe Blufhes and Rofes which Poets and
Writers of Romances onely paint, but the Hunt-
man truely courts? When he heareth the chirping of
fmall Birds pearching upon their dewy Boughs? when
he draws in the fragrancy and coolnefs of the Air ?
How jolly is his Spirit, when he fuffers it to be impor-
ted with the noife of Bugle-Horns, and the baying of Hounds, which leap up and play round about
him!

　　Nothing doth more recreate the Minde, ftrengthen
the Limbs, whet the Stomach, and clear up the Spirit, when it is heavy, dull, and over-caft with gloomy
Cares : from whence it comes, that thefe delights
have merited to be in efteem in all Ages, and even
amongft barbarous Nations, by their Lords, Princes,
and higheft Potentates.

　　Then it is admirable to obferve the natural inftinct
of Enmity and Cunning, whereby one Beaft being
as it were confederate with man, by whom he is main-
tained, ferves him in his defignes upon others.　How
perfect is the Scent or Smell of an Hound, who never leaves it, but follows it through innumerable chan-
ges and varieties of other Scents, even over and in the
Water, and into the Earth ? Again, how foon will a
Hound fix his Eye on the beft and fatteft *Buck* of the
Herd, fingle him out, and follow him, and him onely, without changing, through a whole Herd of rafcal
Game, and leave him not till he kills him ? Moreover,

over, is it not delightful and pleasant to observe the Dociblenefs of Dogs, which is as admirable as their Underftanding? For as a right Huntfman knows the Language of his Hounds, fo they know his, and the meaning of their own kinde, as perfectly as we can diftinguifh the voices of our friends and acquaintance from fuch as are ftrangers.

Again, how fatisfied is a curious Minde, nay exceedingly delighted, to fee the Game fly before him! and after that it hath withdrawn it felf from his fight, to fee the whole Line where it hath paffed over, with all the doublings and crofs works which the amazed and affrighted Beaft hath made, recovered again; and all that Maze wrought out by the intelligence which he holds with Dogs! this is moft pleafant, and as it were a Mafter-piece of natural Magick. Afterwards, what Triumph there is to return with Victory and Spoils, having a good Title both to his Appetite and Repofe! Neither muft it be omitted, that herein there is an efpecial need to hold a ftrict Rein over our affections, that this Pleafure, which is allowable in its feafon, may not intrench upon other Domeftical affairs. There is great danger left we be tranfported with this Paftime, and fo our felves grow Wilde, haunting the Woods till we refemble the Beafts which are Citizens of them; and by continual converfation with Dogs, become altogether addicted to Slaughter and Carnage, which is wholly difhonourable, being a fervile employment. For as it is the priviledge of Man, who is endued with Reafon, and Authorized in the Law of his Creation, to fubdue the Beafts of the Field; fo to tyrannize over them too much, is brutifh in plain Englifh.

Miftake me not, I intend this Reflection not for the Nobility and Gentry of this Nation, whofe expence of time in this noble and delightful Exercife can no

ways

ways prejudice their large Poſſeſſions, ſince it is ſo far from being very chargeable, that it is exceeding profitable to the bodily health of ſuch who can diſpence with their ſtaying at home without any injury to their Families.

I might much enlarge my ſelf in the commendation of Hunting, but that I am loath to detain you too long from the knowledge of what will make a right and perfect Huntſman. I ſhall therefore thus conclude: No Muſick can be more raviſhingly delightful than a Pack of Hounds in full cry, to ſuch a man whoſe Heart and Ears are ſo happy to be ſet to the tune of ſuch charming Inſtruments.

HUNTERS TERMS.

BEfore we ſhall treat of the Method that is to be uſed in the obtaining pleaſure in the proſecution of this Royal Game, it will be very requiſite, as an Introduction to this Work, firſt to underſtand thoſe *Terms of Art* Huntſmen, Foreſters, and Wood men uſe, when they are diſcourſing of their commendable and highly recreative Profeſſion. And firſt, let us conſider

Which are Beaſts of Foreſt, or Venery, or Venary, Chaſe, and Warren.

Old Foreſters and Wood-men, with others well acquainted with Hunting, do reckon that there are five Beaſts of Venery, (that are alſo called Beaſts of Foreſt) which are theſe: the *Hart*, the *Hinde*, the *Hare*, the *Boar*, and *Wolf :* this is the opinion of *Budæus* likewiſe, in his Treatiſe of *Philologie,* ſpeaking
of

of the former Beasts, *Semper Forestæ & Veneris haben-tur Bestiæ* : These (saith he) are always accounted Beasts of Venery and Forest.

Some may here object and say , Why should the *Hart* and *Hinde*, being both of one kinde, be accounted two several Beasts ? To this I answer, That though they are Beasts of one kinde, yet they are of several seasons : for the *Hart* hath his season in Summer, and the season of the *Hinde* begins when the *Hart's* is over.

Here note, that with the *Hart* is included the *Stag*, and all other *Red Deer* of Antlier.

There are also five wild Beasts that are called Beasts of Chase ; the *Buck*, the *Doe*, the *Fox*, the *Martron*, and the *Roe*.

The Beasts and Fowls of Warren, are the *Hare*, the *Coney*, the *Pheasant*, and the *Partridge*; and none other, saith Mr. *Manwood*, are accounted Beasts nor Fowls of Warren.

My Lord *Cook* is of another opinion, in his *Commentary on Littleton* 233. *There be both Beasts and Fowls of the Warren*, saith he : *Beasts , as* Hares, Coneys, *and* Roes : *Fowls of two forts*, Terrestres, (*and they of two forts*) Silvestres , & Campestres : *The first*, Pheasant, Wood-cock, &c. *The second*, Partridge, Quail, Rail, &c. *Then* Aquatiles, *as* Mallard, Hern, &c.

There is great difference between Beasts of Forest, and Chase; the first are *Silvestres tantum* , the latter *Campestres tantum*. The beasts of the Forest make their abode all the day-time in the great Coverts and secret places in the Woods; and in the night-season they repair into the Lawns, Meadows, Pastures, and pleasant feeding places; and therefore they are called *Silvestres* , beasts of the Wood. The beasts of Chase do reside all the day-time in the Fields, and

upon

upon the Hills or high Mountains, where they may see round about them afar off, to prevent danger ; but upon nights approach they feed as the rest in Meadows, &c. and therefore these are called *Campestres*, beasts of the Field.

Let us in the next place discover their Names, Seasons, Degrees, and Ages of Forest or Venery, Chase and Warren : and because the *Hart* is the most noble, worthy, and Stately Beast, I shall place him first ; and must call a

Hart

The first year, a *Hinde-calf*, or *Calf.*
The second year, a *Knobber.*
The third year, a *Brocke.*
The fourth year, a *Staggard.*
The fifth year, a *Stag.*
The sixth, a *Hart.*

If hunted by the King, a *Hart Royal.* If he escape, and Proclamation be made for his safe return without let or detriment, he is then called a *Hart Royal Proclaimed.*

It is a vulgar errour, according to the opinion of Mr. *Guillim*, to think that a *Stag*, of what age soever he be, shall not be called a *Hart* till he be hunted by the King or Queen, and thence he shall derive his Title. Mr. *George Turbervile* saith positively, he shall not obtain that Name till he is hunted or killed by a Prince. But late Huntsmen do agree, he may be called a *Hart* at and after the age of six years old.

Now if the King or Queen shall happen to hunt or chase him, and he escape with life, he shall ever after be called a *Hart Royal :* But if he fly so far from the Forest or Chase, that it is unlikely he will ever return of his own accord to the place aforesaid,

and

and that Proclamation be made in all Towns and Villages thereabouts, that none shall kill or offend him, but that he may safely return if he list; he is then called a *Hart Royal Proclaimed.*

The second Beast of Venery is called a

Hinde.

And she is called the first year, a *Calf.*
The second year, a *Hearse* ; and sometimes we say *Brockets Sister,* &c.
The third year, a *Hinde.*

The next and third, which by old Foresters is called the King of all beasts of Venery, is the

Hare.

And is called the first year, a *Leveret.*
The second year, a *Hare.*
The third year, a *Great Hare.*

The fourth Beast of Venery is called the

Wilde-Boar.

The first year, he is a *Pig of the Sounder.*
The second year, he is a *Hog.*
The third year, he is a *Hogs Steer.*
The fourth year, he is a *Boar* ; at which age, if not before, he leaveth the *Sounder,* and then he is called a *Singler* or *Sanglier.*

The fifth and last Beast of Venery is the

Wolf.

The

The names of the Beasts of Chase according to their Ages.

The first is the

Buck.

It is called the first year, a *Fawn.*
The second year, a *Pricket.*
The third year, a *Sorel.*
The fourth year, a *Sore.*
The fifth year, a *Buck* of the *first Head.*
The sixth year, a *Great Buck.*

The second Beast of Chase is the

Doe or Doo.

She is called the first year, a *Fawn.*
The second year, a *Tegg.*
The third year, a *Doe.*

The third Beast of Chase is the

Fox.

And is called the first year, a *Cub.*
The second year, a *Fox,* and afterwards an old *Fox.*

The fourth Beast of Chase is the

Martern.

The first year, it is called a *Cub.*
The second year, a *Martern.*

The

The fifth and laſt Beaſt of Chaſe is called the

Roe.

The firſt year, it is called a *Kid*.
The ſecond year, a *Gyrle*.
The third year, a *Hemuſe*.
The fourth year, a *Roe-Buck* of the *firſt Head*.
The fifth year, a *Fair Roe-Buck*.

As for the Beaſts of the Warren, the *Hare* hath been ſpoken of already. The *Coney* is called the firſt year a *Rabbet*, and afterwards an old *Coney*.

The ſeaſons of Beaſts.

A *Hart* or *Buck* beginneth at the end of Fencer Moneth, which is 15 days after *Midſummer*-day, and laſteth till *Holy-rood*-day. The *Fox* at *Chriſtmas*, and laſteth till the *Annuntiation* of the *Bleſſed Virgin*. The *Hinde* or *Doe* beginneth at *Holy-rood*-day, and laſteth till *Candlemas*. The *Roe-buck* beginneth at *Eaſter*, and laſteth till *Michaelmas*. The *Roe* beginneth at *Michaelmas*, and laſteth till *Candlemas*. The *Hare* beginneth at *Michaelmas*, and laſteth till the end of *February*. The ſeaſon of the *Wolf* is ſaid to be from *Chriſtmas* till the *Annuntiation* of the Virgin *Mary*. Laſtly, The *Boar* begins at *Chriſtmas*, and continues to the *Purification* of our *Lady*.

Terms to be uſed for Beaſts of Venery and Chaſe, as they are in Company one with the other.

A Herd of *Harts*.
A Herd of all manner of *Deer*.

A Bevy of *Roes.*
A Sounder of *Swine.*
A Rout of *Wolves.*
A Richeſs of *Marterns.*
A Brace or Leaſe of *Bucks.*
A Brace or Leaſe of *Foxes.*
A Brace or Leaſe of *Hares.*
A Couple of *Rabbets.*
A Couple of *Coneys.*

Terms for their Lodging.

A *Hart* Harboureth.
A *Buck* Lodgeth.
A *Roe* Beddeth.
A *Hare* Seateth, or Formeth.
A *Coney* Sitteth.
A *Fox* Kennelleth.
A *Martern* Treeth.
An *Otter* Watcheth.
A *Badger* Eartheth.
A *Boar* Coucheth.

Terms for their Doſlodging.

Unharbour the *Hart.*
Rouze the *Buck.*
Start the *Hare.*
Bolt the *Coney.*
Unkennel the *Fox.*
Tree the *Martern.*
Vent the *Otter.*
Dig the *Badger.*
Rear the *Boar.*

Terms

Terms for their Noise at Rutting time.

A *Hart* Belleth.
A *Buck* Growneth or Troateth.
A *Roe* Belloweth.
A *Hare* Beateth or Tappeth.
An *Otter* Whineth.
A *Boar* Freameth.
A *Fox* Barketh.
A *Badger* Shricketh.
A *Wolf* Howleth.
A *Goat* Ratleth.

Terms for Copulation.

A *Hart* or *Buck* goeth to Rut.
A *Roe* goeth to Tourn.
A *Boar* goeth to Brim.
A *Hare* and *Coney* goeth to Buck.
A *Fox* goeth to Clickitting.
A *Wolf* goeth to Match or to Make.
An *Otter* hunteth for his Kinde.

Terms for the Footing and Treading of all Beasts of Venery and Chase.

Of a *Hart*, the Slot.
Of a *Buck* and all *Fallow Deer*, the View.
Of all *Deer*, if on the Grafs, and fcarce vifible, then
it is called Foiling.
Of a *Fox*, the Print ; and other fuch Vermin, the
Footing.
Of an *Otter*, the Marks.
Of a *Boar*, the Tract.
Of a *Hare*, diverfly ; for when fhe is in open field,
fhe

she Soreth: When she winds about to deceive the
Hounds, then she Doubleth: When she beateth on the
hard High-way, and her Footing can be perceived,
then she Pricketh ; and in the Snow, it is called the
Trace of the *Hare*.

Terms of the Tail.

Of a *Hart*, *Buck*, or other *Deer*, the Single.
Of a *Boar*, the Wreath.
Of a *Fox*, the Brush or Drag ; and the Tip at the
   end is called the Chape.
Of a *Wolf*, the Stern.
Of a *Hare* and *Coney*, the Scut.

Terms for their Ordure.

Of a *Hart*, and all *Deer*, their Excrement is called
   Fewmets or Fewishing.
Of a *Hare*, Crotiles or Crotising.
Of a *Boar*, Lesses.
Of a *Fox*, the Billiting ; and all other such Vermin,
   the Fuants.
Of an *Otter*, the Spraints.

Terms for the Attire of Deer.

Of a *Stag*, if perfect, the Bur, the Pearls, (the
little Knobs on it) the Beam, the Gutters, the Antlier,
the Sur-Antlier, Royal, Sur-Royal, and all at top the
Croches.

Of a *Buck*, the Bur, the Beam, the Brow-Antlier,
the Back-Antlier, the Advancer, Palm, and Spellers.

If the Croches grow in form of a mans Hand, it
is then called a Palmed Head. Heads bearing not a-
bove three or four, the Croches being plac'd aloft all
of

of one height, are called Crown'd Heads. Heads having doubling Croches, are called Forked Heads, becaufe the Croches are planted on the top of the Beam like Forks.

If you are asked what a *Stag* bears, you are onely to reckon Croches he bears, and never to exprefs an odde number: As, if he hath four Croches on his near Horn, and five on his far, you muft fay, he beareth ten, a falfe Right on his near Horn (for all that the Beam bears are called *Rights*) If but four on the near Horn, and fix on the far Horn, you muft fay he bears twelve, a double falfe Right on the near Horn ; for you muft not onely make the number even, but alfo the Horns even with that diftinction.

When a *Hart* breaketh Herd, and draweth to the Thickets or Coverts, we ufually fay he taketh his Hold, or he goeth to Harbour.

All kinde of *Deers* fat is called Sewit ; and yet you may fay, This Deer was a high Deer of Greafe. The fat of a *Boar* is called Greafe. The fat of a *Roe* onely is called Beavy Greafe.

We fay the *Deer* is broken up. The *Fox* and *Hare* is cafed.

It is
{
A Litter of *Cubs.*
A Neft of *Rabbets.*
A *Squirrels* Dray.
}

Venifcn, or Venaifon, is fo called, from the means whereby the beafts are taken, *quoniam ex Venatione capiuntur* ; and being hunted, are moft wholfome.

Beafts of Venary (not Venery, as fome call it) are fo termed, becaufe they are gotten by hunting.

No beaft of the Foreft that is *folivagam & nocivum* is Venifon, as the *Fox,* the *Wolf,* the *Martin,* becaufe they are no meat. The *Bear* is no Venifon, becaufe not onely that he is *Animal noctvum & folivagam* ; but

but becaufe he is no beaft of the Foreft, and whatfoever is Venifon muft be a beaft of the Foreft ; *fed non è
converfo.* On the other fide, *Animalia gregalia non
funt nociva*, as the Wilde *Boar* ; for naturally the firft
three years he is *Animal gregale* ; and after trufting to
his own ftrength, and for the pleafure of man, becom-
eth *Solivagum.* He is then called *Sanglier*, becaufe he
is *Singularis :* but he is Venifon, and to be eaten.
The *Hare* is Venifon too, which *Martial* preferreth
before all others.

Inter Quadrupedes gloria prima Lepus.

So are the *Red-Deer* and *Fallow-Deer* Venifon : *vide
Cook* Inft. 4. pag. 316. Give me leave to infert here
out of the fame Author two Conclufions in the Law
of the Foreft, which follow from hence. Firft, Whatfoever Beaft of the Foreft is for the food of man, that
is Venifon : and therewith agreeth *Virgil*, defcribing
of a Feaft,

Implentur Veteris Bacchi pinguifque ferinæ.

They had their belly full of old Wine and fat Venifon. So Venifon was the principal Difh of the
Feaft. Secondly, whatfoever beaft is not for the food
of man, is not Venifon. Therefore *Capriolus*, or
the *Roe*, being no beaft of the Foreft, is by the Law
of the Foreft no Venifon unlefs hunted. Nature hath
endewed the beafts of the Foreft with two qualities,
Swiftnefs, and Fear ; and their Fear increafeth their
Swiftnefs.

——*Pedibus timor addidit alas.*

Vert is any thing that beareth green Leaf, but efpecially of great and thick Coverts, and is derived *à Viri-
ditate*

ditate. Vert is of divers kinds; some that beareth
Fruit that may serve for food both for man and beasts,
as *Service-trees, Nut-trees, Crab-trees,* &c. and for the
shelter and defence of the Game. Some called *Hautboys,* serving for Food and browse of and for the
Game, and for the defence of them; as *Oaks, Beeches,* &c.
Some *Hautboys* for Browse, Shelter, and Defence only; as *Ashes, Poplars,* &c. Of *Sub-boys,* some for
Browse and Food of the Game, and for Shelter and
Defence; as *Maples,* &c. Some for Browse and Defence; as *Birch, Sallow, Willow,* &c. Some for Shelter and Defence onely; as *Elder, Alder,* &c. Of Bushes and other Vegetables, some for Food and Shelter,
as the *Haw-thorn, Black-thorn,* &c. Some for hiding
and shelter, as *Brakes, Gorse, Heath,* &c. *Vert,* as I
said, comes *à Viridi* ; thence *Viridarii,* because their
Office is to look after the preservation of the *Vert,*
which in truth is the preservation of Venison.

Terms for Flaying, Stripping, and Casing of all manner of Chases.

The *Hart* and all manner of *Deer* are slain : Huntsmen commonly say, Take off that *Deer's* Skin. The
Hare is Stripped or Cased ; and so is the *Boar* too,
according to the opinion of the Antients. The *Fox,*
the *Badger,* and all manner of Vermin are cased, beginning at the Snout or Nose of the Beast, and so turn
his Skin over his Ears down to the Body till you come
to the Tail.

Proper Terms for the Noises of Hounds.

When Hounds are first cast off, and finde some
Game or Chase, we say, *They Challenge.* If they are
too busie before they finde the scent good, we say, *They*
C
Bawl

Bawl. If they be too busie after they finde good scent, we say, *They Babble.* If they run it end-ways orderly, making it good, and then hold in together merrily, we say, *They are in full cry.* When Spaniels open in the string, (or a Grey-hound in his course) we say, *They Lapse.* When Hounds hang behinde, and beat too much upon the scent or place, we say, *They Plod.* And when they have either Earthed a Vermin, or brought a *Deer,* *Boar,* or such-like to turn head against them, then we say, *They Bay.*

Different Terms for Hounds and Grey-hounds.

Of Grey-hounds, two make a *Brace*; of Hounds, a *Couple.* Of Grey-hounds, three make a *Leace*; and of Hounds, a *Couple and half.*

We let slip a Grey-hound, and cast off a Hound. The string wherewith we lead a Grey-hound, is called a *Leace*; and for a Hound, a *Lyome.* The Grey-hound hath his *Collar*, and the Hound hath his *Couples.* We say, a Kennel of Hounds, and a Pack of Beagles. Some other differences there are, but these are the most usual.

Where we finde *Deer* have lately passed into Thickets, *&c.* by which we guess their greatness, and then put the Hounds or Beagles thereto for the View, we account such places *Entries.*

The Impression where any *Deer* hath reposed or harboured, we call a *Layr.*

When the Hounds or Beagles hit the scent of their Chase contrary, as to hit it up the wind when they should it down, we then say, they *Draw amiss.*

When the Hounds or Beagles take fresh scent, hunting another Chase, untill they stick and hit it again, we say, they *Hunt Change.*

When the Hounds or Beagles hunt it by the Heel, we say, they *Hunt Counter.*　　　　　　When

When the Chase goes off, and comes on again traverfing the fame ground, to deceive the Hounds or Beagles, we fay, they *Hunt* the *Foil*.

When we fet Hounds in readinefs where we expect the *Deer* will come by, and then caft them off when the other Hounds are pafs'd by, we account that a *Relay*.

When Hounds or Beagles have finifh'd their Chafe by the death of what they purfued, and then in requital are fed by the hands of the Huntfman or other, we call that their *Reward*.

Huntfmen when they go drawing in their Springs at *Hart*-hunting, ufually make Dew-rounds, which we call *Ringwalks*.

When any *Deer* is hard hunted, and then betakes himfelf to fwimming in any River, *&c.* then we fay, he takes *Soyl*.

When *Deer* caft their Horns, we fay, they *Mew*.

The firft head of a *Fallow-Deer* is called *Prick*.

When Huntfmen endeavour to finde a *Hart* by the Slot, *&c.* and then minde his ftep to know whether he is great & long, they then fay, they know him by his *Gate*.

When *Deer* rub and pufh their Heads againft Trees to caufe the Pills of their new Horns come off, we fay, they *Fray*.

When *Deer*, after being hard run, turn head againft the Hounds, we fay, they *Bay*.

When Hounds or Beagles run long without opening or making any cry, we fay, they run *Mute*.

When Hounds or Beagles at firft finding the fcent of their Game prefently open and cry, we then fay, they *Challenge*.

When Hounds run at a whole Herd of *Deer*, we fay, they *Run Riot*.

When the Hounds touch the fcent, and draw on till they rouze or put up the Chafe, we fay, they *Draw on the Slot*.

C 2   When

When a *Roe* crosses and doubles, it is called *Trajoning.*

When a *Hare*, as sometimes (though seldom) takes the Ground like a *Coney*, we then say, she *Goes to the Vault.*

When we beat the Bushes, &c. after the *Fox*, we call it *Drawing.*

When a *Hare* runs on rotten ground, or in a Frost sometimes, and then it sticks to her Feet, we say, she *Carryeth.*

When the *Fox* hath young ones in her, we say, she *is with Cub.*

When Beagles bark and cry at their Prey, we say, they *Yearn.*

A Red Male *Hart* of an year old, is called a *Spitter.*

A *Rayn-Deer*, is a Beast like an *Hart*, but hath his Head fuller of Antliers.

A *Pricker*, is a Huntsman on Horse-back.

Engines that we take *Deer* withal, are called *Wiles.*

When we set Hounds or Beagles in readiness, expecting the Chase to come by, and then cast them off before the rest come in, we call it a *Vauntlay.*

When Hounds or Beagles finde where the Chase hath been, and made a proffer to enter, but returned, we say, there is a *Blemish.*

We say *How* to a *Deer.*

When we start a *Hare*, we say, *That, that,* or *There, there.*

The *Call*, a Lesson blowed on the Horn to comfort the Hounds.

A *Recheat*, a Lesson likewise blown on the Horn. The *Mort* or *Death*, is blown at the death of any *Deer.* There are several other Lessons, which you may finde in the Sculpture of Notes for blowing on the Horn.

There

There are several Hounds and Beagles which we have different Titles for ; as Gaze-hound, Blood-hound, Staunch-hound , Harrier , and Terrier, &c. But we generally in all our Kennels and Packs rank them under these heads : *Enterers, Drivers, Fylers, Tyers*, &c.

And now to conclude our discourse of general Terms at this place, give us leave to insert , for such young Gentlemen as in time may keep a Kennel, some usual Names of Hounds and Beagles.

A Catalogue of some general Names of *Hounds* and *Beagles.*

Beauty
Blue-man
Boman
Bouncer

Captain
Countess
Cæsar.

Dido
Driver
Drunkard
Drummer
Damosel
Darling
Dutchess
Dancer
Daphne.

Fuddle.

Gallant.

Hector.

Juggler
Jewel
Jocky
Joler
Jollyboy
Jupiter
Juno.

Keeper.

Lively
Lady
Lilly
Lillups.

Madam
Merryboy
Musick.

Nancy.

C 3

Plunder

Plunder	*Thunder*
	Thisbe
Rockwood	*Truman*
Ringwood	*Truelove*
Rover	*Tickler*
Ranter	*Tattler*
Royal	*Tulip.*
Rapper	
Ruffler.	*Venus.*
Spanker	*Wanton*
Soundwel	*Wonder.*
Stately.	
	Younker.
Troler	

Some other Terms and Descriptions relating more particularly to Forest and Forest-Laws.

A *Forest*, is a place priviledged by Royal Authority, and differs from Park, Warren, and Chase, and is on purpose allotted for the peaceable abiding and nourishment of the Beasts and Fowls thereto belonging. For which there are certain peculiar Laws, Officers, and Orders; part of which appear in the Great Charter of the Forest.

A *Forester*, is an Officer of the Forest, sworn to preserve the Vert and Venison therein, and to attend the wilde beasts within his Bailiwick, and to watch, and endeavour to keep them safe by day and night. He is likewise to apprehend all Offenders in Vert and Venison, and to present them to the Courts of the Forest, to the end they may be punished according to their offences.

A

A *Purlieu*, is all that ground adjoyning to Forests, which being made Forest by *Henry* the second, *Richard* the first, or King *John*, were by perambulations granted by *Henry* the third, and severed again from the same.

A *Purlieu*-man, is he that hath ground within the *Purlieu*, and hath 40 s. a year Free-hold ; and such a one with some caution may hunt within his own *Purlieu*.

A *Regarder*, is an Officer of the Kings Forest, that is sworn to take care of the Vert and Venison, and to view and enquire of all the offences committed within the Forest , and of all the Concealments of them ; and whether all other Officers do execute their Office or not.

Woodgeld, is the gathering or cutting of Wood in the Forest, or the money paid for it to the use of the Foresters ; or an Immunity for this by the King's Grant.

A *Raunger*. In some Forests there are twelve *Raungers*, whose Offices are to look after the *Purlieu* , and drive back the wilde Beasts into the Forest again ; and to see, hear, and enquire of offenders there , and to present their offences.

A *Verderor*, is an Officer of the King's Forest, and chosen by the Free-holders of the County where the Forest is, by the Kings Writ directed to the Sheriff for that purpose. Their Office is chiefly to look after the Wood and Grass in the Forest.

An *Agistor*, is an Officer of the Forest that takes in to feed the Cattle of Strangers , and receives for the Kings use all such tack Money as becomes due from those Strangers.

A *Chase*, is a place used for the receipt of *Deer* and Beasts of the Forest : It differs from a Forest and Park. It may be in the hands of a Subject, which a

C 4   Forest

Foreft in its proper nature cannot be. Neither is it inclofed as a Park always is ; and it hath a larger compafs, more ftore of Game, and more Keepers and O-verfeers.

Expeditate , is (faith Mr. *Crompton*) the cutting out the ball of the Foot of great Dogs in the Foreft ; but (faith Mr. *Manwood*) it is the cutting off the three fore-Claws by the Skin ; and that the Owner of every fuch Dog, unexpeditated in the Foreft, fhall forfeit 3 *s.* 4 *d.*

Fence Moneth, hath 31 days, begins 15 days before *Midfummer,* and ends 15 days after : In which time it is unlawful for any to hunt in the Foreft, or to go amongft the *Deer* to difquiet them; becaufe it is the time of Fawning.

Frank Chafe, is a liberty of free Chafe in a Circuit annexed to a Foreft, whereby all men that have ground within the circuit are forbidden to cut down Wood, or difcover,*&c.* within the view of the Forefter, though it be his own Demefne.

Green-hue, or *Vert* , they both fignifie one thing, it being every thing that doth grow and bear green Leaf within the Foreft, that may cover and hide the *Deer.*

Over Vert, is all manner of high Wood.

Nether Vert, is all forts of under-wood. Brufhwood is called *Cablifh.*

Horngeld, is a Tax within the Foreft for all manner of horned beafts.

Footgeld, is an Amercement on fuch as live within the Foreft, for not expeditating their Dogs. And to be quit of *Footgeld* , is a priviledge to keep Dogs there unlawed without Punifhment or Controlement.

Pawnage, is Money taken by the Agiftors for the feed of Hogs with the Maft of the Kings Foreft ;

but

but (Mr. *Crompton* faith) it is moft properly the Maft, Woods, Lands , or hedg'd Rowes, or Money due to the Owners of the fame for it.

A *Scotale*, is where any Officer of the Foreft doth keep an Ale-houfe in the Foreft by colour of his Office, caufing men to come to his Houfe, and to fpend their money there for fear of having Difpleafure ; but this is forbidden by *Charta Foreft.*

Perambulation , is the admeafurement and fetting down of Bounds and Limits to the Foreft.

Drift of the Foreft, is an exact view and examination taken at certain times, as occafion fhall ferve, to know what beafts are there ; that none Common there but fuch as have right ; and that the Foreft be not over-charged with the beafts of Forreigners.

An *Affart*, is a great offence committed in the Foreft, by grubbing up the Woods, Coverts, and Thickets, and making them plain as Arable Land , or the like.

Minoverie, is a Trefpafs or Offence committed by fome Engine fet up in the Foreft to catch *Deer*, or the like.

Tritis, is a freedom that one hath from holding a Grey-hound in ones hand when the Lord of the Foreft is hunting there, or to be amerced for his default.

Protoforeftarius , was a great Officer heretofore in *Windfor* Foreft.

Stableftand, is when one is found ftanding in the Foreft with his Bow ready bent to fhoot at any *Deer*, or with his Grey-hound in a Leafe ready to flip.

Swainmote , or *Swannimote*, is a Court appointed to be held thrice in a year within a Foreft ; the firft, 15 days before *Michaelmas* ; the fecond, about *Martinmas* ; and the third, 15 days before St. *John Baptift.*

Chiminage, is taken by Forefters in fee throughout
their

their Bailywick for Bushes, Timber, &c. and signifies the same with Toll.

Afforest, is to turn Land into Forest.

Disafforest, is to turn Land from being Forest to other uses.

Let what hath been said be sufficient for an Introduction, and let us conclude it with a perswasion to all generous Souls not to slight this noble and worthy Exercise, (wherein is contained so much health and pleasure) for the besotting Sensualities, and wicked Debaucheries of a City, in which the course of Nature seems to be inverted, Day turn'd into Night, and Night into Day; where there is little other Recreation but what Women, Wine, and a bawdy Play can afford them; whereby, for want of Labour and Exercise, Mens Bodies contain as many Diseases as are in a sickly Hospital.

Of DOGS in general.

AS there is no Country in the world wherein there is not plenty of Dogs, so no Animal can boast of greater variety both in shape and kinde.

Some Dogs are very great, as the *Wolf*-dog, which is shaped like a Grey-hound, but by much taller, longer, and thicker; some are for the *Buck*, others for the *Boar, Bear,* and *Bull*; some for the *Hare, Coney,* and *Hedge-hog*; some are both for Water and Land, and they are called Spaniels; other are called Lurchers, Tumblers, Brachers, Beagles, &c. As for Shepherds dogs, foisting Curs, and such whom some fond Ladies make their daily, nay nightly Companions

too

too, I shall pass over, being neither worthy to be inserted in this Subject, nor agreeable thereunto: wherefore I shall onely treat of such whose natures do incline them to Game, for mans Pastime and Recreation.

In the first place, let us consider the nature of Dogs in general, wherein they agree, and their common properties of nature, such as are not destroyed in the distinction of kinds, but remain like infallible Truths, and invariable in every kinde and Country through the Universe. Dogs (as it is to be observed) are generally rough; and their Hair indifferently long (which in Winter they lose every year) is a signe of a good constitution; but if it grow over-long, the Mange will follow. The outward proportion of the Head altereth as the kinde altereth, having no commissure or seam in the Skull, being a continued bone without separation.

The best Dogs (in *Pliny*'s opinion) have flat Nostrils, yet round, solid, and blunt: Their Teeth are like Saws, which they change in the fourth month of their age: and by them is their age discerned; for while they are white and sharp, it discovers the youth of a Dog; but when they grow blackish or dusky, broken and torn, they demonstrate the elder age.

The Breast of a Dog is narrow, so is his Ventricle: for which cause he is always in pain in the discharging his Excrements.

After they have run a Course, they relieve themselves by tumbling and rowling to and fro. When they lie down, they turn round in a circle two or three times together; which they do for no other cause, but that they may the more commodiously lie round, and from the Wind.

In their sleep they often dream, as may appear by their barking. Here observe, that they who love to

keep

keep Dogs, muſt have a ſpecial care that they let them
not ſleep too much, eſpecially after their Meat, when
they are young: for as they are very hot, ſo in their
ſleep doth their heat draw much pain into their Stomack and Ventricle. The time of their Copulation is for the moſt part at a year old; yet the
Females will luſt after it ſooner; but they ſhould be
reſtrained from it, becauſe it debilitates their Body, and dulls their Generoſity. After the expiration of a year, they may be permitted to copulate;
it matters not whether in Winter or Summer, but
it is beſt in the beginning of the Spring: but with
this caution, that Whelps of a Litter, or of one and
the ſame Bitch, be never ſuffered to couple; for Nature delights in variety.

In antient time, for the more ennobling of their
race of Dogs, they would not permit them to ingender till the Male was four year old, and the
Female three; for by that means the Whelps would
prove more ſtrong and lively. By Hunting, Labour,
and Travel, the Males are made more fit for Generation, and they prove beſt which have their Sires
of equal age. When they grow proud, give them
Leaven mingled with Milk and Salt, and they will
not ſtray and ramble abroad.

It is not good to preſerve the firſt or ſecond Litter, but the third: and after they have littered, it
is good to give the Bitch Whey and Barley-bread; for
that will comfort her, and increaſe her Milk: or take
the Bones of broken Meat, and ſeeth them in Goats-
Milk; which nutriment will ſtrengthen very much
both Dam and Whelps.

There is no great regard to be had as to the
Food of a Dog, for he will eat any thing but the
Fleſh of his own kinde; for that cannot be ſo
dreſſed by the art of Man, but they find it out
by

by their Nose, and avoid it. It is good to let the Whelps suck two Months before they be weaned, and that of their own Dam.

Put *Cummin* now and then in their bread, it will cure or prevent Wind in their Bellies ; and if Oyl be mingled with that Water they lap, they will prove more able and swift to run. If he refuse and loath his Meat, give him a little hot Bread, or dip brown Bread in Vinegar, and sqeeze the liquor thereof into his Nose, and it will ease him.

There is some difficulty to chuse a Whelp under the Dam that will prove the best of the Litter. Some observe that which seeth last, and take that for the best : others remove the Whelps from the Kennel, and lay them several and apart one from the other ; then watch they which of them the Bitch first taketh and carrieth into her Kennel again, and that they take for the best ; or else that which vomiteth last of all. Some again give for a certain rule to know the best, that the same which weigheth least while it sucketh will prove the best, according to the Verses of *Nemesian :*

> *Pondere nam Catuli poteris perpendere viris,*
> *Corporibusque leves gravibus pernoscere cursu.*

But this is certain, that the lighter Whelp will prove the swifter, and the heavier will be the stronger.

As soon as the Bitch hath littered, it is requisite to chuse them you intend to preserve, and throw away the rest : keep the black, brown, or of one colour, for the spotted are not much to be accounted of ; but of Hounds, Spotted are to be valued.

There is not any Creature irrational, more loving to his Master, nor more serviceable than a Dog, enduring blows from his hands, and using no other means

to

to pacifie his difpleafure, than Humiliation and pro-ftration; and after beating, turneth a Revenge into a more fervent Love. Irrational, did I fay? I may miftake, if what *Ælianus* reports be true, who thought Dogs have Reafon, and ufe Logick in their hunting; for they will caft about for the Game, as a Difputant doth for the truth; as if they fhould fay, the *Hare* is gone either on the left hand, the right, or ftraight forward; but not on the left or right, Therefore ftraight forward. Whereupon he runneth forthright after the true and infallible footfteps of the *Hare*.

Of Dogs for Hunting. Of the *Hound* Rache *and* Sluth-hound, *fo called in* Scot-land, *and by the* Germans Schlathund.

THere are in *England* and *Scotland* two kindes of hunting-Dogs, and no where elfe in all the World: The firft kinde is called *Ane Rache*, and this is a foot-fcenting creature both of wilde-Beafts, Birds, and Fifhes alfo, which lie hid among the Rocks: *The Female hereof in* England *is called a* Brache. A *Brach*, is a mannerly name for all Hound-bitches. The fecond in *Scotland* is called a *Sluth hound*, being a lit-tle greater than the Hunting-hound, and in colour for the moft part brown or fandy fpotted. The fenfe of Smelling is fo quick in thefe, that they can follow the foot-fteps of Thieves, and purfue them with violence until they overtake them: nay, fhould the Thief take the Water, fo eager they are in their purfuit, that they will fwim after them; and are reftlefs till they finde the

thing

thing they feek after: For this is common in the borders of *England* and *Scotland*, where the people were wont to live much upon Theft: and if the Dog brought his Leader to any houfe where they may not be fuffered to enter, they take it for granted that there is both the ftolen Goods, and the Thief alfo.

Of the BLOOD-HOUND.

THe Blood-hound differeth nothing in quality from the Scotifh Sluth-hound, faving that they are more largely fized, and not always of one and the fame colour: for they are fometimes Red, Sanded, Black, White, Spotted, and of all colours with other Hounds, but moft commonly either brown or red.

The *Germans* call this Beaft *Langhund*, becaufe their Ears are long, thin, and hanging down; and they differ not from vulgar Dogs in any other outward proportion, than only in their Cry and Barking. Their nature is, being fet on by the voice and words of their Leader, to caft about for the fitting of the prefent Game; and having found it, will never ceafe purfuing it with full cry, till it is tired, without changing for any other. They feldome bark, except in their Chafe, and are very obedient and attentive to the Voice of the Leader.

They which are white, are faid to be the quickeft fcented, and fureft Nos'd, and therefore beft for the *Hare*: The black ones for the *Boar*; and the red for the *Hart* and *Roe*. This is the opinion of fome, but none of mine; becaufe their colour (efpecially the latter) are too like the Game they hunt: although there can be nothing certain collected of their colour, yet is the black Hound hardier, and better able to endure cold than the other which is white. They

muft

mult be tied up till they hunt, yet fo as they be let loofe now and then a little to eafe their Bellies ; for it is neceffary that their Kennel be kept fweet and dry. It is queftionable how to difcern a Hound of excellent fenfe : yet fome are of the opinion that the fquare and flat Nofe is the beft figne thereof ; like-wife a fmall Head, having all his Legs of equal length ; his Breaft not deeper than his Belly, and his Back plain to his Tail ; his Eyes quick, his Ears hanging long ; his Tail nimble, and the beak of his Nofe always to the Earth ; and efpecially fuch as are moft filent, and bark leaft.

Confider now the divers and variable difpofitions of Hounds in their finding out the Beaft. Some are of that nature, that when they have found the Game, they will ftand ftill till the Huntfman come up, to whom in filence, by their Face, Eye, and Tail, they fhew the Game : others, when they have found the foot-fteps, go forward without any voice or other fhew of Ear or Tail : Another fort when, when they have found the footings of the Beaft, prick up their Ears a little, and either bark or wag their Tails ; and others will wag their Tails, and not move their Ears.

There are fome again that do none of thefe, but wander up and down barking about the fureft marks, and confounding their own foot-fteps with the Beafts they hunt ; or elfe forfake the way, and fo run back again to the firft head ; but when they fee the *Hare*, are affraid, not daring to come neer her, except fhe ftart firft. Thefe, with the other which hinder the cun-ning labours of their Colleagues, trufting to their Feet, and running before their betters, deface the beft mark, or elfe hunt counter, and take up any falfe fcent for the truth ; or, which is more reprehenfible, never for-fake the High-ways, and yet have not learned to be

filent.

filent: Unto thefe you may alfo adde thofe which cannot difcern the Footing or Pricking of a *Hare*, yet will they run fpeedy when they fee her, purfuing her hotly in the beginning, and afterwards tire, or hunt lazily. All thefe are not to be admitted into a Kennel of good Hounds.

On the contrary, thofe Hounds which are good when they have found the *Hare*, make fhew thereof to the Huntfman, by running more fpeedily, and with gefture of Head, Eyes, Ears, and Tail, winding to the Fourm or *Hares* Mufe, never give over profecution with a gallant noife: they have good and hard Feet, and ftately Stomacks.

Now whereas the nature of the *Hare* is fometimes to leap and make headings, fometimes to tread foftly with but a very fmall impreffion in the Earth, or fometimes to lie down, and ever to leap or jump out and into her own Fourm, the poor Hound is fo much the more bufied and troubled to retain the fmall fcent of her pricking which fhe leaveth behinde her; for this caufe it is requifite that you help the Hound, not onely with Voice, Eye, and Hand, but with a feafonable Time alfo: for in frofty weather the fcent freezeth with the Earth, fo that there is no certainty of hunting till it thaw, or that the Sun arife. Likewife if very much Rain fall between the ftarting of the *Hare* and time of hunting, it is not convenient to hunt till the Water be dried up; for the drops difperfe the fcent of the *Hare*, and dry weather colle-cteth it again. The Summer-time alfo is not for hunting, becaufe the heat of the weather confumeth the Scent; and the Night being then but fhort, the *Hare* travelleth not far, feeding onely in the Morning and Evening: befides, the fragrancy of Flowers and Herbs then growing, obliterates the fcent the Hounds are guided by.

Thf

The beſt time for hunting with theſe Hounds is in Autumn, becauſe then the former Odours are weakned, and the Earth barer than at other time.

Theſe Hounds do not onely chaſe their Game while it liveth, but being dead alſo by any manner of caſualty, make recourſe to the place where it lieth, having in this point an aſſured and infallible Guide, namely, the *Scent* and *Savour* of the Blood ſprinkled here and there upon the ground: for whether the Beaſt being wounded doth notwithſtanding enjoy life, and eſcapeth the hands of the Huntſman; or whether the ſaid Beaſt, being ſlain, is conveyed cleanly out of the Park, (ſo that there be ſome marks of bloodſhed) theſe Dogs, with no leſs facility and eaſineſs, than avidity and greedineſs, diſcloſe and bewray the ſame by Smelling, applying to their purſuit agility and nimbleneſs, without tedeouſneſs; for which conſideration, of a ſingular ſpecialty they deſerved to be called *Sanguinarii*, Blood-hounds: And although a piece of fleſh be ſubtilly ſtolen, and cunningly conveyed away, with ſuch proviſo's and precaveats, as thereby all appearances of Blood is thereby prevented or concealed; yet theſe kinde of Dogs, by certain direction of an inward aſſured notice and private mark, purſue theſe deſperate *Deer*-ſtealers through craggy Ways, and crooked Meanders, till they have found them out: yea, ſo effectual is their foreſight, that they can diſcover, ſeparate, and pick them out from an infinite multitude; creep they never ſo far into the thickeſt throng, they will finde them out notwithſtanding.

Of

Of the GAZE-HOUND.

THis Dog is little beholding in hunting to his Nose or Smelling, but to sharpness of Sight altogether, by the vertue whereof it makes excellent sport with the *Fox* and *Hare*.

This Dog will chuse and separate from amongst a great Flock or Herd, and such a one will it take by election, as is not lank or lean, but full, fat, and round.

If a Beast be wounded and go astray, this Dog will seek after it by the stedfastness of the Eye; if it happen to return, and be mingled with the residue of the Herd, this Dog will soon spy it out, leaving the rest untouched : and after he hath set sure sight upon it, he separateth it from the company; and having so done, never ceaseth till he hath wearied it to death

This Dog is called in Latine *Agasæus*, because the b ams of the Sight are so stedfastly settled, and unmoveably fastned. These Dogs are much used in the Northern parts of *England*, much more than in the Southern; and on Champion ground ratherthan in bushy and woody places : Horsemen use them more than Footmen.

It it happen so at any time that this Dog take a wrong way, the Master making some usual signe, and familiar token, he returneth forthwith, and taketh the right and ready course, beginning his Chase afresh, and with a clear Voice, and a swift Foot, followeth the Game with as much courage and nimbleness as he did at the first.

Of the GREY-HOUND.

AMong the divers kindes of Hunting-dogs, the Grey-hound, by reason of his Swiftnes, Strength, and Sagacity to follow and pursue his Game, deserveth the first place ; for such are the conditions of this Dog, as a Philosopher observeth, that he is reasonably scented to finde out, speedy and quick of foot to follow, and fierce and strong to take and overcome ; and yet silent , coming upon his Prey at unawares, according to the observation of *Gratius* :

Sic Canis illa suos taciturna supervenit hostes.

The best *Grey-hound* hath a long Body, strong, and reasonable great, not so big as the *Wolf* dog in *Ireland* ; a neat sharp head, and splendant Eyes ; a long Mouth, and sharp Teeth ; little Ears , and thin Gristles in them ; a straight Neck, and a broad and strong Breast ; his fore Legs straight and short, his hinder Legs long and straight ; broad Shoulders, round Ribs , fleshy Buttocks, but not fat ; a long Tail, strong , and full of Sinews. Thus *Nemesian* eloquently describes the best of *Grey-hounds* :

——————— *Sit cruribus altis,*
Costarum sub fine decenter prona carinam :
Renibus ampla satis validis deductaq; coras
Sit rigidis, multamq; gerat sub pectore lato,
Quæ sensim rursus sicca se colligat alvo :
Cuiq; nimis molles fluitent in cursibus Aures.
Elige tunc cursu facilem, facilemq; recursu,
Dum superant vires, dum læto flore juventus.

Of

Of this kinde, that is always the beſt to be choſen among the Whelps, which weigheth lighteſt; for it will be ſooneſt at the Game, and ſo hang upon it, hindering its ſwiftneſs, till the ſtronger and heavier Dogs come to help and offer their aſſiſtance; and therefore beſides the marks or neceſſary good parts of a *Grey-hound* already ſpoken of, it is requiſite that he have large ſides, and a broad Midriff, that ſo he may take his Breath in and out more eaſily: his Belly muſt be ſmall; if otherwiſe, it will hinder the ſwiftneſs of his courſe: likewiſe he muſt have long Legs, thin and ſoft Hairs. And theſe muſt the Huntſman lead on the left hand, if he be afoot; and on the right, if on Horſe-back.

The beſt time to try them and train them to their Game, is at twelve Moneths old; yet ſome begin ſooner with them, that is, at ten Moneths if they are Males, and at eight if Females: yet it is ſureſt not to ſtrain them, or permit them to run a long Courſe, till they be twenty Moneths old. Keep them alſo in the Slip while they are abroad, until they can ſee their Courſe; and looſen not a young Dog, until the Game have been on foot for a good ſeaſon, leſt being over-greedy of the Prey, he ſtrain his Limbs too much.

The *Grey-hounds* which are moſt in requeſt among the *Germans*, are called *Windſpil*, alluding to compare their ſwiftneſs with the Wind; but the *French* make moſt account of thoſe that are bred in the Mountains of *Dalmatia*, or in any other Mountains, eſpecially of *Turkie*; for ſuch have hard Feet, long Ears, and brittle Tails.

The *Grey-hound* (called by the Latins *Leporarius*) hath his name from the word *Gre*, which word ſoundeth *Gradus* in Latine, in Engliſh *Degree*; becauſe among all Dogs, theſe are the moſt principal, having the chiefeſt place, and being ſimply and abſolutely the beſt of the gentle kind of Hounds. D 3 Of

Of the HARRIER and TERRIER.

THE *Harrier* in Latine is called *Leverarius*, or *Sa-gax*; by the *Greeks, Ichneuten*, of tracing or cha-sing by the Foot.

Nature hath endewed this Creature with an admi-rable gift of Smelling, and is bold and courageous in the pursuit of his Game. There are several sorts of them, and all differ in their Services: some are for the *Hare*, the *Fox*, the *Wolf*, the *Hart*, the *Buck*, the *Badger*, the *Otter*, the *Polecat*, the *Weasle*, the *Coney*, &c. some for one thing, some for another.

As for the *Coney*, we use not to hunt, but take it sometimes with a Net, sometimes with a *Ferret*, and sometimes with a Lurcher or Tumbler. Among the several sorts of *Harriers*, there are some which are apt to hunt two divers Beasts, as the *Fox* some-times, and otherwhiles the *Hare*; but they hunt not with that good success and towardness, who stick not to one sort of Game.

The *Terrier* hunteth the *Fox* and the *Badger* or *Gray* onely: And they are called *Terriers*, because they (after the manner and custom of *Ferrets* in searching for *Coneys*) creep into the ground, and by that means affright, nip, and bite the *Fox* and the *Badger*, in such sort, that either they tear them in pieces with their Teeth, (being in the bosome of the Earth) or else hale and pull them by force out of their lurking Angles, dark Dungeons, and close Caves; or at the least, through conceived fear, drive them out of their hollow Harbours, insomuch, if they are not taken by Net or otherwise, they are compelled to prepare for
                                                          flight,

flight ; and being defirous of the next , though not the fafeft, refuge , they are oft-times entrapped with Snares and Nets laid over Holes for the fame purpofe.

Of the LEVINER or LYEMMER.

THe *Leviner* is fingular in Smelling, and in Swiftnefs incomparable. This is as it were a middle kinde between the *Harrier* and the *Grey-hound* , as well for his kinde, as the frame and fhape of his Body. It is called in Latine *Levinarius, à Levitate*, of lightnefs, and therefore may well be called a *Light-hound.* This Dog, for the excellency of his Conditions , namely, Smelling, and fwift Running, doth follow the Game with more eagernefs, and taketh the Prey with a jolly quicknefs.

Of the TUMBLER.

THe word *Tumbler* undoubtedly had its derivation from the French word *Tumbier*, which fignifies to Tumble ; to which the Latine name agrees, *Vertagus*, from *Vertere* to turn ; and fo they do : for in hunting they turn and tumble, winding their Bodies about circularly, and then fiercely and violently venturing on the Beaft , do fuddenly gripe it at the very entrance or mouth of their Holes or Receptacles, before they can make any recovery of felf-fecurity.

This Dog ufeth another craft and fubtilty, namely,

D 4 when

when he runneth into a Warren, or fetcheth a courſe about a *Coney*-borough, he hunts not after them, he no ways affrights them , he ſhews no ſpight againſt them ; but diſſembling friendſhip, and pretending favour, paſſeth by with ſilence and quietneſs, marking their Holes diligently, wherein he ſeldom is deceived. When he cometh to a place where there is a certainty of *Coneys*, he coucheth down cloſe with his Belly to the ground, provided always by his Skill and Policy that the Wind be againſt him in that Enterprize, and that the *Coneys* diſcover him not where he lurketh ; by which means he gets the benefit of the ſcent of the *Coneys*, which is carried to him by the Wind and Air, either going to their Holes, or coming out, either paſſing this way, or running that way ; and ſo ordereth the buſineſs by his circumſpection, that the ſilly *Coney* is debarred quite from his Hole. (which is the Haven of their hope, and the Harbour of their ſafety) and fraudulently circumvented and taken before they can get the advantage of their Holes. Thus having caught his Prey, he carrieth it ſpeedily to his Maſter, waiting his Dogs return in ſome convenient lurking corner.

These Dogs are ſomewhat leſſer than the Hounds, being lanker, leaner, and ſomewhat prick-ear'd. By the form and faſhion of their Bodies they may be juſtly called *Mungrel-Grey-hounds*, if they were ſomewhat bigger. But notwithſtanding they countervail not the *Grey-hound* in greatneſs , yet will he take in one days ſpace as many *Coneys* as ſhall ariſe to as big a burthen, and as heavy a load as a Horſe can carry : For Craft and Subtilty are the Inſtruments whereby he maketh this ſpoil , which pernicious properties ſupply the places of more commendable qualities.

Let this ſuffice for a taſte : now, after ſuch Dogs as ſerve Hunting, will follow ſuch as ſerve for Hawking and

and Fowling ; among which, the principal and chiefeſt
is the *Spaniel*, called in Latine *Hiſpaniolus* , borrowing
his name from *Hiſpania* ; wherein we Engliſh-men,
not pronouncing the Aſpiration *H*, nor the Vowel *I*,
for quickneſs and readineſs of ſpeech, ſay, *Spaniel*.

Of the SPANIEL.

THere are two ſorts of Dogs which neceſſarily
ſerve for Fowling. The firſt findeth Game on
the Land, the other on the Water. Such as delight
on the Land, play their parts either by ſwiftneſs of
foot, or by often queſting to ſearch out and to ſpring
the Bird for further hope of reward, or elſe by ſome
ſecret ſigne and privy token, diſcover the place where
they fall. The firſt kinde of ſuch ſerve the *Hawk* ;
the ſecond, the Net or Train. The firſt kinde have
no peculiar names aſſigned them, except they are
named after the Bird which by natural appointment
he is allotted to take ; for which conſideration, ſome
are called Dogs for the *Falcon*, the *Pheaſant*, the *Par-*
tridge, and ſuch-like : they are commonly called by
one name, *viz*. *Spaniels*, as if they originally came
from *Spain*.

The *Spaniel*, whoſe ſervice is required in Fowling
on the Water, partly through natural inclination, and
partly by diligently teaching, is properly called *Aqua-*
ticus, as *Water-Spaniel*, becauſe he hath uſual recourſe
to the Water, where all his Game lieth, namely,
Water-fowl, which are taken by their help in their
kinde.

His ſize is ſomewhat big, and of a meaſurable greatneſs, having long, rough, and curled Hair, which
muſt

muſt be clipt in due ſeaſon : for by leſſening that ſuperfluity of Hair, they become more light and ſwift, and are leſs hindred in ſwimming. *Ducks* and *Drakes* are his principal Game ; whereupon he is likewiſe named a Dog for a *Duck*, becauſe in that quality he is excellent.

of the WHITE-HOUND.

THoſe Hounds which are all of one colour, as all white, are the beſt Hounds ; in like manner thoſe which are ſpotted with red : but thoſe which are ſpotted with a dun colour, are of little value, being faint-hearted, and cannot endure much labour. But ſhould they happen to be whelpt coal-black, which is but ſeldom , they commonly prove incomparable Hounds. But if white Hounds are ſpotted with black, experience tells us, they are never the beſt *Hare*-hunters. White , and black and white , and grey ſtreak'd white, are alſo the moſt beautiful.

of FALLOW-HOUNDS.

THey are hardy, and of good ſcent, keeping well their Chace without change ; but not ſo ſwift as the white. They are of a ſtrong conſtitution, and do not fear the Water ; running ſurely , and are very hardy, commonly loving the *Hart* beyond any other Chaſe.

The beſt complexion for theſe *Fallow-hounds*, is the lively

lively red, and such as have a white spot in their Forehead, or have a Ring about their Neck : but those which are yellowish, and spotted with black or dun, are of little estimation. Those which are well joynted, having good Claws, are fit to make Blood-hounds : and those which have shagged Tails, are generally swift runners. These Hounds are fitter for Princes than private Gentlemen, because they seldom run more than one Chace ; neither have they any great stomack to the *Hare* or other small Chases : and, which is worst of all, they are apt to run at tame Beasts.

Of the DUN-HOUND.

THese are good for all Chases, and therefore of general use. The best coloured are such as are dun on the Back, having their four quarters tann'd, or of the complexion of a *Hare*'s Legs : But if the Hair on the Back be black, and their Legs freckled with red and black, they then usually prove excellent Hounds : and indeed there are few dun-coloured to be found bad; the worst of them are such whose Legs are of a whitish colour. It is wonderful, in these creatures, to observe how much they stick upon the knowledge of their Master, especially his Voice, and Horn, and none's else. Nay, farther, they know the distinct Voices of their Fellows, and do know who are Babblers and Liars, and who not; and will follow the one, and not the other.

Now for Hounds, the West-country, *Cheshire*, & *Lancashire*, with other Wood-land and Mountainous Countries, breed our *Slow-hound*; which is a large great Dog, tall and heavy. *Worcester-shire, Bedford shire,* and

and many well-mixt soils, where the Champaign and Covert are of equal largeness , produce a middle-sized Dog , of a more nimble compofure than the former.   Laftly , the North-parts , as *York-fhire*, *Cumberland*, *Northumberland*, and many other plain Champaigne Countries , breed the Light , Nimble, Swift , Slender , Fleet Hound.   After all thefe, the little Beagle is attributed to our Country; this is that Hound , which in Latine is called *Canis Agafæus* , or the *Gaze-hound.* Befides our Maftiff, which feems to be an *Indigena*, or Native of *England* , we train up moft excellent Grey-Hounds, (which feem to have been brought hither by the *Galls*) in our open Champaigns.   All thefe Dogs have deferved to be famous in adjacent and remote Countries , whither they are fent for great rarities, and ambitioufly fought for by their Lords and Princes; although onely the fighting Dogs feem to have been known to the antient Authors; and perhaps in that age Hunting was not fo much cultivated by our own Country-men.

The marks of a good and fair Hound.

His Head ought to be of a middle proportion, rather long than round; his Noftrils wide; his Ears large; his Back bowed; the Fillets great; the Haunches large; the Thighs well truffed; the Ham ftraight; the Tail big near the Reins, and the reft flender to the end; the Leg big; the Soal of the Foot dry, and formed like a *Fox's*, with the Claws great.

Of the Election of a Dog and Bitch for good Whelps.

Your Bitch muſt come of a good kinde, being ſtrong, and well-proportioned in all parts, having her Ribs and Flanks great and large. Let the Dog that lines her be of a good fair breed; and let him be young, if you intend to have light and hot Hounds: for if the Dog be old, the Whelps will participate of his dull and heavy nature.

If your Bitch grow not naturally Proud ſo ſoon as you would have, you may make her ſo, by taking two heads of Garlick, half a Caſtor's Stone, the juice of Creſſes, and about twelve Spaniſh Flies, or Cantharides: boil theſe together in a Pipkin which holds a pint, with ſome Mutton, and make Broth thereof; and of this give to the Bitch twice or thrice, and ſhe will infallibly grow proud. The ſame Pottage given to the Dog, will make him deſirous of copulation.

When your Bitch is lined, and with Puppy, you muſt not let her hunt, for that will be the way to make her caſt her Whelps; but let her unconfined walk up and down in the Houſe and Court, and never lock her up in her Kennel; for ſhe is then impatient of food; and therefore you muſt make her ſome hot Broth once a day.

If you would ſpay your Bitch, it muſt be done before ſhe ever had Litter of Whelps: And in ſpaying her, take not away all the Roots or Strings of the Veins; for if you do, it will much prejudice her Reins, and hinder her ſwiftneſs ever after: but by leaving ſome behinde, it will make her much the ſtronger and more hardy. Whatever you do, ſpay her not when ſhe is proud; for that will endanger her life: but you may do it fifteen days after. But the beſt time of all is, when the Whelps are ſhaped within her.

How to enter young Hounds to hunt the Hart ; *and what Quarries and Rewards you ſhall give them.*

Having firſt taught your Hounds to know your Hallow, and the ſound of your Horn , then , about eighteen moneths old , you muſt lead them once a Week into the fields, and not oftner.

The beſt manner to teach your Hounds, is to take a live *Hare*, and trail her after you upon the Earth, now one way, now another ; and ſo, having drawn it a convenient ſpace, hide it in the Earth : afterward ſet forth your Hound neer the Trail , who taking Wind, runneth to and fro neer the Woods, Fields, Paſtures, Path-ways, and Hedges, until he finde which way the *Hare* is gone ; but with a ſoft and gentle pace, until at length coming neer the lodged *Hare*, he mendeth his pace, and beſtirreth himſelf more ſpeedily, leaping on his Prey , and killing it , loadeth himſelf with his conqueſt, and bringing it to his Maſter with Triumph, he muſt receive both Dog and it with all tokens of love into his Boſom.

When you hunt, let your *Hart* be in prime of greaſe, for then he is heavier than in *April* or *May*, and cannot ſtand up ſo long.

Then chuſe your Foreſt wherein the Relays are of equal proportion : then place all your young Hounds with five or ſix old to enter them ; and then lead them to the fartheſt and laſt Relay , and cauſe the *Hart* to be hunted unto them. Being come up, uncouple your old Hounds ; and having found the Track of the *Hart*, being well entered in cry , uncouple likewiſe your

　　　　　　　　　　　　　　　　　　young

young Hounds: and if you finde any of them lag behinde, you muſt beat or whip them forward.

In what place ſoever you kill the *Hart*, immediately flay his Neck, and reward your Hounds: for it is beſt whilſt it is hot ſo to do.

There are ſeveral ways of entring Hounds. As firſt, by taking a *Hart* in Nets, and after you have cut off one of his Feet, let him go: a quarter of an hour after, aſſemble your young Hounds; and having found out the View or Slot of the *Hart* or *Buck* by your Bloud-hounds, uncouple your young Hounds, and let them hunt. Secondly, you may bring them to quarry, by taking half a dozen Huntſmen, ſwift of foot, each whereof ſhall have two couple to lead in Liams; and having unlodg'd the *Hart*, purſue him fair and ſoftly, ſo that you tire not too much your young Hounds. After the *Hart* hath ran two or three hours, and that you finde he begins to ſink, you may then caſt off your young Hounds: but beware it be not when he is at Bay, and his Head full ſummed; for ſo you may endanger the lives of your Hounds.

But the beſt way of entring Hounds is at the Hare; for thereby they will learn all Doubles and Turns, better know the Hallow, will be more tender-noſed, and better ſcented, by uſing the beaten ways and Champion grounds.

Here note, that with whatſoever you firſt enter your Hounds, and therewith reward them, they will ever after love that moſt. Wherefore, if you intend them for the *Hart*, enter them not firſt with the *Hinde*. And for the better hunting the *Hart*, enter not your young Hounds within a Toil; for there a *Hart* doth nothing but turn and caſt about, ſince he cannot run end-long, and ſo they are always in ſight of him. If then afterwards you ſhould run him at force out of a Toil, and at length, and out of ſight, you will finde the Hounds to give him over quickly. Laſtly,

Laſtly, enter not your Hounds nor teach them in the Morning; for if ſo, you will finde them apt to give over in the heat of the day.

Of COURSING *with* Grey-Hounds.

I Need not declare the Excellencies which are contained in the noble and worthy Exercife of Courfing with *Grey-hounds*, fince it is fo well known to all Gentlemen who take delight in this pleaſant and healthy Paſtime : I ſhall therefore onely inſiſt upon the breed of *Grey-hounds*, their Shape, their Diet, and the Laws belonging to the fame, according as they were commanded , allowed , and ſubſcribed by the Duke of *Norfolk*, in the Reign of Queen *Elizabeth*.

Firſt, for the Breeding of *Grey-hounds* , in this you muſt have reſpect to the Country, which ſhould be Champain, Plain, or high Downs.   The beſt Valleys are thoſe of *Belvoir*, *White-horſe*, and *Eveſholm*, or any other where there are no Coverts, ſo that a *Hare* may ſtand forth and endure a Courſe of two or three miles : as for high Downs or Heaths, the beſt are about *Marlborough*, *Salisbury*, *Cirenceſter*, and *Lincoln*.

Though theſe places are very commodious for the breeding and training up of *Grey-hounds* ; yet, in my opinion, the middle, or moſt part arable grounds are the beſt : and yet thoſe Gentlemen who dwell on Downs or plain grounds, to keep up the reputation of their own Dogs, affirm, that they are more nimble and cunning in turning than the Vale-dogs are : and Mr. *Markham* confeſſeth that he hath feen a Vale-dog fo much deceived, that upon a turn he hath

loſt

loſt more ground than hath been recoverable in the
whole Courſe after : however, with a little care, in a
ſhort time this errour may be rectified ; and then you
will experimentally finde *The good Dogs upon the Deeps
will ever beat the good Dogs upon the Plains.*

It is a received opinion, that the *Grey-hound*-Bitch
will beat the *Grey-hound*-Dog, by reaſon ſhe excelleth
him in nimbleneſs : but if you conſider that the
Dog is longer and ſtronger, you muſt look upon that
opinion no more than as a vulgar errour.

Here note, as to the breeding of your *Grey-hounds*,
that the beſt Dog upon an indifferent Bitch, will not
get ſo good a Whelp as an indifferent Dog upon the
beſt Bitch.

Obſerve this in general as to breeding, let your Dogs
and Bitches, as near as you can, be of an equal age;
not exceeding four years old : however, to breed with
a young Dog and an old Bitch , may be the means of
producing excellent Whelps , the goodneſs whereof
you ſhall know by their Shapes in this manner.

If they are raw-bon'd, lean, looſe-made, ſickle or
crooked-hough'd, and generally unknit in every Member ; theſe are the proper marks of excellent ſhape
and goodneſs : but if after three or four months they
appear round and cloſe-truſt, fat, ſtraight , and as it
were full ſummed and knit in every Member, they
never prove good, ſwift , nor comely.

The goodneſs of ſhape in a *Grey-hound* after a year
and a half old, is this : his Head muſt be lean and long,
with a ſharp Noſe, ruſh-grown from the Eye downward ; a full clear Eye, with long Eye-lids ; a ſharp
Ear, ſhort and cloſe falling ; a long Neck a little bending, with a looſe hanging Weaſand ; a broad Breaſt;
ſtraight Fore-legs, hollow Side, ſtraight Ribs ; a ſquare
flat Back, ſhort and ſtrong Fillets, a broad ſpace between
the Hips, a ſtrong Stern or Tail, a round Foot, and
good large Clefts.   E   The

The Dieting of *Grey-hounds* conſiſts in theſe four things: *Food, Exerciſe, Airing*, and *Kennelling*.

Food of a *Grey-hound* is two fold: general, that is, the maintaining of a Dog in good bodily condition; and particular, when the Dog is dieted for a Wager, or it may be for ſome Diſtemper he is afflicted with.

A *Grey-hound*'s general Food ought to be Chippings, Cruſts of Bread, ſoft Bones and Griſtles. Your Chippings ought to be ſcalded in Beef, Mutton, Veal or Veniſon-Broth; and when it is indifferent cool, then make your Bread onely float with good Milk, and give it your *Grey-hounds* Morning and Evening; and this will keep them in good ſtate of body.

But if your Dog be poor, ſickly, and weak, then take Sheeps-heads, Wooll and all, clean waſh'd, and having broken them to pieces, put them into a Pot; and when it boils, ſcum the Pot, and put therein good ſtore of Oatmeal, and ſuch Herbs as Pottage is uſually made of; boil theſe till the Fleſh be very tender: then with the Meat and Broth feed your Dogs Morning and Evening, and it will recover them.

If you deſigne your *Grey-hound* for a Wager, then give him this Diet-bread: Take half a peck of the fineſt and drieſt Oat-meal, and a peck of good Wheat, having ground them together, boult the Meal, and ſcattering an indifferent quantity of Liquoriſh and Anniſeeds well beaten together; knead it up with the Whites of Eggs, new Ale and Barm mix'd together, and bake it in ſmall Loaves indifferent hard; then take it and ſoak it in Beef or any of the aforeſaid Broths; and half an hour after Sun-riſing, and half an hour before its ſetting, having firſt walkt and air'd your *Grey-hound*, give it him to eat. This will not onely increaſe his ſtrength, but enlarge his Wind.

Having thus ſpoken of a *Grey-hound*'s Feeding,
either

either generally or particularly , either for keeping him in health, or reſtoring it when it is loſt, I ſhall in the next place proceed to his Exerciſe; and this likewiſe conſiſts in two things, that is, Courſing, and Airing.

As to the firſt, he ought to be Courſed thrice a week, in ſuch manner that you uſually reward him with Blood , which will animate and encourage him to proſecute his Game : but be not unmindful to give the *Hare* all juſt and lawful advantage, ſo that ſhe may ſtand long before the *Grey-hound*, that thereby he may ſhew his utmoſt ſtrength and skill before he reap the benefit of his labour.

If he kill , ſuffer him not to break the *Hare*, but take her from him; and having cleans'd his Chaps from the Wooll of the *Hare* , then give him the Liver, Lights, and Heart, and ſo take him up in your Leaſh ; and having led him home, waſh his Feet with ſome Butter and Beer, and then put him into the Kennel, and feed him half an hour afterwards.

Upon your *Grey-hounds* Courſing-days , give him in the Morning before you air him, a Toaſt and Butter or Oyl, and nothing elſe; then Kennel him till he go to his Courſe.

The reaſon of Kennelling your *Grey-hounds* is this, becauſe it breeds in Dogs Luſt, Spirit, and Nimbleneſs; beſides, it prevents ſeveral dangerous Caſualties, and keeps the Pores from ſpending till time of neceſſity : and therefore do not permit your Dog to ſtir out of the Kennel but in the hours of Feeding , Walking, Courſing, or other neceſſary buſineſs.

The Laws of the Leaſh or Courſing.

Though the Laws of Courſing may alter according to ſome mens ſwaying Fancies ; yet theſe, ſubfcribed by the chief of the Gentry, were ever held authentical. Take them thus in order, according to my collection out of Mr. *Markham.*

First, it was ordered, that he who was chosen *Fewterer*, or Letter-loose of the *Grey-hounds*, should receive the *Grey-hounds* Match to run together into his Leash as soon as he came into the Field, and follow next to the *Hare-finder* till he came unto the Form: and no Horse-man or Foot-man, on pain of disgrace, to go before them, or on any side, but directly behinde, the space of forty yards or thereabouts.

2. That not above one Brace of *Grey-hounds* do course a *Hare* at one instant.

3. That the *Hare-finder* should give the *Hare* three *Sohoe's* before he put her from her *Lear*, to make the *Grey-hounds* gaze and attend her rising.

4. That the *Fewterer* shall give twelve-score Law ere he loose the *Grey-hounds*, except it be in danger of losing sight.

5. That Dog that giveth the first *Turn*, if after the Turn be given there be neither *Coat*, *Slip*, nor *Wrench* extraordinary; I say, he which gave the first *Turn* shall be held to win the Wager.

6. If one Dog give the first *Turn*, and the other bear the *Hare*, then he which bare the *Hare* shall win.

7. If one give both the first and last *Turn*, and no other advantage be between them, the odde *Turn* shall win the Wager.

8. That a *Coat* shall be more than two *Turns*, and a *Go-by*, or the *Bearing* of the *Hare* equal with two *Turns.*

9. If neither Dog turn the *Hare*, then he which leadeth last at the *Covert* shall be held to win the Wager.

10. If one Dog turn the *Hare*, serve himself, and
turn

turn her again, thoſe two *Turns* ſhall be as much as a *Coat*.

11. If all the Courſe be equal, then he which *bears* the *Hare* ſhall win onely ; and if ſhe be not *born*, the Courſe muſt be adjudged dead.

12. If he which comes firſt in to the death of the *Hare* takes her up, and ſaves her from breaking, cheriſheth the Dogs, and cleanſeth their Mouths from the Woll, or other filth of the *Hare*, for ſuch courteſie done he ſhall in right challenge the *Hare* : but not doing it, he ſhall have no Right, Priviledge, or Title therein.

13. If any Dog ſhall take a fall in the Courſe, and yet perform his part, he ſhall challenge the advantage of a *Turn* more than he giveth.

14. If one Dog turn the *Hare*, ſerve himſelf, and give divers *Coats*, yet in the end ſtand ſtill in the field, the other Dog, without *Turn* giving, running home to the *Covert* ; that Dog which ſtood ſtill in the field ſhall be adjudged to loſe the Wager.

15. If any man ſhall ride over a Dog, and overthrow him in his Courſe, (though the Dog were the worſe Dog in opinion, yet) the party for the offence ſhall either receive the diſgrace of the Field, or pay the Wager ; for between the *Parties* it ſhall be adjudged no Courſe.

16. Laſtly, thoſe which are choſen *Judges* of the *Leaſh* ſhall give their judgements preſently before they depart from the Field, or elſe he in whoſe default it lieth ſhall pay the Wager by a general Voice and Sentence.

Here note, that it lieth in the power of him that hath the office of the Leaſh conferred on him, to make Laws according to the Cuſtoms of Countries, and the Rule of Reaſon.

Of

Of the Stiles of Hunting different from the English both Antique and Forrein.

THe Hunting used by the Antients was much like that way which is at present taken with the *Rain-Deer*, which is seldom hunted at force or with Hounds, but onely drawn after with a Blood-hound, and forestall'd with Nets and Engines. So did they with all Beasts, and therefore a Dog is never commended by them for opening before he hath by signes discovered where the beast lieth in his *Layre*, as by their drawing stiff our Harbourers are brought to give right judgement. Therefore I do not finde that they were curious in the Musick of their Hounds, or in a composition of their Kennel or Pack, either for deepness, or loudness, or sweetness of cry like to ours. Their Huntsmen were accustomed to shout and make a great noise, as *Virgil* observes in the third of his *Georgicks*:

Ingentem clamore premes ad retia Cervum.

So that it was onely with that confusion to bring the *Deer* to the Nets laid for him.

But we comfort our Hounds with loud and courageous Cries and Noises, both of Voice and Horn, that they may follow over the same way that they saw the *Hart* pass, without crossing or coasting.

The *Sicilian* way of Hunting was thus: when the Nobles or Gentry were informed which way a Herd of *Deer* passed, giving notice to one another, they appointed a meeting, and every one brought with him

him a Crofs-bow, or a Long-bow, and a bundle of Staves. Thefe Staves had an Iron-fpike at the bottom, and their Head is bored, with a Cord drawn through all of them; their length is about four foot: Being thus provided, they come to the Herd, and there cafting themfelves about into a large Ring, they furround the *Deer*; and then every one of them recieves a peculiar ftand, and there, unbinding his Faggot, ties the end of his Cord to the other who is fet in the next ftation; then to fupport it, fticks into the ground each Staff, about the diftance of ten foot one from the other. Then they take out Feathers, which they bring with them, died in Crimfon for this very purpofe, and faftned upon a Thred which is tied to the Cord, fo that with the leaft breath of Wind they are whirled round about. Thofe which keep the feveral Stands, withdraw and hide themfelves in the next Covert. After this, the chief Ranger enters within the Line, taking with him onely fuch Hounds which draw after the Herd; and coming near with their cry, rouze them: Upon which the *Deer* fly till they come towards the Line, where they turn off towards the left, and ftill gazing upon the fhaking and fhining Feathers, wander about them as if they were kept in with a Wall or Pale. The chief Ranger purfues, and calling to every one by name, as he paffeth by their Stand, cries to them, that they fhoot the firft, third, or fixth, as he fhall pleafe; and if any of them mifs, and fingle out any other than that which was affigned by the Ranger, it is counted a difgrace to him: by which means, as they pafs by the feveral Stations, the whole Herd is killed by feveral hands. This Relation is of undoubted truth, as you may finde it in *Pierius* his *Hieroglyphicks*, Lib. 7. Chap. 6.

Boar-hunting is very ufual in *France*, and they call it *Sanglier*. In this fort of hunting the way is to

ufe

ufe furious terrible Sounds and Noifes, as well of Voice as of Horn, to make the Chafe turn and fly; becaufe they are flow, and truft to their Tusks and defence: which is *Agere Aprum*, to bait the *Boar*. Yet this muft be done after his Den or Hold is difcovered, and the Nets be pitched.

The Huntf-men give judgement of the *Wild-boar* by the print of his Foot, by his Rooting. A wilde Swine roots deeper than our ordinary Hogs, becaufe their Snouts are longer; and when he comes into a Corn-field, (as the *Caledonian-Boar* in *Ovid*) turns up one continued Furrow, not as our Hogs, routing here and there; and then by his foil he foils and wallows him in the myre: thefe are his *Volutabra Silveftria*, where his greatnefs is meafured out; then coming forth, he rubs againft fome Tree, which marks his height; as alfo when he fticks his Tusk into it, that fhews the greatnefs thereof. They obferve the bignefs of his Leffes, and the depth of his Den; where note, that they call his Dung by the name of *Leffes*.

Whenfoever the *Boar* is hunted and ftands at Bay, the Huntf-men ride in, and with Swords and Spears ftriking on that fide which is from their Horfes, wound or kill him. This is in the French hunting: but the antient *Romans* ftanding on foot, or fetting their Knees to the ground, and charging directly with their Spear, did *Opponere ferrum*, and *Excipere Aprum*: for fuch is the nature of a *Boar*, that he fpits himfelf with fury, running upon the Weapon to come at his Adverfary; and fo, feeking his revenge, he meets with his own deftruction.

Though thefe Wild-*Boars* are frequent in *France*, we have none in *England*; yet it may be fuppofed that heretofore we had, and did not think it convenient to preferve that Game: For our old Authors of hunting reckon them amongft the beafts of Venery; and

we

we have the proper terms belonging to them, as you may finde them at the beginning of the Book. Of *Boar*-hunting you will read more hereafter.

There are no *Roe-Deer* in *England*; but there are plenty of them in *Scotland*, as Sir *James Lindsay* an old Scotish Writer testifies.

Yet it may be thought that they have been more common in *England*, becaufe our antient Hunts-men acknowledge the proper terms for this Chafe; and in the firft place we have diftinct Ages for thefe *Dorces*, which you fhall finde in the Terms aforefaid. They make good Chafe, ftand long, and fly end-way. *Compellere Dorcas*, is to force the *Bevy*, and to drive them into the *Toyls*.

Although we have no *Wolves* in *England* at this prefent, yet it is certain that heretofore we had Routs of them, as they have to this very day in *Ireland*; and in that Country are bred a race of *Grey-hounds*, (which are commonly called *Wolf-dogs*) which are ftrong, fleet, and bear a natural enmity to the *Wolf*. Now in thefe the *Grey-hounds* of that Nation there is an incredible force and boldnefs,fo that they are in great eftimation, and much fought after in forrein parts, fo that the King of *Poland* makes ufe of them in his hunting of great Beafts by force. Wherefore it may well be intended of the great fiercenefs which thefe Dogs have in affaulting, that when the *Romans* faw them play, they thought them fo wonderful violent, as that they muft needs have been *Ferreis caveis advecti*, brought up in Iron Dens.

In *Poland* when the King hunts, his fervants are wont to furround a Wood, though a Mile in compafs, with Toyls which are pitched on firm Stakes. This being done, the whole Town, all Sexes and Ages promifcuoufly rufh into the Inclofure, and with their loud fhouts rear all the Beafts within thatWood ; which

making

making forth, are intercepted in the Nets. Their small and great Beasts are entangled together, after the same manner as when amongst us we draw a Net over a Pond, and after beating it all over with Poles, we bring out not onely *Pike* and *Carp*, but lesser **Fry**; so they inclose at once *Deer, Boar, Roe-buck,* and *Hare*: For so they order their Nets, that the space of those Meshes which are twisted with greater Cords, for the entangling of greater Beasts, that space, **I say**, is made up with smaller Whip-cord, for the catching smaller Prey.

He hath a great race of English Mastiffs, which in that Country retain their generosity, and are brought up to play upon greater Beasts. It is not counted among them disagreeable to the Laws of the Chase, to use Guns. I shall now proceed to the manner of English-hunting both antient and modern, according to the best information I could gather either out of Books, experienced Huntsmen, and my own practice.

Of Hart-*hunting*.

A *Hart* can naturally swim a great way; insomuch that I have heard of some so sore hunted in Forests near the Sea, that they have plung'd into it, and have been killed by Fisher-men a dozen miles from land.

It is reported of them when they go to Rut, and must for that purpose cross some great River or Arm of the Sea, they assemble in great Herds, the strongest goes in first, and the next of strength follows him, and so one after the other, relieving themselves by
staying

staying their Heads on the Buttocks of each other.

The *Hinde* commonly carries her Calf eight or nine moneths, which usually falls in *May*, although some later: some of them have two at once, eating the Skin up wherein the Calf did lie.

As the Calf grows up, she teacheth it to run, leap, and the way it must keep to defend it self from the Hounds.

Harts and *Hindes* are very long-liv'd, living commonly an hundred years and upwards.

The Nature of a Hart.

The *Hart* is strangely amazed when he hears any one call, or whistle in his Fist; For trial of which, some seeing a *Hart* in the Plain in motion, have called after him, saying, *Ware*, *Ware*, or *Take heed*; and thereupon have seen him instantly turn back, making some little stand. He heareth very perfectly when his Head and Ears are erected; but heareth imperfectly when he holdeth them down. When he is on foot, and not afraid, he wonders at every thing he seeth, and taketh pleasure to gaze at them.

They bear sometimes few, and sometimes more Croches; and that is the reason that many men have erred in their judgements as to their age.

Harts are bred in most Countries; but the Antients do prefer those of *Britain* before all others, where they are of divers colours.

These do excel all others in the beauty of Horns; which are very high, yet do not grow to their Bones or Scalps, but to their Skin, branching forth into many Speers, being solid throughout, and as hard as Stones, and fall off once a year: but if they remain abroad in the Air, and that thereby they are sometimes

wet

wet and dry, they grow as light as any vanifhing or
other fubftance, as I have proved by experience, finding fome which have been loft by them in the Woods;
wherefore I gather, that they are of an earthly fubftance, concrete, and hardned with a ftrong heat, made
like unto Bones. They lofe thefe Horns every year
in the Spring. At one year old they have nothing
but Bunches, that are fmall fignificators of Horns to
come: at two years they appear more perfectly, but
ftraight and fimple: at three years they grow into two
Spears: at four, into three; and fo increafe every year
in their Branches till they be fix; and above that time
their age is not certainly to be difcerned by their
Head.

Having loft their Horns in the day-time, they
hide themfelves, inhabiting the fhades, to avoid the
annoyance of Flies, and feed, during that time onely,
in the night. Their new Horns come out at firft
like Bunches, and afterwards (as I faid before) by
the increafe of the Sun's heat they grow more hard,
covered with a rough Skin, which is called a *Velvet-
head*; and as that Skin drieth, they daily try the ftrength
of their new Heads upon Trees; which not onely
fcrapeth off the roughnefs, but by the pain they feel thus
rubbing them, they are taught how long to forbear the
company of their fellows: for at laft, when in their
chafing and fretting of their new Horn againft the
Tree they can feel no longer pain and fmart in them,
they take it for high time to forfake their folitary
dwellings, and return again to their former condition.

The reafons why *Harts* and *Deers* do lofe their
Horns yearly, are thefe: Firft, becaufe of the matter
whereof they confift; for it is dry and earthy, like
the fubftance of green Leaves which have an yearly
fall, likewife, wanting glewing or holding moifture

to

to continue them; wherefore the Horn of a *Hart* cannot be bent. Secondly, from the place they grow upon; for they are not rooted upon the Skull, but onely within the Skin. Thirdly, from the efficient cause; for they are hardned both with the heat of Summer, and cold of Winter; by means whereof the Pores to receive their nourishing Liquor are utterly shut up and stopped, so as of necessity their native heat dieth; which falleth not out in other Beasts, whose Horns are for the most part hollow, and fitted for longer continuance; but these are of lesser, and the new Bunches swelling up towards the Spring, do thrust off the old Horns, having the assistance of Boughs of Trees, weight of the Horns, or by the willing excussion of the Beast that beareth them.

It is observed, that when a *Hart* pricketh up his Ears, he windeth sharp, very far, and sure, and discovereth all treachery against him; but if they hang down and wag, he perceiveth no danger. By their Teeth is their Age discerned, and they have four on both sides wherewith they grinde their meat, besides two other, much greater in the Male than in the Female. All these Beasts have Worms in their Head underneath their Tongue, in a hollow place where the Neck-bone is joyned to the Head, which are no bigger than Fly-blows. His Blood is not like other Beasts, for it hath no fibres in it, and therefore it is hardly congealed. His Heart is very great, and so are all those of fearful Beasts, having in it a Bone like a Cross. He hath no Gall, and that is one of the causes of the length of his life; and therefore are his Bowels so bitter, that the Dogs will not touch them unless they be very fat. The Genital-part is all nervy; the Tail small; and the *Hinde* hath Udders betwixt her Thighs, with four Speans like a Cow. These are above all other four-footed Beasts, both

ingenious

ingenious and fearful, who although they have large
Horns, yet their defence againſt other four-footed
Beaſts is to run away.

And now if you will credit *Geſner* as a Huntſ-man,
pray here obſerve what account he gives of hunting
the *Hart : This wilde deceitful and ſubtile Beaſt* (ſays
he) *by windings and turnings does often deceive its
Hunter, as the Harts of* Meandros *flying from the terrible cry of* Diana's *Hounds.* Wherefore the prudent
Hunter muſt frame his Dogs as *Pythagoras* did his
Scholars, with words of Art to ſet them on, and take
them off again at his pleaſure ; wherefore he muſt
firſt of all compaſs in the Beaſt (*en ſon giſte*) in her own
Layr, and ſo unharbour her in the view of the Dogs,
that ſo they may never loſe her Slot or Footing : neither muſt he ſet upon every one , either of the Herd
or thoſe that wander ſolitary alone, or a little one ;
but partly by ſight, and partly by their Footing and
Fumets, judge of their Game ; alſo he muſt obſerve
the largeneſs of his Layr. Being thus informed, then
Diſcouples les chiens , take off your Dog-Couplings ;
and ſome on Horſe-back, others on foot, follow the
Cry with greateſt art, obſervation and ſpeed, remem-
bring and preventing (*cer fraze*) the ſubtile turnings
and headings of the *Hart* ; ſtraining with all dexterity to leap Hedge, Pale , Ditch, nay Rocks ; neither
fearing Thorns, down Hills , nor Woods , but providing freſh Horſe if the firſt tire, follow the largeſt Head of the whole Herd, which you muſt endeavour to ſingle out for the Chaſe ; which the Dogs
perceiving muſt follow , taking for a prohibition to
follow any other.

The Dogs are animated by the winding of Horns,
and voices of the Huntſ-men, like Souldiers to the
Battle, by the noiſe of Trumpets and other Warlike
Inſtruments. But ſometimes the craſty great Beaſt
ſendeth

fendeth forth his little Squire to be facrificed to the
Dogs and Huntf-men, inftead of himfelf; lying clofe in
the mean time: Then muft a Retreat be founded, and
(*rompre le chiens*) the Dogs be broken off, and taken in
(*le Limier*) that is, Leame again, until they be brought
to the fairer Game; who arifeth in fear, yet ftill ftri-
veth by flight, until he be wearied and breathlefs.

The Nobles call this Beaft (*Cerf fage*) a wife
Hart, who, to avoid all his Enemies, runneth into the
greateft Herds, and fo bringeth a Cloud of errour
on the Dogs, to keep them from further profecution;
fometimes alfo beating fome of the Herd into his
Footings, that fo he may the more eafily efcape, and
procure a Labyrinth to the Dogs; after which he be-
taketh himfelf to his Heels again, running ftill with
the Wind, not onely for refrigeration, but becaufe he
may the more eafily hear the voice of his purfuers,
whether they be far or neer. At laft, being for all
this found out again by the obfervance of the Hunters, and skilful Scent of the Dogs, he flieth into the
Herds of Cattle, as Cows, Sheep, &c. leaping on an
Ox or Cow, laying the foreparts of his body thereon, that fo touching the Earth onely with his hinder
Feet, to leave a very fmall or no fcent at all behinde
for the Hounds to defcern.

The chief Huntf-man to *Lewis* the twelfth, called (*le Grand Venieur*) affirmeth, that on a time,
they having a *Hart* in chafe, fuddenly the Hounds
were at a fault, fo as the Game was out of fight, and
not a Dog would once ftir his foot, whereat the
Hunters were all amazed; at laft, by cafting about,
(as it is ufual in fuch cafes) they found the fraud of
this crafty Beaft, which is worth the memory.

There was a great White-thorn, which grew in a
fhadowy place as high as a tree, and was environed with
other fmall fhrubs about it; into the which the faid
Hart

Hart leaped, and there ftood aloft the Boughs fpreading from one another, and there remained till he was thruft through by a Huntf-man, rather than he would yield to the angry and greedy Hounds. Yet their manner is when they fee themfelves every where intercepted, to make force at him with their Horns who firft comes unto him, except prevented by Sword or Spear ; which being done, the Hunter with his Horn windeth the fall of the Beaft, and then every one approacheth, luring with triumph for fuch a conqueft, of whom the skilfulleft openeth the beaft, rewarding the Hounds with what properly belongeth unto them for their future encouragement ; and for that purpofe the Huntf men dip Bread in the Skin and Blood of the Beaft, to give unto the Hounds their full fatisfaction.

Veloces Spartæ catulos, acremq; Molloffum
Pafce fero pingui, &c.

Much more might be faid of this prefent fubject, which is not proper in this place ; wherefore I fhall refer you to what followeth, and your own experience.

Of the Rut of Harts.

The time of their Rutting is about the midft of *September*, and continues two months : the older they are, the hotter, and the better beloved by the Hindes ; and therefore they go to Rut before the young ones ; and, being very fiery, will not fuffer any of them to come near the *Hindes* till they have fatisfied their Venery. But the young ones are even with the old ; for when they perceive the old are grown weak by excefs of Rutting, the young will frequently attaque them,

them, and make them quit the place, that they may be masters of the sport.

They are easily kill'd in Rutting-time: for they follow the scent of the *Hindes* with such greediness, laying their Noses to the ground, that they minde that solely, and nothing else.

They are such great lovers of the sport, it is very dangerous for any man to come near them at this season, for then they will make at any living creature of different kind.

In some places, in *October* their Lust ariseth, and also in *May*; and then, whereas at other times the Males live apart from the Females, they go about like lascivious Lovers, seeking the company of their Females, as it were at the market of *Venus*.

The Males in their raging desired Lust have a peculiar noise, which the French call *Reere*. One Male will cover a many Females, continuing in this carnal appetite a month or two. The Females are chaste, and unwilling to admit of Copulation, by reason of the rigour of the Male's Genital; and therefore they sink down on their Buttocks when they begin to feel his Seed, as it hath been often observed in Tame *Harts*; and if they can, the Females run away, the Males striving to hold them back within their Fore-feet. It cannot be well said, that they are covered standing, lying, or going, but rather running; for so are they filled with greatest severity. When one month or six weeks is over of their Rutting, they grow tamer by much, and laying aside all fierceness, they return to their solitary places, digging every one by himself a several Hole or Ditch, wherein they lie, to asswage the strong favour of their Lust; for they stink like Goats, and their Face beginneth to look blacker than at other times: and in those places they live till some Showers distil from the Clouds; after which, they return to

F   their

their Pasture again, living in Flocks as before.

The Female, thus filled, never keepeth company a-
gain with the Male until she is delivered of her burthen, which is eight months; and but one at a time,
seldom two, which she lodgeth cunningly in some
Covert: If she perceive them stubborn and wilde,
she will beat them with her Feet till they lie close and
quiet.

Oftentimes she leadeth forth her young, teaching
it to run and leap over Bushes, Stones, and small
Shrubs; and so continueth all the Summer long,
while their own strength is most considerable.

It is very pleasant to observe them when they go to
Rut, and make their Vaut. For when they smell the
Hinde, they raise their Nose up into the Air, looking
aloft, as though they gave thanks to the God of Nature, who gave them so great delight and pleasure.
And if it be a great *Hart*, he will turn his Head and
look about to see whether there be none neer to in-
terrupt or spoil his sport. Hereat the young fly a-
way for fear: but if there be any of equal bigness,
they then strive which shall Vaut first; and in the op-
posing each other, they scrape the ground with their
Feet, shocking and butting each other so furiously,
that you shall hear the noise they make with their
Horns a good half mile, so long, till one of them is
Victor. The *Hinde*, beholding this Pastime, never
stirs from her station, expecting, as it were, the Vaut-
ing of him who hath the Mastery; and having got
it, he bellows, and then instantly covers her.

During the time of their Rut, they eat but very
little; for they feed onely on what they see before
them, minding more the track of the *Hindes*. Their
chief meat is the red Mushrome, which helps them to
evacuate their Grease: they are then extraordinary
hot, insomuch, that every where as they pass and finde
Waters, they tumble and lie therein.   *The*

The time of Harts *Mewing, or Casting the Head.*

The old *Hart* casteth his Head sooner than the young : and the time is about the month's of *February* and *March*.

Here note, that if you geld an *Hart* before he hath an Head, he will never bear any ; and if you geld him when he hath it, he will never after Mew or cast it : and so, if you geld him when he hath a Velvet-head, it will ever be so, without fraying or burnish-ing.

Having cast their Heads, they instantly withdraw unto the Thickets, hiding themselves in such conve-nient places where they may have good Water, and strong Feeding, near some ground where Wheat or Pease is sown : But young *Harts* do never betake themselves to the Thickets till they have born their third Head, which is in the fourth year.

After they have Mewed, they will begin to But-ton in *March* and *April* ; and as the Sun grows strong, and the season of the year puts forward the Crop of the Earth, so will their Heads increase in all respects : so that in the midst of *June* their Heads will be sum-med as much as they will bear all the year.

Of the Coats and Colour of Harts.

The Coats of *Harts* are of three sundry sorts, *Brown, Red*, and *Fallow* ; and of every of these Coats there proceeds two sorts of *Harts*, the one are great, the other little.

Of brown *Harts*, there are some great, long, and hairy, bearing a high Head, red of colour, and well

beam'd,

beam'd, who will stand before Hounds very long, being longer of breath, and swifter of foot than those of a shorter stature.

There are another sort of brown *Harts*, which are little, short, and well-set; bearing commonly a black Main, and are fatter and better Venison than the former, by reason of their better feeding in young Copses.

They are very crafty, especially when in grease; and will be hardly found, because they know they are then most enquired after: besides, they are very sensible they cannot then stand long before the Hounds. If they be old, and feed in good ground, then are their Heads black, fair, and well branched, and commonly palmed at the top.

The Fallow-*Harts* bear their Heads high, and of a whitish colour, their Beams small, their Antliers long, slender, and ill-grown, having neither Heart, Courage, nor Force. But those which are of a lively Red-fallow, having a black or brown List down the Ridge of the Back, are strong, bearing fair and high Heads, well furnished and beam'd.

Of the Heads and Branches of Harts, and their diversities.

As there are several sorts of *Harts*, so have they their Heads in a divers sort and manner, according to their Age, Country, Rest, and Feeding. Here note, that they bear not their first Head, which we call Broches, and in a Fallow-*Deer* Pricks, until they enter the second year of their Age. In the third year they bear four, six, or eight small Branches: At the fourth, they bear eight or ten: at the fifth, ten or twelve: at six, fourteen or sixteen: and at the seventh year they bear their Heads Beam'd, Branched, and Summed with as much as ever they will bear, and do never multiply but in greatness onely.

How

How to know an old Hart *by the Slot, Entries, Abatures and Foils, Fewmets, Gate and Walks, Fraying-(tocks, Head and Branches.*

I shall proceed in order, and first of the *Slot.* You must carefully look on the Treadings of the *Hart's* Foot : If you find the Treadings of two, the one long, the other round, yet both of one bigness; yet shall the long Slot declare the *Hart* to be much larger than the round.

Moreover, the old *Hart's* hind-foot doth never over-reach the fore-foot; the young one's doth.

But above all, take this Observation : When you are in the Wood, and have found the Slot of a *Hart,* mark what manner of Footing it is, whether worn, or sharp; and accordingly observe the Country, and thereby judge whether either may be occasioned thereby. For *Harts* bred in mountainous and stony Countries, have their Toes and sides of their Feet worn, by reason of their continual climbing and resting themselves thereon, and not on the Heel: whereas in other places they stay themselves more on the Heel than Toes : For in soft or sandy ground they slip upon the Heel, by reason of their weight; and thus by frequent staying themselves thereon, it makes the Heel grow broader and greater. And thus you may know the age of a *Hart* by his Slot or Treading.

The next thing to be considered, is the Fewmishing; and this is to be judged of in *April* or *May.* If the Fewmets be great, large, and thick, they signifie the *Hart* to be old.

In the midst of *June* and *July*, they make their Fewmets or Fewmishing in great Croteys, very soft; and from that time to the end of *August*, they make them great, long, knotty, anointed and gilded, let-

ting

ting them fall but few and fcattered. In *September*
and *October* there is no longer judging, by reafon of
the Rut.

Thirdly, If you would know the height and thick-
nefs of the *Hart*, obferve his Entries and Galleries
into the Thickets, and what Boughs he hath over-
ftridden, and mark from thence the height of his Belly
from the ground.

By the height of the Entries, we judge the age of a
Hart : for a young *Deer* is fuch as creeps ufually ; but
the old is ftiff and ftately.

His greatnefs is known by the height of his creeping as he paffes to his Harbour ; the young *Deer*
creeping low, which the old will not ftoop to.

Fourthly, Take notice of his Gate, by which you
may know whether the *Hart* be great and long, and
whether he will ftand long before the Hounds or not.
For all *Harts* which have a long ftep will ftand up very long, being fwift, light, and well breath'd ; but
if he leave a great Slot, which is the figne of an old
Deer, he will never ftand long when he is chafed.

Laftly, Take notice of his Fraying-poft : Where
note, the elder the *Hart* is, the fooner he goeth to
Fray, and the greater is the Tree he feeketh to Fray
upon, and fuch as he cannot bend with his Head.

All *Stags* as they are burnifh'd, beat their Heads
dry againft fome Tree or other, which is called their
Fraying-poft : The younger *Deer* againft weaker and
leffer Trees, and lower ; the elder againft bigger and
ftronger, and Fray higher ; fo that accordingly we
confidently judge of their age, and of the neernefs of
their Harbour ; for that is the laft Ceremony they ufe
before they enter it.

As to the Head and Branches, the *Hart* is old, Firft,
when the compafs of the Bur is large, great, and well
pearl'd.

Secondly,

Secondly, when the Beam is great, burnished, and well pearl'd, being straight, and not made crooked by the Antliers.

Thirdly, when the Gutters therein are great and deep.

Fourthly, when the first Antlier, called *Antoiller* , is great, long, and near to the Bur; the Surantlier near unto the Antlier: and they ought to be both well pearled.

Fifthly, The rest of the Branches which are higher, being well ordered and set, and well grown, according to the bigness and proportion of the Head; and the Croches, Palm or Crown being great and large according to the bigness of the Beam, are the signes of an old *Hart.*

Now since many men cannot understand the names and diversities of Heads according to the Terms of Hunting, I shall in the following Chapter give you a brief account thereof.

The Names and diversities of Heads, according to Hunting-Terms.

The thing that beareth the Antliers, Royals , and Tops, is called the *Beam* ; and the little streaks therein are called *Gutters.*

That which is about the Crust of the Beam , is termed *Pearls* : and that which is about the Bur it self, formed like little Pearls, is called *Pearls bigger than the rest.*

The Bur is next the Head; and that which is about the Bur, is called *Pearls.* The first is called *Antlier*; the second, *Surantlier:* All the rest which grow afterwards, until you come to the Crown, Palm, or Croche, are called *Royals,* and *Sur-royals* : The little Buds or Broches about the Top, are called *Croches.*

F 4 Their

Their Heads go by several Names: The first Head is called a *Crowned Top*, because the Croches are ranged in form of a Crown.

The second is called a *Palmed Top*, because the Croches are formed like a mans Hand.

Thirdly, all Heads which bear not above three or four, the Croches being placed aloft, all of one height, in form of a cluster of Nuts, are to be called *Heads* of so many *Croches*.

Fourthly, all Heads which bear two in the Top, or having their Croches doubling, are to be called *Forked Heads*.

Fifthly, all Heads which have double Burs, or the Antliers, Royals, and Croches turned downwards, contrary to other Heads, are only called *Heads*.

How to seek a Hart *in his Haunts or Feeding-places according to the seasons of the year.*

All *Harts* do change their manner of Feeding every month; and therefore I shall treat orderly of every one till I have concluded the year; beginning with that month which is the conclusion of their Rutting-time, and that is *November*, in which month they feed in Heaths and broomy places.

In *December* they herd together, and withdraw themselves into the strength of the Forests, to shelter themselves from the cold Winds, Snows, and Frosts, and do feed on the Holm-trees, Elder-trees, Brambles, with whatsoever other green thing they can finde; and if it snow, they will skin the Trees like a Goat.

In *January*, *February*, and *March*, they leave herding, but will keep four or five in company, and in the corners of the Forest will feed on the Winter-pasture; sometimes making their incursions into the neighbouring Corn-fields, if they can perceive the

blades

blades of Wheat, Rie, or such-like, appear above ground.

In *April* and *May* they rest in their Thickets, and other bushy and shady places, during that season, and stir very little till Rutting-time, unless they are disturb'd.

There are some *Harts* are so cunning, that they will have two several Layrs to harbour in, a good distance one from the other; and will frequently change (for their greater security) from the one to the other, taking still the benefit of the Wind.

In these months they go not to the Soil, by reason of the moisture of the Spring, and the Dew that continually overspreadeth the Grass.

In *June*, *July*, and *August*, they are in their pride of grease, and do resort to Spring-Copses, and Corn-fields; only they seldom go where Rye or Barley grow.

In *September* and *October* they leave their Thickets, and go to Rut; during which season they have no certain place either for food or harbour.

In what manner the Hunts-man shall go drawing in the Springs.

Let him not come too early into the Springs or Hewts where he thinketh the *Hart* feedeth, and is at relief. For they usually go to their Layrs in the Springs; and if they be old crafty *Deer*, they will return to the border of the Copse, and there listen whether they can hear any approaching danger: and if they chance once to vent the Hunts-man or the Hound, they will instantly dislodge.

Now is the Hunts-man's proper time. Let him beat the outsides of the Springs or Thickets; if he finde the Track of an *Hart* or *Deer*, let him observe

whether

whether it be new ; which he may know thus ; the Dew will be beaten off, the Foil fresh, or the ground broken or printed, with other tokens : so he may judge his Game lately went that way.

Having found this Slot or Treading, and the Hound sticking well upon it, let him hold him short, for he shall better draw being so held, than if he were let at length of the Lyam : and thus let him draw till he is come to the Covert , if possible , taking notice by the way of the Slot, Foils, Entries , and the like, till he hath harboured him. That done , let him plash down small Twigs, some above, and some below, as he shall think fit : and then, whilst the Hound is hot, let him beat the outsides , and make his Ring-walks twice or thrice about the Wood , one while by the great and open ways, that he may help himself by the Eye ; another while through the thick and Covert, for fear left his Hound should overshoot it, having still better Scent in the Coverts than High-ways.

If he doubt the *Hart* is gone out of the Ring-walks, or fears he hath drawn amiss ; then let him go to the Marks which he plashed, and draw counter , till he may take up the Fewmet.

The directions for Harbouring a Stag *are these.*

The Harbourer having taught his Hound to draw mute always round the outside of the Covert, as soon as his Hound challenges, which he knows by his eager flourishing, and straining his Lyam , he then is to seek for his Slot : If he findes the Heel thick, and the Toe spreading broad, it argues an old *Deer*, especially if it is fringed, (that is, broken on the sides.) However, if the ground be too hard to make any judgment from the Slot, he is to draw into the Covert, as he passes observing the size of the Entries ; the larger

and

and higher, the elder the *Deer*; as also his Croppings of the Tenders as he passes: (the younger the *Deer*, the lower; the elder the *Deer*, the higher he branches.) Also observe all his Fewmishings as you pass, whose largeness bespeak the largeness of the *Deer*; also be curious in observing his Fraying-post, which usually is the last opportunity you have to judge by, the eldest *Deer* Fraying highest against the biggest Trees; and that found, you may conclude his Harbour not far off; therefore draw with more circumspection, checking your Draught-hound to secure him from spending when he comes so near as to have the *Deer* in the Wind: and then by his eagerness you having discovered that, ought to draw him; and having retired some distance back, you are with your Hound to round the place first at a considerable distance; and then, if you finde him not disturbed, a little within that make your second round; which will not onely secure you that he is in his Harbour, but will also secure his continuance there; for he will not (unforc'd) pass that Taint your Hound hath left in the rounding of him. So that having broken a Bough for his direction, he may at any time unharbour that *Hart*.

How to finde a Hart lost the night before.

A Huntsman may fail of killing a *Hart* divers ways; sometimes by reason of great heat, or overtaken with the night, and the like. If any such thing should happen, then thus you must do. First, they which follow the Hounds, must mark the place where they left the Chase, and at break of day bring your Bloodhound to it with your Kennel after him. If any hound vents, whom he knows to be no Lier or Babler, he shall put his Hound to it, whooping twice, or blowing two Notes with his Horn, to call all his fellows about

about him : and if he finde where the *Hart* is gone
into some likely Covert or Grove, then must he draw
his Hounds about it, and beat cross through it.   And
if there he renews his Slot or View, let him first consider whether it be the right or not : if it be the right, let
him blow his Horn.   Now if he finde five or six Layrs,
let it not seem strange; for *Harts* hunted and spent, do
freequently make many Layrs together , because they
cannot stand, but lie and feed.

Harts which are hunted , most commonly run up
the Wind , and straight forwards as far as they are
able, and finding any Water or Soil, do stay a long
time therein; by which means their Joynts are so be-
nummed and stiffned, that coming out they cannot go
far, nor stand up long; and therefore are compelled
to take any Harbour they can finde, which may be a
present Covert to them.

How to finde a Hart in high Woods.

In the seeking of a *Hart* in high Woods, regard must
be had to two things; that is, the Thickets of the Forest, and the Season.

If it be in very hot weather, Gnats, Horse-flies, and
such-like, drive the *Deer* out of the high Wood, and
they disperse themselves into small Groves and Thickets near places of good feeding.   According to the
Coverts which are in the Forest , so accordingly the
Huntf-man must make his enquiry.   For sometimes
the *Harts* lie in the Tufts of White-thorn; sometimes
under little Trees; otherwhiles under great Trees in
the high Woods; and sometimes in the Skirts of the
Forest under the shelter of little Groves and Copses.
And therefore the Huntf-man must make his Ring-
walk great or small, according to the largeness of those
Harbours or Coverts.

How

How to Unharbour a Hart, and cast off the Hounds.

When the Relays are well set and placed, let the Huntf-man with his Pole walk before the Kennel of Hounds: Being come to the Blemifhes, let him take notice of the Slot, and fuch other marks as may be obferved from the View of the *Deer*, to the intent he may know whether the Hounds run Riot or not. Then let the Horfe-men caft abroad about the Covert, to difcover the *Hart* when he is unharboured, the better to diftinguifh him by his Head or otherwife. The Huntf-man having unharboured him, all the Hounds fhall be caft off, they crying one and all, *To him, to him*; *That's he, that's he*, with fuch words of encouragement.

If the Blood-hound as he draweth chance to overfhoot, and draw wrong or counter, then muft the Huntf-man draw him back, and fay, *Back, back, Soft, foft*, until he hath fet him right again: and if he perceive that the Hound hath mended his fault, by his kneeling down, and obferving the Slot or Ports, he muft then cherifh him, by clapping him on the Back, and giving him fome encouraging words. Thus let him draw on with his Hound till the *Deer* be defcried.

Now fome are fo cunning and crafty, that when they are unharboured from their Layr, they will coaft round about to finde fome other *Deer*, whereby the Hounds may be confounded in the change of hunts.

If the Huntf-man have the *Hart* in view, let him ftill draw upon the Slot, blowing and hollowing until the Hounds are come in. When he feeth they are in full cry, and take it right, he may then mount, keeping under the Wind, and coaft to crofs the Hounds that are in chafe, to help them at default, if need require.

What

What subtleties are used in hunting a Hart at force.

Let the Huntf-man never come nearer the Hounds in cry, than fifty or threefcore paces, efpecially at the firft uncoupling, or at cafting off their Relays. For if a *Hart* make Doublings, or wheel about, or crofs before the Hounds, as he feldom doth ; if then you come in too haftily, you will fpoil the Slot or View ; and fo the Hounds, for want of Scent, will be apt to over-fhoot the Chafe : but if after hunting an hour, the Huntf-man perceive that the *Hart* makes out end-ways before the Hounds, and that they follow in full cry, taking it right, then he may come in nearer, and blow a Recheat to the Hounds to encourage them. Here-upon the *Hart* will frequently feek other *Deer* at Layr, and rouze them, on purpofe to make the Hounds hunt change, and will lie down flat in fome of their Layrs upon his Belly, and fo let the Hounds over-fhoot him : and becaufe they fhall neither fcent or vent him, he will gather up all his four Feet under his Belly, and will blow and breath on fome moift place of the ground, in fuch fort, that I have feen the Hounds pafs by fuch a *Hart* within a yard, and never vent him.

For which caufe Huntfmen fhould blemifh at fuch places they fee the *Hart* enter into a Thicket, to this end, that if the Hounds fhould fall to change, they may return to thofe Blemifhes, and put their Hounds to the right Slot and View, until they have rouzed or found him again.

The *Hart* hath another way to bring the Hounds to change ; and that is, when he feeth himfelf clofely purfued, and that he cannot fhun them, he will break into one Thicket after another to finde *Deer*, rouzing and herding with them, continuing fo to do fome-times above an hour before he will part from them, or

break

break Herd. Finding himself spent, he will break
herd, and fall a doubling and crossing in some hard
High-way that is much beaten, or else in some River
or Brook, in which he will keep as long as his Breath
will permit him : and if he be far before the Hounds,
it may be then he will use his former device, in gathering his Legs up under his Belly as he lies flat along
upon some hard and dry place. Sometimes he will
take soil, and so cover himself under water, that you
shall perceive nothing but his Nose.

In this case the Huntf-man must have a special regard to his old Hounds, who will hunt leisurely and
fearfully ; whereas the young Hounds will over-shoot
their Game.

If it so chance that the Hounds are at a default, and
hunt in several companies, then it may be guessed that
the *Hart* hath broken herd from the fresh *Deer*, and
that the fresh *Deer* have separated themselves also :
then regard how the old *Staunch*-hounds make it, and
observe the Slot ; and where you see any of the old
Hounds Challenge, cherish and encourage him, hasten-
ing the rest in to him, by crying *Hark* to such a Hound,
calling him by his Name.

Here is to be noted, that they cannot make it so
good in the hard High-ways as in other places, because
they cannot have there so perfect a scent, either by
reason of the Tracks or Footing of divers sorts of
Beasts, or by reason of the Sun drying up the moisture, so that the Dust covereth the Slot : now in such
places (such is the natural subtilty of that Beast for
self-preservation) the *Hart* will make many Crosses
and Doublings, holding them long together, to make
the Hounds give over the Chase.

In this case, the first care of the Huntf-man is, to
make good the Head, and then draw round apace, first
down the Wind, though usually *Deer* go up the Wind :
and

and if the way is too hard to Slot, be sure to try far enough back. This expert Hounds will frequently do of themselves.

But if a *Hart* break out into the Champion-country, and that it be in the heat of the day, between Noon and three of the clock; then if the Huntf-man perceive his Hounds out of breath, he muft not force them much, but comfort them; and though they do not call upon the Slot or view, yet it is fufficient if they but wag their Tails; for, being almoft fpent, it is painful for them to call.

The laft Refuge of a *Hart* forely hunted is the Water, (which, according to Art, is termed the *Soil*) fwimming oftneft down the Stream, keeping the middle, fearing left by touching any Bough by the Water-fide he may give fcent unto the Hounds.

Always when you come to a Soil, (according to the old Rule: *He that will his Chafe finde, let him firft try up the River, and down the Winde*) be fure if your Hounds challenge but a yard above his going in, that he is gone up the River: for though he fhould keep the very middle of the Stream, yet will that, with the help of the Wind, lodge part of the Stream, and Imbofh that comes from him on the Banks, it may be a quarter of a mile lower, which hath deceived many. Therefore firft try up the Stream: and where a *Deer* firft breafts foil, both Man and Hound will beft perceive it.

Now the ways to know when a *Hart* is fpent, are thefe: *Firft*, He will run ftiff, high, and lompering. *Secondly*, If his Mouth be black and dry without any Foam upon it, and his Tongue hanging out; but they will often clofe their Mouths, to deceive the Spectators. *Thirdly*, By his Slot: for oftentimes he will clofe his Claws together, as if he went at leifure; and ftraightway again open them wide, making great glidings,

glidings, and hitting his Dew-claws upon the ground, following the beaten Paths without Doublings ; and sometimes going all along by a Ditch-side, seeking some Gap, having not strength to leap it otherways : yet it hath been often seen, that Dead-run *Deer* have taken very great leaps.

Thus must a Huntt-man govern himself according to the Subtlety and Craft of the *Deer*, observing their Doublings and Crossings, and the places where they are made ; making his Rings little or great, according to the nature of the place , time , and season : For Hounds are subject to shoot where Herbs and Flowers have their most lively scent and odoriferous smell. Neither must you be unmindful of the perfection and imperfection of your Hounds. Thus doing, it will be very hard luck if you loose a *Hart* by default.

How to kill a Hart *at Bay.*

It is very dangerous to go in to a *Hart* at Bay, and especially at Rutting-time ; for then they are most fierce.

There are two sorts of Bays ; one on the Land, the other on the Water. If now the *Hart* be in a deep Water, where you cannot well come to him, then couple up your Dogs ; for should they long continue in the Water, it would endanger furbating or foundering. Get then a Boat, or swim to him with a Dagger ; or else with a Rope that hath a Noose, and throw it over his Horns : for if the Water be so deep that the *Hart* swims, there is no danger in approaching him ; otherwise you must have a care.

As to the Land-bay, if the *Hart* be burnished, then must you consider the place : For if it be in a plain and open place, where there is no Wood nor Covert, it is dangerous and hard to come in to him ; but it

G is

it be in a Hedge-fide or Thicket, then, whilft the *Hart* is ftaring on the Hounds, you may come covertly a-mong the Bufhes behinde him, and cut his Throat. If you mifs your aim, and the *Hart* turn head upon you, then make fome Tree your refuge ; or when the *Hart* is at Bay, couple up your Hounds ; and when you fee the *Hart* turn head to fly, gallop in roundly to him, and kill him with your Sword.

Directions at the Death of Buck *or* Hart.

The firft Ceremony when the Huntf-men come in to the Death of a *Deer*, is to cry *Ware Haunch*, that the Hounds may not break into the *Deer* ; which ha-ving fecured, the next is cutting his Throat, and there blooding the youngeft hounds, that they may the bet-ter love a *Deer*, and learn to leap at his Throat ; then, having blown the Mort, and all the company come in, the beft perfon, that hath not taken Say before, is to take up the Knife that the Keeper or Huntf-man is to lay crofs the Belly of the *Deer*, ftanding clofe to the left Shoulder of the *Deer*, fome holding by the Fore-legs, and the Keeper or Huntf-man drawing down the Pizle, the perfon that takes Say, is to draw the edge of the Knife leifurely along the very middle of the Belly, beginning near the Brisket ; and drawing a little upon it, enough in length and depth to difco-ver how fat the *Deer* is, then he that is to break up the *Deer* firft flits the Skin from the cutting of the Throat downward, making the Arber, that fo the Ordure may not break forth ; and then he is to pounch him, rewarding the Hounds therewith. Next, he is to prefent the fame perfon that took the Say with a drawn Hanger, to cut off the Head ; which done, and the Hounds rewarded therewith, the concluding Ceremony is, if a *Buck* a double, if a *Stag* a treble

Mort

Mort blown by one , and then a whole Recheat in Confort by all that have Horns; and that finished, immediately a general *Whoo whoop*.

It was formerly termed, *Winde a Horn*, becaufe (as I fuppofe) all Horns were then compaffed; but fince ftraight Horns are come into fafhion, we fay, *Blow a Horn*, and fometimes, *Sound a Horn*.

In many cafes heretofore, *Leafing* was obferved; that is, one muft be held, either crofs a Saddle, or on a mans Back, and with a pair of Dog-couples receive ten pound and a Purfe; that is, ten ftripes, (according to the nature of the Crime, more or lefs fevere) and an eleventh, that ufed to be as bad as the other ten, called a *Purfe*.

There are many Faults, as coming too late into the Field, miftaking any term of Art; thefe are of the leffer fize : of the greater magnitude, Hallowing a wrong *Deer*, or leaving the Field before the death of the *Deer*, &c.

Buck-*Hunting*.

THis Beaft is common in moft Countries, being as corpulent as a *Hart*; but in quantity refembleth more a *Roe*, except in colour.

The Males have Horns, which they lofe yearly; but the Females none at all. Their Colours are divers, but moft commonly branded or fandy on the back, having a black Lift all down along on the Back; their Bellies and Sides fpotted with White, which they lofe by their old age : and the *Does* do efpecially vary in colour, being fometimes all white, and therefore like unto Goats, except in their Hair, which is fhorter.

In their Horns they differ not much from a *Hart*,

except

except in quantity, and that they grow out of their Heads like Fingers out of the Hand ; such is this *Fallow-Deer*, being therefore called *Cervus Palmatus*. As for their other parts, they much resemble a *Roe-buck*. Their flesh is excellent for nourishment , but their blood ingenders too much Melancholy.

Now know, the *Buck* is Fawn'd about the latter end of *May*, and its nature and properties differ little from the *Hart*.

There is not so much art and skill in Lodging a *Buck*, as in the Harbouring a *Hart* ; neither is there required so much drawing after, but onely you are to judge by the View, and mark what Grove or Covert he entreth ; for he will not wander and rove up and down so often as a *Hart*, nor so frequently change his Layr.

He maketh his Fewmishings in divers manners and forms, as the *Hart* doth, according to the diversity of Food, and time of the day, Morning and Evening ; but most commonly they are round.

The *Hart* and *Buck* differ thus in parallel. When the *Buck* is hunted, he oft-times betakes himself to such strong Holds and Coverts as he is most acquainted with, not flying far before the Hounds , not crossing nor doubling, using no such subtleties as the *Hart* is accustomed to.

The *Buck* will beat a Brook , (but seldom a great River, as the *Hart*) but it must not be so deep ; nor can he stay so long at Soil as the *Hart* will do : onely he leapeth lightlier at Rut than the *Hart* ; and groaneth or Troateth, as a *Hart* Belleth, but with a lower Voice, rattling in the Throat. And here is to be noted, they love not one another, nor will they come near each other's Layr.

Buck-Venison is incomparable food, and is dressed like *Hart*-Venison ; onely this last will be preserved longer than the former. **The**

The *Buck* herds more than the *Hart*, and lieth in the driest places: but if he be at large, unconfined within the limitary Precincts of a Park, he will herd but little from *May* to *August*, because the flies trouble him. He takes great delight in hilly places; but the Dales are his joy to feed in.

Bucks have seldome or never any other Relays than the old Hounds.

The greatest subtlety a Huntf-man need use in the hunting of the *Buck*, is to beware of hunting Counter or Change, because of the plenty of *Fallow-Deer*, which use to come more directly upon the Hounds than the *Red-Deer* doth. Now upon the breaking up of a *Buck* the Hounds Reward is the same with that of the *Hart*.

Roe-*Hunting*.

THe *Roe-Buck* is called by the Greeks and Latines by one name, *viz. Dorcas* These Beasts are very plentiful in *Africa*, *Germany*, and *Helvetian* Alps.

Their swiftness doth not onely appear upon the Earth, but also in the Waters, cutting them when they swim as with Oars; and therefore they love the Lakes and strong Streams, breaking the Floods to come at fresh Pasture, feeding deliciously on sweet Rushes, and Bull-rushes. Horns onely grow upon the Male, and are set with six or seven Branches, not palmed, but branchy, yet shorter than *Fallow-Deer*: They differ not much from common *Deer*, but in their Horn: and whereas the Horns of other Beasts are hollow towards the root, whereinto entereth a certain long substance; the Horns of these, as also of the vulgar *Buck* and *Elk*,

G 3   are

are folid without any fuch emptinefs, onely they are full of Pores.

It is fuppofed by the Learned, that a *Roe* was called in Greek *Dorcas*, by reafon of the quicknefs of her fight; and that fhe can fee as perfectly in the night as in the day. Phyfitians have obferved a certain vifcous humour about her Bowels, which by anointing Eyes that are dark, heavy, and near blinde, quickens the fight moft wonderfully.

It is reported of them, that they never wink, no not when they fleep; for which conceit their Blood is prefcribed for them who are dim-fighted or pur-blinde. The Tail of this Beaft is leffer and fhorter than a *Fallow-Deer's*; infomuch that it is doubtful whether it be a Tail or not.

They keep for the moft part in the Mountains among the Rocks, being very fwift; and when they are hunted (*Martial* faith) they hang upon the Rocks with their Horns, to delude the Dogs, after a ftrange manner, ready to fall and kill themfelves, and yet receive no harm, where the Dogs dare not approach, as appeareth in his Epigram.

Pendentem fumma Capream, de rupe videbis,
Cafuram fperes, decipit illa Canes.

This might be more properly meant of the Wilde-Goat.

They are moft eafily taken in the Woods. When they are chafed, they defire to run againft the Wind, becaufe the coldnefs of the Air refrefheth them in their courfe; and therefore they who hunt them place their Dogs with the Wind. They are often taken by the counterfeiting of their Voice, which the skilful Huntf-man doth by the affiftance of a Leafe in his Mouth.

This

This Beast is very easie to hunt, and goeth to Rut (or *Tourn* most properly) in *October*, the extent whereof consists of fifteen days, and never parteth with the *Doe* till Fawning-time.

The *Doe*, finding her self near her time, secretly departs from the *Buck*, and fawneth as far from him and his knowledge as she can; for could he finde the *Fawn*, he would kill it. Now when the *Fawn* grows big, and can run and feed, she then returns to the *Buck* again very lovingly, with all expedition: the cause whereof, is the *Roes* fawning Twins, which are commonly *Buck* and *Doe*; so that being accustomed together in youth, they do love to keep company ever after.

As soon as the *Roe-Buck* cometh from Rut, he casts his Horns; and there are few after two years old which Mew not at *Alhallontide*, but their Heads grow quickly out again.

The Venison of a *Roe* is never out of season, being never fat, and therefore they are to be hunted at any time: onely this, some favour ought to be shewn the *Doe* whilst she is big with *Fawn*, and afterwards till her *Fawn* is able to shift for himself: besides, some *Roe-Does* have been killed with five *Fawns* in their Belly.

They usually when hunted, take a large first Ring, and afterwards hunt the Hounds.

When they are hunted, they turn much and often, and come back upon the Dogs directly: When they can no longer endure, they then take Soil, as the *Hart* doth, and will hang by a Bough in such manner, that nothing shall appear of them above Water but their Snout, and will suffer the Dogs to come just upon them before they will stir.

He is not called by the skilful in the art of Hunting a *Great Roe-Buck*, but a *Fair Roe-Buck*. The Herd of them is called a *Beavy*: And if he hath not Beavy-greafe on his Tail when he is broken up, he is more fit to be Dogs-meat than Mans-meat.

The Hounds muft be rewarded with the Bowels, the Blood, and Feet flit afunder, and boiled all together. This is more properly called a *Dofe* than a *Reward*. For what might be faid farther concerning *Roe*-hunting, I fhall refer you to the Chapters of *Hart* and *Buck*-hunting.

Rain-Deer-*Hunting*.

THe *Rain-Deer* is not unlike a *Hart*, onely his Head is fuller of Antliers, being bigger and wider in compafs; for he bears four and twenty Branches and more according to his age, having a great Palm on the top, as a *Hart*, and his Fore-Antliers are palmed alfo.

He flieth end-ways when he is hunted, by reafon of the great weight of his Head. When he hath ftood up a great while, doubled, croffed, and ufed other crafty tricks to fhun the Hounds, he makes a Tree his laft refuge; fo planting himfelf, that nothing can affault him but juft before, placing his Buttock and Haunches againft the Tree, and hanging down his Head low to the ground, whereby all his Body is covered.

As the *Hart* ftrikes with his Head, the *Rain-deer* ftrikes with his Feet againft any one that comes in to him to help the Dogs, not in the leaft turning his Head, that being his chiefeft defence, and feems very terrible to the Hounds.

He feedeth like the *Hart*, and maketh his Fewmets fometimes long, and fometimes flat, and beareth fatter

Venifon

Venifon, when he is in pride of Greafe, than any other
Deer doth, and is very long-liv'd. He is more commonly drawn after with a Blood-hound, than hunted,
and intrapped with Nets and Engines, and that in
the thick and greateft Holds, if it may be; which
is the beft and fpeedieft way, by reafon of his great and
fpreading Head. Since there are but few of them in
England, I fhall defift from difcourfing farther concerning him.

Of the Nature and Properties of a Hare.

AN *Hare* is called in Hebrew *Arnebet* in the Femi-
nine gender, which word poffeffed a great many
that all *Hares* were Females: He is called *Lagus* by
the Greeks, for his immoderate Luft; and by the fame
Nation *Ptoox*, for his Fear; and by the Latines *Lepus*,
quafi Levi-pes, fignifying Swiftnefs of Feet (*alias*)
Light-foot.

There are four forts of *Hares*; fome live in the
Mountains, fome in the Fields, fome in the Marfhes,
fome every where, without any certain place of abode.
They of the Mountains, are moft fwift; they of the
Fields, lefs nimble; they of the Marfhes, moft flow;
and the wandering *Hares* are moft dangerous to follow; for they are fo cunning in the ways and mufes
of the Fields, running up the Hills and Rocks, becaufe
by cuftome they know the nearer way, with other
tricks, to the confufion of the Dogs, and dif-encou-
ragement of the Hunters.

In the next place, a defcription of the parts of an
Hare will not be unneceffary, fince it is admirable to
behold how every Limb and Member of this Beaft is
compofed

composed for celerity. In the first place, the Head is round, nimble, short, yet of convenient longitude, prone to turn every way. The Ears long, and lofty, like an Asses : for Nature hath so provided, that every fearful and unarmed creature should have long and large Ears, that by hearing it might prevent its Enemies, and save it self by flight. The Lips continually move sleeping and waking; and from the Slit they have in the middle of their Nose, cometh the term of *Hare-lips* which are so divided in men.

The Neck of an *Hare* is long, small, round, soft, and flexible : The Shoulder-bone straight and broad, for her more easie turning : her Legs before soft, and stand broader behinde than before, and the hinder Legs longer than the former : a Breast not narrow, but fitted to take more breath than any Beast of that bigness : a nimble Back, and fleshy Belly, tender Loins, hollow Sides, fat Buttocks, filled up, strong and nervous Lines. Their Eyes are brown, and they are subtile, but not bold ; seldom looking forward, because going by jumps. Their Eye-lids coming from the Brows are too short to cover their Eyes, and therefore this Sense is very weak in them : when they watch they shut their Eyes, and when they sleep they open them.

They have certain little Bladders in their Belly filled with matter, out of which both the one and the other Sex suck a certain humour, and anoint their Bodies all over therewith, and so are defended against Rain.

Though their sight be dim, yet they have *visum indefessum*, an indefatigable sense of Seeing ; so that the continuance in a mean degree, countervaileth in them the want of excellency.

They feed abroad, because they would conceal their forms ; and never drink, but content themselves with

the

the Dew, and for that cause they often fall rotten. As
it is before, every Limb of a *Hare* is composed for celerity, and therefore she never travelleth, but jumpeth:
her Ears lead her the way in her Chase; for with one
of them she hearkneth to the cry of the Dogs, and
the other she stretcheth forth like a Sail, to hasten her
course; always stretching her hinder beyond her former,
and yet not hindering them at all; and in Paths and
High-ways she runs more speedily.

The *Hares* of the Mountains do often exercise
themselves in the Valleys and Plains, and through practice grow acquainted with the nearest ways to their
Forms or places of constant abode. So that when at
any time they are hunted in the Fields, such is their
subtile dodging, that they will dally with the Huntsmen till they seem to be almost taken, and then on a
sudden take the nearest way to the Mountains, and
so take Sanctuary in the inaccessible places, whither
Dogs nor Horse dare ascend.

Hares which frequent Bushes and Brakes, are not
able to endure labour, and not very swift, by reason of
the pain in their Feet, growing fat through idleness
and discontinuance of running. The *Campestrial* or
Field-*Hare*, being leaner of Body, and oftner chased,
is taken with more difficulty, by reason of her singular
agility; she therefore when she beginneth her course,
leapeth up from the ground as if she flew, afterwards
passeth through Brambles, and over thick Bushes and
Hedges with all expedition; and if at any time she
come into deep Grass or Corn, she easily delivereth her
self, and slideth through it, always holding up one
Ear, and bending it at her pleasure to be the Moderator of her Chase. Neither is she so unprovident and
prodigal of her strength, as to spend it all in on
Course, but observeth the force of her Prosecutor
who if he be slow and sluggish, she is not profuse o

he

her celerity, but onely walketh gently before the Dogs, and yet safely from their Clutches, reserving her greatest strength to her greatest necessity : for she knoweth she can out-run the Dogs at her pleasure, and therefore will not trouble her self more than she is urged. But if there be a Dog following her more swiftly than the residue, then she setteth forward with all the force she can ; and when she hath left both Hunters and Dogs a great way behinde her, she getteth to some little Hill or rising of the Earth, where she raiseth her self upon her hinder-Legs, that thereby she may observe how far or near her Pursuers are distant from her.

The younger *Hares*, by reason of their weak Members , tread heavier on the Earth than the elder ; and therefore leave the greater Scent behinde them, At a year old they run very swift , and their Scent is stronger in the Woods than in the plain Fields ; and if they lie down upon the Earth (as they love to do) in Red Fallow-grounds, they are easily descried.

Their foot-steps in the Winter-time are more apparent than in the Summer, because, as the Nights are longer, so they travel farther : neither do they scent in the Winter-mornings so soon as it is day, until the Frost be somewhat thawed ; but especially their footsteps are uncertain at the Full of the Moon, for then they leap and play together, scattering and putting out their scent or savour ; and in the Spring-time also, when they do ingender, they confound one anothers footsteps by multitudes.

Hare-*Hunting*.

IT is the judgement of all, that a *Hare* doth naturally know the change of Weather from twenty four hours to twenty four hours. When she goeth to her Form, she will suffer the Dew to touch her as little as she can, but followeth the High-ways and beaten Paths.

They go to Buck commonly in *January*, *February*, and *March*, and sometimes all the warm Months; sometimes seeking the Buck seven or eight miles distant from the place where they usually sit, following the High-ways, &c.

If when a *Hare* riseth out of her Form, she couches her Ears and Scut, and runs not very fast at first, it is an infallible signe that she is old and crafty.

You may know a Buck-*hare* as you hunt him to his Form by his beating the hard High-ways. He seedeth farther out into the Plains, and maketh his Doublings and Crossings much wider, and of greater compass than the Female doth: for she will keep close by some Covert-side, turning and winding in the Bushes like a *Coney*; and if she go to Relief in the Corn-fields, she seldom crosseth over the Furrows, but followeth them along, staying upon the thickest tufts of Corn to feed.

Likewise you may know a Buck at the rising out of his Form by his Hinder-parts, which are more whitely; or if you observe his Shoulders before he rise, which will be redder than the Does, having some loose long Hairs growing on them. Again, his Head is shorter, and better trussed; his Hairs about his Lips longer;

longer; and his Ears shorter and more gray. The Hairs upon the Female's Chine will be of a blackish gray.

Besides, when Hounds hunt a Female-*Hare*, she will use more Crossing and Doubling, seldom making out end-ways before the Hounds: whereas the Male acts contrary; for having once made a Turn or two a-bout his Form, then farewel Hounds; for he will frequently lead them five or six miles before ever he will turn his head.

When you see that your Hounds have found where an *Hare* hath pass'd to Relief upon the High-way-side, and hath much doubled and crossed upon dry places, and never much broken out nor relieved in the Corn, it is a signe she is but lately come thither; and then commonly she will stay upon some high place to look about her, and to chuse out a place to form in, which she will be loth to part with.

Of the Craft and Subtlety of an Hare.

As of all Chases the *Hare* makes the greatest pastime and pleasure; so it is a great delight and satisfaction to see the craft of this little poor Beast in her own self-preservation.

And that you may understand what these Subtleties are, you must first take notice what Weather it is. If it be rainy, then the *Hare* will hold the High-ways more than at any other time: and if she come to the side of any young Grove or Spring, she will scarcely enter, but squat down by the side thereof until the Hounds have over-shot her; and then she will return the self-same way she came to the place from whence she was started, and will not by the way go into any Covert, for fear of the wet and Dew that hang upon the Boughs.

In

In this cafe, let the Huntf-man ftay a hundred paces before he comes to the Wood-fide, by which means he fhall perceive whether fhe return as aforefaid ; which if fhe do, let him hallow in his Hounds, and call them back, and that prefently , that the Hounds may not think it the Counter fhe came firft.

The next thing to be obferved, is the place where the Hare fitteth, and upon what wind fhe makes her Form: for if fhe form either upon the North or South-wind, fhe will not willingly run into the Wind, but run upon a fide or down the Wind. But if fhe form in the Water, it is a figne fhe is foul and meafled. If you hunt fuch a one, have a fpecial regard all the day to the Brook-fides, for there and near Plafhes fhe will make all her Croffings, Doublings, &c.

I have feen a *Hare* fo crafty,that as foon as fhe heard the found of a Horn, fhe would inftantly ftart out of her Form, though it was a quarter of a mile diftant, and go fwim in fome Pool, and there reft her felf upon fome Rufh-bed in the midft thereof, from whence fhe would not ftir till fhe heard the Horn again ; and then I have feen her ftart out again fwimming to Land, and fhe hath ftood up before the Hounds four hours before we could kill her, fwimming, and ufing all her Subtleties and Croffings in the Water.

Such is the natural craft and fubtlety of a *Hare*, that fometimes , after fhe hath been hunted three hours, fhe will ftart a frefh *Hare*, and fquat in the fame Form. Others, having been hunted a confiderable time, will creep under the Door of a Sheep-coat, and there hide themfelves among the Sheep ; or when they are hard hunted,will run in among a flock of fheep,and cannot be gotten out from among them by any means, till the Hounds are coupled up, and the Sheep driven into their Pens. Some (and that is fomething ftrange) will take the ground like a *Coney* , and that is called

going

going to the Vault. Some *Hares* will go up one side
of the Hedge, and come down the other, the thickness
of the Hedge being the onely distance between the
courses.

I have seen a *Hare*, that being forely hunted, got
upon a Quick-set-hedge, and ran a good way upon the
top thereof, and then leapt off upon the ground. And
they will frequently betake themselves to Furz-bushes,
and will leap from one to the other, whereby the
Hounds are frequently in default. Nay, which is more,
I have heard of a *Hare*, that being hunted two hours
or more, at length, to save her self, got upon an old
Wall six foot high from the ground, and hid her self
in the hole that was made for a Scaffold : and that several have swam over *Trent* and *Severn.*

A *Hare* liveth not above seven years at most, especially the Buck ; and if he and the Doe shall keep one
quarter together, they will never suffer any strange
Hare to sit by them : and therefore it is proverbially
said, *The more you hunt, the more* Hares *you shall have* ;
because when you have killed one *Hare*, another will
come and possess his Form.

An *Hare* hath greater Scent, and is more eagerly
hunted by the Hounds, when she feeds and relieveth
upon green Corn, than at any other time in the year :
and yet there are some *Hares* which naturally give a
greater Scent than others ; as the great Wood-*hares*,
and such as are foul and measled, and keep near to the
Waters : But the little red *Hare*, which is not much
bigger than a *Coney*, is neither of so strong a Scent,
nor so eagerly hunted. Such as feed upon the small
Branches of wilde Time, or such-like Herbs, are commonly very swift, and will stand long up before the
Hounds. In like manner you have some *Hares* more
subtile and cunning than others : Young *Hares* which
have not been hunted are foolish, and are neither of
force

force nor capacity to ufe fuch fubtleties and crafts, but hold on end-ways before the Hounds moft commonly, and do fquat and ftart again oftentimes, which doth much encourage the Hounds, and enters them better than if the *Hare* flies end-ways, as fometimes they will five or fix mile an end.

The Females are more crafty and politick than the Bucks; for they double and turn fhorter than they, which is difpleafant to the Hounds; for it is trouble-fome for them to turn often, delighting more in an endway-chafe, running with all their force: for fuch *Hares* as double and crofs fo often, it is requifite at default to caft the greater compafs about, when you beat to make it out, for fo you will finde all her fub-tleties, and yet need to ftick upon none of them, but onely where fhe went on forwards: By this means you will abate her force, and compel her to leave doubling and croffing.

How to enter Hounds to the Hare.

Let the Huntfman be fure in the firft place to make his Hounds very well acquainted with him and his Voice, and let them underftand the Horn; and to this end let him never blow his Horn or hallow but when there is good caufe for fo doing, and let him be fure that his Hounds want no encouragement.

Here by the way obferve two remarkable things. The firft is, if you intend to enter a young Kennel of Hounds, you muft take notice of the Country where you will make your firft Quarry, and whereof you make it. For according to the places wherein they are firft entred, and the nature of the Quarry given them, they will prove accordingly for the future. Thus if they are firft entred in the Plains and Champain-coun tries, they will ever after more delight to hunt there

H   than

than in any other place: and so it is the same with the Coverts.

But, say some of our Huntsmen, all strange Countries that differ from that to which Hounds are accustomed, causes them at first to be at seek: But good Hounds will soon be master of any Country; and therefore he that would have the best Hounds, must use them to all kindes of Hunting: And it is easie to bring Hounds to enjoy a Scent from a bleak Down to a fresh Pasture. And therefore many of us love to enter in the worst Countries.

Do not accustom your Hounds to hunt in the Morning, because of the Dew and moisture of the Earth: and besides, you will finde by experience, that if afterwards you hunt them in the heat of the day, they will soon give over the chace; neither will they call on willingly or chearfully, but seek out the Shades to sleep in. Yet many of us agree, that to hunt both early and late in the Morning by Trayling, advantageth the Hounds to use their Noses; and by keeping them sometimes in the heat of the day, or till night, moves them to stoutness.

The best season to enter your young Hounds is in *September* and *October*; for then the Weather is temperate, neither too hot nor too cold; and then is the time to finde young *Hares* which have never been hunted, which are foolish, and ignorant of the politick Crossings, Doublings, *&c.* of their Sires, running commonly end-ways, frequently squatting, and as often starting, by which encouragement the Hounds are the better entered.

A *Hare* hath greater Scent, and is more eagerly hunted by the Hounds, when she feedeth and relieveth on green Corn, than at any other time of the year.

Moreover, some *Hares* have naturally a greater Scent than

than others, as the great Wood-*Hares*, and such as are
foul and measled, having their greatest resort near the
Water and Plashes.

The little small red *Hare*, not much bigger than a
Coney, is very feeble, and not much coveted by the
Hounds, having a bad scent : but such as feed on the
small Branches of wilde Time are commonly very
swift, and will stand up a long time before the Hounds.

The Does are much craftier than the Bucks, doubling and turning oftner and shorter, which is very
vexatious and troublesome to the Hounds. Now for
such *Hares* as double and cross so often, it is requisite
at a default to cast the greater compass about when you
draw to make it out ; so shall you finde all their subtleties ; though it is needless to stick upon any, but
where they went onwards : by so doing you will a-
bate the force of a *Hare*, and force her from Crossing
and Doubling.

Some *Hares* hold the high beaten ways onely, where
the Hounds can have no scent : wherefore when the
Huntsman findes his Hounds at a default in the High-
way, let him hunt on until he finde where the *Hare*
hath broken from the High-way, or hath found some
Dale or fresh place where the Hounds may recover
Scent, looking narrowly on the Ground as he goeth,
if he can finde the Footing or Pricking of the *Hare*.

There are other places wherein a Hound can finde
no Scent ; and that is in fat and rotten ground, and it
sticketh to the Foot of the *Hare*, which is called *Carrying*, and so consequently she leaves no Scent behinde
her. So likewise there are certain Moneths wherein
a Hound can finde no Scent, and that is in the Spring
time, by reason of the fragrant smell of Flowers, and
the like.

Shun, as much as you can, hunting in hard frosty Weather, for so you will surbate or founder your Hounds,

and

and make them lose their Claws : besides, at that time a *Hare* runneth better than at any other time, the Soals of her Feet being hairy.

To conclude, the best way of entring your young Hounds, is by the help of old Staunch-Hounds ; so will they the better learn to cast for it at a Doubling or Default.

What time of the year is best for Hare-*hunting : How to finde her, start her, and chase her.*

The best time to begin *Hare*-hunting, is about the middle of *September* , ending towards the latter end of *February*, lest you destroy the early brood of *Leverets.* Moreover, upon the approach of Winter the moistness and coolness of the Earth increaseth, which is agreable to the nature of the Hounds, and very acceptable, they ever hating extream Heats and hot weather.

Your Hounds being two years old and upwards, you may exercise them thrice a Week, and they will be the better for so often hunting, provided you feed well ; and keep out your Hounds the greatest part of the day , both to try their stoutness , and to make them stout.

If there be any Hound which hath found the Trail of a *Hare* where she hath relieved that night , let the Huntsman then forbear being over-hasty , but let the Hounds make it of themselves : and when he shall perceive that they begin to draw in together, and to call on freshly, then let him encourage them, especially that Hound which hunteth best, frequently calling him by his name.

Here note, that a *Hare* leaveth better scent when
she

ſhe goeth to Relief, than when ſhe goeth towards her Form : for when ſhe relieveth in the Field, ſhe coucheth her Body low upon the ground , paſſing often over one piece of ground, to finde where lieth the beſt food ; and thus leaveth the better Scent, crotying alſo ſometimes.

Beſides, when ſhe goes to her Form, ſhe commonly takes the High-ways, doubling, croſſing , and leaping as lightly as ſhe can ; in which places the Hounds can have no Scent, (as is ſaid before) by reaſon of the Duſt, *&c.* And yet they will ſquat by the ſides of High-ways ; and therefore let the Huntſman beat very well the ſides of thoſe High-ways.

Now having found where a *Hare* hath relieved in ſome Paſture or Corn-field, then muſt you conſider the ſeaſon of the year, and what Weather it is : for if it be in the Spring-time, or Summer, a *Hare* will not then ſit in the Buſhes, becauſe they are frequently offended with Piſmires, Snakes and Adders, but will ſit in Corn-fields and open places.

In Winter they love to ſit near Towns and Villages in Tufts of Thorns and Brambles, eſpecially when the Wind is Northerly or Southerly.

According to the ſeaſon and nature of the place where the *Hare* is accuſtomed to ſit, there beat with your Hounds and ſtart her ; which is much better ſport than Trailing of her from her Relief to her Form.

When the *Hare* is ſtarted and on foot , then ſtep in where you ſaw her paſs, and hallow in your Hounds untill they have all undertaken it and go on with it in full cry : then recheat to them with your Horn, following fair and ſoftly at firſt, making neither too much haſte nor noiſe with Horn or Voice : for at the firſt Hounds are apt to over-ſhoot the chace through too much heat. But having ran the ſpace of an hour, and that you see the Hounds are well in with it, stick-ing well upon it, then you may come in nearer with the Hounds, because by that time their heat will be cooled, and they will hunt more soberly. But above all things mark the first Doubling, which must be your direction for the whole day; for all the Doub-lings that she afterwards shall make will be like the former: and according to the policies that you shall see her use, and the place where you hunt, you must make your Compasses great or little, long or short, to help the defaults, always seeking the moistest and most commodious places for the Hounds to scent in.

To conclude, those who delight in the commenda-ble Exercise of hunting the *Hare*, must rise early, lest they be deprived of the Scent of her foot-steps, by which means the Dogs will be incapacitated to follow their Game; for the nature of the Scent is such, that it will not remain long, but suddainly, in a manner every hour, vanisheth away.

Of Parks and Warrens.

HAving thus discoursed of the Nature and Pro-perties of the *Hare*, together with the manner of hunting them; in the next place I hold it not im-proper in short to speak something of Parks and en-closed Warrens, wherein *Hares, Coneys, Deer,* &c. may always be ready as it were out of a Store-house or Se-minary to serve the use and pleasure of their Ma-sters.

The first *Roman* that ever enclosed wilde Beasts, was *Fulvius Herpinus*; and *Varro* had the first Warren of *Hares*. The largest *Hare*-Parks that ever I heard

of,

of, and the beſt furniſhed with thoſe fearful, yet ſubtile, Creatures, are in *Ireland* ; the one belongs to the
Lord-Lieutenant of that Kingdom, near *Dublin* ; and
the other in the North, and belongs to the Lord of
Mazareen. It will be a tedious task for me to give
you an account of the variety of Parks and Warrens
within the three Kingdoms ; I ſhall therefore onely
tell you in what manner they are erected, and that
very briefly.

The Walls or Pales muſt be high, or cloſe joynted,
ſo as neither Badger nor Cat can creep through, nor
Wolf, nor *Fox* can leap over ; wherein ought alſo to be
Buſhes and broad trees to cover the Beaſts againſt heat
and cold, and other ſecret places to ſatisfie their natures, and to defend the leſſer Beaſts, as *Hares, Coneys,* &c. from *Hawks , Kites ,* and other ravening
Fowls : in which three or four couple of *Hares* will
quickly multiply into a great Warren.

It is very good to ſow Gourds, Miſceline, Corn,
Barley, Peaſe, and ſuch-like, wherein *Hares* delight,
and will thereby quickly grow fat.

Warreners have a very crafty device to fatten *Hares*,
which by experience is found effectual, and that is by
putting Wax into their Ears, and ſo make them deaf ;
then turn them into the place where they ſhould feed,
where being freed from the fear of Sounds (for want
of hearing) they grow fat before other of their
kinde.

Here note, that when you have pitched your Hays
for *Coneys*, ſound a Trumpet in ſome of the Burroughs,
and ſcarce a *Coney* in the whole Warren but will ſtart
abroad.

I ſhall end this Chapter with *Martial*'s praiſe of a
Hare and a *Thruſh.*

Inter Aves Turdus si quis in Judice certet,
Inter Quadrupedes gloria prima Lepus.

Amongst all Birds none with the *Thrush* compare,
And no Beast hath more glory than the *Hare*.

Of Coney-*catching.*

BEfore we speak of the Hunting of the *Coney*, it
will not be amiss to take notice of her nature and
properties, which are these: she carrieth her young
in her Belly thirty days; as soon as she hath kindned she
goes to Buck. They begin to breed in *England* at a year
old, (but sooner in other places) and so continue, bearing
at least seven times in a year if they Litter in *March*;
this is the reason that a small stock will serve to increase
a large Warren. The Does cannot suckle their young
till they have been with the Buck, which must be done
presently, or she will not be inclined 14 days after.

When the Buck goes to Doe, he will beat very
strongly with his Fore-foot upon the ground, and by
that means he heateth himself. When he hath buckt,
he is accustomed to fall backwards, and lie as if he
were in a Trance or half dead, at which time he is easily taken.

The Latines call a *Coney, Cuniculus*, because it maketh
Holes in the Earth; and *Cuniculus* was a Latine word
for a Hole or Cave in the Earth, before it was taken for
a *Coney*.

The Bucks will kill the young if they can come at
them, like to your Bore-cats; and therefore the Doe
prevents that mischief, by covering her Stop or Nest
with

with Earth or Gravel, that so they may not easily be discovered.

Those who keep *Coneys* tame for profit, may give them to eat Vine-leaves, Fruits, Herbs, Grass, Bran, Oat-meal, Mallows, Milk-thistles, Apple-parings, Cabbage, Lettise, or Carret-tops. In Winter they will eat Hay, Oats, and Chaff, being given to them thrice a day: but when they eat green things, they must not drink at all, because of the Dropsie which will follow: At all other times a little drink must serve their turn, and that must be always fresh. Here note; give them not too much green juicy meat, unless you intermix therewith what is dry, as Oats, Chaff, &c. otherwise they will be *Cathed*, or tun-bellied.

Now the way of taking them is either by small Curs or Spaniels bred up for that sport; and their places for hunting are among Bushes and Hedges; or else by coursing them with small Grey-hounds. In their default they are commonly driven into their Burrows; and therefore it will be very requisite to set Purse-nets on the Holes, then put in a Ferret close muzzled, and she will make the *Coneys* bolt out again into the Purse-nets, and so you may take them. Some say the Drone of a Bag-pipe, put into a *Coney*-burrow, and blown on a sudden, will make *Coneys* bolt.

For want of a Ferret, you may take the powder of Orpine and some Brimstone, and therewith make a smother in the Burrows, and so they will bolt out. But this way is not to be approved of; for by that means the *Coneys* will forsake those Burrows, and so in a little time a Warren will be destroyed, should this course be used frequently.

But above Nets and Ferrets, Hays are to be preferred for the taking of *Coneys*; neither is the drawing Ferret to be despised when they are young. Likewise there is excellent sport to be made with our Tumblers, who will kill *Coneys* abundantly.

Let

Let this suffice, since any farther discourse hereof is neither proper, nor pertinent to my present purpose.

Of the Ferret.

THE *Ferret* is a little creature that is not bred in *Spain*, *Italy*, *France*, nor *Germany*; but in *England* they breed naturally, and are tamed for the benefit of such who keep Warrens, and others.

It is a bold and audacious Beast, Enemy to all others but his own kinde, drinking and sucking in the Blood of the beast it biteth, but eateth not the flesh.

When the Warrener hath an occasion to use his *Ferret*, he first makes a noise in the Warren to frighten what *Coneys* are abroad into their Burrows, and then he pitcheth his Nets; after that, he puts his *Ferret* into the Earth, having a long Strick, with Bells about her Neck, whose Mouth must be muzzled, so that he may not seize, but frighten the *Coneys* out of their Burrows, and afterwards driven by Dogs into the Nets or Hays so planted for them.

The Body is longer for the proportion than the quantity may afford. Their colour is variable, sometimes black and white on the Belly, but most commonly of a yellowish sandy colour, like Wooll died in Urine. The Head is little, like a Mouse's; and therefore into whatsoever Hole she can put it in, all her Body will easily follow after. The Eyes are small, but fiery like red-hot Iron, and therefore she seeth most clearly in the dark. Her Voice is a whining cry without changing it: She hath onely two Teeth in her nether Chap, standing out, and not joyned and growing

ing

ing together. The Genital of the Male is of a bony
fubftance, and therefore it always ftandeth ftiff, and
is not leffer at one time than another. The pleafure
of the fenfe in Copulation is not in the Genital-part,
but in the Mufcles, Tunicles, and Nerves wherein the
faid Genital runneth. When they are in Copulation
the Female lieth down, or bendeth her Knees, and continually crieth like a Cat, either becaufe the Male claw-
eth her with his Nails, or by reafon of the roughnefs
of his Genital.

She ufually brings forth feven or eight at a time,
carrying them forty days in her little Belly: The
young ones newly littered are blinde thirty days together; and within forty days after they can fee, they
may be ufed as their Dam for profit and recreation.

When tamed, they are nourifhed with Milk or with
Barley-bread, and they can faft a very long time. When
they go, they contract their long Back, and make it
ftand upright in the middle round like a Bowl:
when they are touched, they fmell like a *Martel*; and
they fleep very much. Thus much of the *Ferret*,
which I thought good to place after the Chapter of
Coney-catching, becaufe this little Animal is fuch a
neceffary Inftrument for that purpofe.

Of Fox-*hunting.*

HIs Shape and Proportion is fo well known, being
a beaft fo common, that it will be needlefs to
defcribe him.

His nature in many refpects is like that of a *Wolf*;
for they bring as many Cubs at a Litter one as the o-
ther: but thus they differ; the *Fox* Litters deep under
the ground, fo doth not the *Wolf*.   A

A Bitch-*Fox* is hardly to be taken when she is bragged and with Cub; for then she will lie near her Burrow, into which she runs upon the hearing of the least noise. And indeed at any time it is somewhat difficult; for the *Fox* (and so the *Wolf*) is a very subtile crafty creature.

Fox-hunting is very pleasant; for by reason of his strong hot Scent he maketh an excellent Cry : And as his Scent is hottest at hand, so it dies soonest. Besides, he never flies far before the Hounds, trusting not on his Legs, Strength, or Champion-ground, but strongest Coverts. When he can no longer stand up before the Hounds, he then taketh Earth, and then must he be digged out.

If Grey-hounds course him on a Plain, his last refuge is to piss on his Tail, and flap it in their Faces as they come near him; sometimes squirting his thicker Excrement upon them, to make them give over the Course or pursuit.

When a Bitch-*Fox* goes a clicketing and seeketh for a Dog, she cryeth with a hollow Voice, not unlike the howling of a mad Dog; and in the same manner she cries when she misseth any of her Cubs : but never makes any cry at all when she is killing, but defends her self to the last gasp.

A *Fox* will prey upon any thing he can overcome, and feeds upon all sorts of Carrion; but their Dainties, and the food which they most delight in, is Poultry. They are very destructive and injurious to *Coney*-Warrens, and will sometimes kill *Hares* by deceit and subtlety, and not by swift running.

The *Fox* is taken with Hounds, Grey-hounds, Terriers, Nets, and Gins.

Of Terriers there are two sorts. The one is crooked-leg'd, and commonly short-hair'd : and these will

take

take Earth well, and will lie very long at *Fox* or *Badger*. The other fort is fhagged and ftraight Legg'd: and thefe will not onely hunt above ground as other Hounds, but alfo enter the Earth with much more fury than the former; but cannot ftay in fo long, by reafon of their great eagernefs.

The time of entring thefe Terriers, is when they are neer a twelve-month old; for if you enter him not in within this time, you will hardly after bring him to take the Earth. And to encourage the young Terrier the more, put in an old one before him, that can better endure the fury of the *Fox* or *Badger :* and be careful that neither of them be old when you engage your young Terrier with him.

The entring and flefhing them may be done feveral ways. In the firft place thus : When *Foxes* and *Badgers* have young Cubs, then take your old Terriers and enter them in the ground; and when they begin to bay, you muft then hold every one of your Terriers at a fundry Hole or Mouth of the Earth, that they may liften and hear the old ones Bay. Having taken the old *Fox* or *Badger*, and that nothing remains within but the young Cubs, then couple up all your old Terriers, and put in the young in their ftead, encouraging them by crying, *To him, to him, to him.* And if they take any young Cub within the ground, let them alone to do what they pleafe with him; and forget not to give the old Terriers their reward, which is the Blood and Livers, fryed with Cheefe and fome of their own Greafe, fhewing them the Heads and Skins to encourage them. Before you reward them, wafh them with Soap and warm Water, to clear their Skins from Earth and Clay that is clodded to the Hair, otherwife they are apt to be mangie. You may alfo enter them in this manner : Take an old *Fox*, or *Badger*, and cut away the nether Jaw, but meddle not with the other,

leaving

leaving the upper to shew the fury of the Beaft, although it can do no harm therewith. Then dig an Earth in some convenient place in your own grounds, and be careful to make it wide enough, to the intent the Terriers may turn therein the better, and that there may be room enough for two to enter together: then cover the Hole with Boards and Turf, putting the *Fox* or *Badger* firft therein, and afterwards put in your Terriers both young and old, encouraging them with words that are the usual terms of Art. When they have bay'd sufficiently, then begin to dig with Spades and Mattocks, to encourage them againft such time as you are to dig over them: then take out the *Fox* or *Badger* with the Clamps or Pinchers, killing it before them, or let a Grey-hound kill it in their fight, and make them reward thereof. Here note, that inftead of cutting away the Jaw, it will be every whit as well to break out all his Teeth, to prevent him from biting the Terriers.

Now to fay the truth, there is not much paftime or pleafure in hunting of a *Fox* under ground; for as soon as that subtle creature perceiveth the Terriers, if they bay hard, and lie near unto them, they will bolt out immediately, unlefs it be when the Bitch hath young Cubs, then they will sooner die than ftir.

They make their Earths as near as they can in ground that is hard to dig, as in Clay, Stony-ground, or amongft the Roots of Trees; and their Earths have commonly but one Hole, and that is ftraight a long way in before it come at their Couch. Sometimes craftily they poffefs themfelves of a *Badger*'s old Burrow, which hath variety of Chambers, Holes, and Angles.

When a good Terrier doth once binde the *Fox*, he then yearns, and defends himfelf very notably, but not fo ftrenuoufly as the *Badger*, nor is his biting half fo

dange-

dangerous. Here note, if you take a Bitch-*Fox* when she goeth a Clicketing, and cut out that Gut which containeth her Sperm, together with the Kidneys which Gelders deprive Bitches of when they spay them, and cut them into small gobbets, mingling therewith the Gum of Mastick, and put them hot as they are into a Pot, and cover the same close, it will serve for an excellent Train for a *Fox*, and will keep the whole year round. Take the Skin of Bacon, and broil it well on a Gridiron, then dip it in the ingredients of the Pot aforesaid, and make a Train thereof, you will experimentally finde, that if there be any *Fox* neer to any place where the Train is drawn, he will follow it; but let him who makes the Train rub the soals of his Feet with Cow-dung, lest the *Fox* vent his footing: and thus you may Train a *Fox* to a Standing, and kill him in an Evening with Gun or Cross-bow. It is likewise found by experience, that if a Terrier be rubbed with Brimstone, or with Oil of Cade, and then put him into an Earth where either a *Fox* or *Badger* is, they will leave that Earth, and come not to it again a good while after.

I shall conclude this discourse with what I have observed in *Gesner's* History of *Beasts* tending to the same purpose: saith he, *As he frequently cheats the* Badger *of his Habitation by laying his Excrements at the mouth of his Earth or Burrow; so, for as much as the* Wolf *is an Enemy to the* Fox, *he layeth in the mouth of his Earth an Herb called a Sea-onion, which a* Wolf *naturally hates, and is so averse thereunto, that he will never come near the place where it either lies or grows.*

Of Fox-hunting above ground.

To this purpose you must draw with your Hounds about Groves, Thickets, and Bushes near Villages: for

a

a *Fox* will lurk in such places, to prey on young Pigs and Pullein.

But it will be necessary to stop up his Earths, if you can finde them, the night before you intend to hunt; and the best time will be about midnight, for then the *Fox* goeth out to seek his Prey. You may stop his Holes by laying two white sticks acrofs before them, which will make him imagine it is some Gin or Trap laid for him : or elfe you may stop them up close with Black-thorns and Earth together.

The best hunting a *Fox* above-ground, is in *January*, *February*, and *March*, for then you shall best see your Hounds hunting, and best finde his Earthing; befides, at those times the *Fox*'s Skin is best in feafon.

Again, the Hounds best hunt the *Fox* in the coldest Weather, because he leaveth a very strong scent behind him; yet in cold Weather it chills fastest.

At first onely cast off your sure Finders, and as the Drag mends, so adde more as you dare trust them.

Shun casting off too many Hounds at once, because Woods and Coverts are full of fundry Chases, and so you may engage them in too many at one time.

Let such as you cast off at first be old staunch-Hounds, which are sure; and if you hear such a Hound call on merrily, you may cast off some other to him; and when they run it on the full cry, cast off the rest : and thus you shall compleat your pastime.

The words of comfort are the same which are used in the other chases, attended with the same Hallowings and other ceremonies.

Let the Hounds kill the *Fox* themselves, and worry and hare him as much as they please : many Hounds will eat him with eagernefs.

When he is dead, hang him at the end of a strong Pike-staff, and hallow in all your Hounds to bay him : but reward them not with any thing belonging to the *Fox*; for it is not good, neither will they eat it.   *Of*

Of Badger-*hunting.*

A Badger is called by several names, *viz.* a *Gray,* Brock, Boreson or Bauson, and in *France* Taußon. The Male is called a *Badger* or *Boar-pig*; and the Female is called a *Sow.*

These Beasts are plentiful in *Naples, Sicily, Lucane,* and in the *Alpine* and *Helvetian* Coasts; so are they also here in *England.*

There are two kindes of this beast, (saith *Gesner*) one resembling a Dog in his feet, and the other a Hog in his cloven Hoof: they differ too in their Snout and colour; for the one resembles the Snout of a Dog, the other of a Swine: the one hath a greyer Coat, or whiter Coat than the other, and goeth farther out in seeking of its Prey. They differ also in their meat, the one eating Flesh and Carrion like a Dog, the other Roots and Fruits like a Hog: both these kindes have been found in *Normandy, France,* and *Sicily.*

Mr. *Turbervil* makes mention of two sorts of Badgers likewise, but in a different manner. *For the one* (saith he) *casteth his Fiaunts long like a* Fox, *and have their residence in Rocks, making their Burrows very deep. The other sort make their Burrows in light ground, and have more variety of Cells and Chambers than the former.* The one of these is called the *Badger-Pig,* and the other the *Badger-whelp*; or call one *Canine,* and the other *Swinish.* The first hath his Nôse, Throat, and Ears yellowish like a *Martern's* Throat; and are much blacker, and higher Leg'd than the *Badger-*whelp. Both sorts live upon all Flesh, hunting greedily after Carrion. They are very mischievous and hurtful to Warrens, especially when they are big with young.

Badgers when they Earth, after by digging they have entred a good depth, for the clearing of the Earth cast, one of them falleth on the Back, and the other layeth Earth on the Belly, and so taking his hinder feet in his Mouth, draweth the Belly laden-*Badger* out of the Hole or Cave; and having disburdened her self, re-enters, and doth the like till all be finished.

These *Badgers* are very sleepy, especially in the day-time, and seldom stir abroad but in the night; for which cause they are called *Lucifugæ*, avoiders of the Light.

It is very pleasant to behold them when they gather materials for their Couch, as Straw, Leaves, Moss, and such-like; for with their Feet and their Head they will wrap as much together as a man can well carry under his Arm, and will make shift to get it into their Cells and Couches.

He hath very sharp Teeth, and therefore is accounted a deep biting Beast : his Back is broad, and his Legs are longer on the right side than the left, and therefore he runneth best when he gets on the side of an Hill, or a Cart-road-way. His Fore-legs have very sharp Nails, bare, and apt to dig withal, being five both before and behinde, but the hinder very much shorter, and covered with Hair. His favour is strong, and much troubled with Lice about the Secrets. Both Male and Female have under their Hole another Hole outwardly, but not inwardly in the Male. If she be hunted abroad with Hounds, she biteth them most grievously where-ever she lays hold on them. For the prevention thereof, the careful Huntsmen put great broad Collars made of *Grays* Skins about their Dogs Necks. Her manner is to fight on her Back, using thereby both her Teeth and her Nails; and by blowing up her Skin after a strange and wonderful manner, she defendeth

her

her felf againſt any blow and Teeth of Dogs; onely a ſmall ſtroke on her Noſe will diſpatch her preſently; you may thraſh your heart weary on her Back, which ſhe values as a matter of nothing.

In *Italy* they eat the fleſh of *Badgers*, and ſo they do in *Germany*, boiling it with Pears: ſome have eaten it here in *England*, but like it not, being of a ſweet rankiſh taſte.

The Fleſh is beſt in *September* if it be fat; and of the two kinds, the Swiniſh *Badger* is better fleſh than the other.

They love Hogs-fleſh above any other; for take but a peice of Pork and train it over a *Badger*'s Burrow, if he be within, you ſhall quickly ſee him appear without.

Their nature is very cold; and therefore when it ſnoweth they will not come out of their Holes for three or four days together.

They live long, and by mere age will grow blinde; then will they not ſtir out of their Holes, but are fed by thoſe who have their ſight.

This ſubtlety they have, that when they perceive the Terriers begin to yearn them, they will ſtop the Hole between the Terriers and them: if the Terriers continue baying, they will remove their Baggage with them, and go into another Appartment or Chamber of the Burrow, (for know that ſome of their Houſes have half a dozen Rooms at leaſt;) and ſo will remove from one to the other, till they can go no further, barricadoing the way as they go.

The hunting of a *Badger* muſt be after this manner: You muſt firſt ſeek the Earths and Burrows where he lieth, and in a clear Moon-ſhine night go and ſtop all the Holes but one or two, and therein place ſome Sacks faſtned with ſome drawing Strings, which may ſhut him in as ſoon as he ſtraineth the Bag.

The Sacks or Bags being thus ſet, caſt off your

I 2 Hounds,

Hounds, and beat all the Groves, Hedges, and Tufts within a mile or two about. What *Badgers* are abroad, being alarm'd·by the Dogs, will straight repair to their Earths or Burrows, and so be taken.

Let him that standeth to watch the Sacks, stand close, and upon a clear Wind , for else the *Badger* will soon finde him, and fly some other way for safety. But if the Hounds either encounter him, or undertake the chase before he can get into his Earth, he will then stand at bay like a *Boar*, and make most incomparable sport.

What Instruments are to be used in digging, and how to dig for Badger *or* Fox.

In the first place, you must have such as are able to dig : next, you must have so many Terriers garnished with Bells hung in Collars, to make the *Fox* or *Badger* bolt the sooner ; besides, the Collars will be some small defence unto the Terriers.

The Instruments to dig withal are these : a sharp-pointed Spade, which serveth to begin the Trench where the ground is hardest, and broader Tools will not so well enter ; the round hollowed Spade, which is useful to dig amongst Roots , having very sharp edges ; the flat broad Spade, to dig withal when the Trench is better opened, and the ground softer ; Mattocks and Pick-axes, to dig in hard ground where a Spade will do but little service ; the Coal-rake, to cleanse the Hole, and to keep it from stopping up ; the Clamps, whereby you may take a *Fox* or *Badger* out alive·to make sport therewith afterwards. And it would not be amiss to have a Pail of Water, to refresh your Terriers after they are come out of the Earth to take breath.

In this order you may besiege a *Fox* or *Badger* in
their

their ftrongeft Holes or Caftles, and may break their Cafmats, Platforms, Parapets, and work to them with Mines and Counter-mines, until you have obtained your fatisfaction. But there is a fhorter method than this, which by reafon of its commonnefs I fhall forbear to mention.

Of the Otter:

IT is fuppofed by fome that the *Otter* is of the kinde of *Beavers*, being it is an amphibious creature living both in the Water and on the Land ; befides, the outward form of the parts beareth a fimilitude of that beaft. Some fay, were his Tail off, he were in all parts like a *Beaver*, differing in nothing but habitation : For the *Beaver* frequenteth both the Saltwater and the Frefh ; but the *Otter* never goeth to the Salt.

Though the *Otter* live in the Water, yet it doth not breath like Fifhes through the benefit of the Water, it doth breath like other four-footed beafts, yet it will remain a long time underneath the Water without refpiration.

If he want Prey in the Waters, then will he quit them for the Land ; and if by painful hunting afhore he cannot fill his Belly, he will feed on Herbs, Snails, or Frogs : neither will he take lefs pains in the Water to fatisfie hunger ; for he will fwim two miles together againft the ftream, that fo, when his Belly is full, the current of the Stream may carry him down again to his defigned Lodging, which is neer the Water, very artificially built with Bows, Sprigs, and Sticks couching together in excellent order, wherein he fitteth to keep him from the wet.   I 3   In

In the hunting of Fish he often pops his Nose above Water to take breath: It is a creature of wonderful swiftness and nimbleness in taking his Prey, and for greediness takes more than he knows what to do with.

It is a very subtile and crafty beast, and indowed with a wonderful sagacity and sense of smelling, insomuch that he can directly wind the Fishes in the Waters a mile or two off.

The flesh of this beast is both cold and filthy, because it feedeth on stinking Fish, and therefore not fit to be eaten; yet it is eaten in *Germany*; and the *Carthusian* Fryers, who are forbidden to eat all manner of flesh of other four-footed beasts, yet they are not prohibited the eating of *Otters*. There are those in *England*, who lately have highly valued an *Otter*-pie, much good may it do them with it.

These *Otters* must be hunted by special Dogs, such as are called *Otter*-hounds, and also with special Instruments called *Otter*-spears. When they finde themselves wounded with a Spear, they then come to Land, where they fight with the Dogs furiously; and except they be first wounded, they forsake not the Water: for they are not ignorant how safe a refuge the Waters are unto them, and how unequal a combat they shall sustain with Men and Dogs upon the Land: yet, because the cold Water annoyeth their green wounds, therefore they spin out their lives to the length of the Thread, chusing rather to die in torments among Dogs, than to die in the Waters.

The Food of an *Otter* (as I said) is Fish; and her abode is commonly under the Root of some Tree neer Rivers, Brooks, Pools, Meers, or Fish-ponds; and sometimes she will lie in a hollow Tree four or five foot above ground: and no Vermin can be more destructive to a Warren, than the *Otter* is to a Fish-pond;

for

for she diveth and hunteth under water after that most wonderful manner, that few fish escape her, unless they are very swift and great.

An *Otter* and *Ferret* grow salt much about the same time, and bring forth their young much after the same manner, neither having their constant number.

There is much craft and cunning in the hunting them; yet with pains-taking you may ensnare them under the Water, and by River-sides, as you may a *Hare* with *Hare*-pipes and such-like Gins. They bite sore and venomously, and when occasion serves they will defend themselves stoutly. If after their ensnaring they chance to abide there long, they will soon enlarge themselves with their Teeth.

These creatures are footed like your Water-fowl, having a Web between their Claws, and have no Heel, but a round Ball under the Soal of their Feet : and their Track is called their *Mark*, as the Slot of a *Hart*; and their Excrements are called *Spraints*.

An *Otter* will not abide long in a place; for he is apt to be afraid and take distaste, (having an excellent Ear and Nose, for hearing and smelling;) and then he will forsake his Couch, and shift a mile or two up or down the River : and this he will do according as he findes scarcity of fishing.

In hunting of the *Otter* observe this, to send some to one side of the River whilst you are on the other, and so beat on the Banks with your Dogs, and so you will soon finde if there be an *Otter* in that quarter : for an *Otter* cannot endure long in the Water, but must come forth to make his Spraints, and in the night sometimes to feed on Grass and such Herbs as the fields afford.

If any of the Hounds finde out an *Otter*, then look in the soft grounds and moist places to see which way he bent his head : if the marks make no discovery,

I 4   you

you may partly perceive it by the Spraints, and so follow the Hounds, and lodge him as a *Hart* or *Deer.*
If you finde not the *Otter* quickly, you may then imagine he is gone to couch somewhere farther off from
the River : for sometimes he will seek his food a mile
from the place of his rest, chusing rather to go up the
River than down, because upwards he meets with better scent of Fish ; and bearing his Nose into the Wind,
he shall the sooner finde any fault that is above
him.

Remember, in the hunting of the *Otter,* that you
and your friends carry your *Otter*-spears to watch his
Vents , for that is the chief advantage : and if you
perceive where the *Otter* swims under water , then
strive to get to a Stand before him where he would
vent, and there endeavour to strike him with your
Spear ; but if you miss, pursue him with the Hounds,
which if they be good *Otter*-hounds , and perfectly
entred, will come chaunting and trailing along by the
River-side , and will beat every Tree-root, every O-
sier-bed and tuft of Bull-rushes ; nay, sometimes they
will take the Water, and beat it like a Spaniel.   And
by these means the *Otter* can hardly escape you.

Of the Squirrel.

THe first Author that ever wrote of this little Animal was *Oppianus,* who lived in the days of *Anto-
ninus Cæsar,* and wrote a Book also of Hunting.

A *Squirrel* is greater in compass than a *Weasle,* but
the latter is longer than the other ; the back-parts and
all the body is reddish except the Belly , which is
white.   In *Helvetia* they are black and branded, and
they

they are hunted at the fall of the Leaf, when the Trees grow naked : for they run and leap from Bough to Bough in a moſt admirable and agile manner ; and when the Leaves are on, they cannot be ſo well diſcerned. They are of three colours, in the firſt age black, in the ſecond of a ruſty Iron-colour , and laſtly, when old, they are full of white hoar Hairs. Their Teeth are like the Teeth of Mice, having the two under-Teeth very long and ſharp. Their Tail is always as big as their Body, and it lieth continually on their Back when they ſleep or ſit ſtill, and ſeemeth to be given them for a covering.

In the Summer-time they build them Neſts (which by ſome are called *Drays*) in the Tops of the Trees very artificially with Sticks and Moſs , with other things the Woods afford , and then they fill it with Nuts for Winter-proviſion, and do ſleep like the *Alpine* Mouſe moſt part thereof very ſoundly, in ſuch ſort, that the beating of the outſide of their Drays will not wake them.

When they leap from Tree to Tree, they uſe their Tail inſtead of Wings, leaping a great diſtance, and are ſupported without ſinking to any one's appearance ; nay, they will frequently leap from a very high Tree down to the ground, and receive no harm.

Many muſt go together to hunt them, and muſt carry Dogs with them : and the fitteſt place for the exerciſe of this ſport, is in little and ſmall ſlender Woods, ſuch as may be ſhaken by the hand. Bows are requiſite to remove them when they reſt in the twiſts of Trees ; for they will not be much terrified with all the hallowing, except they be ſtruck now and then by one means or other. Well do they know what harbour a high Oak is unto them, and how ſecure they can lodge therein from Men and Dogs ; wherefore ſince it is too troubleſome to climb every Tree,

that

that labour muſt be ſupplied with Bows and Bolts, that when the *Squirrel* reſteth, preſently he may be thumpt by the blow of an Arrow : the Archer need not fear to do her much harm, except he hit her on the Head ; for by reaſon of a ſtrong back-bone, and fleſhy parts, ſhe will abide as great a ſtroak as a Dog.

If they be driven to the ground from the Trees, and they creep into Hedges, it is a ſigne of their wearineſs : for ſuch is the lofty minde of this little beaſt, that while her ſtrength laſteth ſhe ſaveth her ſelf in the tops of high Trees ; but being wearied, ſhe deſcendeth, and falls into the Mouths of the yelping Curs that attend her.

The admirable wit of the *Squirrel* appeareth (if it be true) in her ſwimming, or paſſing over a River ; for when hunger conſtraineth her ſo to do, ſhe ſeeks out ſome Rind, or ſmall Bark of a Tree, which ſhe ſetteth upon the Water, and then goeth into it, and holding up her Tail like a Sail, letteth the wind drive her to the other ſide ; and carry meat in their mouths, to prevent Famine whatſoever ſhould befal them.

Of the Martern and Wilde-Cat.

A *Martern* is about the bigneſs of a Cat, having a longer Body, but ſhorter Legs, with Head and Tail like a *Fox* ; its Skin is commonly brown, white on the Throat, and ſomewhat yellowiſh on the Back.

Their Teeth are exceeding white, and unequal, being above meaſure ſharp ; the canine Teeth both above and below hang out very long.

This and the wild-*Cat* are a ſort of Vermine which we uſe here in *England* commonly to hunt, and as
neceſſary

neceſſary to be hunted as any Vermin can be : For the queſtion may be doubtful, whether either *Fox* or *Badger* do more hurt than the wild-*Cat* doth , ſince there are ſo many Warrens every where throughout the Kingdom of *England* which are very much infeſted by the wild-*Cat*.

It is the opinion of long-experienced Huntſmen, that ſhe leaveth as great Scent, and maketh as good a Cry for the time as any Vermin that is hunted, eſpecially the *Martern* paſſeth all other Vermin for ſweetneſs of Scent, and her Caſe is a noble Fur. The wild-*Cat*'s Caſe is not ſo good, but it is very warm, and medicinable for ſeveral Aches and Pains in the Bones and Joynts : alſo her Greaſe is very good for Sinews that are ſhrunk.

Theſe two Chaſes are not to be ſought purpoſely, unleſs the Huntſman do ſee them where they prey, and can go readily to them ; but if a Hound chance to croſs them, he will hunt it as ſoon as any Chaſe, and they make a noble cry as long as they ſtand up ; when they can do it no longer, they will take a Tree, and ſo deceive the Hounds ; but if the Hounds hold in to them, and will not give it over ſo, then they will leap from one Tree to another, and make great ſhift for their Lives, with much paſtime to the Huntſmen.

When they are killed you muſt hold them up upon a piked Staff , and hallow in all your Hounds, and then reward them with ſome meat ; for the fleſh of theſe Vermin is naught for Hounds.

A short Account of some particular
Beasts that are not hunted in *England*, but in Forrain Countries.

The Nature and Properties of a Wolf, and the manner of its Hunting.

HEretofore I read that there were many *Wolves* in *England*, but now there are none; however they are still in *Ireland*, but their number is very much decreased within these thirty years; and that they may more and more decrease, being so pernicious to all sorts of Cattle, I thought good to publish the nature and manner of their hunting.

First, as to their Nature; they go a Clicketing in *February*, and continue in that manner ten or twelve days. Where many *Wolves* are, many will follow one Bitch, as Dogs will follow a Bitch that is salt, but she will be onely Lined with one.

A notable story I have heard when I was in *Ireland*, and attested for a truth by the Inhabitants: That a Bitch-*Wolf* proud, will suffer a great many of the Male to follow her, and will carry them after her sometimes eight or ten days without Meat, Drink, or Rest; and when they are so tired that they cannot travel farther, she will first lie down, then will the rest follow her example: when she perceives that they are all asleep, and through weariness snore, then will she arise and awake that *Wolf* which she observed to follow her most, and having so done, entice him with her far from the rest, and suffer him to Line her: the rest awaking and finding her missing, pursue her by the Scent, and finding
how

how she hath cunningly deluded them, they fall instantly on her Companion who hath been before-hand
with them, and revenge themselves on him by depri-
ving him of his life; which verifies the proverb:
Never Wolf yet ever saw his Sire.

Their Whelps are able to ingender at twelve
months end, at which age they part with their Dam,
that is, when those Teeth are grown which they cast
the first half year, and being grown, they never shed
them again: and here see their gratitude, (though
bloody cruel creatures) after they have preyed for
themselves, if they chance to meet their Dam or Sire
(for *Turbervile* doth not believe the aforesaid story)
they will fawn upon them and lick them, rejoycing at
the sight of them.

The Dog will never bring any of his Prey to his
Whelps till he hath filled his own Belly; whereas the
Bitch will not eat a bit till she hath served them first:
they go nine weeks with Whelp, and sometimes a little longer, and grow salt but once a year. As to number of Whelps, they have more or less as Dogs have;
for doubtless both the *Wolf* and the *Fox* are but a kinde
of wild Mastiffs and wild Curs.

They prey upon all kind of things, and will feed
on Carrion, Vermin, &c. They will kill a Cow or a
Bullock; and as for a Sheep, Goat, or good Porket,
they will roundly carry him off in their Mouths, not
touching ground with it, and will run so fast away,
notwithstanding the load, that they are hardly to be
stopped but by Mastiffs or Horse-men. There is no
Beast which runneth faster than the *Wolf*, and holdeth
wonderfully also. When he is hunted with Hounds,
he flieth not far before them; and unless he be coursed
with Grey-hounds or Mastiffs, he keepeth the Covert
like the *Bear*, or *Boar*, and especially the beaten ways
therein. Night is the usual time of his preying,
                                                          though

though hunger will force him to prey by day. They are more fubtile and crafty (if more can be) than the *Fox* or any other Beaft: When they are hunted, they will take all their advantages; at other times they will never run over-haftily, but keep themfelves in breath and force always.

A *Wolf* will ftand up a whole day before a good Kennel of Hounds, unlefs that Grey-hounds or *Wolf-dogs* courfe him. If he ftand at Bay, have a care of being bitten by him; for being then mad, the wound is defperate, and hard to be cured.

When a *Wolf* falls into a flock of Sheep, with his good will he would kill them all before he feed upon any of them, and therefore all means fhould be ufed to deftroy them, as by hunting at force, or with Grey-hounds or Maftiffs, or caught in Gins and Snares; but they had need be ftrong. For encouragement to the meaner fort in *Ireland*, whofoever took a fucking-Whelp, or preying Cub, a Dog or a Bitch-*Wolf*, and brought but the Heads of either to the next Juftice of Peace, for reward for the firft, he received twenty fhillings; for the fecond, forty; for the third, five pound; and for the laft, fix pounds: which late encouragement hath in a manner cleared that Kingdom of them.

They bark and howl like unto Dogs; and if there be but two of them together, they make fuch a terrible hideous noife, that you would think there could be no lefs than twenty of them in a body.

When any one would hunt the *Wolf*, he muft train him by thefe means: Firft let him look out fome fair place, a mile or more from the great Woods, where there is fome clofe ftanding to place a brace of good Grey-hounds in, if need be, the which fhould be clofely environed, and fome Pond of Water by it: there he muft kill a Horfe that is worth little, and

take

take the four Legs thereof and carry them into the Woods and Forests adjoyning; then let four men take every man a Leg of the Beast and draw it at his Horse-tail all along the Paths and Ways in the Woods, until they come back again to the place where the Carcass of the said Beast lieth; there let them lay down their Trains. Now when the *Wolves* go out in the night to prey, they will follow the scent of the Train till they come to the Carkass where it lieth. Then let those who love the sport, with their Huntsmen come early and privately near the place; and if they are discernable as they are feeding, in the first place let them consider which way will be the fairest course for the Grey hounds, and place them accordingly, and as near as they can let them forestal with their Grey-hounds the same way that the *Wolves* did or are flying either then or the night before; but if the *Wolves* be in the Coverts near the Carrion that was laid for them to feed upon, then let there be Hewers set round the Coverts to make a noise on every side, but onely that where the Grey hounds do stand; and let them stand thick together, making what noise they can to force them to the Grey-hounds: Then let the Huntsman go with his Leam-hound, and draw from the Carrion to the Thickets-sides where the *Wolves* have gone in, and there the Huntsman shall cast off the third part of their best Hounds; for a *Wolf* will sometimes hold a Covert a long time before he will come out.

The Huntsmen must hold near in to the Hounds, blowing hard, and encouraging them with their Voice: for many Hounds will strain courtesie at this Chase, although they are strong and fit for all other Chases.

When the *Wolf* cometh to the Grey-hounds, they who hold them will do well to suffer the *Wolf* to pass by the first rank until he come further, and let the last

Rank

Rank let flip their Grey-hounds full in the face of the *Wolf*, and at the same instant let all the other Ranks let flip also: so that the first Rank staying him but ever so little, he may be assaulted on all sides at once, and by that means they shall the more easily take him.

It is best entring of Hounds at young *Wolves* which are not yet past half a year or a year old; for a Hound will hunt such more willing, and with less fear than an old *Wolf*; or you may take *Wolves* alive in Engines, and breaking their Teeth, enter your Hounds at them.

A man may know a Dog-*Wolf* from a Bitch by the Tracks of his Feet; for the Dog hath a greater Heel, a greater Toe, greater Nails, and a rounder Foot. Besides, the Bitch casteth her Fiaunts commonly in the midst of an High-way, whereas the Dog casteth them either on the one side or the other of the Path.

The Reward of the Dogs is thus: when they have bit and shaked the dead *Wolf*, let the Huntsman then open his Belly straight along, and taking out his Bowels, let him throw in Bread, Cheese, and other Scraps, and so let the Dogs feed therein.

Wild-Goat-*hunting.*

I Never could read or hear that there was ever any such Chase in *England* as the hunting of the wild-*Goat*: But since there may be such sport in *Wales*, as there hath been elsewhere, it will not be much amiss to give some short account thereof.

The Wild-*Goat* is as big as a *Hart*, but not so long, or so long Leg'd, but is as fleshy. They have Wreaths and

and Wrinkles on their Horns , which declare what their age is : for according to the quantity of the Wreaths, fuch is the number of their years; which Wreaths he Meweth, but not his Beam , the which may be, if he be an old *Goat*, as big as a mans Leg.

They have a great long Beard, and are of a brownifh gray colour very fhaggy, having a long black Lift down the ridge of the Back, and the Track is bigger than the Slot of a *Hart*.

They Fawn as a *Hinde* or *Doe* in *May*, and have but one Fawn, which they fuckle and bring up as the tame *Goat* doth her Kid.

They feed like *Deer*, onely they will eat befides Ivy, Mofs, and fuch-like. In Spring they make their Fumets round, and afterwards broad and flat, as the *Hart* when he comes to feed well.

They go to Rut about *Alballontide*, and continue therein a Month or five Weeks ; that feafon being over, they defcend from the Mountains and Rocks , their abode for the Summer-feafon , and herd themfelves, not onely to avoid the Snow, but becaufe they can find no Food any longer ; and yet they come not very low, but keep at the foot of the Mountains, feeding there till *Eafter* : then they return again, every one chufing fome ftrong Hold in the Rocks, as the *Harts* in the Thickets.

About Fawning-time the Females feparate from the Males , attending till Rutting-time : in this interval they will run at Man or Beaft , and fight as *Harts* do one amongft the other.

When he goeth to Rut, his Throat and Neck is much bigger than ufual : he is very ftrong backt ; and (which is wonderful) though he fhould fall from on high ten Poles length, he will receive no harm ; and will walk as fecurely on the fharp tops of Rocks, as a Horfe in the High-way.

K

Alballon-

Alhallontide is the chiefest season for hunting these Wild-*Goats*, observing very well before you hunt, the advantages of the Coasts, the Rocks and places where the *Goats* do lie.

Having thus done, set Nets and Toils toward the Rivers and Bottoms; for you cannot expect your Hounds should follow a *Goat* down every place of the Mountains.

Also it will be needful that some stand on the Top of the Rocks, and throw down Stones as they see occasion. Where the *Goat* goeth down to the small Brooks or waters in the Bottom, there place your Relays, and let the Relays never tarry till the Hounds come in which were cast off: and this is your best help; for a man can neither follow on foot nor horse-back.

Hunting of the Wild-Boar.

THe *Boar* is ever pigg'd with as many Teeth at first as he shall have ever after, which will onely increase in bigness, not number. Amongst the rest, they have four which are called *Tushes*, or *Tusks*, whereof the two biggest do not hurt when he strikes, but serve onely to whet the other two lowest, with which they frequently kill.

They feed upon all kinde of Corn and Fruits which they can come at; also Roots. In *April* and *May* they feed on the Buds of Plumb-trees, and Chesnut-trees, and all other sweet Buds they can finde, especially on the Buds of Broom and Juniper, and are never measled, as our tame Swine. Being near the Sea-coast, they will feed on all manner of Shell-fish.

Their season beginneth in the midst of *September*,

and

and endeth about the beginning of *December*, at which time they go a *Brimming*. A *Boar* will commonly abide the Bay before he goes out of his Den; and he lies most commonly in the strongest Holds of Thorns and thick Bushes.

If it so chance that there is a *Sounder* of them together, then if any break Sounder, the rest will run that way : and if you hunt a *Boar* from a thick and strong Covert, he will not fail to go back by the same way he came thither : and when he is rear'd he never stays, but flies continually till he comes to the place where he was farrow'd and brought up. This Mr. *Turbervile* observed himself when he was in *France*; attesting he saw a *Boar* hunted from a Thicket, which returned the same way he came to the place of his Farrowing, which was distant seven French Leagues. And this was performed by the Track of his Feet.

If he be hunted in a Forest or Hold where he was bred, he will hardly be forced out of it. Sometimes he will take head, and seem to go out, and will draw to the outsides of the Wood; but it is onely to hearken on every side : and if he hear the noise of the Hounds, then will he return, and will not be compell'd to go that way till night. But having broken out of a Forest and taken head end-ways, he will not be put out of his way either by Man, Dog, Voice, Blowing, or any thing.

A *Boar*, especially a great one, will not cry when you kill him : The Sows and young Swine will sometimes.

Terms to be used in Boar-*hunting.*

If it should be demanded what you will call a *Boar* of three years old; you may answer, He is a *young Boar which hath lately left the Sounder.* An old *Boar*

K 2

you

you must call a *Singular*, or *Sanglier*, *that hath left the Sounder four or five years since.* In making of a report, if you are asked where the *Boar* fed the night before, you may say, he *fed* in the Corn; but if in the Fields or Meadows, you must then say, he hath been *Routing* and *Worming* in such a place, or such a Fern-field. Where note, that whatsoever he feeds on, excepting Roots, is called *Feeding*; the other is called *Routing*, *Worming*, or *Fearning*: but when he feedeth and routeth not, you must then call that *Grasing*.

Boar-*hunting with Hounds at force.*

Be advised not to hunt a young *Boar* of three years old at force; for he will stand up as long, if not longer than any light young *Deer* which beareth but three in the top: but in the fourth year you may hunt him at force, as you do a *Hart* of ten.

In the rearing of your *Boar*, you need not be affraid to come near him, for he values you not, and will lie still, and will not be rear'd by you alone.

Here note, that if a *Boar* intends to abide in his Den, Couch, or Fort, then will he make some Crossing or doubling at the entry thereof upon some High-way or beaten Path: by such means a Huntsman, being early in the Woods, may judge of the Subtlety of the *Boar*, and accordingly may make preparations for his Game.

If he be a great *Boar*, and one that hath lain long to rest, let him hunt him with good store of Hounds, and such as will stick close to him; and let him on Horse-back be ever amongst them, charging the *Boar*, to discourage him: for if you hunt such a *Boar* with half a dozen couple of Dogs, he will not value them; and they having chased him, he will take courage and keep them still at Bays, running upon any thing he

seeth

feeth before him. But if he be charged home, and hard laid unto with the Hounds, he will turn head and fly.

If you ſtrike at him with your Sword or *Boar* ſpear, ſtrike not low, for then you will hit him on the Snout, which he little values; for he watcheth to take blows upon his Tusks or thereabouts: but lifting up your hand, ſtrike right down, and have a ſpecial care of your Horſe; for if you ſtrike and hurt him, ſo will he you if he can.

It behoveth the Hunters of *Boars* to be very wary; for he will run fiercely without fear upon his purſuers: in which encounter, if he receive not his deaths wound, he overthroweth his adverſary, except he fall flat on the ground, and then he need not fear much harm; for his Teeth cannot cut upward but downward: but it is otherwiſe with a Female; for ſhe will bite and tear any way.

It is good to raiſe this Beaſt early in the Morning before he hath made Water, for the burning of his Bladder doth quickly make him weary.

When the *Boar* is firſt raiſed out of the Wood, he ſnuffeth in the wind, lifting up his Noſe to ſmell what is with him, and what againſt him; and rarely ſtrikes a man till he be firſt wounded himſelf.

The Hunting-ſpear muſt be very ſharp and broad, branching forth into certain Forks, ſo that the *Boar* may not break through them upon the Huntſman: The beſt places to wound him in therewith, are the middle of his Forehead betwixt his Eye-lids, or elſe upon the Shoulder; either of theſe Wounds is mortal.

If the *Boar* make head againſt the Hunter, he muſt not fly for it, but muſt meet him with his Spear, holding one hand on the middle of it, and the other at the end; ſtanding one foot before another, having an especial eye to the Head of the Beast which way soever he windeth or turneth the same: for such is the nature of the *Boar*, that sometimes he snatcheth the Spear out of their hands, or else recoileth the force back again upon the Hunter, by both which means he is in great danger of life: whensoever this hapneth there is but one remedy, which is; another of his Companions must come and charge the *Boar* with his Spear, and then pretend to wound him with his Dart, but not casting it for fear of hurting the Hunter. The *Boar* seeing this, forsaketh the first man, and rusheth upon the second, who must look to defend himself with all dexterity, composing his Body, and ordering his Weapons according to artificial *Boar*-hunting: in the mean time he that was overthrown must rise again, taking fresh hold on his Spear, and with all courage assault his Adversary, and assist his Friend who was the cause of the saving of his life.

When he feeleth himself so wounded that he cannot live, were it not for the Forks of the *Boar*-spear, he would press it on his Vanquisher, and so revenge his death: For such is the fury of this Beast, that he will endeavour to wound and kill, although he feel upon him the pangs of death; and what place soever he biteth, whether Man or Dog, the heat of his Teeth causeth the Wound to be inflamed: and for this cause, if he but touch the Hair of a Dog, he burneth it off: nay, Huntsmen have tried the heat of his Teeth, by laying Hairs on them as soon as he was dead, and they have shrivel'd up as with a hot-Iron.

To conclude; the same Devises, Diligence, Labour, Prosecution, and Observations are to be used in the hunting of the *Boar*, which are prescribed for the hunting of the *Hart*. Not but that there are several policies and Stratagems which have been invented, and are still used in several Countries, whereby to take

them

them without the pursuit of Dogs; to the knowledge whereof I shall refer the Reader to *Blondus*, *Oppianus*, *Gesner*, *Turbervile*, and many others both antient and modern Writers, who have largely treated on this Subject.

Of the Nature and Properties of a Bear, and after what manner hunted.

THere are two sorts of *Bears*, a greater and a lesser; the last is more apt to climb Trees than the other.

Bears are bred in many Countries; in the *Helvetian Alpine* Region they are so strong and courageous, that they can tear in pieces both Oxen and Horses; for which cause the Inhabitants are studiously laborious in the taking them.

A *Bear* is of a most Venereous and Lustful disposition; for night and day the Females with most ardent inflam'd desires do provoke the Males to copulation; and for this cause at that time they are most fierce and angry. The time of their Copulation is in the beginning of Winter, and the manner of it is like to a man's; the Male moving himself upon the Belly of the Female, which lieth flat on her Back, and they embrace each other with their Fore-feet: they remain a very long time in that act; in so much (as some have observed, how true I cannot say) that if they were very fat at their first entrance, they dis-joyn not themselves again till they be lean.

There is a strange report in History, (if it be true) That in the Mountains of *Savoy* a *Bear* carried a young Maid into his Den by violence, where in a venereal

K 4   manner

manner he had the carnal use of her Body; and while he kept her in his Den, he daily went forth and brought her the best fruits he could get, presenting them to her as Food , as courtly as he could do it; but always when he went to forrage , he rowled a very great Stone to the mouth of his Den, that the Virgin should not make her escape from him : at length her Parents, with long search, found their Daughter in the *Bear*'s Den, who delivered her from that beastial captivity.

They are naturally very cruel and mischievous unto all tame Beasts, and are very strong in all parts of their Body but their head, whereon a small blow will kill them.

They go to mate in the beginning of the Winter, some sooner, some later, according to their rest and feeding; and their heat lasteth not passing fifteen days.

When the she-Bear perceiveth her self with whelp, she withdraws her self into some Cave, or hollow Rock, and there remains till she brings forth her Whelps, where without meat they grow very fat, especially the Males, onely by sucking their Fore-feet. When they enter into their Den, they convey themselves backward, that so they may put out their Foot-steps from the sight of the Hunters.

The nature of all of them is to avoid cold , and therefore in the Winter-time they hide themselves, chusing rather to suffer Famine than cold; lying for the most part three or four months together and never see the light, whereby in a manner their Guts are clung together : coming forth, they are so dazled by long darkness, being in the light again, that they stagger and reel to and fro; and then by a secret instinct they remedy the straightness of their Guts by eating an Herb called *Arum*, in English *Wake-Robbin* or *Calves-foot,*

foot, by the acidity whereof their Guts are enlarged; and being recovered, they remain more fierce and cruel than at other times, during the time their young are with them: and this is the Herb, some say, which they eat to make them sleep so long in Winter without sense of cold or hunger.

They are Whelped most commonly in *March*, sometimes two, and not above five in number; the most part of them are dead one whole day after they are whelped; but the *Bear* doth so lick them and warm them with her breath, and hug them in her Bosome, that she quickly revives them again.

It is commonly received as a truth, (though it be a palpable vulgar errour) *That the Whelps of* Bears *at their first littering are without all form and fashion, and nothing but a little congealed Blood like a lump of Flesh, which afterwards the old one frameth with her Tongue by licking them to her own likeness.* This opinion may be easily disproved; for they are onely littered blind without Hair, and the Hinder-legs not perfect, the Fore-feet folded up like a Fist, and other Members deformed, by reason of the immoderate Humour or moistness in them; which also is one cause why she cannot retain in her Womb the Seed to the perfection of the young ones, whereof *Joachimus Rheticus* is an Eye-witness.

As soon as the Dam perceiveth her Cubs to grow strong, she suckleth them no longer, by reason of their curstness; for they will sorely bite her if they cannot get Suck enough. After this she preyeth abroad upon any thing she can meet with, which she eats, and casts up again to her young ones, and so feeds them till they can prey for themselves: They will climb a Tree for the Fruit.

If they be hunted, they will follow a man, but not run upon him unless they are wounded. They are

very

very ftrong in their Paws, in fuch fort, that they will fo hug a man or Dog till they have broke his Back, or fqueez'd his Guts out of his Belly: with a fingle Paw they will pull a lufty Dog to their tearing and devouring Mouth. They bite very feverely; for they will bite a mans Head to the very Brains; and for an Arm or Leg, they will crafh it as a Dog may do a flender bone of Mutton.

When they are hunted, they are fo heavy that they make no fpeed, and fo are always in fight of the Dogs: They ftand not at Bay as a *Boar*, but fly wallowing; but if the Hounds ftick in, they will fight valiantly in their own defence; fometimes they ftand up ftraight on their hinder-feet, and then take that as a figne of fear and cowardife; they fight ftouteft and ftrongeft on all four.

They have an excellent fcent, and fmell further off than any other Beaft except the *Boar*; for in a whole Forreft they will fmell out a Tree laden with Maft.

They may be hunted with Hounds, Maftiffs, or Grey-hounds; and they are chafed and killed with Bows, *Boar*-fpears, Darts, and Swords; fo are they alfo taken in Snares, Caves, and Pits, with other Engines.

They do naturally abide in great Mountains; but when it fnoweth, or in hard Weather, then they defcend into Valleys and Forefts for provifion. They caft their Leffes fometimes in round Croteys, and fometimes flat like a Bullock, according to their feeding.

They go fometimes a gallop, and at other times an amble; but they go moft at eafe when they wallow.

When they come from their feeding they beat commonly the High-ways and beaten Paths: and wherefoever they go out of the High-ways, there you may be fure they are gone to their Dens; for they ufe no doublings nor fubtleties.

They

They tumble and wallow in Water and Mire as Swine, and they feed like a Dog. Some say their flesh is very good food, let who will eat it for me, who are not so nicely palated as my self.

The best finding of a *Bear* is with a Leam-hound; and yet he who is without one may trail after a *Bear* as we do after a *Buck* or *Roe*, and you may lodge and hunt them as you do a *Bear*. For the more speedy execution, mingle Mastiffs among your Hounds; for they will pinch the *Bar*, and so provoke her to anger, until at last they bring her to the bay; or else drive her out of the Plain into the Covert, not letting her be at rest till she fight in her own defence.

Of the Beaver.

A *Beaver* differeth but a little from an *Otter* but in his Tail: his colour is somewhat yellow and white aspersed with Ash-colour, which stand out beyond the shorter Hairs, double their length; and are neat and soft like an *Otters*.

There is plenty of them in the River *Pontus*, whence the *Beaver* by some is called *Canis Ponticus*: They are also bred in *Spain*, some few in *France*, *Germany*, *Polonia*, *Sclavonia*, *Russia*, *Prussia*, *Lithuania*; and abundance of them in *New-England*.

These Beasts are Amphibious, living both on Land and Water both fresh and salt, keeping the last in the day-time, and the first in the night: Without Water they cannot live; for they participate much of the nature of Fish, which may be gathered from their Tails and Hinder-legs.

They are about the bigness of a Country Cur; their

their Head short; their Ears small and round; their
Teeth very long, the under-Teeth standing out beyond
their Lips three fingers breadth, and the upper about
half a finger, being very broad, crooked, strong, and
sharp, standing very deep in their Mouth, wherewith
they defend themselves against Beasts, take Fishes as it
were upon Hooks, and will gnaw in sunder Trees as
big as a man's Thigh.

Their Fore-feet are like Dogs, and their hinder like
Geese, made as it were on purpose to go on the Land,
and swim in the Water; but the Tail of this Beast is
most strange of all, being without Hair, and covered
over with a Skin like the Scales of a Fish, it being like
a Soal, and for the most part six fingers broad, and
half a foot long.   They are accounted a very delicate
dish, and eat like Barbels: the manner of their dressing is by roasting them first, and boiling or stewing
them afterwards; they must be food that is very
sweet, since this Proverb proceeded from them: *Sweet
is that Fish which is no Fish at all.*

As for the wonderful manner of their building, I
shall let that alone, since it is at large described by *Gefner* in his *History of Beasts*, pag. 36.

There is nothing so valuable in this Beast as his
Stones; for they are in great esteem, and a precious
commodity.

It hath been the opinion of some, that when a
Beaver is hunted, and is in danger to be taken, he biteth off his own Stones, knowing that for them onely
is he thus pursued: but this is found to be a meer Fi-
ction; for their Stones being small, and placed like a
Boar's, it is impossible for them to come at them.

They are taken for their Skins, Tails, and Cods, and
that many ways. First, when their Caves are found:
(in which are several Chambers built one over another by the Water-side, to ascend or descend according

as

as the Water rifeth or falleth) I fay, their abode being found, they make a breach therein, wherein is put a little Dog, which the *Beaver* perceiving, flies inftantly to the end of her Cave, and there defendeth her felf with her Teeth, till all her building be rafed and fhe laid open to her Enemies, who kill her with Inftruments for that purpofe. Thefe Dogs for the *Beaver* are the fame which hunt *Otters.*

They cannot dive long time under Water, but muft put up their Heads for Breath; which being feen by thofe who are hunting them, they kill them with Gun-fhot or *Otter*-fpears: His nature is, if he hear any noife, to put up his Head above Water, whereby he is difcovered, and fo lofeth his life. Thofe Skins are belt which are blackeft.

Of the Elk:

THis Beaft is twice as big as a *Hart*, whofe Upperlip is fo great, and hangeth over the nether fo far, that he cannot eat going forward; but as he eateth he goeth backward, and fo gathereth up his fuftenance.

His Mane is divers both on the top of his Neck, and underneath his Throat, which buncheth like a Beard, or curled lock of hair; his Neck is very fhort, difproportionable to his Body.

He hath two very large Horns bending towards the Back in a plain edge, and the fpires ftand forward to the Face: both Males and Females have them; they are folid at the Root and round, but afterwards branched; they are broader than a *Hart's*, and are very heavy, being not above two foot long; and thefe

Horns

Horns they mew every year : He is coloured for the most part like a *Hart*, and hath cloven Feet, but without Joynts (like an Elephant) in his Fore-legs, and therefore keepeth leaning to Posts or Trees; and fighteth not with his Horns, but Fore-feet.

It is a most timorous creature, not desiring to stir much, unless provoked thereunto by hunting. There is no danger in hunting this Beast, except a man come right before him : for if this Beast fasten his Fore-feet on him, he cannot escape alive; but if it receive any small wound, it instantly dies.

They are taken by Nets and Toils, or as Elephants are taken : for when they have found the Trees whereunto they lean, they so cut and saw them, that when the *Elk* cometh, he overthroweth the Tree and falleth with it; and being not able to rise, is so taken alive. When they are chafed eagerly, and can finde no place to rest themselves in and lie secret, they run to the Waters, and therein stand, taking up waters into their mouths; and in a little time do so heat it, that squirting it out upon the Dogs, the heat thereof so scaldeth them, that they dare not come nigh or approach them any more.

Many more Exotick Beasts I might here insert, describing their natures, and the manner of their Forrain hunting; but, since they are not to be found in *England*, let these suffice which I have already described.

Dogs

Dogs Diseases remedied, and their Hurts healed, according to the best Prescriptions of Ancient and Modern Huntsmen.

Of a five-fold Madness in a Dog : the Symptomes of the Maladies, and their Cure.

THe Antients have derived *Rabies*, madness, from *Ravies*, hoarseness of Voice, for mad Dogs have no perfect Voice: but it is more probable, that *Rabies* cometh *à Rapiendo*; because when a Dog beginneth to go mad, he biteth, runneth, snatcheth, and roves to and fro, to his own perdition. A mad Dog is most dangerous in the Dog-days; for at that time the very Foam or Spittle falling on a man breeds danger.

There are properly seven sorts of Madnesses which afflict a Dog, whereof two of them are incurable, and therefore I shall speak little of them; onely so much as may give you warning to shift them from your other Dogs, because their Disease is infectious; and that you may beware of them your self, lest they injure you; for their biting is dangerous.

The first of these incurable Madnesses is called the *Hot burning Madness*, and is known by these Symptoms. First, when they run, they raise their Tails bolt-upright, and run upon any thing that stands before them, having no respect where nor which way they run : also their Mouths will be very black, having no foam in nor about them. They will not continue thus above three or four days, after which time they die, their pain being so intolerable. Where note, that

all

all thoſe Dogs they have bitten and drew blood from, will be mad in like manner.

The ſecond is called the *Running Madneß*, and is leſs dangerous, however incurable. The Dogs that are troubled with this Madneſs run not on Men, but Dogs, and on no other Beaſts. The Symptoms are, they will ſmell on other Dogs, and having ſmelt them, will ſhake and bite them, yet ſhaking their Tails, and ſeeming to offer no harm : with other tokens I omit for brevity ſake.

Of the Dumb Madneſs.

The five Madneſſes (or rather Sickneſſes) which are curable, are theſe.

The firſt is called the *Dumb* Madneſs, and is thus known : the Dog that is troubled therewith will not feed, but holds his Mouth wide open continually, putting his Feet to his Mouth frequently, as if he had a Bone in his Throat.

The Cure is thus : Take four ounces of the juice of *Spathula putrida*, and put it into a Pot ; then take the like quantity of the juice of black Hellebore, and as much of the juice of Rue : having ſtrained them all well through a fine cloath, put them into a Glaſs : then take two drams of Scammony unprepared, and having mingled it with the former juices, put it into a Horn or Funnel, and convey it down his Throat, keeping his Head up ſtraight, leſt he caſt it up again : then bleed him in the Mouth, cutting three or four Veins in his Gums that he may bleed the better ; and in a ſhort time you will find amendment. Or you may onely take eight drams of the juice of an Herb called Harts-horn, or Dogs-tooth, and you will finde it a moſt excellent Receipt againſt any madneſs whatſo-ever.

Of the Falling Madness.

The second is called the *Falling* Madness: the Disease lieth in their Heads, which maketh them reel as they go, and fall.

The Cure is thus: Take four ounces of the juice of Piony, with the like quantity of the juice of Briony, the like of the juice of *Cruciata*, and four drams of Stavefacre pulverized: mingle these together, and give it your Hound or Dog as aforesaid: then let him blood in the Ears or the two Veins which come down the Shoulders; and if he is not cured at first, give it him a second or third time.

Of the Lank Madness.

The third kinde of Madness is called the *Lank* Madness, by reason of the Leanness of their Bodies occasioned by *Skummering*.

The Cure is thus: First, purge your Dog with this Potion: Take an ounce and half of *Caffia fistularis* well cleansed, two drams and a half of Stavefacre pulverized, and the like quantity of Scammony prepared in White-wine-vinegar, and four ounces of Oyl-olive; temper these and warm them over the Fire, and give it your Dog. In the morning put him into this Bath fasting as followeth: Put into fix Pails full of Water ten handfulls of Mugwort, of Rosemary, of red-Sage, of the Roots or Leaves of Marsh-mallows, of the Roots or Leaves of Wall-wort, of the Roots or Stalks of Fennel, of the Leaves or Stalks of Elecampane, Baulm and Rue, Sorrel, Buglofs and Mellilot; let these boil together in two thirds of Water and the other Wine, until one third be confumed: the Bath being no hotter than your Dog can endure it, bathe him

L   therein

therein for the space of an hour; then taking him out, put him in some warm place for fear of catching cold. Do this four or five times in the same Bath, and it will cure.

Of the Sleeping *Madness.*

The fourth Madness is called the *Sleeping* Madness, and is caused by some little Worms breeding in the mouth of the Stomack from corrupt Humours, the vapours and fumes whereof ascending into the Head, make the Dog sleep continually, and frequently he dieth sleeping.

For the Cure, you must take five ounces of the juice of Wormwood, with two ounces of the powder of Harts-horn burned, and two drams of Agarick: mingle these together; and if they be too thick, thin them with White-wine, and give it your Dog to drink.

Of the Rheumatick *or* Slavering *Madness.*

This Madness is called so, because, when a Dog hath got it, his Head swelleth, his Eyes are as yellow as a Kite's-foot, and he commonly slavereth at the mouth.

The Cure is thus: Take six ounces of the juice of Fennel-roots, and the like quantity of the juice of Misseltoe, four ounces of the juice of Ivy, four ounces of the Powder of the Roots of Polypodie; boil these in White-wine, and give it your Dog to drink as hot as he can suffer it.

Here note, that when a Dog hath any of these kinds of Madnesses he will have no desire to eat, fasting frequently eight or nine days, and so starving to death. Nay, if they are troubled with any distemper they will refuse their meat, nay, the daintiest bit you can give them, until they have eaten Grass, and have cleared

their

their Stomack of what did offend it, and then they will eat.

Concerning the Madneſs of Dogs, and their Venomous Bitings.

I think no reaſonable man ought to queſtion why the Teeth of a mad Dog ſhould do more harm than thoſe of a ſound one; becauſe in rage and anger the Teeth of every Beaſt and creature receive Venome and Poyſon from the Head, whereby when they bite at that time they do much more harm.

Againſt the ſimple biting of a Dog, take the Urine of a Dog, which is ſufficient, ſince there is but little Venome in thoſe Wounds. To lay the Hair of the ſame Dog thereon, (though ſo much talkt on) I look upon as a meer foppery. Or being bit by a Dog, take Vinegar, and with your Hand rub the wound very well; then pour into it Vinegar mixed with Water or Nitre; then wet a Spunge in the ſame liquids, and ſo let it remain bound up three days; then take Pellitory of the Wall, mingled and beaten with Salt, or any other Plaiſter for green Wounds.

Divers are the Cures and Remedies for biting of mad Dogs; which I omit in this place, as belonging not to my Subject, but to Phyſick.

A Remedy againſt the common Mange.

This Diſtemper befalls a Dog frequently for want of freſh water to drink when he deſires it, and ſometimes by foul Kennelling, and ſometimes by Foundering and melting his Greaſe.

You may cure it in this manner: Take two handfuls of wild Creſſes, two handfuls of Elecampane, and as much of the Leaves and Roots of Roerb and

Sorrel, and two pound of the Roots of Frodels; make
them all boil well in Lye and Vinegar : having strai-
ned the Decoction, put therein two pound of gray
Soap ; and when it is melted therein, then rub your
Dogs with it four or five days together, and it will
cure them.

---

*A brief discourse of the cure of Maladies
belonging to* Spaniels, *with other accidents happening.*

HOw necessary a thing a *Spaniel* is to Faulconry,
and for those that delight in that noble Recreation, keeping Hawks for their pastime and pleasure,
I think no body need question, as well to spring and
retrive a Fowl being flown to the mark , as also divers
other ways to help and assist Faulcons and Gos-hawks.

Now since they are subject to many diseases and
casualties, I shall endeavour to propound a suitable
Cure for them; and first, I shall begin with the Mange,
as the capital Enemy to the quiet and beauty of a
brave *Spaniel*, wherewith poor creatures they are often
grievously troubled, and as frequently infect others.

For the cure of this distemper , take a pound of
Barrow Flick, common Oyl three ounces, Brimstone
well pulverized four ounces, Salt well beaten to powder, Ashes well sifted and searced , of each two ounces; boil all these in a Kettle or Earthen-pot , and
when they are all well incorporated together, anoint
your *Spaniel* with this thrice every other day, either
against the Sun or Fire : having so done, wash him all
over with good strong Lye, and this will kill the
Mange. Remember you shift his Kennel and Litter
often.   If

If the *Spaniel* lose its Hair, as it often happens, then bathe your *Spaniel* in the water of Lupines or Hops, and anoint him with stale Barrows Flick.

This Ointment, besides the cure, maketh his Skin look slick and beautiful, and kills the Fleas, the Dogs disquieters, and Enemies to his ease.

If this be not strong enough to destroy this malady, then take two quarts of strong Vinegar, common Oyl six ounces, Brimstone three ounces, Soot six ounces, brayd Salt and searced two handfuls : boil all these together in the Vinegar, and anoint your Dog as aforesaid. This Receipt must not be administred in cold weather, for it may hazard his life in so doing.

If a *Spaniel* be not much troubled with the Mange, then it is easie to cure him thus :

Make bread with Wheaten-bran, with the Roots, Leaves, and Fruit of Agrimony, beating them well in a Mortar, and, making it into a Paste or Dough, bake it in an Oven, and so made, give thereof to your *Spaniel*, giving him no other bread for some time, letting him eat as long as he will.

Cure of the Formica.

In the Summer-time there is a scurvy malady which very much afflicts a *Spaniel*'s Ears, and is occasioned by Flys and their own scratching with their Feet : We term it a *Mange*, the *Italians*, *Formica*, and the *French*, *Fourmier*.

For the Cure, take Gum Dragaganth four ounces infused in the strongest Vinegar may be gotten, for the space of eight days, and afterwards bruised on a Marble-stone, as Painters do their Colours, adding unto it Roch-Allum and Galls beaten to powder, of either two ounces ; mingle all these well together, and lay it on the place afflicted.

For

For Swelling in the Throat.

By reason of a Humour distilling from the Brain, the Throat of a *Spaniel* will often swell unreasonably. For cure whereof, anoint the grieved place with Oyl of Camomile; then wash it with Vinegar not over-strong mixed with Salt. *Probatum est.*

Of Worms breeding in the Hurts and Mangy parts of a Spaniel.

These Worms do hinder the cure of the Mange or Wounds, causing them to continue at one stay, or to grow worse and worse. To remove this hindrance, take the Gum of Ivy and convey it into the Wound, and let it there remain a day or two, washing the Wound with Wine; and after that anoint it with Bacon-grease, Oyl of Earth-worms, and Rue.

The powder of wild Cucumbers is excellent good to kill these Worms, and will prove a good Corrosive, also eating away the dead flesh, and increasing the good.

If the Worms be within the body, you must destroy them in this manner : Cause your *Spaniel*, by fair means or foul, when fasting, to eat the Yolk of an Egg with two scruples of Saffron pulverized and confected with the same Egg, keeping him after it fasting till night.

When a *Spaniel* is hurt, as long as he can come to lick the Wound with his Tongue he needs no other remedy; his tongue is his best Chirurgeon : but when he cannot do that, then such wounds as are not venomous you may cure with the powder of *Matresilva* dried in an Oven, or in the Sun. If it be a bite of a *Fox*, anoint it with Oyl wherein Earth-worms and Rue have been boiled together. If by a mad Dog, let him lap twice or thrice of the

broth

broth of Germander, and eat the Germander too boiled.

Others bore the Skin of his Neck through with a hot-Iron just betwixt his Ears, so as the fire may touch both sides of the Hole made: after that, plucking up the Skin of the Dog's Shoulders and Flanks backwards, thrust it through with a hot-Iron in like manner: by giving the Venom this vent, it is a ready way to cure him.

To help a Spaniel that hath lost his sense of Smelling.

Spaniels, sometimes, by reason of too much rest and grease, or some other accident, do lose their sense of Smelling, so as they cannot spring or retrive a Fowl after their usual manner : To recover it again, take Agarick two drams, Sal Gemma one scruple ; beat these into powder, and incorporate them with Oxymel, making a Pill as big as a Nut, cover it with Butter, and give it the Dog by fair means or foul. This will bring him into a quick scent, as I have oftentimes proved it.

The benefit of cutting off the tip of a Spaniel's Tail or Stern.

It is necessary for several reasons to cut off the tip of a Spaniel's Stern when it is a Whelp. First, by so doing Worms are prevented from breeding there ; in the next place, if it be not cut, he will be the less forward in pressing hastily into the Covert after his Game ; besides this benefit, the Dog appears more beautiful.

L 4

An

An Abſtract of ſuch penal
L A W S
As relate to
HUNTERS & HUNTING.

STat. 13 R. 2. cap. 13. No man who hath not Lands of 40 s. per ann. nor Clerk who hath not 10 l. revenue per ann. ſhall have or keep any Grey-hound, Hound, Dog, Ferret, Net, or Engine to deſtroy Deer, Hares, Coneys, or any other Gentlemans Game, in pain of one whole years impriſonment, which Juſtices of Peace have power to inflict.

Stat. 1 H. 7. cop. 7. If any ſhall hunt within Foreſts, Parks, or Warrens in the night-time, or diſguiſed, one of the Kings Council, or a Juſtice of Peace to whom information ſhall be made, ſhall by his Warrant cauſe the Offender to be brought before himſelf, or ſome other Councellor or Juſtice of Peace to be examined; where if he conceal the Fact, ſuch hunting ſhall be deemed Felony; but being confeſſed, the Offence is onely finable at the next general Seſſions. And here a Reſcous of the Execution of any ſuch Warrant ſhall be alſo deemed Felony.

Stat. 19 H. 7. cap. 11. None ſhall keep any Deer-hays, or Buck-ſtalls (ſave in his own Foreſt or Park) in pain to forfeit for every Month

Month they are so kept 40 s. Neither shall any stalk with any Bush or Beast to any Deer, except in his own Forest or Park, in pain of 10 l.

Stat. 14, 15 H. 8. cap. 10. None shall trace, destroy, or kill any Hare in the Snow, in pain of 6 s. 8 d. for every such Offence: which penalty assessed in Sessions shall go to the King; but in a Leet, to the Lord thereof.

Stat. 3 Jacob. cap. 13. None shall (without the Owners License) kill or chase any Deer or Coneys in any Parks, or inclosed Grounds, in pain to suffer three months imprisonment, to pay treble damages to the party grieved, and to be bound with two good Sureties to the good behaviour for seven years: But the party grieved, having satisfaction, hath liberty to release the Behaviour.

II. By the same Statute it appears, that if any person not having 40 l. per annum in Lands, or 200 l. in Goods, or some inclosed Ground used for Deer or Coneys worth 40 s. per ann. at least, shall use any Gun, Bow, or Cross-bow to kill any Deer or Coneys, or shall keep any Buck-stall, Ferret, Dog, Net, or other Engine, it shall be lawful for any person (having Lands worth 100 l. per ann.) to take such Gun, &c. from any such person, and to convert it to his own use.

Stat. 13 Car. 2. cap. 20. None shall unlawfully Course, Kill, Hunt, or carry away any Deer in any Forest, Chase, Purlieu, Wood, Park, or other Ground where Deer have been usually kept, within England and Wales, without the consent of the Owners or Partie

ty chiefly trusted with the custody thereof,
or be aiding or assisting therein, upon pain,
being convicted by confession, or one Witness, before any Justice of the Peace within six moneths after the Offence, of 20 l. to
be levied by distress by Warrant of the said
Justices: one moity to the Informer, the
other to the Owner of the Deer: And for
want of distress, to be committed to the
House of Correction, or common Goal, for
one year, and not discharged till sufficient
Sureties be given for the good behaviour.

II. It is nevertheless provided, that upon
punishment of this Statute the penalty of
no other Law be incurred.

Stat. 22 & 23 Car. 2. cap. 25. It is Enacted,
That all Lords of Mannours or other Roy-
alties, not under the degree of an Esquire,
may by Writing under their Hands and
Seals, Authorize one or more Game-keepers
within their respective Mannours or Roy-
alties; who being thereunto so Authorized,
may take and seize all such Guns, Bows,
Grey hounds, Setting-dogs, Lurchers, or
other Dogs to kill Hares or Coneys, Ferrets, Trammels, Low-bells, Hayes, or o-
ther Nets, Hare-pipes, Snares, or other
Engines for the taking and killing of Coneys, Hares, Pheasants, Partridges, or
other Game, as within the Precincts of such
respective Mannours shall be used by any
person or persons who by this Act are prohibited to keep or use the same. And if any
person or persons by this Act prohibited to
keep or use any Guns, Dogs, &c. as aforesaid, be upon good ground suspected to have

or

or keep in his or their custody, any Guns, Bows, or any sort of Dogs, &c. to destroy Hares, Coneys, &c. Then may the said Game-keeper or Game-keepers, or other person (being thereunto Authorized by Warrant under the Hand and Seal of any Justice of the Peace of the same County, Division, or Place) in the day-time, search the Houses, Out-houses, or other places of such persons so suspected: and if any Gun, Grey-hound, Bows, Setting-dogs, &c. be there found, the same he shall seize, detain, and keep, to and for the use of the Lord of the Mannour or Royalty where the same shall be so found or taken; or otherwise to cut in pieces or destroy, as things by this Act prohibited to be kept by their degree.

II. None having Lands or Tenements, or some other Estate of Inheritance in his own or his Wifes right, of the clear value of 100 l. per ann. or for term of life, or having Lease or Leases of 99 years at least of the clear value of 150 l. Nor the Son and Heir apparent of an Esquire, or other person of higher degree, who are hereby declared to be persons declared by the Laws of this Realm not allowed to have or keep any Guns, Bows, Grey-hounds, Setting-dogs, Ferrets, Coney-dogs, Lurchers, Hayes, Nets, Low-bells, Hare-pipes, Snares, or other Engines aforesaid: But shall be, and are hereby prohibited to have, keep, or use the same. All Owners and Keepers of Forests, Parks, Warrens, or Chases, being stockt with Deer or Coneys for their necessary

sary use, in respect of the said Forests, Parks, Warrens, or Chases are allowed to keep, &c.

III. None may enter wrongfully into any Warren or ground lawfully used or kept for the breeding or keeping of Coneys ; (although the same be not enclosed) nor take, kill, or chase any Coneys there without the consent of the Owner thereof, not having any lawful Title or Authority so to do, on pain to yield to the party grieved treble damages and cost ; besides shall suffer three months Imprisonment, and after till they find Sureties for their good abearing : the person offending being convict by one Witness upon Oath, or his own confession is sufficient.

IV No person or persons shall take in the night-time any Coneys upon the borders of any Warren, or other grounds, lawfully used for the breeding or keeping of any Coneys, except such as shall be owners of the Soil, or lawful occupier or possessor of the ground, or any persons employed by him, her, or them, whereon such Coneys shall be so killed or taken ; upon pain that every Offender, lawfully convict as aforesaid, shall give the party or parties injured such recompence or satisfaction for his or their damages, and within such time as shall be appointed by the Justice before whom such Offender shall be convicted ; and over and above pay down presently to the Overseers for the use of the Poor of the Parish where such Offence shall be committed, such sum of mony, not exceeding 10 s. as the said Justice shall think meet. And if such Offender or Offenders do not
make

make recompence or satisfaction to the said party or parties injured, and also pay the said sum to the Poor as aforesaid; then the said Justice shall commit the said Offender or Offendors to the house of Correction, for such time as the said Justice shall think fit, not exceeding one month.

V. Provided that what is mentioned in this Act of 22 & 23 Car. 2. extend not to abridge any Royalty or Prerogative of his Majesty; nor to abridge, change, or alter any Forest-Laws, but the same to be of force, and remain as if this Act had not been made.

A further Abstract of some penal LAWS as concern Forests, Chases, &c.

1. THere shall be 3 Swainmotes in the year, viz. one 15 days before Michaelmass; another about Martinmass; and the third 15 days before Midsummer. At the first two of which none shall appear by distress, but the Fosters, Verdors, and Gest-takers; and at the other onely the Fosters and Verdors: howbeit the Fosters and Verdors shall meet every forty days, to see the Attachment of the Forests, as well for Green-hue, as Hunting: And the Swainmotes shall not be kept, but in the Counties where they have used to be kept.

II. Lawing of Dogs shall be made in Forests, from 3 years to 3 years by the view and testimony of lawful men, and not otherwise: Howbeit such Lawing of Dogs shall not be
but

but where it hath been used from the Coronation of Hen. 2 d.

III. No Foster or Beadle shall make Scotal, or gather Garbe, Oats, Lamb, or Pig, but by the sight of the 12 Rangers when they shall make their Range: And there shall be so many Rangers assigned for the keeping of Forests, as shall seem reasonably sufficient for the same.

IV. Any person having a Wood in the Forest may agest it, and take his pawnage there at his pleasure; he may also drive his Hogs through the Kings Woods, or elsewhere for that purpose; and if they ly all night in the Forest, he shall not be questioned for it.

V. None shall lose Life or Member for killing of Deer, but shall be fined for it if he have any thing; if not, he shall be imprisoned a year and a day: and (if he can finde good Sureties) shall then be delivered; but if not, he shall abjure the Realm.

VI. A Peer of the Realm, being sent for by the King, in coming and returning may kill a Deer or two in the Forest through which he passeth: howbeit, it must not be done privily, but by the view of the Foster, if present; but if absent, by causing one to blow a Horn for him, lest he seem to steal the Deer.

VII. No Chimage or Toll shall be taken in Forests, but by a Forester in fee, that farms his Bailiwick, and onely of such as buy their Bushes, Timber, Bark, or Coals, to sell it again, viz. 2 d. for a Cart, and 1 d. for an Horse, to be taken half-yearly; and it shall onely be taken where it hath used to

be

be taken, and not elsewhere: Neither shall any Chimage be taken of such as carry burthens of Bushes, Bark or Coal, albeit they sell it, unless they take them out of the Kings Demesne Woods. Thus far *Charta Foresta.*

A Forester, Parker, or Warrener shall not be questioned for killing a Trespasser, who (after the peace cryed to him) will not yield himself, so it be not done out of some other former malice. Stat. 21 Ed. 1.

No Minister of the Forest shall be put upon any Assize, Jury, or Inquest to be taken without the Forest. Ordin: Foresta.

Stat. 1 Ed. 3. cap. 8. None shall be taken or Imprisoned for Vert or Venison, unless he be taken with the manner, or else indicted according to the form of the Stat. 34. Ed. 1. And then the Warden of the Forest shall take him to Mainprise, until the Eyre of the Forest, without taking any thing for his deliverance. And if the Warden will not so do, he shall have a Writ out of the Chancery of Old ordained for persons indicted to be bailed till the Eyre.

Stat. 1 Ed. 3. cap. 2. Any man having Wood within the Forest, may take Horse-boot and Hay-boot in his said Wood, without being Attached for the same by the Ministers of the Forest, so that it be done by the view of the Foresters.

Stat. 7 R. 2. cap. 4. No Officer of the Forest shall take or imprison any without due Indictment, or per main ouvre (with his hand at the work) that is, being taken with the manner, or trespassing in the Forest; nor shall constrain any to make Obligation or

Ran

Ranfome againſt his will, and the Aſſiſe of the Foreſt, in pain to pay the party grieved double damages, and to be ranſomed at the Kings will.

16 & 17 Car. cap. 16. An Act for the certainty of Foreſts, and of the Meers, limits and bounds thereof: See the Statute at large.

17 Car. cap. 16. No place within England or Wales, where no Juſtice Seat, Swainmote, Court, or Attachment hath been made, or Windoſers choſen, or Regard made within 20 years, ſhall be accounted Foreſt.

II. Tenants and Owners of all excluded Land, ſhall enjoy their common and other profits.

Stat. 20 Car. 2. cap. 3. Ten Thouſand Acres of waſte Lands in the Foreſt of Dean ſhall be encloſed, and kept in ſeveralty, for the growth and preſervation of Timber; and be under the regard and Government of Foreſt-Law.

FINIS.

THE
GENTLEMAN'S
Recreation:

BEING,

A TREATISE

OF

HAWKING

AND

FAULCONRY.

Fitted for the Delight and Pleasure of all Noblemen and Gentlemen.

Collected from Ancient and Modern Authors, and Rectified by the Experience of the most Skilful Artists of these Times.

With an Abstract of such Statute Laws as concern this Recreation.

The Second P A R T.

L O N D O N: Printed by *J. C.* for *N. C.*

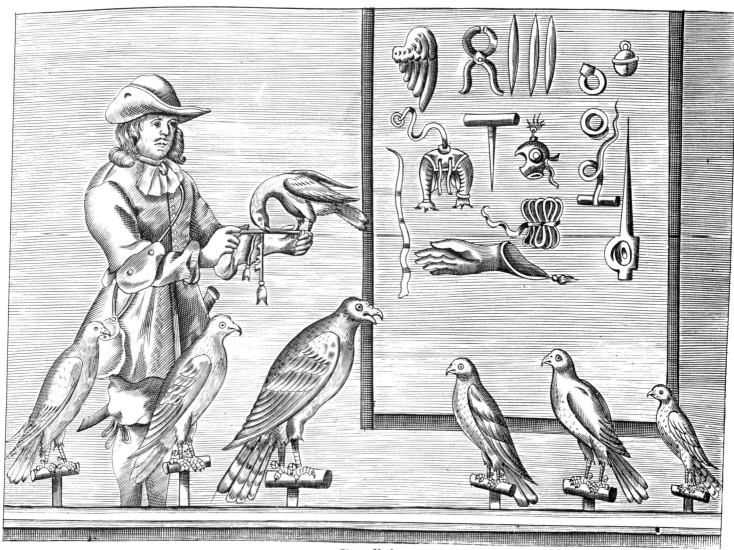

W Dolle fe

OF
HAWKING.

The Introduction.

THe Element wherein the *Faulconer* ufeth to trade, is the *Air*; and though he dealeth fometimes in the *Water*, yet he prefers the Air before it, that yielding him moft Recreation; for it is unable to ftop the high foaring of his generous Faulcon: in it fhe flies to fuch a height, that, being loft to the fight of Mortals, fhe feems to converfe with Heaven alone; and, like *Icarus*, endangers her Wings to be fcorcht by the Sun-beams; and yet is fearlefs, cutting the fluid Air with her nimble Pinions, making her High-way over the fteepeft Mountains and deepeft Rivers, and in her lofty career looks down with a feeming contempt on the greateft Glories we moft eftimate: and yet fuch is her Loyalty and Obedience to her Mafter, that a word from his mouth fhall make her ftoop and condefcend.

This Element of Air is not onely to be praifed for the Recreation it affords the Faulconers, but for its Ufefulnefs to all, no creature being in a condition to live without it: for if the infpiring or expiring Organ of any crea-

ture

ture be ſtopt, it muſt ſpeedily die, and pay the Debt that's due to Nature.

And as this Element juſtly merits praiſe, ſo do its wing'd Inhabitants, both feeding and refreſhing Mankind : with their Bodies they perform the firſt, and the latter with their harmonious Voices.

The number of Heaven's airy Quire is ſo great, I cannot here well enumerate them : yet I muſt not paſs by theſe nimble Muſicians of the Air, which warble forth ſuch curious Notes as puzzle Art to imitate.

I mean to ſpeak of few, and firſt of the *Lark*. When ſhe means to recreate her ſelf and hearers, ſhe quits the Earth, and ſings as ſhe aſcends ; and having made an end of her heavenly Ditty, ſhe ſeems to ſwound to think ſhe muſt deſcend again unto the dull Earth, which ſhe would ſcorn to tread but for neceſſity.

Again, obſerve how the *Black-bird* and the *Thruſh* contend who ſhall with their unimitable Voices bid the beſt welcome to the fragrant Spring.

Nor doth the *Nightingale* come ſhort in breathing out her loud Muſick through the ſmall Organ of her Throat. How have I oft admired in a ſtill night the clearneſs of her Airs, the ſweetneſs of her Deſcants, her natural Riſings and Fallings, her Doublings and Redoublings !

Much more might be ſaid of theſe, which I ſhall wave, being a digreſſion from my purpoſe, which is to treat of another Bird of pleaſure, *viz.* the *Hawk*.

HEre note, that the *Hawk* is diſtinguiſhed into two kindes ; the *Long-winged*, and *Short-winged Hawk*.

Of the first kinde there are these, which are here amongst us most in use :

> The *Gerfaulcon* and *Jerkin*,
> *Faulcon* and *Tiercel gentle*,
> *Lanner* and *Lanneret*,
> *Bockerel* and *Bockeret*,
> *Saker* and *Sakaret*,
> *Merlin* and *Jack-merlin*,
> *Hobby* and *Jack*,
> The *Stelletto* or *Spain*,
> The bloud-red *Rook* or *Turkie*,
> The *Waskite* from *Virginia*.

Of the *Short-winged Hawks* there are these :

> The *Eagle* and *Iron*,
> *Goshawk* and *Tiercel*,
> The *Sparrow-hawk* and *Musket*,
> Two forts of the *French Pie*.

Of inferiour fort there are these :

> The *Stanyel* or *Ring tail*,
> The *Raven* and *Buzzard*,
> The *Forked Kite* and bold *Buzzard*,
> The *Hen-driver*, &c.

It is not to be expected that we should treat of all these and many others bearing different nam s, but onely such which are most in use, of which I shall regularly treat concerning their Eyries, Mewings, Castings, Renovation of Feathers, &c. with their Reclaiming, Dieting, Diseases, Cures, and Method of Practice.

Terms

Terms of Art in Faulconry, as they were used by Ancient *Faulconers*, and are now by modern Practitioners, with their Explanations.

THe *Age* of a *Hawk*:
       The first year, a *Soarage*.
       The second year, an *Enterview*.
       The third year, a *White Hawk.*
       The fourth year, a *Hawk of the first Coat.*
Arms, are the Legs from the Thigh to the Foot.

Bate, is when the *Hawk* fluttereth with her Wings either from Pearch or Fist, as it were striving to get away.

Bathing, is when the *Hawk* washeth her self at home or abroad.

Beak, is the upper part of the Bill that is crooked.

Beam Feathers, are the long Feathers of the *Hawks* Wings.

Beavy of Quails, are a brood of young *Quails.*

Bewits, are the Leathers with Bells buttoned about the *Hawks* legs.

Binde.

Bowet, is when a young *Hawk* draws any thing out of her Nest, and covets to clamber on the bowes.

Bowsing, is when the *Hawk* drinks often, and yet continually thirsteth for more.

Branch

Branch or Stand, is to make the *Hawk* leap from Tree to Tree till the Dog springs the *Partridge*.

Brancher, is a young *Hawk* newly taken out of the Nest.

Cadge, is that circular piece of Wood on which *Hawks* are carried when they are exposed to sale.

Carry, is flying away with the Quarry.

Cast your Hawk to the Pearch, is to put your *Hawk* on the Pearch.

Casting, is when you give your *Hawk* any thing to cleanse and purge her Gorge.

Carvist ; a *Hawk* may be so called at the beginning of the year, and signifies as much as to carry on the Fist.

Cataract, a Disease in *Hawks* so called.

Cauterizing-Irons, are Irons to fear with.

Cawking time, is Treading time.

Canceleer.

Crabbing, is when *Hawks*, standing too neer, fight with one another.

Creance, is a fine small long Line of strong and even-wound Pack-thread wich is fastned to the *Hawk's* Leafe or Leash when she is first Lured.

Check, that is when the *Hawk* forsakes her proper Game to fly at Pies, Crows, or the like, crossing her in her flight.

Clap, is the nether part of the *Hawk's* Beak.

Coping-Irons, are used in coping, or paring the *Hawks* Beak, Pounces, or Talons, when over-grown.

Cowring, is when young *Hawks* quiver and shake their Wings in testimony of obedience towards the old ones.

Crinets, are the small black Feathers like Hairs about the Sere.

Disclosed, is when the young just peep through the shell. M 4 *Drop-*

Dropping, is when the *Hawk* muteth directly downward in several drops, not yerking it straight forwards.

Endew, is when the *Hawk* digesteth her meat, that she not onely dischargeth her *Gorge* thereof, but likewise cleanseth her *Pannel*.

Enseame, is the purging of a *Hawk* of her glut and Grease.

Enter a Hawk is when she first begins to kill.

Eyess, is a young *Hawk* newly taken out of the Nest, not able to prey for himself.

Eyrie, is that place where *Hawks* build, and hatch their young.

Feaking, is when the *Hawk* wipeth her Beak after feeding.

Filanders, a sort of little red Worms that usually breed in *Hawks*.

Flags, Feathers next the principal Feathers in the *Hawk's* Wing.

Fly on head, is missing her *Quarry*, and betaking her self to the next Check, as Crows, *&c.*

Formale, is the Female-*Hawk*.

Formica, a Disease in *Hawks* so called.

Frounce, is a Disease common in the Mouth or Throat of a *Hawk*.

Gleam, after a *Hawk* hath cast, she Gleamith, or throweth up filth from her Gorge.

Glut, is the slimy substance that lies in the *Hawk's* Pannel.

Gorge, is called in other Fowl the *Craw* or *Crop*.

Gurgiting, is when she is stuft and suffocated.

Hack, is the place where the *Hawk's* Meat is laid.

Hawk

Hawk keeps her mark, is when she waits at the p'ac where the lays in *Partridge,* or the like, until it be retrived.

Hern at seidge, is when you finde a *Hern* standing by the water-side watching for Prey, or the like.

Jack , is the Male-*hawk.*

Jesses, are those short Straps of Leather which are fastned to the *Hawks* Legs, and so to the Lease or Leash by Varvils, and such-like.

Imp, is to insert a Feather into the Wing of a *Hawk* in the place of one that is broken.

Inke, is the Neck from the Head to the Body of any Bird which the *Hawk* doth prey upon.

Intermewing, is from the first exchange of the *Hawks* Coat, till she turn white: and this is so called from the first Mewing.

Jouketh, is when she sleepeth.

Lure, that is when a young *Hawk* is called by the Faulconer thereunto, and is made of Feathers and Leather not much unlike a Fowl, which he casteth up into the Air.

Lease or *Leash,* is a small long thong of Leather by which the Faulconer holdeth his *Hawk* fast, folding it many times about his Finger.

Lean, is when the *Hawk* holds in to you.

A *Make-Hawk,* is an old Staunch-*Hawk* which used to fly. will easily instruct a young *Hawk.*

Managing a Hawk, is to use her with art and skill.

Make out, is when the *Hawk* goes forth at Check.

Mailes, are the Breast-feathers.

Manning, is making a *Hawk* to endure company.

Mantleth, is when the *Hawk* stretcheth one of her Wings after her Legs, and so the other.

Mew,

Mew, is the place where you set down your *Hawk* during the time she raiseth her Feathers.

Muting, is the Excrements or Dung of a *Hawk*, and so it is of a *Hern*.

Mites, are a sort of Vermin that trouble the Head and Nares of a *Hawk*.

Nares, are the little holes in a *Hawk*'s Beak.

Pearch, is the *Hawks* resting-place when she is off the Faulconers Fist.

Pelt, is the dead body of any Fowl the *Hawk* hath killed.

Pill or *Pelf*, is what the *Hawk* hath left of her prey after she is relieved.

Plume, is the general mixture of Feathers and Colours by which the Constitution of a *Hawk* is known.

Plumage, are small Feathers given the *Hawk* to make her cast.

Pluming, is after the *Hawk* hath seized her Prey, and dismantles it of the Feathers.

Pannel, is the Pipe next the Fundament of a *Hawk* where she digesteth her meat from her body.

Pantas, a Disease in *Hawks* so called.

Pendant-feathers, those Feathers behinde the Thigh of a *Hawk*.

Petty-singles, are the Toes of the *Hawk*.

Pounces, are the Claws of the *Hawk*.

Principal-feathers, are the two longest Feathers in the *Hawk*'s Wings.

Pruneth, is when the *Hawk* picketh her self.

Put over, is when a *Hawk* removeth her Meat from the Gorge into her Bowels by traversing with her Body, but chiefly with her Neck.

Quarry, is the Fowl which the *Hawk* flies at dead or alive.

Raised

Raised in flesh, is when a *Hawk* grows fat.

Rake, is when the *Hawk* flies out too far from the Fowl.

Ramage, is when a *Hawk* is wild, and difficult to be reclaimed.

Rangle, is when we give a *Hawk* Gravel to bring her to her Stomack.

Retrive, is when Partridges, having been sprung, are to finde again.

Rouze, is when a *Hawk* lifteth her self up and shaketh her self.

Ruff, is when the *Hawk* hits the Prey, and yet not trusses it.

Rufter-hood, is a plain and easie Leather-hood, being large, wide, and open behinde, and is to be won by a *Hawk* when you first draw her.

Reclaim, is to make a *Hawk* tame, gentle and familiar.

Sails, are the Wings of a *Hawk*.

Sear or *Sere*, is the yellow between the Beak and Eyes of the *Hawk*.

Seeling, is when a *Hawk* first taken is so blinded with a Thread run through the Eye-lids, that she sees not, or very little, the better to make her endure the Hood.

Seizing, is when a *Hawk* gripes her Prey, or any thing else, fast within her Foot.

Setting down, is when the *Hawk* is put into the Mew.

Slice, is when a *Hawk* muteth a great distance from her.

Sliming, is when a *Hawk* muteth without dropping.

Sniting, is when a *Hawk* as it were sneezeth.

Soar hawk, that is from the first taking her from the Eyrie till she hath Mewed her Feathers.

Spring, is when any Partridge or Pheasant rise.

Stooping, is when the *Hawk* is aloft upon her Wing, and then descends to strike her Prey.

Suu-

Summ'd, is when the *Hawk* is in all her Plumes.

Swivel, is that which keepeth a *Hawk* from twisting.

Tiercel or *Tissel*, is the Male *Hawk*.

Tiring, is when you give your *Hawk* a Leg or Pinion of a Pullet, Pidgeon, &c. to pluck at.

Train is the Tail of the *Hawk*.

Trussing, is when she raiseth any Fowl aloft, and soaring with it, at length descendeth with it to the ground.

Varvels, little Rings of Silver at the end of the Jesses, whereon the owners of the *Hawk* have their Names ingraven.

Unreclaimed, is when a *Hawk* is wilde.

Unseeling, is when you take away a Thread that runs through the *Hawks* Eye-lids, and hinders her sight.

Unstrike the Hood, is to draw the Strings, that it may be in a readiness to pull off.

Unsumm'd, is when the Feathers of a *Hawk* are not fully grown.

Urines, are Nets to catch *Hawks* withal.

Warbling, is after a *Hawk* hath mantled her self she crosses her Wings together over her back.

Weathering, is when you air your *Hawk* in Frost, Sun, or by the Fire-side.

Whur, is the rising and fluttering of Partridge or Pheasant.

The

The Names and Natures of Hawks *in general :*
and first of the Haggard-Faulcon.

I Begin with the *Haggard-Faulcon*, since it is a Hawk
which most men now-a days covet, to fit and prepare for their delight and pleasure; although heretofore I hear less spoken of her praise by the Antients
than she deserves.

Some of old have preferred the *Faulcon-gentle* for
mettle and courage, being of a loving disposition,
strong and daring, and hardy in all seasons; and by a
meer mistake have undervalued the *Haggard-faulcon*,
condemning her as being a Bird too tender to endure
rough and boisterous weather.

Experience confutes this opinion, she being known
to be able to endure as much the extremity of weather
or more than the *Tiercel*, *Faulcon gentle*, or most o-
ther Hawks whatsoever; and therefore she shall first
take place in this manner.

The *Haggard Faulcon*, wild, and unreclaimed, takes
a large liberty to her self for her abode, either by Sea
or Land; and is so absolute in her power, that where-ever she comes, all flying Fowl stoop under her subjection.
Nay, the *Tiercel-gentle*, although her natural companion, dares not fit by her or come near her residence
but in cawking-time, and that is in the Spring; and
then, for procreation sake, she will admit him to come
near her with submission, which he manifests by bow-
ing his Head at his approach, and by calling and cowring with his Wings, as the young ones do, in testimony how fearful he is of incurring her displeasure.

Whilst she is very young (and so will a *Paffenger-*
Soar-

Soar-faulcon) she will prey upon Birds wich are too big to encounter withal; and this she doth for want of understanding: and she continues this rashness and folly till experience and a sound beating have reclaimed her.

The *Haggard-faulcon* will prey on any other Fowl she can meet with advantageously, especially tame Pigeons, or such as belong to a Dove-house; for these they frequently meet withal.

This Hawk is an incessant Pains-taker; no weather discourageth her from her Game, but that onely wherein no Fowl can well stir abroad to seek for sustenance; otherwise she is continually working, either in the Air or elsewhere, unless she stoop and miss of her Prey, and then she will rest a little, to take breath and renew her courage. Nay, if she hath laboured in boisterous and tempestuous weather three or four days together, she will be so far from being the worse for it, that she will appear much better, and more lively. And therefore it is a vulgar errour, for men not to fly their Hawks but after three or four days rest, some a week or fortnight. For old Staunch-hawks I judge a little rest will do no harm; but for the young, till she is blouded give her but little; and if you can fly her every day, you will find it so much the better.

When the Faulcon unreclaimed hath seized her Prey and broke her Neck, (in artificial terms, her *Ink*) she then falls on the Crop, and feeds first on what is there contained, afterwards on other parts; and having filled her Gorge, she will fly to some solitary place which is near water, or what liketh her best, and there she will sit all day: upon the approach of night she takes Wing, and flies to some convenient place she hath afore purposed, to pearch therein till the morning.

Thus much of her as she is wild and unreclaimed.

In

In the next place it will be requisite to inform you with the manner of reclaiming of a *Haggard faulcon*, and her entry to the Lure.

Having taken or purchased one of them, set her down, and let her rest quietly the first night in a Rufter-hood.

The next day take her up easily on your Fist, and carry her up and down that whole day; using a Feather to stroke her withal instead of your hand. When you finde her not impatient of being toucht, take her Hood off speedily, and put it on again as speedily, observing thus to do till she is willing to feed: then frequently offer her food, but let her have but a little at a time; never pulling her Hood off or on but you must gain her love with a bit or two, using your voice unto her when you are taking off her Hood, and all the while she is feeding, and no longer; that by that means, after she is reclaimed, she may know by your voice she shall be fed.

Having thus done, teach her to come to your Fist from the Pearch by doing thus: Let her stand on a Pearch about breast-high; if lower, kneel, for this low posture will less affright than any other: after this, unstrike her Hood, and lure her, using your voice; and have a special care that you affright her not or distaste her, and so cause her to bate from you. But you must, before you unstrike her Hood, encourage her with a bit or two, which will make her the more eager to come to you: For it is her Stomack that rules her, and is the Bridle that keeps her in subjection, pricking her forward to perform her duty: wherefore if you keep not her Appetite sharp and truly edged, instead of submission you will finde disobedience. When you finde she will willingly feed from and come to your Hand, you may then let her sit bare-fac'd, now and then diverting her staring about by giving her a

bit

bit or two, to direct her face towards you : after this you may let her to the Lure.

When you finde she will come readily to the Lure, garnisht with meat in the *Creance*, tearing left she scorn this way of Luring, fix a live Pigeon to the Lure, and lure her therewith. When she hath killed the Pigeon and eaten the Head, take her up gently with a bit of meat, and put on her Hood; then unstrike her Hood and lure her to the Pelt, doing thus twice or thrice, and no more : if you do it oftner, she will become in time very loth to part with the Pelt, and by this means you will provoke her to carry. This is a great fault, and more incident to and worse in Field-Hawks than such as are fitted for the River.

But be sure you lure her not far till her Stomack be perfect; for otherwise she may discover something by the way which she hath a greater esteem for, and so be lost for that time; which will be very detrimental to her, although you should happen to recover and reclaim her afterwards.

Here observe, in the time of her making (while she is on the ground either pluming or feeding) forget not to walk round her, using your Voice, and giving her many bits with your hand; continuing so to do till you have won her to a more than ordinary familiarity.

But above all, mark this; spring her some living Doves between the Man and the Lure, and let them be given in a long Creance, that she may kill them near you, in such manner that she may truss them over your head : by this means she will not be afraid when you come to her from afar off; the neglect whereof will make her timorous: thence will proceed her dragging and carrying from you; nay sometimes she will leave her Prey, and totally forsake you.

There are some Hawks will not be taken up without

out ſtriking or rapping in the Creance, which muſt be infallibly the loſs of ſuch a Hawk without ſuch a device : this is a great fault in the Hawk , and argueth great negligence in the Faulconer, in ſuffering, and not remedying that ill property in her firſt making.

Rules for ordering a Haggard-faulcon *in the Luring : with the Cauſes and Remedies of Carrying, and other ill qualities.*

Having thus far acquainted your Hawk with the Lure, take her out ſome convenient Evening, and be no farther from her than ſhe can ſee and hear you ; then hold in your Lure , and ſuffer her to fly about you, holding her as near you as you can with your Voice and Lure, teaching her to do her buſineſs, and work it on your head, and then caſt up a live Dove : Which ſome diſapprove of, becauſe (ſay they) the lightneſs of the Dove inclines the Hawk to that ill quality of Carrying ; but I rather impute that fault to the ignorance, or negligence and harſhneſs of the Faulconer , who hath been either unskilful, remiſs, or hath not uſed that gentleneſs which is requiſite in Reclaiming a Hawk in her firſt Making ; ſo that inſtead of gaining her love by fair Allurements, he hath converted it into Hatred, Abhorrency, and Diſdainful Coyneſs.

Another cauſe of this Dragging or Carrying proceeds from the Keeper's ill or ſlender Rewarding his Hawk in the Luring, in giving her the Pelt of a Pigeon or ſome other dead thing, which gives her no deligh . It is the pleaſure ſhe takes in the Reward that engages her coming to you : if then ſhe chance to finde her expectation fruſtrated in her uſual ſatisfaction , ſhe will ever after ſhun you ; and though you ſhould throw her a live Pigeon, ſhe may ſeize it, and keep cloſe

N   to

to it, or remove it as you approach, for fear that your unkindness should deprive her of it. Wherefore you must have a special care you disoblige her not in her Luring.

There are several other errours which must be rectified in a *Haggard-faulcon*, *Faulcon-gentle*, or *Slight-Faulcons*, (which naturally are all of one kinde, yet differ much in quality and condition) which I shall leave to the study of the ingenious and industrious Faulconer or Keeper. I say, the first fault is, that though you have lured your Hawk well, and given her all the content and satisfaction imaginable, yet will she not tarry with you, but take her flight and forsake you. This argueth an aversion in her from you to something else. This fault Mr. *Turbervile*, and Mr. *Latham* say they have known remedied: but because I look upon the trouble therein to be so great, and the future satisfaction so small and uncertain, I shall not lay down what means are commonly made use of in the cure of this ill quality.

But there is another fault, which at first may be easily prevented; and that is, an aspiring quality and working humour, when although the Hawk never shewed any dislike to the Keeper or discontent, yet by observation she hath been found conceited, and would not endure the society of another Hawk; and having been well blouded on Fowl, she would not be kept down neer her Keeper. To remedy this, let no scope be given to the *Haggard* in the time of making; let her not fly high, but be held down and neer you: and if you should let this Hawk in to another Hawk, and finde her fall to her work without any regard or notice taken of the other Hawk, suspect her instantly, and let her see Fowl in due time, lest when she comes to her due place, she go her way; for she will prove impatient: wherefore the shorter work you make

with

with her, the greater delight you give her, and so consequently you engage her love continually towards you.

Having taught your Hawk to sit bare-faced in the Evening among company undisturbed, and that she knows your Voice, and will come to the Lure, then give her every night Stones, till you finde her Stomack good: after that, proser her *Casting*, and let her not receive it unless she likes it well; otherwise she is apt to take a dislike, and will never afterwards receive it willingly.

These Stones aforesaid prepare and make ready the way for casting, stirring, and dissolving whatever is offensive within, and fitting it to be carried downward in her Mutes, or upward in her Castings. The time for giving these Stones is when she hath put away her Supper from above; then give her halt a dozen above the hand, if you have so much skill; if not, otherwise as you are able. Do thus often, until such time as you shall give her such things whereof she shall take Plumage in her living or training. But of this, more hereafter.

How to know the nature and disposition of several H A W K S, and what must be observed from thence.

T'Here is a certain Hawk called a *Blank Hawk*, which is a kinde, loving, and docible Hawk; for she will diligently listen and give ear unto you and your voice; she will soon learn to come to hand, being very eager and hot to seize on what you shall either

ther

ther throw or give her, and will be very familiar: laftly, having done your will on the ground, fhe will lock up for your Fift, and will readily jump thereon.

They are much fubject to little Grubs, which are ingendered in the Guts, and difcover themfelves in their Mutes, crawling out from them, fhrinking themfelves up, and fo inftantly dying. Thefe Worms do little harm, and that Hawk which hath them is feldam bad. The colour of thefe Worms is red in a *Slight Faulcon*, and red in a *Barbary-Faulcon*; and when dead, in both white.

There is a fort of *Swarthy, black-plum'd Hawk*, that is good-mettled, and a high flier, yet hard to be reclaimed: for fhe will neither minde you nor your voice; but when you lure her, will look any other way than that fhe fhould. However, you muft fhew your felf very loving towards her, though you fhall get no more from her than what you extort by force. For her due reclaiming, leffen her pride by ordering her Diet with meafure, with refpect had unto the Weather; which if it be mild and temperate, you need not fear to hold her down until you have quarried her: and as you fhall fee her amend her manners, alter her Diet, and adde to her ftrength according to reafonable expedition; which will be foon obtained if fhe be found, and the weather moderate. But if the weather be frofty, have a care of abating flefh.

When at any time you fly any one of thefe black or tawny Hawks, and fhe ftoops foul and fails in her flight, you muft take her down with fome living thing.

If fhe be young, fuffer not her (or any other Hawk) to fly too long; for nothing is more prejudicial and diftafteful to a young Hawk at her firft making, than to let her toil and make many ftoopings before fhe be

ferved

ferved : by this diflike fhe is induced to fly wide and carelefly, and frequently to go away through difplea-fure.

Now to the intent I may go on methodically, and with as little confufion as may be, I fhall in the next place here nominate what *Hawks* I intend to treat of; and in the fame order as I name them, in like manner will difcourfe of them. Take them thus :

		Their Males	
Faulcon,			*Tiercel-gentle,*
Gerfaulcon,			*Jerkin,*
Mylion,			*Tiercel,*
Merlin,			*Jack,*
Hobby,			*Robbin,*
Goshawk			*Tiercel,*
Sparrow-hawk,			*Musket,*
Lanner.			*Lanneret.*

Here note, that the Female of all Birds of Prey are much larger, and of greater bulk than the Male, and are more ferviceable, being more watchful, hardy, and bold : but of fuch Birds as do not prey, the Cocks are the larger.

The *Faulcon, Gerfaulcon, Mylion, Merlin,* and *Hobby* do ftoop and feize their Prey with their Foot, breaking with their beak the Neck-bone of the Fowl, without pluming or tiring thereupon till the Fowl hath left busking and bating on the foot.

The *Goshawk* with her Male the *Tiercel,* and the *Sparrow-hawk,* kill their Game by ftrength and force of Wing at random , and do inftantly plume and tire up-on their Prey.

Of

Of the Faulcon.

THere are seven kinds of *Faulcons*, viz.

Faulcon-gentle,		*Gerfaulcon*,
Haggard-faulcon,		*Saker*,
Barbary or *Tar-*		*Lanner*, and
taret-faulcon,		*Tunician*.

The *Faulcon-gentle* is so called for her familiar courteous disposition; she is withal valiant, strong, and better able to endure any sort of weather than any other Hawk.

She hath a natural inclination and love to fly the Hern every way, either from her Wings to the downcome, or from the Fist and afore-head. She is most excellent at the Brook or River, especially at large Fowl, as the Shoveler, Wild-goose, &c. If she be an *Eyess*, you may venture her at the Crane; otherwise she will not be so hardy and bold. Where note, Hawks prove valiant or cowards according as they are first quarried: and if you take them out of the Eyrie before they are fully summed and hard penned, you must never expect their Wings should grow to perfection, but their Legs will be apt to wear crooked, and their Train, their long Feathers and their Flags also will be full of Taints.

In the choice of your Faulcon, observe that she have wide Nares; high and large Eye-lids; a great black Eye; a round Head, somewhat full on the top; a short, thick, azure Beak; and indifferent high Neck; barb Feathers under the clap of the Beak; a good

large,

large, round, fleshy Breast: let her be strong, hard, and stiff bonded, broad-shouldered; having slender Sails, full Sides, long and great Thighs; strong and short Arms; large Feet, with the Sear of the Foot soft and blewish; black Pounces; long Wings, and crossing the Train, which Train must be short and very pliable.

Here observe, that Faulcons of one kinde differ much and are diversly named, according to the time of their first Reclaiming, places of Haunt, and Countries from whence they come; as *Mew'd hawks*, *Rammage-hawks*, *Soar-hawks*, *Eyesses*: and these again are divided into large Hawks, mean Hawks, and slender Hawks. All these have different Males and Plumes, according to the nature of the Countries from whence they come; as some are black, some blank, or russet: and they differ in disposition; some are best for the Field, others for the River.

Names are bestowed on a Faulcon according to her Age or Taking.

The first is an *Eyess*, which name lasts as long as she is in the Eyrie. These are very troublesom in their feeding, do cry very much, and are difficultly entred; but being well entred and quarried, prove excellent Hawks for the *Hern*, River, or any sort of Fowl, and are hardy and full of mettle.

The second is a *Rammage-faulcon*, and reserves the name after she hath left the Eyrie, being so called *May*, *June*, *July*, and *August*. These are hard to be manned, but being well reclaimed, they are not inferiour to any Hawk.

The third is a *Soar hawk*, so called *September*, *October*, and *November*. The first Plumes they have when they forsake the Eyrie they keep a whole year before they mew them, which are called *Soar feathers*.

The fourth is termed *Marzarolt*, (the latest term

N 4   is

is *Carvist*, as much as to say, *Carry on the Fist :*) they are so called *January*, *February*, *March*, *April*, and till the middle of *May*, during which time they must be kept on the Fist. They are for the most part very great Baters, and therefore little eaters : They are bad Hawks, frequently troubled with *Filanders* and worms, and are rarely brought to be good for any thing.

The fifth are called *Enter mewers*, from the middle of *May*, to the latter end of *December*. They are so call'd because they cast their Coats. They were excellent Hawks, could they be trusted ; therefore they must be kept hard under, and must make your Fist their Pearch. Having discours'd of the Names and Nature of the Faulcon, I next come to his Manning, Luring, Flights, and Mewing in every condition : which course I shall orderly take in my ensuing discourse of the other Hawks I have onely named heretofore. And because what Diseases or Casualties are incident to one are likewise to all, I shall put their Cures at the latter end all together.

Of the Manning, Luring, Flights and Mewing of a Faulcon, with other things properly belonging to an Ostrager.

Having taken a Faulcon, you must Seel her, in such manner, that as the Seeling slackens, the Faulcon may be able to see what provision is straight before her, which she will better see so than any other way : and be sure you Seel her not too hard.

A Hawk newly taken ought to have all new Furniture, as new Jesses of good Leather, mailed Leases with Buttons at the end, and new Bewets. You must have a small round Stick likewise hanging in a string, with which you must frequently stroak your Hawk :

the

the oftner you do it, the sooner and better you will man her. She muſt have two good Bells, that ſhe may the better be found and heard when ſhe either ſtireth or ſcratteth : Her Hood muſt be well faſhioned, raiſed and boſſed againſt her Eyes, deep, and yet ſtraight enough beneath, that it may the better faſten about her Head without hurting her : and you muſt cope a little her Beak and Talons, but not ſo near as to make them bleed.

Take notice, if you take a *Soar-faulcon* which hath already paſt the Seas, although ſhe be very hard to be reclaim'd, yet ſhe is the beſt of Faulcons.

Her food muſt be good and warm twice or thrice a day, until ſhe be full gorg'd ; which food muſt be either Pigeons, Larks, or other live Birds : and the reaſon is, becauſe you muſt break her by degrees off from her accuſtomed feeding.

When you feed her, you muſt whoop and lure as you do when you call a Hawk, that ſhe may know when you will give her meat.

You muſt unhood her gently, giving her two or three bits ; and putting on her Hood again, you muſt give her as much more , and be ſure that ſhe be cloſe Seeled : and after three or four days leſſen her diet : and when you go to bed, ſet her on ſome Pearch by you, that you may awaken her often in the night. Thus you muſt do till you obſerve her grow tame and gentle : and when you finde ſhe begins to feed eagerly, then give her a Sheep's-heart. And now you may begin to unhood her by day-time, but it muſt be far from company ; firſt giving her a bit or two, then hood her again gently, and give her as much more. Be ſure not to affright her with any thing when you unhood her. And when you perceive her to be acquainted with company, and that ſhe is ſharp ſet, unhood her, and give her ſome meat, holding her juſt againſt your Face and

Eyes,

Eyes, which will make her lefs afraid of the countenances of others. If you can, reclaim her without over-watching.

You muft bear her continually on the Fift till fhe be throughly Manned, caufing her to feed in company, giving her in the Morning about Sun-rifing the Wing of a Pullet, and in the Evening the Foot of a Coney or Hare cut off above the joynt, flay'd and laid in Water; which having fqueez'd, give it her with the Pinion of a Hen's Wing.

For two or three days give her wafht meat, and then Plumage, according as you think her foul within. If fhe Caft, hood her again, and give her nothing till fhe Gleam after her Cafting: having gleamed and cafted, then give her a beaching of hot meat in company; and towards the Evening let her plume a Hen's Wing in company alfo.

If the Feathers of her Cafting be foul or flimy and of a yellowifh complexion, then be fure to cleanfe her well with wafht meat and Cafting: if clean within, give her gentle Caftings, as the Pinions of an old Hens Wing, or the Neck-bone chopped four or five times between the joynts, wafht and fteeped in fair Water.

Having well reclaim'd her, throughly manned her, and made her eager and fharp fet, then you may venture to feed her on the Lure.

But before you fhew her the Lure you muft confider thefe three things: 1. That fhe be bold in and familiar with company, and no ways afraid of Dogs and Horfes. 2. That fhe be fharp fet and hungry, regarding the hour of the Morning and Evening when you will lure her. 3. And laftly, fhe muft be clean within, and the Lure muft be well garnifhed with meat on both fides, and you muft abfcond your felf when you intend to give her the length of the Leafe.

You

You muſt firſt unhood her, giving her a bit or two on the Lure as ſhe ſitteth on your Fiſt : afterwards take the Lure from her, and ſo hide it that ſhe ſee it not ; and when ſhe is unſeized, caſt the Lure ſo near her that ſhe may catch it within the length of her Leaſe. When ſhe hath ſeis'd it, uſe your voice according to the cuſtome of Faulconers, and feed her upon the Lure on the ground with the Heart and warm Thigh of a Pullet. Having ſo lured her, in the Evening give her but a little meat; and let this luring be ſo timely, that you may give her Plumage and a Juck of a joynt.

In the Morning betimes take her on your Fiſt, and when ſhe hath caſt and gleamed, give her a little beaching of warm meat. Towards Noon take a Creance and tie it to her Leaſe, and go into ſome pleaſant Field or Meadow, and give her a bit or two on the Lure ; then unſeize her : and if you find ſhe is ſharp ſet, and hath ſeiz'd on the Lure eagerly, then give her ſome one to hold, to let her off to the Lure ; then unwind the Creance, and draw it after you a good way, and let him which holds the Hawk hold his right hand on the Taſſel of the Hawk's Hood in readineſs, ſo that he may unhood her aſſoon as you begin to lure : and if ſhe come well to the Lure, and ſtoop upon it roundly, and ſeize it eagerly, then let her eat two or three bits thereon; then unſeize her and take her off the Lure, hood her, and deliver her to him again that held her, and going farther off lure her, feeding her as before with the accuſtomed voice. Thus lure her every day farther and farther off, till ſhe is accuſtomed to come freely and eagerly to the Lure.

After this, lure her in company, but have a care that nothing affright her : and when you have uſed her to the Lure on foot, then lure her on Horſe-back; which you may effect the ſooner, by cauſing Horſe-

men

men to be about you when you lure her on foot : alfo you may do it the fooner by rewarding her upon the Lure on Horfe-back among Horfemen.   When this way fhe grows familiar, let fome body afoot hold the Hawk, and he that is on Horfe-back muft call and caft the Lure about his Head ; then muft the holder take off the Hood by the Taffel : and if fhe feize eagerly on the Lure without fear of man or Horfe , then take off the Creance, and lure her at a greater diftance, And if you would have her love Dogs as well as the Lure , call Dogs when you give her Tiring or Plumage.

Of Bathing a Faulcon lately reclaimed ; how to make her Flying , and to hate the Check.

Having wean'd your Faulcon from her Rammage-fooleries , being both ways lured , rewarded , and throughly reclaim'd, offer her fome Water to bathe her felf in, in a Bafon wherein fhe may ftand up to the Thighs , chufing a temperate clear day for that purpofe.   Then having lured your Hawk, and rewarded her with warm meat, in the morning carry her to fome Bank, and there hold her in the Sun till fhe hath endewed her Gorge, taking off her Hood that fhe may prune and pick her felf : that being done, hood her again, and fet her near the Bafon, and taking off her Hood, let her bathe again as long as fhe pleafeth : After this, take her up, and let her pick her felf as before, and then feed her.   If fhe refufe the Bafon to bathe in, fhew her fome fmall River or Brook for that purpofe.

By this ufe of bathing fhe gains ftrength and a fharp appetite, and thereby grows bold : but that day wherein fhe batheth give her no wafht meat.   If

If you will make your Faulcon upwards, the next day after she hath bath'd get on Horse-back, either in the morning or Evening, and chuse out some field wherein are no Rooks or Pigeons; then take your Lure well garnished on both sides, and having un-hooded your *Hawk*, give her a bit or two on the Lure, then hood her: afterwards go leisurely against the Wind, then unhood her: and before she bate, or finde any Check in her Eye, whistle her off from your Fist fairly and softly. As she flieth about you, trot on with your Horse, and cast out your Lure, not suffering her to fly long about you at first: continue thus doing Morning and Evening for seven or eight days. But if you finde your Hawk unwilling to fly about you or stoop to the Lure, then must you let her fly with some *Hawk* that loves the company of others, and will not rove at any change or check; and that must first be done at the Partridge, for they will not fly far before the *Hawk*. If she hath flown twice or thrice, cast out the Lure, and reward her on Horse-back. If the Fowl you flew her at be killed by another *Hawk*, let her feed with him a little, and then farther reward her on the Lure.

If you would have your Faulcon prove upwards and a high-flying *Hawk*, you must let her fly with such as are so qualified. If she love the company of others, and is taught to hold in the Head, then if the Fowl be in Pool, Pit, or Plash, cast off your high-flying *Hawk*, and let him that hath your new-lur'd *Hawk* get under the Wind, and when he seeth his advantage, let him unhood her; and if she bate, then it is to get up to the other *Hawk*.

Let him then cast her off, and before she get up to the other near his full pitch, lay out the Fowl: if she kill her Game, reward her with the Heart, and let her participate of the Breast with the other *Hawks*.

To

To take your Faulcon from going out to any Check thus you must do : If she hath kill'd a Check, and hath fed thereon before you could come in, rebuke her not severely at first, but take her down to the Lure, give her a bit or two, hood her, and fly her not in three or four days ; and if you do, let it be where no Checks are : but if you come in before she hath tasted the Check she hath killed, then take the Gall of an Hen, and anoint the Breast of that Check she hath killed, (any other bitter thing will do) and this will make her hate to go at Check again.

How to enseam a Faulcon with her Castings and Scowrings.

When you feed your Faulcon, call and lure as if you called her to the Lure, and every day profer her Water, and every night give her Castings accordingly as she endeweth. Take off her Hood frequently in company ; and that you may hinder her from bating, hold always the Hood ready by the Tassel in your hand.

In the Evening by candle-light take off her Hood among company, until she Rouze and Mewt; then set her on the Pearch, and not before, setting a light before her.

Every Faulcon ought to have a *Make-Hawk* to teach her to hold in the Head : if that will not do, cut off some part of her two Principals in each Wing, the long Feather and that next to it, which will force her to hold in.

Be sure to reward your *Hawk* well at the beginning, and let her feed well on the Quarry ; which will so encourage her, that she will have no fancy to go out to the Check. When she is well in bloud and well quarried, then let her fly with other *Hawks*.　　　**If**

If you would make your Faulcon to the Crane, her Lure should be a counterfeit Crane. If you would make her to the Hare, her Lure should be then a Hares Skin stuft with some light matter: When she is well lured, and you would enter her, tie the Hare's Skin so stuft to the end of a Creance, and fasten it to your Saddle-pummel, by which means when you gallop it will resemble a running Hare: then unhood your *Hawk*, and cry, *Back with the Dogs, back with the Dogs.* When you finde she hath seized it, let go your Creance, and suffer her to fasten thereon; then instantly reward her upon it, and encourage her as much as is possible.

When she is well entred after this manner, take a living Hare and break one of her hinder Legs, and having before well acquainted your Faulcon with your Dogs by continual feeding among them, I say then put your Hare out in some fair place with your Dogs, and the Faulcon will stoop and ruff her until the Dogs may take her; then take the Hare from the Dogs, and cast her out to the Faulcon, crying, *Back, Back there.*

If you would make your Hawk flying to the Partridge or Pheasant after she is reclaimed and made, then every time you lure her cast your Lure into some low Tree or Bush, that she may learn to take the Tree or Stand: if she take the Stand before she sees the Lure, let her stand a while; and afterwards draw the Lure out before her, and cry with what words you have acquainted her to understand you by, and then reward her well. After this manner she will learn to take stand.

Feed her always on the ground, or in some thick place; for in such places she must encounter with the Pheasant at Pearch.

At first fly with her at young Pheasant or Partridge,

to encourage her by advantage, and afterwards at the old.

If a Faulcon will not take Stand, but keep on the Wing, then muft you fly her in plain places where you may always fee her upon you.

Draw your Faulcon out of the Mew twenty days before you Enfeam her : If fhe trufs and carry, the remedy is to cope her Talons, her Powlfe and Petty-fingle.

Never reward your *Hawk* upon River-fowl but upon the Lure, that fhe may the better love and efteem thereof.

The Crane ought to be flown at before Sun-rifing; for fhe is a flothful Bird, and you may caft off to her a Caft or Leafe of Faulcons, or a Gofhawk from the Fift, without Dogs. You muft fly but once a day at the Crane, after which you muft reward your Hawk very well, ever fuccouring her with a Grey-hound, which is the beft of Dogs for that purpofe.

Give your Faulcon a Beaching very early in the morning, and it will make her very eager to fly when it is time for it.

If you would have her a high-flying *Hawk*, you muft not feed her highly, but fhe fhould be fed nine days together before Sun-rifing, and at night late in the cool of the Evening.

The Faulcon will kill the Hern naturally if fhe be a Peregrin or Traveller : yet you will do well to give her Trains.

A Faulcon may fly ten times in a day at a River, if the feafon be not extream ; but more is inconvenient.

A *Hawk* ought to have forty Caftings before fhe be perfectly made. And indeed all *Hawks* ought to have Caftings every night, if you would have them clean and found : for *Hawks* which have not this continual

noctur-

nocturnal Casting will be surcharged with abundance
of superfluous Humours, which ascending to the Brain,
breed so great a disturbance that they cannot fligh so
high as otherways they would. And it is good to
give them Tiring or Plumage at night, especially field-
Hawks, but not River-*Hawks*, for fear of weakning
their Backs.

When your *Hawk* hath flown or bated, feed her
not so long as she panteth, (but let her be first in breath
again;) otherways you may bring her into a Disease
called the *Pantas*.

If a Faulcon or other *Hawk* will not Seize nor
Gorge, take the Quill of a Wild-goose, and tie it under her long Single; then will she Seize and Gripe.
When she beginneth to seize, take away the said Quill,
and she will seize long afterwards.

If you cannot give Covert to your Faulcon or Goshawk, then cast her off with the Sun in her back.

When you draw your *Hawk* out of the Mew, if she
be greazy, (which you shall know by her round fat
Thighs and her full Body, the Flesh being round, and
as high as her Breast-bone) and if she be well mew'd,
and have all her Feathers summed, then give her at
feeding-time in the morning two or three bits of hot
meat; and at night give her less, unless it be very
cold; and if she feed well and without compulsion,
give her washt meat. Thus prepared, take the Wings of
a Hen for her Dinner and wash them in two Waters.
In the morning give her the Legs of a Hen very hot,
at Noon meat temperately warm, a good Gorge; then
let her fast till it be late in the Evening. If she have
put over her meat, and there is nothing left in her
Gorge, then give her warm meat, as in the morning.
Thus diet her till it be convenient to give her Plumage, the which you may know by these tokens:
First, the Flesh of the end of the Pinion of the *Hawk's*

O

Wing

Wing will feem fofter and tenderer than it did before fhe did eat wafht meat. Secondly, if her Mewts be white, and the black thereof be very black, and not mingled with any other colour. Laftly, if fhe be fharp fet, and doth plume eagerly, you may give her Cafting either of a Hare's or Coney's Foot, or the fmall Feathers on the joynt of the Wing of an old Hen.

Having fet her on the Pearch, fweep clean underneath, that you may fee whether the Mewt be full of ftreaks, or skins, or flimy: if it be, then continue this fort of Cafting three or four nights together; but if you finde the Feathers digefted and foft, and that her Cafting is great, then take the Neck of an old Hen, and cut it between the joynts, then lay it in cold water, and give it your Faulcon three nights together; in the day-time give her wafht meat, after this Cafting or Plumage, as you fhall fee requifite: and this will bear all down into the Pannel.

When you have drawn her out of the Mew, and her principal Feathers are fummed, give her no wafht meats, but quick Birds with good Gorges, and fet her out in open places.

General Inftructions for an Oftrager or Faulconer.

LEt his *Jeffes* and *Bewets* be of good Leather, having Bells big and fhrill according to the proportion of the *Hawk*, with a Hood that is boffed at the Eyes, and fizable for the Head.

He muft ufe his *Hawk* in fuch manner, that he may make her grow familiar with him alone or in company, and

and to that end he muſt often unhood and hood her again.

In nine nights the Faulconer ought not to let his *Hawk* Jouk at all, nor ſuffer her to pearch, but keep her during that time continually on his Fiſt.

When the Faulconer would call his *Hawk*, let him ſet her on the Pearch, unhood her, and ſhew her ſome meat within his Fiſt, call her ſo long till ſhe come to it, then feed her therewith : if ſhe come not, let her ſtand without food till ſhe be very ſharp ſet. Obſerve this order for about nine days.

When you would lure her, give her ſome man to hold, and call her with a Lure well garniſhed with meat on both ſides, and give her a bit : uſe her to this ſix or ſeven days ; then cauſe her to be held farther from you, and caſt the Lure about your Head , and throw it on the ground a little way from you : if ſhe come to it roundly, reward her bountifully. Having uſed her to this ſome certain days, take your Lure garniſhed as aforeſaid, and every day call her to you as far as it is poſſible for her to ſee or hear you, and let her be looſe from all her Furniture, without Loins or Creance. If ſhe come freely, reward her, and ſtop her now and then in her feeding ; for that will make her come the better. You may do well to ſtop the Lure upon her ſometimes, and let her fly upon you. Here note, it is requiſite to bathe her before you take this courſe, leſt when ſhe is at liberty ſhe rangle to ſeek Water, and in the mean time you loſe your *Hawk* ; wherefore bathe her every ſeven or eight days, for her nature requireth it.

When you have thus manned, reclaimed, and lured your *Hawk*, go out with her into the fields, and whiſtle her off your Fiſt, ſtanding ſtill to ſee what ſhe will do, and whether ſhe will rake out or not : but if ſhe fly round about you, as a good *Hawk* ought to do, let

her

her fly a turn or two, and fling her out the Lure, and let her foot a Chicken or Pullet, and having killed it, let her feed thereon.

Unhood her often as you bear her; continue so doing till she hath endewed and mewted sufficiently.

Your *Hawk* being thus made and manned, go abroad with her every morning when it is fair, and let the place where you intend to fly her be plashy, or some narrow Brook; and when you cast her off, go into the Wind so far, that the Fowl may not discover you. When she is cast off, and beginneth to recover her Gate, make then to the Brook or Plash where the Fowl lie, always making your *Hawk* to lean in upon you: and when you see her at a reasonable pitch, (her Head being in) lay out the Fowl, and land it if you can; and if you cannot, take down your *Hawk*, and let her kill some Train; to which end you must always carry some live Fowl with you, as a Duck &c. And having slipt one of her Wing-feathers, thrust it through her Nares, and cast her up as high as you can underneath your *Hawk*, that she may the better know your hand.

If you would have your *Hawk* fly at one particular Fowl more than at another, you must then feed her well upon a Train of the same kind, as thus: Take a Creance, and tie that Fowl you would accustom her to fly to by the Beak, with meat on her Back, and cause one to stand close that shall hold the Creance; then standing afar off, unhood your *Hawk*, and let the Fowl be stirred and drawn with the Creance until your *Hawk* perceive it stir; and if she foot it, make another Train thus: Take a living Fowl that can fly, half feel it and cast it out; then let your *Hawk* fly to it; and if she kill it, reward her well upon it.

Of

Of the Rammage-faulcon.

If a Faulconer chance to recover a *Rammage-han*
that was never handled before, let him immediately
feel her; and at that instant put on her Jesses made of
soft leather; at the end thereof fix two Varvels, the
one may bear your Coat of Arms, the other your
Name, that if she chance to be lost, they that take her
up may know where to return her: put her on also a
pair of Bells with two proper Bewets. Having thus
furnished her, you must begin her manning by gentle
handling. To avoid the danger of her Beak, you must
have a smooth Stick about half a foot in length, with
which you must stroak your *Hawk* about the Pinions
of her Wings, and so downwards thwart her Train.
If she offer to snap at the Stick, withdraw not your
hand, and let her bite thereon, the hardness whereof
will soon make her weary of that sport.

If you would man her well, you should watch all
the night, keeping her continually on your Fist.

You must teach her to feed feel'd; and having a
great and easie Rufter-hood, you must hood and unhood her often, feel'd as she is, handling her gently
about the head, coying her always when you unhood
her, to the intent she may not be displeased with her
Keeper.

Let her plume and tire sometimes upon a Wing on
your Fist, keeping her so day and night, without pearching, until she be weary, and will suffer you to hood
her without stirring.

If your *Hawk* be so rammage that she will not leave
her snapping or biting, then take a little *Aloes succotrina*, and when she offers to snap, give it her to bite
the bitterness whereof will quickly make her leave
that ill quality. Garlick I have heard will do the

O 3

like,

like, the ſtrong ſcent thereof being equally offenſive.

How to hood a Hawk.

Having ſeel'd your *Hawk*, fit her with a large eaſie
Hood, which you muſt take off and put on very often,
watching her two nights, handling her frequently
and gently about the Head as aforeſaid. When you
perceive ſhe hath no averſion to the Hood, unſeel her
in an Evening by Candle-light; continue handling her
ſoftly, often hooding and unhooding her, until ſhe
takes no offence at the Hood, and will patiently endure
handling.

Take this Obſervation by the way, that it is the
duty of a Faulconer to be endowed with a great deal
of Patience; and in the next place he ought to have
a natural love and inclination to *Hawks*: Without
theſe two qualifications all the Profeſſors of this Art
will prove *Mar-Hawks* inſtead of good Faulconers.

But to return where I left off: If your ſeel'd *Hawk*
feeds well, abides the Hood and handling without
ſtriking or biting, then by Candle-light in an Evening unſeel her, and with your Finger and Spittle a-
noint the place where the Seeling-thread was drawn
through; then hood her, and hold her on your Fiſt all
night, often hooding, unhooding, and handling her,
ſtroaking her gently about the Wings and Body, giving
her ſometimes a bit or two, alſo Tiring or Plumage.
Being well reclaimed, let her ſit upon a Pearch; but
every night keep her on the Fiſt three or four hours,
ſtroaking, hooding, and unhooding, &c. as aforeſaid:
and thus you may do in the day-time, when ſhe hath
learn'd to feed eagerly without fear.

How to make a Hawk *know your Voice, and her own Feeding.*

Having mann'd your *Hawk* fo that fhe feeds bold-ly, acquaint her with your Voice, Whiftle, and fuch words as Faulconers ufe : you may do it by frequently repeating them to her as fhe is feeding on your Fift, &c. But I think the beft way of making her acquainted with them is by your experience and practice.

When fhe feeds boldly, and knows your Voice and whiftle, then teach her to know her Feeding, and to bite at it, in this manner. Shew her fome meat with your right hand, crying and luring to her aloud : if fhe bate or ftrike at it, then let her quickly and neatly toot it, and feed on it for four or five bits. Do thus often, and fhe will know her Feeding the better.

After this give her every night fome Cafting either of Feathers, or Cotton with Cloves or Aloes wrapt up therein, &c. Thefe Caftings make a *Hawk* clean and eager.

How to make your Hawk *bold and venturous.*

In the firft place, to make her hardy, you muft per-mit her to plume a Pullet or large Chicken in a place where there is not much light : her Hood in a readi-nefs, you muft have either of the aforefaid alive in your hand ; then kneeling on the ground, luring and crying aloud to her, make her plume and pull the Pullet a lit-tle ; then with your Teeth drawing the Strings, un-hood her foftly, fuffering her to pluck it with her Beak three or four times more ; then throw out the Pullet on the ground, and encourage her to feize it. When you perceive fhe breaks it and takes blood, you muft

O 4　　　　　　　　　lure

lure and cry aloud to her, encouraging her all the ways
imaginable : then hood her gently, and give her Tiring
of the Wing or Foot of the said Pullet.

How to make a Hawk know the Lure.

Your *Hawk* having three or four times thus killed a
Pullet or large Chicken in some secret place, then thus
teach her to know the Lure.

Having fastned a Pullet unto your Lure, go apart,
giving your *Hawk* unto another, who must draw loose
the strings of her Hood in readiness : Being gone a
little way, take half the length of the String, and cast
it about your Head, luring with your Voice at the same
time ; then let your *Hawk* be unhooded as you are
throwing your Lure a little way from her, not ceasing
luring all the while. If she stoop to the Lure and
seize, suffer her to plume the Pullet, still coying and
luring with your voice ; then let her feed on the Pullet upon the Lure : After that, take her on your Fist
together with her meat, then hood her, and let her tire
as aforesaid. And thus you may teach her to come by
degrees to a very great distance.

How to make a Hawk flying.

When your *Hawk* or *Haggard-faulcon* will come
and stoop to the Lure roundly without any fear or
coyness, you must put her on a great pair of Luring-
bells ; the like you must do to a *Soar-hawk* : by so
much greater must the Bells be, by how much your
Hawk is giddy-headed, and apt to rake out at Check.

That being done, and she sharp set, go in a fair morning into some large Field on Horseback, which Field
must be very little incumbred with Wood or Trees :
having your *Hawk* on your Fist, ride up into the wind,

and

and having loofned her Hood, whiftle foftly to provoke her to fly ; and then you will obferve fhe will
begin to bate, or at leaft to flap with her Flags and
Sails, and to raife her felf on your Fift : then fuffer her
until fhe rouze or Mewt : when fhe hath done either
of them, unhood her, and let her fly with her Head
into the Wind ; for thereby fhe will be the better able
to get upon the Wing ; then will fhe naturally climbe
upwards, flying in a circle.

When fhe hath flown three or four Turns, then cry
and lure with your Voice, cafting the Lure about your
head, unto which you muft firft tie a Pullet : and if
your Faulcon come in and approach neer you, then caft
out the Lure into the Wind ; and if fhe ftoop to it, reward her as before.

There is one great fault you will often finde in the
making of a *Hawk* flying , and that is , when fhe
flieth from the Fift fhe will not get up, but take ftand
on the ground ; a frequent fault in Soar-faulcons. You
muft then fright her up with your Wand, riding in to
her ; and when you have forced her to make a Turn
or two, take her down to the Lure and feed her. But
if this do no good, then you muft have in readinefs a
Duck feeled, fo that fhe may fee no way but backwards, and that will make her mount the higher.
This Duck you muft hold by one of the Wings near
the body in your right hand, then lure with your voice
to make your Faulcon turn the head : when fhe is at
a reafonable pitch, caft up your Duck juft under her,
that fhe may perceive it : if fhe ftrike, ftoop, or trufs
the Duck, permit her to kill it, and reward her, giving
her a reafonable Gorge. Ufe this cuftom twice or
thrice, and your *Hawk* will leave the Stand, delighting
on the Wing, and will become very obedient.

Here note, that for the firft or fecond time it is not
convenient to fhew your *Hawk* great or large Fowl,

for it often happens that they flip from the *Hawk* into the wind; the *Hawk* not recovering them, raketh after them, which puts the Faulconer to much trouble, and frequently occafions the lofs of his *Hawk*.

But if it fo chance that your *Hawk* fo rake out with a Fowl that fhe cannot recover it, but gives it over and comes in again directly upon you, then caft out a feeled Duck; and if fhe ftoop and trufs it, crofs the Wings, and permit her to take her pleafure, rewarding her alfo with the Heart, Brains, Tongue, and Liver. For want of a quick Duck, take her down with the dry Lure, and let her plume a Pullet, and feed her upon it.

By fo doing your *Hawk* will learn to give over a Fowl that rakes out, and hearing the Lure of the Faulconer, will make back again to the River, and know the better to hold in the Head.

A Flight for a Haggard.

When you intend a Flight for a Haggard, for the firft, fecond, and third time make choice of fuch a place where there are no Crows, Rooks, or the like, to take away all occafion of her raking out after fuch Check.

Let her not fly out too far on head at the firft, but run after and cry, *Why lo, why lo*, to make her turn Head. When fhe is come in, take her down with the Lure, unto which muft be faftned a live Pullet, and let her tire, plume, and feed as aforefaid.

Sometimes a Haggard out of pride and a gadding humour will rangle out from her Keeper: then clog her with great Luring-bells, and make her a Train or two with a Duck feeled, to teach her to hold in and know her Keeper: take her down often with the dry Lure, and reward her bountifully, and let her be ever

well

well in bloud, or you may whoop for your *Hawk* to no purpose.

How to make a Soar-faulcon *or* Haggard *kill her Game at the very first.*

If she be well lured, flieth a good Gate, and stoopeth well, then cast off a well-quarried *Hawk*, and let her stoop a Fowl on Brook or Plash, and watch her till she put it to the plunge: then take down your *Make-Hawk*, reward her, hood her, and set her: so you may make use of her if need require.

Then take your *Hawk* unentred, and going up the wind half a Bow-shot, loose her Hood, and softly whistle her off your Fist, until she have rouzed or mewted: then let her fly with her Head into the Wind, having first given notice or warning to the company to be in readiness against the *Hawk* be in a good Gate, and to shew Water, and to lay out the Fowl.

When she is at a good pitch, and covering the Fowl, then notifie that all the company make in at once to the Brook upon the Fowl, to land her: if your Faulcon strike, stoop, or truss her Game, run in to help her, and crossing the Fowl's Wing, let her take her pleasure thereon.

If she kill not the Fowl at first stooping, give her then respite to recover her Gate. When she hath got it, and her Head in, then lay out the Fowl as aforesaid, until you land it at last; not forgetting to help her as soon as she hath seized it, giving also her due Reward.

Remedy

Remedy for a Hawk's *taking Stand in a Tree.*

In the first place you must chuse such places where are no Wood or Trees, or as little as may be. If you cannot avoid it, then have two or three live Trains, and give them to as many men, placing them conveniently for to use them. When therefore your *Hawk* hath stooped, and endeavours to go to stand, let him to whom the *Hawk* most bends cast out his Train-Duck seeled : if the *Hawk* kill her, reward her therewith. If this course will not remedy that fault in her by twice or thrice so doing, my advice is then to part with the Buzzard.

How to help a Hawk *froward and coy through pride of Grease.*

There is a scurvy quality in some *Hawks*, proceeding from pride of Grease, or being high kept, which is a disdainful coyness. Such a *Hawk* therefore must not be rewarded although she kill ; yet give her leave to plume a little ; and then let the Faulconer take a Sheeps-Heart cold, or the Leg of a Pullet, and whilst the *Hawk* is busie in pluming, let either of them be conveyed into the Body of the Fowl, that it may favour thereof ; and when the *Hawk* hath eaten the Brains, Heart, and Tongue of the Fowl, then take out your Inclosure, and call your *Hawk* with it to your Fist , and feed her therewith : after this give her some Feathers of the Neck of the Fowl to scowr and make her cast.

To

To make a Hawk hold in her Head, and not minde Check.

Take a piece of a Leafe, and faſten it to your Lure-ſtring, the other end to the Wing of a Pigeon, which you may put in and pull out of your Hawking-bag at your conveniency : when you finde your *Hawk* apt to go out, ſhew your Pigeon. I would not have you uſe it often ; for it draws a *Hawk* from her place if well flown.

How to continue and keep a Hawk in her high-flying.

If your *Hawk* be a ſtately high-flying *Hawk*, you ought not to engage her in more Flights than one in a morning: for often flying brings her off from her ſtately pitch. If ſhe be well made for the River, fly her not above twice in a morning ; yet feed her up though ſhe kill not.

When a high-flying *Hawk*, being whiſtled to, ga-thers upwards to a great Gate, you muſt continue her therein, never flying her but upon broad Waters and open Rivers ; and when ſhe is at the higheſt, take her down with your Lure ; where when ſhe hath plumed and broken the Fowl a little, then feed her up, and by that means you ſhall maintain your Faulcon high-flying, inwards, and very fond of the Lure.

Some will have this high-flying Faulcon ſeldom to kill, and not to ſtoop : yet if ſhe kill every day, al-though ſhe ſtoop from a high Gate, yet if ſhe be not rebuked or met herewith, ſhe will, I can aſſure you, become a better Flier every day than other : but ſhe will grow leſs fond of the Lure. Wherefore your
high-

high flying *Hawks* fhould be made inwards, it being a commendable quality in them to make in and turn head at the fecond or third tofs of the Lure, and when fhe poureth down upon it as if fhe had killed.

And as the teaching of a Faulcon, or any other *Hawk*, to come readily to and love the Lure, is an art highly commendable, becaufe it is the effect of great labour and induftry : fo it is the caufe of faving many a *Hawk*, which otherways would be loft irrecoverably.

Mark this by the way, that fome naturally high-flying *Hawks* will be long before they be made upwards, ftill fifhing and playing the flugs; and when they fhould get up to cover the Fowl, they will ftoop before the Fowl be put out : And this may proceed from two caufes. In the firft place, fhe may be too fharp fet; and in the next place, it may be fhe is flown untimely, either too foon or too late.

When you fee a *Hawk* ufe thofe evil Tatches without any vifible caufe, caft her out a dead Fowl for a dead Quarry, and hood her up inftantly without Reward, to difcourage her from practifing the like another time : half an hour afterwards call her to the Lure and feed her, and ferve her after this manner as often as fhe fifheth in that fafhion.

Befides, to correct this errour the Faulconer ought to confult the natures and difpofitions of his *Hawks*, and fhould carefully obferve which flie high when in good plight, and which beft when they are kept low; which when fharpeft fet, and which on the contrary in a mean between both; which early at Sun-rifing, which when the Sun is but two hours high; which fooner, and which later in an evening.

For know that the natures of *Hawks* are different; fo are the times to fly each one : for to fly a *Hawk* in her proper time, and to fly her out of it, is as difagree-
able

able as the flight of a *Gerfaulcon* and a *Buzzard.* Therefore the Oftrager muft fly his *Hawks* according to
their natures and difpofitions, keeping them always
in good order.

Where by the bye take notice, all *Hawks*, as well
Soar-hawks as *Mew'd-hawks* and *Haggards*, fhould be
fet out in the evening two or three hours, fome more,
fome lefs, having refpect to their nature as it is ftronger or weaker ; and in the morning alfo according as
they caft, hooding them firft, and then fetting them
abroad a weathering, until you get on Horfeback to
profecute your Recreation.

A Flight for the Hern.

This Flight hath lefs of Art in it than Pleafure to
the beholders ; and, to fay the truth, the Flight is ftately and moft noble.

As it is lefs difficult to teach a *Hawk* to fly at Fowl
than it is to come unto and love the Lure, the firft being
natural, and not the laft ; fo there is lefs induftry to be
ufed in making a *Hawk* fly the Hern than Water-fowl.
To the firft fhe is inftigated by a natural propenfity and
inclination ; to the latter fhe is brought with art, pains,
and much diligence.

At the beginning of *March* Herns begin to make
their Paffage : if therefore you will adapt your Faulcons for the Hern , you muft not let them fly longer at the River, and withal you muft pull them down
to make them light ; which is done by giving them
Hearts and flefh of Lambs and Calves, alfo Chickens ;
but give them no wild meats.

To the intent you may acquaint them one with the
other, fo that they may the better fly the Hern and
help one another, you muft call a caft of them to the
Lure at once ; but have a care they crab not together,

ther, for so they may endanger one another in their flight.

When your *Hawk* is scowred and clean and sharp set, you must then get a live Hern, upon the upper part of whose long sharp Bill you must place a joynt of a hollw Cane, which will prevent her from hurting the *Hawk*: that being done, tie the Hern in a Creance; then setting her on the ground, unhood your *Hawk*, who will fly the Hern as soon as she sees her. If she seize her, make in apace to succour her, and let her plume and take bloud of the Hern: then take the Brains, the Marrow of the Bones, and the Heart, and laying it on your Hawking-glove, give it your Faulcon. After this, rip her Breast, and let your *Hawk* feed thereon till she be well gorged: this being done, hood her up upon the Hern, permitting her to plume at her pleasure; then take her on your Fist, and let her tire on the Foot or Pinion.

Because Herns are not very plentiful, you may preserve one for a Train three or four times, by arming Bill, Head, and Neck, and painting it of the same colour that the Hern is of: and when the Faulcon seizeth her, you must be very nimble to make in, and deceive her by a live Pigeon clapt under the Wing of the Hern for the Faulcon, which must be her Reward.

The *Hawk* having thus several times taken her Train without discovery of the delusion, you may then let the Hern loose in some fair Field without a Creance, or without arming her: when she is up of a reasonable height, you may cast off your Faulcon; who if she bind with the Hern and bring her down, then make in apace to rescue her, thrusting the Hern's Bill into the ground, and breaking his Wings and Legs, that the *Hawk* may with more ease plume and foot him. Then reward her as before, with the Brains,

Mar-

Marrow of the Bones, and Heart, making thereof an *Italian Soppa.*

Thus much of a Train-Hern. Now to fly the wild Hern it is thus : If you finde a wild Hern at Siege, win in as nigh unto her as you can, and go with your *Hawk* under the Wind ; and having first loosed her Hood in a readiness, as soon as the Hern leaveth the Siege, off with her Hood, and let her fly. If she climbe to the Hern and bring her down, run in (as I said before) to rescue her, thrusting her Bill into the ground, breaking her Wings and Legs, and rewarding her as aforesaid on your Hawking-glove.

Now if your Faulcon beat not down the Hern, or do give him over, never fly your Faulcon again at a Hern unless with a *Make-hawk* well entred ; for the Coward by this means, seeing another fly at the Hern and bind with her, takes fresh courage. And if they kill the Hern flying both together, then must you reward them both together while the Quarry is hot, making for them a *Soppa* as aforesaid. This is the onely way to make them both bold and perfect Herners.

Of the HAGGARD-FAULCON, *why so called; her good Shape and Properties : And what difference there is between a* Haggard *and a* Faulcon-gentle.

THe *Haggard* is by some called the *Peregrin-faulcon,* because, say some, she is brought from a Country forrein and remote ; and therefore others call them *Travellers,* or *Passengers.* But if there be no

other

other reason for the name but this, all other *Hawks* coming from exotick places might borrow that appellation.

Upon a threefold confideration I conceive they are called *Haggard* or *Peregrin-faulcons*.

Firft, becaufe their Eyrie was never found in any Country by any man that ever I could hear or read of.

Secondly, becaufe thefe Faulcons rangle and wander more than any other Faulcon doth, ftill feeking ftrange and forrein Coafts ; fo that where-ever they come they may be juftly called *Pilgrims* or *Forreiners*.

Thirdly, and laftly, fhe never takes up her habitation long in a place.

This *Haggard* is not inferiour to any other Faulcon, but very tender, and cannot endure hard weather, fay fome ; but my experience hath found it otherwife. The reafon that may be alledged is this ; firft, fhe travels far, as a Stranger, and comes into Countries commonly in the hardeft time of the year : next, fhe is a hot *Hawk,* which may be gathered from her high flying, where the Air is much colder than below, and therefore ought to be more hardy : laftly, fhe meweth with more expedition (if fhe once begin to caft her Feathers) than other Faulcons do.

They are of fhape like other Faulcons ; but as to mould they are of three forts, large, middle-fiz'd, and little ; fome long-fhaped, fome fhort-truffed ; fome larger, fome lefs.

They have a four-fold Mail, blank, ruffet, brown and Turtle.

The goodnefs of her Shape confifts in having her Head plum'd dark or blank, flat on the top, with a white Wreath environing the fame, a large blue bending Beak, wide Nares, a great black full Eye, high ftately Neck, large Breaft, broad Shoulders, a great
Turtle-

Turtle-coloured Feather, long Veins and Sails, but slender shaped, a long Train, high Thighs, and white on the Pendant Feathers, a large wide Foot, with slender Stretchers, and Talons tending somewhat to an azure colour.

You may know her in her flight from another by the stirring of her Wings; for she useth no thick stroak, but getteth up to her *Mountee* leisurely, without any great making out: besides she may be known by her extraordinary large Sails.

The differences between the *Haggard* and *Faulcongentle* are these.

First, the *Haggard* is larger, being longer-armed with longer Beak and Talons, having a higher Neck, with a long and fair-seasoned Head.

Secondly, her Beam-feathers in flight are longer than the *Faulcon-gentle*'s, her Train somewhat larger: again, the *Haggard* hath a flat Thigh, and the other's is round.

Thirdly, the *Haggard* will lie longer on the Wing.

Fourthly, the *Haggard* at long flight exceeds the *Faulcon-gentle*; which last flieth with more speed from the Fist than the other. For maintenance of Flight and goodness of Wing the *Haggard* exceeds all other Hawks.

Fifthly, and lastly, the *Haggard* is more deliberate and advised in her Stooping than the *Faulcon gentle*, who is more hot and hasty in her Actions, and missing the Fowl, is apt presently to fly on head at the Check.

Of

Of the BARBARY-FAULCON.

THE *Barbary*, or, as some call her, the *Tartaret-Faulcon*, is a Bird seldom found in any Country, and is called a *Passenger* as well as the *Haggard*. They are somewhat lesser than the *Tiercel-gentle*, and plum'd red under the Wings, strong-armed, with long Talons and Stretchers.

The *Barbary-faulcon* is venturously bold, and you may fly her with the *Haggard* all *May* and *June*. They are *Hawks* very slack in Mewing at first; but when once they begin, they mew their Feathers very fast.

They are called *Barbary-faulcons* because they make their passage through that Country and *Tunis*, where they are more frequently taken than in any other place, namely in the Isles of the *Levant*, *Candy*, *Cyprus*, and *Rhodes*. In my opinion she is a *Hawk* of not much value, and therefore I shall leave her, to speak of another of greater reputation.

Of the GERFAULCON.

THE *Gerfaulcon* is a very fair *Hawk*, and of great force, especially being mewed: she is strong-armed, having long Stretchers and Singles; she is fierce and hardy of nature, and therefore difficultly to be reclaimed. She is a lovely Bird to behold, larger than any kind of Faulcon: her Eyes and Head are like the *Haggard*'s.

Her

Her Beak is great and bending: she hath large Nares, and a Mail like a *Lanner's* ; her Sails are long and sharp-pointed ; her Train much like the *Lanners* ; she hath a large Foot marble-seared, and is plumed blank, brown, and russet. She expects great civility from her Keeper, who must exercise a great deal of patience on her.

The *Gerfaulcon's* Eyrie is in some parts of *Prussia*, and on the borders of *Russia* ; and some come from the Mountains of *Norway*, and from *Germany :* These may be also called *Passengers.*

By reason of the fierceness and hardiness of this Bird, she is very hardly manned and reclaimed ; but being once overcome, she proves an excellent *Hawk,* and will scarce refuse to fly at any thing.

Their Beaks are blue, so are the Sears of their Legs and Feet, having Pounces and Talons very long.

These *Hawks* do not fly the River, but always from the Fift fly the Herns, Shovelers, *&c.*

In going up to their Gate they do not hold that course or way which others do ; for they climbe up upon the Train when they find any Fowl, and as soon as they have reacht her they pluck her down , if not at the first, yet at the second or third encounter. You must feed and reward them like other Faulcons.

They are very crafty, and covet to keep their Castings long through sloth ; therefore instead of Cotton give them a Casting of Tow, and be sure to keep them sharp set.

In the Manning and Reclaiming you must by kindness make her gentle and familiar with you. When you have taught her to be lured loose, then learn her to come to the Pelts of Hens, or any other Fowl : but let her not touch any living flesh, for fear that draw her love away from your Voice and Hand.

All

All this time you muſt be cloſe by her, about her, and upon your Knees, uſing your Voice unto her, with her dinner and ſupper clean dreſt and waſht, giving her ſtill ſome bits thereof with your hand, that ſhe may the more delight therein. By doing thus frequently you will ſo win her, that ſhould ſhe be guilty of Carrying, yet by this means ſhe will be reclaimed, and forget that errour.

Let the Oſtrager have eſpecial care how he make his *Gerfaulcon* at firſt, and indeed all other *Hawks*; for as they are made then, he ſhall ever finde them after; and if they are well made, they are twice made, and for ever made: and therefore have a care of too much precipitation in poſting them forward from one leſſon to another, before they are perfect in any thing.

If you train her with Doves, ſhe will not carry a feather from you. But firſt before you ſpring her any Doves, let her kill four or five at Lure cloſe by your foot, having a pair of ſhort Creances at your Lure.

Here note, that the *Gerfaulcon* is moſt deſired for her high-flying, and is beſt at Hern and the Mountee: and that you may bring her to perfection herein, play with your entermewed *Gerfaulcon* the firſt year, ſhewing her all imaginable kindneſs, and uſing all poſſible means to make her love you. When you have brought her forward, give her often Caſtings to cleanſe and purge her, alſo to prevent the growth of too much glut and fatneſs in her inward parts, which will indanger her life.

Of

Of the SAKER.

THe *Saker* is a Paſſenger or Peregrin-hawk, for her Eyrie hath not been found by any. They are found in the Iſles of the *Levant*, *Cyprus*, *Rhodes*, and *Candia*, and in ſeveral other Iſlands in the Sea.

She is ſomewhat larger than the Haggard-faulcon; her Plume is ruſty and ragged; the Sear of her foot and beak like the Lanner; her Pounces are ſhort, however ſhe hath great ſtrength, and is hardy to all kind of Fowl. She is more diſpoſed to the Field a great deal than to the Brook, and delights to prey on great Fowl, as the Hern, the Gooſe, &c. As for the Crane, ſhe is not ſo free to fly at her as the Haggard-faulcon. The *Saker* is good alſo for leſſer Fowl, as Pheaſant, Partridge, &c. and is nothing ſo dainty of her diet as *Hawks* long-winged.

This *Hawk* will make excellent ſport with a Kite, who, as ſoon as ſhe ſees the *Saker* (the Male whereof is called a *Sakeret*) caſt off, immediately betakes her ſelf to and truſts in the goodneſs of her Wings, and getteth to her pitch as high as poſſibly ſhe may, by making many Turns and Wrenches in the Air: which if well obſerved, together with the variety of conteſts and bickerings that are between them, it cannot but be very pleaſant and delightful to the beholder. I have known in a clear day, and little wind ſtirring, that both the *Saker* and Kite have ſoar'd ſo high that the ſharpeſt Eye could not diſcern them, yet hath the Saker in the encounter conquered the Kite, and I have ſeen her come tumbling down to the ground with a ſtrange precipitancy.

Of

Of all Birds the *Saker* hath the longest Train. This *Hawk* will fly at Hern, Kite, Pheasant, Partridge, Quail, and sometimes at the Hare; but her chiefest excellency consists in her flying at the Crane.   Now because we have but few of them in *England*, I shall desist from speaking farther of the *Saker*, onely that she is made to the Lure as other *Hawks* are : and indeed all Faulcons are made after the same manner, yet are not flown withal alike; for *Sakers*, *Lanners*, *Gerfaulcons*, *Mylions*, and *Merlins* do not fly the River; if any do, it is very rarely.

Of the LANNER, LANNERET, *and* TUNISIAN.

THe *Lanner* is a *Hawk* common in all Countries, especially in *France*, making her Eyrie on high Trees in Forests, or on high Cliffs near the Seaside.

She is lesser than the Faulcon-gentle, fair-plumed when an Enter-mewer, and of shorter Talons than any other Falcon.   Those who have the largest and best-seasoned Heads are the best Lanners.

With the *Lanner* or *Lanneret* you may fly the River; and both are very good also for the Land.

They are not very choice in their Food, and can better away with grofs Victuals than any other *Hawk.*

Mew'd *Lanners* are hardly known from the *Soarhawks*, (and so likewise the *Saker*) because they do not change their Plume.

You may know the *Lanners* by these three tokens. 1. They are blanker *Hawks* than any other.   2. They have

have lefs Beaks than the reft. 3. And laftly, They are lefs armed and pounced than other Faulcons.

Of all *Hawks* there is none fo fit for a young Faulconer as the *Lanner*, becaufe fhe is not inclined to Surfeits, and feldome melts Greafe by being over-flown.

There are a fort of *Lanners* which Eyrie in the *Alps*, having their Heads white and flat aloft, large and black Eyes, flender Nares, fhort and thick Beaks, and leffer than the *Haggard* or *Faulcon-gentle*. Some are indifferent large, fome lefs, and others middle-fized.

Their Mail is marble or ruffet; their Breaft-feathers white and full of ruffet fpots; the points and extremities of their Feathers full of white drops; their Sails and Train long: they are fhort Leg'd, with a foot lefs than that of a Faulcon, marble-feer'd; but being mew'd the Seer changeth to a yellow.

The *Lanner* never lieth upon the Wing after fhe hath flown to Mark, but after once ftooping fhe maketh a Point, and then, like the *Gofhawk*, waits the Fowl.

If fhe mifs at the firft down-fall and kill not, fhe will confult her advantage to her greateft eafe.

Thefe kind of *Hawks* are highly prized in *France* and *Italy*, neither is fhe defpifeable in *England*; but we look upon them as flothful and hard-mettled: and therefore if you intend to have any good of her, keep a ftrict hand over her; for fhe is of an ungrateful difpofition, and will flight your kindneffes, contrary to the nature of the *Faulcon-gentle*, who for one good ufage will return a treble courtefie, and the better fhe is rewarded the better fhe will fly.

They are flown at Field or Brook, and are *Hawks* that maintain long flights, whereby much Fowl is killed (and more than by a better *Hawk*) by reafon of Dogs and Hawking-poles.

If

If you will fly with a *Lanner*, you muſt keep her very ſharp : and becauſe they keep their Caſtings long, by reaſon they are hard-metled *Hawks*, give them therefore hard Caſtings made of Tow and knots of Hemp.

In the reclaiming the *Lanner* and the *Lanneret* much pains and labour muſt be taken, and the chiefeſt thing is to make her well acquainted with the Lure, which muſt be garniſhed with hard waſhed meat, and let her receive the major part of her Reward in bits from your hand : as for the reſt of her Training, take the ſame courſe which I have directed in the manning and ordering of the *Haggard-faulcon*. But above all take pains to ſtay her, and by your utmoſt art reſtrain her from dragging or carrying any thing from you, to which ill quality ſhe is more inclined than any other *Hawk* whatever.

To conclude this Chapter, I come next to the *Tuniſian-faulcon*, which is not much different in nature from the *Lanner*, yet ſomewhat leſs, but in Foot and Plume much alike. She hath a large round Head, and is more creeſe than the *Lanner*, and more heavy and ſluggiſh in her flight.

She is called a *Tuniſian-faulcon*, from *Tunis* the Metropolis of *Barbary*, the Country where ſhe uſually makes her Eyrie.

They are excellent *Hawks* for the River, lying long upon the Wing, and will fly the Field alſo very well.

They naturally delight to ſeize upon the Hare, and will ſtrike boldly at her. Much more might be ſaid of her, which I here omit, ſhe being a *Hawk* not very common in *England*.

Having curſorily diſcourſt in as good a method as I could of the ſeven ſorts of Faulcons, with their Manning, Reclaiming, Luring, Training, Staying, &c.

A

I shall proceed to give you an account of some other *Hawks*, which I propounded and promised in the beginning of this Treatise : take them thus in order.

Of the MERLIN.

THe *Merlin* in Plume is much like the *Haggard-Faulcon*, also in the Sear of the Foot, Beak and Talons, and is much alike in Conditions.

A *Merlin* well mann'd, lur'd, and carefully lookt after, will prove an excellent *Hawk.* Their flight is swifter than any other *Hawk*, and naturally they fly at Partridge, Thrush and Lark.

It is a Bird very busie and unruly, and therefore the Faulconer ought to take special heed and care of them, left unnaturally they eat off their own Feet and Talons, which several of them have been known to do, and die thereby. For which cause *Merlins* ought not to be mew'd or intermew'd, because in the Mew they often spoil themselves.

She is accounted a *Hawk* of the Fift, and not of the Lure : but to my knowledge she may be brought to love the Lure very well.

She is very venturous and hardy, which may appear by her flying at Birds as big or bigger than her self, with such eagerness as that she will pursue them even into a Town or Village.

If you will fly with a *Merlin* at a Partridge, chuse the *Formal*, which is the Female. The *Jack* is not worth the Training.

When you have made her to the Lure, and that she will patiently endure the Hood, then make her a Train with a Partridge : if she foot and kill it, reward her well,

well, suffering her to take her pleasure thereon. After this fly her at the wild Partridge; if she take or mark it at first or second flight, being retrieved by the Spaniels, feed her upon it with a reasonable Gorge, chearing her with your Voice in such manner that she may know it another time. If she prove not hardy at first Train, try her with a second or third: if she prove not then, she will prove nothing worth.

If you fly the *Merlin* at Lark or Linnet, let it be with a Cast of *Merlins* at once, because they love to fly in company: besides, it is a greater delight to the Spectators to see them fly together; you shall observe the one climbe to the Mountee above the Lark, and the other to lie low for her best advantage.

When your *Merlin* is throughly manned and made gentle, (which you must bring to pass according to the method propounded for other *Hawks*) I say, when she is reclaimed, you may then carry her into the fields; where having found a Lark or Linnet, get as neer as you can into the Wind to the Bird; and as soon as the Bird riseth from the ground, unhood your Cast of *Merlins* and cast them off, and when they have beaten down the Lark let them feed a little thereon.

There is a sort of Larks which I would not advise the Faulconer to fly at, and they are called *Cut-larks*, which do not mount as the long-spur'd field-Lark, but fly straight forward, to the endangering the loss of your *Hawk* without any pastime or pleasure.

Of the Mewing of Merlins, Faulcons, Gerfaulcons, *and* Mylions *at Stock or at Large: and which is the best way of Mewing.*

It is the opinion of some, (but how commendable I will leave the Reader to judge) that *Merlins* cannot

be

be mew'd, or if they be, that they are very rarely good afterwards. Experience tells me the contrary : for if they be hardy, and have flown well in their Soarage, they have proved much better after mewing than before.

The time of mewing for Faulcons should be about the latter end of *April* ; at which time set down your Faulcons, diligently observing whether they be louzy or not : if they are, pepper them, and that will infallibly kill the Lice. You must also scour them before you cast them into the Mew.

Mewings are of two sorts ; the one loose and at large, the other at the Stock or Stone.

Mewing at large is thus in short : If your Room be large , by divisions you may mew four Faulcons at once, each partition consisting of about twelve foot square, and as much in height, with two Windows two foot broad, the one opening to the North, for the benefit of cold Air, the other to the East, for the beneficial warmth of the Sun. At your East-window let there be a Board two foot broad even with the bottom of the Window, with a Lath or Ledge round ; in the middle set a green Turff, laying good store of Gravel and Stones about it, that your *Hawk* may take them at her pleasure.

If your Faulcon be a great Bater, let you Chamber be on the ground , which must be covered four fingers thick with gross Sand, and thereon set a Stone somewhat taper of about a Cubit in height, on which they love to sit by reason of its coolness.

Make her two Pearches, at each Window one, to recreate her self as she pleaseth either with heat or cold.

Every week or fortnight set her a Bason of Water to bathe in, and when she hath bathed therein take it away the night following.

You

Your Mew muſt have a Portal to convey in the Hack, a thing whereon the meat is ſerved. I need not preſcribe the manner how to make it, ſince it is a thing ſo generally known already.

You ought to keep one ſet hour in feeding ; for ſo will ſhe mew ſooner and better : when ſhe hath fed and gorged her ſelf, then remove the Stick from the Hack on which the meat was faſtened, to keep her from dragging it into the Mew.

In the opinion of moſt it is better Mewing at the Stock or Stone, which muſt be performed thus : Make choice of a Ground-room remote from noiſe or con-courſe of people, and therein ſet a Table of what length you think is moſt convenient for the number of your Faulcons, and of about ſix foot in breadth, with thin Boards along the ſides and ends, about four fingers high from the ſuperficies of the Table, which muſt ſtand on Treſſels about three foot high from the ground. Let this Table be covered indifferently thick with great Sand mixt with ſmall Pebbles, in the midſt whereof place a pyramidal Free-ſtone about a yard in height, unto which tie your Falcon, Gerfalcon, Mer-lin or Mylion : then take a ſmall Cord of the bigneſs of a Bow-ſtring, and put it through a Ring or Swivel, and bind it about the Stone in ſuch ſort that the Swi-vel may go round the Stone without let or hindrance, and thereunto tie the Leaſe of your *Hawk*.

Here note, that if you mew more than one *Hawk* in one Room, you muſt ſet your Stones at that di-ſtance, that when they bate they may not crab one another.

The reaſon of placing this Stone is, becauſe the Faulcon delights to ſit thereon for its coolneſs ſake, and the little gravelly ſtones the *Hawk* frequently ſwal-lows to cool her within. The Sand is neceſſary to preſerve their Feathers when they bate, and their Mew-

ets

ets are the more easily cleansed. The little Cord with
the Swivel tied about the Stone is to keep the *Hawk*
from tangling when she bateth, because the Ring will
still follow her.

All day let your *Hawk* stand hooded, onely when
you take her on your Fist to feed : at night unhood
her; and lest any accident should happen in the night
prejudicial to the *Hawk*, the Faulconer ought to lie
in the Mew.

Of the HOBBY.

THe *Hobby* is a *Hawk* of the Lure and not of the
Fist, and is a high flier, and is in every respect
like the *Saker*, but that she is a much lesser Bird.

The *Hobby* hath a blue Beak, but the Seer thereof
and Legs are yellow : the Crinets or little Feathers
under her Eye are very black; the top of her head is
betwixt black and yellow , and she hath two white
seams on her Neck; the Plumes under the Gorge and
about the Brows are reddish without spot or drop;
the Breast-feathers are brown for the most part, yet
powdered with white spots; her Back , Train, and
Wings are black aloft, having no great scales upon the
Legs unless it be a few beginning behind the three
Stretchers and Pounces, which are very large in respect
of her short Legs; her Brail-feathers are engouted betwixt red and black; the Pendant-feathers (which
are those behind the Thigh) are of a rusty smoaky
complexion. The daring *Hobby* may be well called
so , for she is nimble and light of Wing, and dares
encounter Kites, Buzzards, or Crows , and will give
souse for souse, blow for blow, till sometimes they
feize

seize and come tumbling down to the ground both to-gether.

They are chiefly for the Lark, which poor little crea-ture so dreads the sight of a *Hobby* soaring in the Air over her, that she will rather chuse to commit her self to the mercy of Man or Dogs, or to be trampled on by Horses, than venture her self into that element where she sees her mortal Enemy soaring.

The *Hobby* makes excellent sport with Nets and Spaniels, which is performed after this manner. The Dogs range the field to spring the Fowl, and the *Hob-bies* soar over them aloft in the Air: the silly Birds, fearing a conspiracy between the Hawks and Dogs to their utter destruction, dare not commit themselves to their Wings, but think it safer to lie close to the ground, and so are taken in the Nets. This sport is called *Daring*.

Of the GOSHAWK.

THere are several sorts of *Goshawks*, and they are different in goodness, force, and hardiness, ac-cording to the diversity of their choice or Cawking: at which time when *Hawks* begin to fall to liking, all Birds of Prey do assemble themselves with the *Goshawk*, and flock together.

The Female is the best: and although there be some *Goshawks* which come from *Sclavonia*, *Sardinia*, *Lom-bardy*, *Russia*, *Puglia*, *Germany*, *Armenia*, *Persia*, *Greece*, and *Africa*; yet there are none better than those which are bred in the North-parts of *Ireland*, as in the Province of *Ulster*, but more especially in the County of *Tyrone*.

Take

Take these Rules as to the goodness of her proportion or shape.

She ought to have a small Head, her Face long and straight, a large Throat, great Eyes, deep set, the Apple of the Eye black, Nares, Ears, Back, and Feet large and blank; a black long Beak, long Neck, big Breast, hard flesh, long Thighs, fleshy, the bone of the Leg and Knee short, long large Pounces and Talons. From the Stern or Train to the Breast forward she ought to grow round: the Feathers of the Thighs towards the Train should be large, and the Train-feathers short, soft, and somewhat tending to an Iron Mail. The Brayl-feathers ought to be like those of the Breast, and the Covert-feathers of the Train should be spotted and full of black rundles; but the extremity of every Train-feather should be black-streaked.

The signe of force in a *Goshawk* is this: Tie divers of them in several places of one Chamber or Mew, and that *Hawk* that doth slise and mewt highest and farthest off from her, is without question the strongest *Hawk*; for the high and far mewting argues a strong Back.

I might tell you the ill shape of a *Goshawk*; but since I have declared the good, the bad may be collected from thence: *Contraria contrariis dignoscuntur*. However take this general rule, That *Goshawk* that hath pendant Plumes over her Eyes, the whites whereof are waterish and blank, that is red-mail'd or bright tawny, hath the most assured tokens of a *Hawk* that is ill-condition'd.

The *Goshawk* preyeth on the Pheasant, Mallard, Wild-goose, Hare, and Coney; nay, she will venture to seize on a Kid or Goat; which declareth the inestimable courage and valour of this *Hawk*.

She ought to be kept with great care, because she is very choice and dainty, and looks to have a nice hand kept over her.

Q. *How*

How to make the Soar *or* Haggard Goshawk.

First trim them with Jeffes, Bewets, and Bells, as soon as they come to your hands; keep them seeled some time, hooding and unhooding them often, teaching them to feed on the Fist three or four days, or till they have left their Rammageness and become gentle : having so done, unseel them by Candle-light at night, causing them to tire or plume upon a Wing or Leg of a Pullet ; and be sure to deal gently and mildly with them until you have won and throughly manned them : then you may go into some pleasant field, and first giving them a bit or two hooded on your Fist, and the like unhooded, cast them down fair and softly on some Pearch, and make them come from it to your Fist, calling to them with a Faulconer's usual terms ; and when they come, feed them, calling all the while in the same manner to make them acquainted with your voice. The next day you may call them with a Creance at a farther distance, feeding them as before.

When you have thus called your *Goshawk* abroad three or four days, and that you finde her grow cunning, then take her on your Fist, and mount on Horseback, and ride with her an hour or two, unhooding and hooding her sometimes, giving her a bit or two in sight of your Spaniels, that she may not be afraid of them : this being done, set her on a Tree with a short Creance tied to her Loins, and going half a score yards from her on Horseback, call her to your Fist according to art ; if she come, reward her with two or three bits, and cast her up again to the Tree : then throw out a dead Pullet (to which she was used before) about a dozen yards from her ; if she fly to it and seize it, let her feed three or four bits upon it ; ride

the

the mean while about her on Horseback, and rate back your Spaniels, because they shall not rebuke her at first, and make her ever after afraid of them: then alight, and gently take her on your Fist, feed her, hood her, and let her plume or tire.

Here note, that the *Goshawk* is a greater Poulterer, and therefore it would be more requisite to throw out a dead Partridge, or one made artificially with its Wing, Tail and Plumage; which will cause her to know Partridge better, and Poultry less.

How to make a Goshawk *fly to the Partridge.*

Having manned your *Goshawk*, go into the field with her, carrying with you a Train-partridge, and unhooding your *Hawk*, bear her as gently as you can; and you will do well to let her plume or tire, for that will make her the more eager.

If the Partridge spring, let her fly: if she mark one, two, three, or more on the ground, then go to her and make her take Pearch on some Tree thereby: then if you can retrive the Partridge with your Spaniels, as soon as they spring it you must cry, *Howit, Howit,* and retrive it the second time, crying when it springeth as aforesaid: if your *Hawk* kill it, feed her upon it.

If it so happen your Spaniels should take it, (as it is very frequent for hot-Spaniels to light upon the Partridge, being either flown out of breath, or overcharged with fear) then alight from your Horse, and taking it speedily from the Dogs, cast it out to your *Hawk,* crying, *Ware Hawk, ware ,* and let her feed thereon at her pleasure.

After this you must not fly her in two days: for having fed on bloudy meat, she will not so soon be in good case to fly again; for such meat is not so easily endewed by a *Hawk* as the Leg of a Chicken or the like:

Using

Using her thus three or four times, she will be well in bloud, and become an excellent Flier at this pleasant Field-flight.

Here note, that you must do at first with her as with other *Hawks*, that is, feel and watch her, and win her to feed, to the Hood, to the Fist, &c. and then enter her to young Partridges till *November*, at which time both Trees and Fields become bare and empty : then you may enter her to the old *Rewen*, setting her short and eager ; if she kill, feed her up with the Partridge three or four times, and this will bring her to perfection.

If your *Hawk* be a good Partridger, let her not fly at the Powt or Pheasant, for they fly not so long a Flight as the Partridge ; and therefore the *Goshawk*, being more greedy of Prey than any other *Hawk*, (yet desirous of ease) would always covet short Flights, not caring to hold out : not but that there are some good both for long and short flights, but they are rarely found.

Besides, you must have a great care in keeping them in good order, with Flying, Bathing, Weathering, Tiring and Pluming.

How to help a Goshawk *that turneth Tail to Tail, and giveth over her Game.*

It is usual for a *Goshawk* to fly at a Partridge, yet neither kill it, nor fly it to mark, but to turn *Tail to tail* ; that is, having flown it a Bow-shot or more, she giveth over her Game, and takes a Tree : then must you call in your Spaniels to the Retrieve that way your *Hawk* flew the Partridge ; let the Faulconer draw himself that way also, and carrying with him a quick Partridge, let him cast it out to her, which will make

her

her believe it is the fame fhe flew at. When you caft it out cry, *Ware Hawk ware*; make her feize it, and feed her upon it : and this will encourage her to fly out her flight another time. If the next time you fly her (which muft be the third day) fhe ferve you fo again, then muft you do as aforefaid with a live Partridge carried about you for that purpofe: if fhe ferve you fo the third time, I fhould advife you to rid your hands of her as foon as you can.

How to make a Gofhawk fly quickly.

The *Gofhawk* (efpecially Soars and Niaffes) are very loving to and fond of man, and therefore fhould be flown with a little more Rammage, elfe frequently, after two or three ftroaks with their Wings, they will give over the Flight, and return to the Keeper : wherefore you muft fly with them as foon as you can. And yet there is an evil which attends this direction, and that is, by flying over-foon you will pull down your *Hawk* and make her poor, from whence proceeds fearfulnefs and cowardife. To remedy which, you muft give your *Hawk* fome refpite, and fet her up again before you fly her. There are fome *Gofhawks* (but very few) which will not fly when they are in good plight : then muft you bate their flefh, and pinch them with fcouring, wafht meat, and the like. But the beft way of flying fuch an one is when fhe is lufty and high : and to adde to her vivacity and courage, let her be fet abroad in the morning an hour or two, when the weather is not very cold; for being fo weather'd, when fhe hath flown a Partridge to the Mark, fhe will not away until it be retrieved by the Spaniels.

How to fly a Goshawk *to the River.*

A *Goshawk* (but no Tiercel) may fly the River at Mallard , Duck, Goose, or Hern , with other large Water fowl : She is made for that purpose after this manner.

First, make her to the Fist, as is prescribed in her making to the Field : then carry her into the field without Bells, and with a live Duck, which you must give to one of the company, who must hide himself in some Ditch or Pit with the Duck tied to a Creance : then must you draw near him with your *Hawk* un-hooded on your Fist, and giving him some private no-tice to throw out the Duck, cast off your *Hawk*; and if she take it at the Source, let him reward and feed her with a reasonable Gorge : then take her upon your Fist and hood her, permitting her to tire and plume upon the Leg or Wing of the Duck. The third day go again with her into the Field in like manner, or else finde out some Plash or Pool where Wild-fowl lie, taking the advantage of the rising Bank : being near the Fowl, let some of the company raise them up, and your *Hawk* being unhooded, cast her off; if she kill any of them at Source, make in to her quickly, and cross the Fowl's Wings, so that she may foot and plume it at her pleasure, rewarding her as before. After this take her on your Fist, and let her tire and plume the Leg or Wing of the Fowl aforesaid.

When your *Goshawk* is throughly nouzled, and well in bloud, you may fly her twice a day or oftner, re-warding her as before.

An

An excellent way to preserve a Goshawk *in the time of her flying, especially in hot weather.*

Take a pint of Red-rose-Water, put it into a Bottle, bruise one stick or two of green Liquorish and put in it likewise a little Mace, and the quantity of a Wallnut of Sugar-candy, and draw her meat through it twice or thrice a week as you shall finde occasion: It prevents the Pantafs, and several Difeafes they are subject to: befides, it gives a huge Breath, and gently scoureth her.

How to fly the Wild-goofe or Crane with the Goshawk.

Having mann'd your *Goshawk*, brought her to the Fift, and train'd her with a Goofe in the Field, then seek out where Wild-geefe, Cranes, or other large Wild-fowl lie: having found them afar off, alight and carry your *Hawk* unhooded behinde your Horfe, ftalking towards them until you have got pretty nigh them, holding down your *Hawk* covert under the Horfe's Neck or Body, yet fo that fhe may fee the Fowl: then you muft raife them, and cafting off your *Hawk*, if fhe kill reward her. And thus fhe may kill four or five in a day.

In like manner you may make her to the Crane, and may ftalk to Fowl which lie in Ponds or Pits as aforefaid.

Here note, that if you can fly at great, flight the leffer Flights, which will make your *Hawk* the bolder.

Q 4

How

How to mew a Goshawk, *and draw her out of the Mew, and make her Flying.*

Having flown with a *Goshawk*, *Tiercel*, *Soar*, or *Haggard* till *March*, give her some good Quarry in her Foot, and having seen her clean from Lice, cut off the Buttons of her Jesses, and throw her into the Mew; which Room should be on the ground , and scituated towards the North if possible.

Let the Pearches therein be lined with Canvas or Cotton; for otherwise by hurting her Foot she may get the Gout or Pynn.

Let the Mew have also a Window towards the East, and another Northward. There must be also a Bason of Water in the Mew for bathing, which must be shifted every three days. Feed your Hawk with Pigeons, or else with the hot Flesh of Weather-Mutton.

About the beginning of *October* if you finde your *Goshawk* fair-mew'd and hard-penn'd , then give her Chickens, Lambs-hearts, or Calves-hearts, for about twenty days together, to scour her , and make her slise out the slimy substance and glitt out of her Pannel, and enseam her.

Having done thus, some Evening draw her out of the Mew, and new furnish her with Jesses, Bells, Bewets, and all other things needful for her : then keep her seel'd two or three days, till she will endure the Hood patiently; for mewed Hawks are as impatient of the Hood as those newly taken.

When you have won her to endure the Hood, then in an Evening by Candle-light you may unseel her, and the next day shew her the Fist and Glove, making her to tire and plume morning and evening, giving her sometimes in the morning (when her Gorge is empty)

empty) a little Sugar-candy, which will help her in an excellent manner to endew.

When you finde your *Goshawk* feed eagerly, and that you think in your judgement she is enseamed, and that you may boldly fly with her, then go with her into the Field ; she will then bate, (if empty) and fly of her own accord : if she kill, feed and reward her ; but if she fly to the mark with a Partridge, then must you retrive it, and serve her as afore declared.

Some general Observations for an Ostrager or Falconer in keeping and Reclaiming a Goshawk.

It frequently happens that a *Goshawk* or *Tiercel*, where good in their Soarage, become worse after they are mewed : and the reason may be, because she was not cherished nor encouraged, to make her take delight in her Soarage.

For in a manner the major part of a Faulconer's skill consists in coying and kinde usage of his *Hawk*, so cherishing her that she may take delight in her Flight.

At the first entring of his *Hawk* he ought always to have a Train-Partridge in his Bag, to serve her with when need requires, to puchase her love : and let him take such observations which may keep his *Hawk* always in good order. As first, he must know naturally all *Goshawks* are full of moist humours, especially in the Head, and therefore let him ply them with Tiring and Pluming morning and evening ; for that will open them in the Head, and make them cast water thereat. Let the *Goshawk*'s tiring be a Rump of Beef, a Pinion or the Leg of a Chicken, given by the fire, or in the warm Sun : this not onely opens her Head, but keeps her from slothfulness in good exercise.

Give

Give her every night Casting of Feathers or Cotton, and in the morning mark whether it be wrought round or not, whether sweet or not, whether moist or dry, and of what colour the water is that drops out of the Casting: by these means he shall know what condition his *Hawk* is in.

He also ought to regard her Mewts, to see whether they be clean or not, and give remedies accordingly. He ought also to consider the season; for in cold weather he must set his *Hawk* in some warm place where fire is made; he must line the Pearch with Canvas or Cotton, and must set it so far from the Wall that the *Hawk* hurt not her Feathers when she bateth. If the weather be temperate, he may then set her in the Sun-shine for an hour or two in the morning.

Let no Hens or Poultry come near the place where your *Hawk* doth pearch; and in the Spring offer her water every week, or else she will soar away from you when she flieth, and you may go look her.

If your *Hawk* bathe her self spontaneously in cold weather after her flight, go presently to the next house and weather her with her Back to the fire, and not her Gorge, for that will make her sick: and dry your *Hawk*, if you have carried her in the Rain.

A good Faulconer will always keep his *Hawk* high and lusty, yet so that she may be always in a condition to fly best.

Also he must keep his *Hawk* clean, and her Feathers whole: and if a Feather be broken or bruised, he must presently imp it; and to that end he must have his Imping-needles, his Semond, with other Instruments always in readiness.

The first year it is most requisite to fly your *Goshawk* to the Field, and not to the Covert; for so they will learn to hold out, and not turn tail in the midst of their flight: and when they are mewed *Hawks*, you

may

may make them do what you will: and it is better to let her be a little rammage than to be over-manned.

Her feeding is best on hot meats: and if you would instruct her to kill great Fowl, make her Trains thereof; and if you would have her continue those Flights, never fly her at less, for that will take her off from them and spoil her. If you will make her to fly with a Dog to assist her, then feed your *Hawk* with great Fowl, and your Dogs with flesh tied under their Wings. If you train your *Hawk* with them, rewarding her upon the Train, and your Dog with her, this will make them acquainted together.

Thus continue doing till your Dog throughly knows his duty: and be sure to keep your Dog tied up; for if you let him go loose, it will spoil the best Dog that is: and never give him a reward but when he maketh in at such Fowls to rescue the *Hawk*.

Gall your *Goshawk* to no other thing than your Fist, and oftentimes spurt good wine on your *Goshawks* Sears: And note, that in all her Distempers sweet things are best to be administred in her medicines.

Of the SPARROW-HAWK.

THe last *Hawk* which we shall treat of is the *Sparrow-hawk*; of which there are several kindes, and of different Plumes.

For the kindes, there is the *Sclavonian*, *Calabrian*, *Corsican*, *German*, *Vicentian*, and *Veronian*, *Alpisan*, *Sabbean*, and *Bergamascan*, in the black Vale near the confines of *Valtolina*. It is needless to give you a particular account of them.

Their

Their Plumes are different; some are small plumed and blank *Hawks*, others of a larger Feather, some plumed like the Quail, some brown or Canvas-mail'd, and others have just thirteen Feathers in their Train, &c.

To be short, this Character I may justly give the *Sparrow-hawk* in general, that she is in her kinde, and for that Game her strength will give her leave to kill, a very good *Hawk*. Besides, he that knows how to man, reclaim, and fly with a *Sparrow-hawk*, may easily know how to keep and deal with all other *Hawks*.

And herein lieth an excellency in the *Sparrow-hawk*, she serves both for Winter and Summer with great pleasure, and will fly at all kind of Game more than the Faulcon. If the Winter-*Sparrow-hawk* prove good, she will kill the Pie, the Chough, the Jay, Wood-cock, Thrush, Black-bird, Felfare, with divers other Birds of the like nature.

How to make a Sparrow-hawk, whether *Eyess*, Brancher, Soar, *Mew'd*, or Haggard.

Sparrow-hawks are to be considered as all other kinds of *Hawks* are, according to their age and dispo-sition.

The several kinds of *Sparrow-hawks* may be com-prehended under these five heads; the *Eyesses* or *Ny-esses*, *Branchers*, *Soars*, *Mew'd*, and *Haggards*.

Eyesses, are mewed in the Wood, and are taken in the Eyrie.

Branchers, are those which have forsaken the Eyrie, and are fed near it by the old ones on Boughs and Branches.

Soar-hawks, are so called, because, having forsaken
the

the Eyrie, and beginning to prey for themselves, they soar up aloft for pleasure.

Mew'd-hawks, are such which have once or more shifted the Feather.

Lastly, *Haggards*, are they which prey for themselves, and do also mew in the Wood or at large.

This division of kindes is not peculiar to the *Sparrow-hawk*, but common to all : give me leave to run them over in order as I have set them down.

For the *Eyeß* or *Nyeß*, (which is of greatest difficulty to bring to any perfection) you must first feed her in some cool Room which hath two Windows, the one to the North, and the other to the East, which must be open, and barred over with Laths, not so wide for a *Hawk* to get out, or Vermin to come in : strow the Chamber with fresh Leaves, and do in every respect to this Room as I have ordered in a former Chapter for the Mewing the Faulcon.

You must feed your *Eyeß* with Sparrows, young Pigeons, and Sheeps-hearts. Whilst she is very young and little you should cut her meat, or shred it into small Pellets, and feed her twice or thrice a day, according as you finde her endew it or put it over.

When she is full summed and flieth about, then give her whole small Birds, and somtimes feed her on your Fist, suffering her to strain and kill the Birds in your hand ; and sometimes put live Birds into the Chamber where she is, that she may learn to know to foot and to kill them ; and let her feed upon them in your presence : by this course you will not onely neul her, but take her off from that scurvy quality of hiding her Prey when she hath seized it, a natural property belonging to all Eyesses. Likewise every morning go into the Room, call her to your Fist, whistle and use such terms as you would have her hereafter acquainted with. When she hath put forth all her Feathers and is full

summed,

summed, then take her out of the Chamber, and furnish her with Bells, Bewets, Jesses, and Lines.

It will be altogether requisite to feel her at first, that she may the better endure the Hood and handling : and let it be a Rufter-hood that is large and easie, which you must pull off and put on frequently, stroaking her often on the head, till she will stand gently.

In the Evening by Candle-light unseel her, giving her somewhat to tire upon, handling and stroaking her Feathers gently, hooding and unhooding her as often as you think fit.

Before I proceed any farther, I shall inform you how to Seel a *Hawk* after the best manner. Take a Needle threaded with untwisted Thread, and casting your *Hawk*, take her by the Beak, and put the Needle through her Eye-lid, not right against the sight of the Eye, but somewhat nearer the Beak, that she may have liberty to see backward ; and have especial care that you hurt not the Web: then put your Needle through the other Eye-lid, drawing the ends of the Thread together, tie them over the Beak, not with a straight knot, but cut off the Threads near to the end of the knot, and so twist them together, that the Eye-lids may be raised so upwards that the *Hawk* may not see at all, but as the Thread shall slacken, she shall be able to see backwards onely, which is the cause that the Thread is put nearer the beak.

When your *Eyess* is well won to the Hood, and to the Fist, let her kill small Birds thereon ; then call her two or three days or longer, till she will come far off; then take a live Pigeon tied by the Foot with a Creance, and stir it till your *Hawk* will bate at it and seize it, but not far off, that you may quickly help her at the first, lest the Pigeon struggling with her she prove too strong, and so discourage your young *Hawk*:

then

then let her plume and foot her, and feed her thereupon, whistling the while, that she may know it a-
nother time: then hood her, and let her plume and
tire a little.

You may use her to Trains of Chicken and Quail:
and when she will seize readily by often Training, ride
out with her in the morning into the Fields, where
calling your *Sparrow-hawk* to your Fist, and giving
her a bit or two, go with your Spaniels to seek some
Beavy of young Quails, advancing your Fist aloft, that
your *Hawk* may see them when they spring, flying
her at advantage: if she kill, reward her, *&c.* if she
miss, serve her with the Train of a Quail.

Let your Dogs hunt on your right hand when they
range, but especially when they quest and call, to the
end you may the better cast off your *Hawk*. When
your *Hawk* is throughly entred and well nouzled, you
may then hold your hand low, for she will now bate
at the Whur: but whatsoever you do, have a quick
eye and a good regard to the Spaniels, not coveting to
be too near them, but a little above them, that you may
let your *Hawk* fly coasting at the advantage when the
Game springeth.

Of the Brancher, Soar, Mew'd, and Haggard Sparrow-hawk.

Having spoken of the first kind of *Sparrow-hawks*,
viz. the *Eyeß*, the other four in the Title of this Chapter must consequently be discoursed of.

I shall give you but few instructions, for in effect the
same precepts that serve for the *Eyeß* will serve also
for the *Brancher*, *Soar*, *Mew'd*, and *Haggard Hawks*;
onely this, these four last require not so much pains to
be taken to make them know their Game as the *Eyeß*,

becaufe

becaufe they have been accuftomed to prey for them-felves.

Above all things the Faulconer muft take them off from their ill cuftome of carrying, and that may be done by ferving them with great Trains, whereby they will learn to abide on the Quarry.

Be very mindful of coying them as much as you can, for they will remember a kindnefs or injury better than any other *Hawk.*

If the *Hawk* be newly taken, and will not feed, then rub her Feet with warm flefh, whiftling to her, and fometimes putting the flefh unto her Beak : if fhe will not yet feed, rub her Feet with a live Bird ; if at the crying of the Bird the *Hawk* feizeth it with her Feet, it is a figne fhe will feed ; then tear off the Skin and Feathers of the Bird's Breaft, and put the Bird to her Beak, and fhe will eat.

When fhe will feed upon your whiftle and chirp, then hood her with a Rufter-hood, and feed her be-times in the morning ; and when fhe hath endewed, give her a Beaching in the day-time, and every time you hood her, give her a bit or two ; at evening give her the Brains of a Hen for her fupper : and in every thing elfe order thefe *Hawks* aforefaid as you do the Faulcon and the reft.

How to mew Sparrow-hawks.

Some ufe to put their *Sparrow-hawk* into the Mew as foon as they leave flying her, cutting off both her Bewets, Lines, and knots of her Jeffes, and fo leave them in the Mew till they are clean mewed.

If you will have your *Sparrow-hawk* to fly at Quail, Partridge, or Pheafant-powt, then you muft draw her in the beginning of *April,* and bear her on the Fift till fhe be clean and throughly enfeamed.

Others

Others keep their *Sparrow-hawks* on the Pearch until *March*, and then throw them into the Mew, peppering them for Lice if they have any. Her Mew should be a Chamber aloft from the ground, eight or nine foot long, and about six foot broad : her Windows and Pearches must be like the Goshawks.

Her Mew being thus provided, in *May* go in to her in an Evening by Candle-light, and taking her up softly, pull out all her Train-feathers one after another : this shall make her mew the faster, especially if you feed her with hot meat and Birds, observing a certain hour to feed her in.

Once in fourteen days set water before her in the Mew : if you perceive she hath any Feathers or Down which stand staring upon her Back, sitting as if she would rouze, then set her water sooner. If you put water by her continually, it delays her Mewing; and to keep it always from her, causeth her to mew her Feathers uncleanly : but water once in a fortnight is the best Medium for her Mewing between those two extremes.

Thus having given you a summary account of most *Hawks* commonly in use in *England* and in most parts of *Europe*, shewing their Shapes, Complexions, Natures, manner of Manning, Reclaiming, Ordering, Luring, Flying, Mewing, &c. I shall next give you an account of the several Diseases and Maladies they are subject to, with their proper Cures and Remedies : but before I shall enter thereon, give me leave to inform the Ostrager or Faulconer of his necessary duties.

R be

The Duty of a Faulconer ; with neceſſary
Rules and Obſervations for him
to follow.

A Faulconer ought to conſult and conſider the
quality and mettle of his *Hawks*, and to know
which of them he ſhall fly with early, and with which
late.

He muſt be fond of his *Hawk*, patient, and cleanly
in keeping her from Lice, Mites, and the like Vermin.
He muſt rather keep his *Hawks* high and full of fleſh,
than poor and low, which makes them more ſubject to infirmities than when they are in very good
plight.

Every night after flying he muſt give his *Hawk* Caſting, ſometimes Plumage, ſometimes Pellets of Cotton, and ſometimes Phyſick, as he ſhall find her di-
ſeaſed by her Caſting or Mewt.

Every night he muſt make the place very clean under her Pearch, that he may know by her Caſting whether the *Hawk* ſtands in need of Scourings upwards or
downwards.

Let him remember every Evening to weather his
Hawk, excepting ſuch days wherein ſhe hath bathed ;
after which in the evening ſhe ſhould be put into a
warm Room on a Pearch with a Candle burning by
her, where ſhe muſt ſit unhooded, if ſhe be not rammage, to the intent ſhe prune and pick her ſelf, and
rejoyce by enoiling her ſelf after bathing : and in the
morning he ought to weather her, and let her caſt, if
ſhe hath not done it already, keeping her ſtill hooded
till he carry her to the field.

In

In feeding his *Hawk* he must have a care of feeding her with two sorts of meat at one time; and what he giveth her must be very sweet.

If he have an occasion to go abroad, let him have a care that he pearch not his *Hawk* too high from the ground, for fear of bating and hanging by the Heels, whereby she may spoil her self.

He ought to carry to the Field with him Mummy in powder with other Medicines; for frequently the *Hawk* meets with many accidents, as bruises at encounters, *&c.* neither must he forget to carry with him any of his necessary Hawking-implements.

Lastly, he must be able to make his Lures, Hoods of all sorts, Jesses, Bewets, and other needful Furniture for his *Hawk*: neither must he be without his Coping-Irons to cope his *Hawk*'s Beak, if it be over-grown, and to cope her Pounces and Talons, as need shall require: neither must he be without his Cauterizing-Irons.

Let these Instructions suffice, I being willing to leave the rest to the care and observation of the ingenious Faulconer.

Of Diseases *and dangerous* Accidents *incident to* H A W K S , *and their several* Cures.

IT is necessary for a skilful Faulconer not onely to know how to Man, Reclaim, Keep, Fly, Imp, and Mew his *Hawks*, with other things pertinent to that purpose; but also to know their Diseases, with the proper Cures of them, and other Accidents frequently

befal-

befalling *Hawks* , both in their Flights and other-ways.

Before we shall characterize their Maladies and prescribe Rules for their Cures, it will not be irrequisite to tell you that *Hawks*, as well as men, (which seems somewhat strange) have four Complexions, the true indicators of their natures : and as in man his natural Complexion and Constitution is known by his Skin, so is the Temperament and natural Disposition of a *Hawk* by her Coat and Plume. This opinion hath not been onely averr'd by the Ancients, but confirmed by the modern experience of the skilful in the noble Art of Hawking. Take it in this manner.

Faulcons that are *black* are *Melancholick*, and are to be physicked with hot and moist Medicines, because their Complexion is cold and dry ; for which purpose Aloes, Pepper, Cock's-flesh, Pigeons, Sparrows, Goats-flesh, and the like, are very good.

Falcons *blank* are *Phlegmatick*, and must have Physick hot and dry, because Phlegme is cold and moist; to which purpose Cinamon, Cloves, Cardamomum, Goats-flesh, Choughs, &c. are very good.

Faulcons *Ruffet* are *Sanguine* and *Cholerick* indifferently mix'd, and their Physick must be cold, moderately moist and dry, as Myrtles, Cassia fistula, Tamarnds, Vinegar, Lambs-flesh, and Pullets.

Thus much for the Complexions: now for the Diseases and their Cures.

Of Castings, *and* Mewtings, *either good or bad, according to their several Complexions and Smells.*

Castings are of two sorts, *Plumage*, or *Cotton:* the latter is most commonly given in Pellets, which must be about the bigness of an Hazle-nut, made of fine soft white

white Cotton : after she hath supp'd you must convey this into her Gorge.

In the morning diligently observe how she hath rolled and cast it, whereby you shall know whether she be in a bad or good condition : for example, if she cast it round, white, not stinking, nor very moist or waterish, you may conclude her sound; but if she roll it not well, but cast it long, with properties contrary to the former, then she is unsound and full of Diseases.

Besides, if her Casting be either black, green, yellow-ish, slimy, or stinking, it denotes your *Hawk* to be diseased. The former Casting is remedied by hot meats; the latter by feeding her well, and washing her meats in cool water, as of Endive, &c. and give her one or two Castings of Cotton, incorporating there-with Incense and Mummy. But if she continue not-withstanding in this condition, give her an upward Scowring made thus : Take Aloes pulverized one scruple, powder of Clove four grains, powder of Cubebs three grains; incorporate these and wrap them in Cotton, and give it your *Hawk* empty, having no meat in her Pannel.

Casting of *Plumage* is to be observed as the former Casting : that is, if in the morning you find them round and not stinking, it is a good signe; but if long, slimy, with indigested flesh sticking to the same, and having an ill scent, it is very bad. Here note, that by how much the more sweet or stinking the Casting is, by so much is the *Hawk* in a better or worse condition.

Mewts must be observed as well as Castings, in this manner : If the Mewt be white, not very thick nor clear, having no black spot in it, or but very little, it is a signe of the healthy constitution of the *Hawk*; but if it be white and very thick in the middle, though it

doth

doth not import sickness, yet it sheweth her to be too gross and over-full of Grease; which you must remedy by giving her moist meats, as the Heart of a Calf or Lamb, &c. and for two mornings after give her some Sugar-candy, or else the Gut of a Chicken well washt and fill'd with Oyl-Olive: either of these will scour her, and make her to slise freely.

It is a very bad and mortal signe, to see your *Hawk*'s Mewt full of variety of colours: therefore you must speedily prevent ensuing mischiefs by giving her Mummy purified and beaten to powder, wrapping it in Cotton.

If the Mewt be more yellow than white, then doth she abound with Choler proceeding from great Flights in hot weather, also from much Bating. This is remedied by washing her meat in Buglofs, Endive, Borage, and such-like cold Waters, wringing the said meat after you have so washed it.

The *black* Mewt is a most deadly signe, and if it continue four days she will peck over the Pearch and die. If she mewt so but once, there is no great danger, for it proceeds either from the Bloud or Guts of the Fowl in tiring, or else from being gorged with filthy meats: in this case give her good warm meat and Cotton-casting, with the powder of Cloves, Nutmeg, and Ginger, or Mummy alone.

If the Mewt be *green*, it is a bad signe, and denotes her troubled with an infected and corrupt Liver, or with some Apostume, unless she be a Raminage-*Hawk*, and then that signe holds not good. Her cure is, by feeding her with meat powdered with Mummy; if she will not take it with her Food, then give it her in a Scowring or Casting: but if this ill-colour'd Mewting continue still, then give her a Scowring of Agarick, and after that another of Incense pulverized to comfort her.

The

The dark *sanguine* Mewt with a black in it is the most deadly signe of all, and differs but little, if any thing, from the former black Mewt. A *Hawk* mewting after this manner is irrecoverable, and therefore it is needless to prescribe a Cure.

Lastly, the *gray* Mewt like sour Milk, is a mortal token, yet curable, as shall be shewn hereafter.

Thus you see how requisite it is for a Faulconer to observe diligently every morning his *Hawk*'s Castings and Mewtings, that knowing thereby their Maladies, he may timely finde out their Remedies. Let us now proceed to their particular Diseases.

Of the Cataract.

The *Cataract* in the Eyes of a *Hawk*, is a malady not easily removed, and sometimes incurable, when it is too thick and of a long continuance.

It proceedeth from gross Humours in the Head, which frequently do not onely dim, but extinguish the sight: and sometimes the Hood is the cause of this mischief.

The cure must be effected by Scowring her two or three days with Aloes or Agarick : then take the powder of washt Aloes finely beaten one scruple, and two scruples of Sugar-candy ; mingle these together, and with a Quill blow it into your *Hawk*'s Eye afflicted as aforesaid three or four times a day. This is the gentlest and most Soveraign Medicine of any yet I have tried. But if this will not do, you must use stronger medicines, as the juice of Celandine-roots , bathing their Eyes often with warm Rose-water wherein hath been boil'd the seeds of Fenugreek.

Of

Of the Pantas or Asthma.

The *Pantas* is a dangerous Distemper, and few *Hawks* escape which are afflicted therewith. It happens when the Lungs are as it were so baked by excessive heat, that the *Hawk* cannot draw her breath, and when drawn, cannot well emit it again. You may judge of the beginning of this Distemper by the *Hawk*'s labouring much in the Pannel, moving her Train often up and down at each motion of her Pannel ; and she cannot many times mewt or slise, or if she do, she drops it fast by her. It is known likewise by your *Hawk*'s frequent opening her Clap and Beak.

The best Remedy is, to scour your *Hawk* with good Oyl-Olive well washed in several Waters till it become clear and white, which you must do after this manner : Take an earthen Pot with a small hole in the bottom thereof, which you must stop with your Finger ; then pour therein your Oyl with a quantity of Water, and coil these together with a Spoon till the Water grow darkish ; after which remove your Finger, and the Water will run out, but the Oyl remain behind floating on the top ; thus do seven or eight times, till you have throughly purified the Oil : Then take a Sheep's Gut above an Inch long for a Faulcon and Goshawk, but of less length for lesser *Hawks*, and fill it with this Oyl, and fasten it with Thread at both ends. Your *Hawk* having first cast, convey this Gut into her Throat, holding her on the Fist till she make a Mewt ; an hour after she hath done mewting feed her with a Calf's Heart or a Pullet's Leg, giving her every third or fourth day a Cotton casting with Cubebs and Cloves. I shall onely adde one Receipt more for the *Pantas* or *Asthma*, and that is the Oyl of sweet Almonds poured into a washt Chicken's Gut, and given

the

the *Hawk*; which is of great efficacy in the cure of this Disease.

Of Worms.

There are a sort of Worms an Inch long which frequently afflict *Hawks*, proceeding from gross and viscous Humours in the Bowels, occasioned through want of natural heat and ill digestion.

You may know when she is troubled with them by her casting her Gorge, her stinking Breath, her trembling and writhing her Train, her croaking in the night, her offering with her Beak at her Breast or Pannel, and by her Mewt being small and unclean.

You may cure her of them with a Scowring of washt Aloes, Hepatick, Mustard-seed, and Agarick, of each an equal quantity; or the powder of Harts-horn dried; or lastly, a Scowring of white Dittander, Aloes, Hepatick washt four or five times, Cubebs, and a little Saffron wrapt in some flesh, to cause her to take it the better.

Of the Filanders.

There are several sorts of *Filanders*, but I shall speak but of one sticking to the Reins. They are Worms as small as a Thread, and about an Inch long, and lie wrapt up in a thin Skin or Net near the Reins of a *Hawk*, apart from either Gut or Gorge.

You shall know when your *Hawk* is troubled with them by her poverty, by ruffling her Train, by straining the Fist or Pearch with her Pounces, and lastly by croaking in the night when the Filanders prick her. You must remedy this Malady betimes, before these Worms have enlarged themselves from their proper station, roving elsewhere to your *Hawk*'s ruine and destruction.   You

You muſt not kill them as other Worms, for fear of Impoſtumes from their corruption, being incapable to paſs away with the *Hawk*'s Mewt ; but onely ſtupifie them, that they may be offenſive but ſeldom : and that is done thus ; Take a head of Garlick, taking a-way the outmoſt rinde ; then with a Bodkin heated in the fire make holes in ſome Cloves, then ſteep them in Oyl three days, and after this give her one of the Cloves down her Throat, and for forty days after ſhe will not be troubled with the Filanders. Wherefore a Faulconer will ſhew himſelf prudent, if, ſeeing his *Hawk* low and poor, he give her once a month a Clove of this Garlick for prevention of the Filanders.

Another approved Medicine for Filanders or Worms in Hawks.

Take half a dozen cloves of Garlick, boil them in Milk until they are very tender, then take them out and dry the Milk out of them ; then put them into a ſpoonful of the beſt Oyl of Olives you can get, and when ſhe hath caſt, in the morning give theſe to your *Hawk*, feed her not in two hours after, and be ſure it be warm meat, and not much, and keep her warm that day for fear of taking cold ; give her the Oyl with the Garlick : they muſt ſteep all night.

Of Hawks Lice.

Theſe *Lice* do moſt infeſt the Head, the Ply of a *Hawk*'s Wings, and her Train. In the Winter you may kill them thus : Take two drams of Pepper beaten to powder, and mingle it with warm Water, and with this Lotion waſh the places infeſted with theſe Lice or Mites : then ſet your *Hawk* on a Pearch with

her

her Back and Train against the Sun; then hold in your hand a small Stick about a handful long, with a piece of soft Wax at the end of it, and with that (whilst the *Hawk* is weathering her self) take away those Vermin crawling upon the Feathers. You may do well to adde to the Pepper and Water some Staves-acre.

In the Summer-time you may kill the Lice with *Auripigmentum* beaten to powder, and strowed on the places where they lie.

A safe and easie way to kill Lice in Hawks.

Mail your *Hawk* in a piece of Cotton, if not in some Woollen Cloath, and put between the Head and her Hood a little Wooll or Cotton: then take a Pipe of Tobacco, and, putting the little end in at the Tream, blow the Smoak, and what Lice escape killing will creep into the Cloath. This is a certain way.

How to keep and maintain all manner of Hawks in health, good plight, and liking.

In the first place, never give them a great Gorge, especially of gross meats, as Beef, Pork, and such as are hard to be endewed and put over.

Secondly, never feed them with the flesh of any Beast that hath lately gone to Rut; for that will insensibly destroy them.

Thirdly, if you are constrained to give your *Hawk* gross food, let it be well soaked first in clean Water, and afterwards sufficiently wrung; in Summer with cold Water, in Winter with luke-warm Water.

Ever

Ever observe to reward your *Hawks* with some good live meat, or else they will be brought too low: however, the serving them with washt meats is the way to keep them in health.

I shall conclude how to keep *Hawks* in perfect health with this most excellent Receipt. Take Germander, Pelamountain, Basil, Grummel-seed, and Broom-flowers, of each half an ounce; Hyssop, Sassifras, Polypodium, and Horse-mints, of each a quarter of an ounce, and the like of Nutmegs; Cubebs, Borage, Mummy, Mugwort, Sage, and the four kinds of Mirobolans, of each half an ounce; of Aloes Succotrine the fifth part of an ounce, and of Saffron one whole ounce. All these you must pulverize, and every eighth or twelfth day give your *Hawks* the quantity of a Bean thereof with their meat. If they will not take it so, put it into a Hen's Gut tied at both ends, and let him stand empty an hour after.

Of the Formica.

This is a Distemper which commonly seizeth on the Horn of *Hawks* Beaks, which will eat the Beak away, and this is occasioned by a Worm, as most men are of opinion.

You may perceive it by this; the Beak will grow rugged, and it will begin to separate from the Head.

To remedy this Malady, you must take the Gall of a Bull, and break it into a Dish, and adde thereto the powder of Aloes Succotrine: mingle these well together, and anoint the Clap or Beak of your *Hawk* therewith, and the very place where the *Formica* grows, twice a day; but touch not her Eyes or Nares: continue thus doing till your *Hawk* be perfectly cured, and bathe her with Orpiment and Pepper to keep her from other Vermin.

Of

Of the Frownce.

The *Frownce* proceedeth from moist and cold Humours which descend from the *Hawk's* Head to the Palate and root of the Tongue, by means whereof they loose their appetite, and cannot close their Clap. This by some is called the *Eagles-bane*; for she seldom dieth of age, but of the over-growing of her Beak.

You may know if your *Hawk* be troubled with this Distemper by opening her Beak, and seeing whether her Tongue be swoln or no: if it be, she hath it.

There are several ways to cure this Distemper, but the best that ever yet I could finde for it, is, onely to take the powder of Alume reduced to a Salve with strong Wine-vinegar, and wash the *Hawk's* Mouth therewith.

To cure the dry Frownce.

Take a Quill and cut it in the shape of a Pen, and at the other end tie a fine little Rag; with one end scrape off the white Skin which you will see in in the Mouth or Throat of your *Hawk* until it bleedeth: then with the other end wash it with the juice of Lemon or white-wine-Vinegar very clean; then take a little burnt Alume, and some of a Shoo-soal burnt upon Wood-coals and beaten to powder; mix them, and lay them on the place or places; but let your *Hawk* have no meat above, nor be ready to be fed: by this I have cured many.

Of the Pip.

The *Pip* frequently troubleth *Hawks*, at it doth Chickens, and proceedeth from cold and moistness of

the

the Head , or from feeding on grofs meat not well wafht in warm Water in the Winter, and cold Water in the Summer.

The Symptoms of this Diftemper are the *Hawk's* frequent Sniting, and making a noife twice or thrice in her Sniting.

For the Cure hereof, you muft caft your *Hawk* gently, and look upon the tip of her Tongue, and if you finde the Pip there , you muft fcour her with a Pill made of Agarick and *Hiera picra* given two or three days together with her Cafting at night ; this will cleanfe her Head, and the fooner if fhe be made to tire againft the Sun in the Morning : Then bind a little Cotton to the end of a Stick, and dipping it in good Rofe-water wafh her Tongue therewith : after this anoint it three or four days with Oyl of fweet Almonds and Oyl-olive well wafhed as aforefaid. Having fo done, you will finde the Pip all white and foft : then take an Awl, and with the point thereof lift up the Pip foftly, and remove it, as Women pip their Chickens , but remove it not till it be throughly ripe ; and wet her Tongue and Palate twice or thrice a day with the aforefaid Oyl, till fhe be throughly cured.

How to remedy that Hawk which Endeweth not, nor Putteth over as fhe fhould do.

This happens either by being foul within, or by a Surfeit ; or elfe when fhe was low and poor her Keeper over-gorged her, by being too hafty to fet her up, and fhe being weak was not able to put over and endew, and furfeited thereupon.

The Cure whereof is this : You muft feed her with light meats, and a little at once, as with young Rats and

and Mice, Chickens or Mutton dipt in Goats-milk or otherwise; or give her a quarter of a Gorge of the yolk of an Egg.

If you feed her with the flesh of any living Fowl, first steep it well in the bloud of the same Fowl, so shall your *Hawk* mount her flesh apace; if you also scour her with Pills made of Lard, Marrow of Beef, Sugar and Saffron mix'd together, and given her three mornings together, giving her also a reasonable Gorge two hours after.

How to make a Hawk *feed eagerly that hath lost her Appetite, without bringing her low.*

A *Hawk* may lose her Appetite by taking too great Gorges in the Evening, which she cannot well endew; or by being foul in the Pannel; or sometimes by Colds.

To remedy which, take Aloes Succotrina, boil'd Sugar, and Beef marrow, of each alike, onely less of the Aloes; incorporate these, and make them into Balls or Pills as big as Beans, and give of them to your *Hawk*, and hold her in the Sun till she hath cast up the filth and slime within her; then feed her not till noon, at which time give her good meat; and three days after for the same Disease it is good tiring on Stockdoves, small Birds, Rats or Mice.

How to raise a Hawk *that is low and poor.*

The Poverty of a *Hawk* happens several ways: either by the ignorance of the Faulconer of some latent lurking Distemper; or by her soaring away, and so being lost four or five days, in which time, finding little or no Prey, she becomes poor and lean.

To set her up you must feed her, a little at once, and often, with good meat and of light digestion, as small
Birds

Birds, Rats, Mice, &c.   Or thus : take two spoon-
fuls of Honey, four of fresh Butter, and boil them together in a new earthen pot of Water ; then take
Pork well washed, and steep it in that Water, giving
your *Hawk* a reasonable Gorge thereof twice a day,
warming the said Water when you intend to feed your
Hawk ; and get some Snails that breed in running
Waters, and give them her in the morning, and they
will not onely scour away the gross slimy humours
which are within, but also nourish her exceedingly.

How to remedy a Hawk *that is slothful, and is averse to flying.*

A *Hawk* frequently hath no minde to fly, either by
reason of her ill keeping, that is, when she is kept by
those who know not how to give her her Rights, as
bouzing, bathing &c. or because the *Hawk* is too
high and full of grease, or too poor and low : by the
first she becomes proud and coy, and by the latter so
weak that she wants strength and spirit to perform it.

For the curing of which Distemper, she ought to be
throughly view'd by some skilful Faulconer, by whom
such Remedies should be administred to her as are needful for her : but above all, there is nothing like giving
her in a morning three or four Pills of Celandine well
washt.

Of Swoln Feet in a Hawk.

Hawks have Swelling in their Feet upon several ac-
counts : sometimes by chafing their Feet in flying their
Prey, striking it, and taking cold thereupon ; sometimes
for want of rolling or lining the Pearch with some soft
warm cloath ; or else through gross humours and
foulness within, which through exercise drop down into their Feet, and so cause them to swell : lastly, this
Swelling

Swelling happens by pricks when they fly fiercely into Bushes after Game.

For a Remedy, you must scour your Hawk three mornings together with the Pills of Lard, Marrow, Sugar and Saffron, and set her in the Sun : two days after this feed her with good meat: then take Bole-Armoniack, and half the quantity of *Sanguis Draconis*, and having made them into powder, temper them well together with the White of an Egg and Rose-water, and anoint her Feet twice a day three or four days together, setting her on some Cloth to keep her Feet warm.

How to scour Hawks *before you cast them into the Mew.*

When Mewing-time is come, you must scour and cleanse your Hawks; for in luring and flying-time by foul feeding they ingender Filanders and other Distempers, whereof they die for want of timely care and cure.

When you set down your Hawk use the same as you finde Page 246. which will not onely kill the Worm, but scour a Hawk also.

The best way is, (when you mean to cast a Hawk into the Mew) first to scour her well according to former directions, to cope her, and set her up well in flesh, to discharge her as near as you can of all Diseases, also to free her from Mites and Lice, to set her Water, sometimes to feed her with young Rats, Mice, Dogs-flesh, Pigeons, Rabbets, and now and then with some liquid thing and meats laxative.

Take notice of this special Observation : A Haggard is not to be cast in loose to the Mew, but is to be mewed on the Fist; for otherwise she will become too coy and strange : and if she fall to bating

S

and

and beating her self for heat, then must you hood her up, or bespout her with cold water, which is the readiest way to make her leave Bating.

You must continue her on the Fist till she begin to shed her Feathers; then set her down, and tie her to a Stone or Pearch, as you do the rest; and after she hath mewed and comes to fly, then let her stand on a Block or Billet cafed or rolled. In the same manner mew Goshawks, Tierces, and Sparrow-hawks; onely they will not be born on the Fist, but be at liberty in the Mew, and very cleanly served.

Fifteen or twenty days before you draw your Hawk out of the Mew, you must begin to abate her of her diet, the sooner and better to enseam her. And forget not to feed her with washed meat, which will prevent many dangers that may follow.

Many more Diseases there are incident, and Accidents happening to Hawks, of which with their Cures there are large discourses written in Italian, French, and English, and therefore I thought fit to insert in this place no other Maladies than what most usually occur: if you desire to be farther satisfied, I shall refer you to those larger and (it may be) less useful Volumes.

An

An Abstract
Of such
STATUTE-LAWS
As concern
HAWKING.

STat. 11 H. 7. cap. 17. None shall take out of the Nest any Eggs of Faulcon, Goshawk, Lanner, or Swan, in pain of a year and a days imprisonment, and to incur a Fine at the Kings pleasure, to be divided betwixt the King and the owner of the Ground where the Eggs shall be so taken.

II. None shall bare any Hawk of English breed called an Eyess, Goshawk, Tassel, Lanner, Lanneret, or Faulcon, in pain to forfeit the same to the King.

III. He that brings an Eyess from beyond the Sea, shall have a Certificate under the Customers Seal where he lands, or if out of Scotland, then under the Seal of the Lord-Warden or his Lieutenant, testifying that she is a Forrein Hawk, upon the like pain of forfeiting the Hawk.

IV. None shall take or fear away any of the Hawks abovesaid from their Coverts where they use to breed, in pain of 10 l. to be recovered before Justices of Peace, and divided betwixt the King and the Prosecutor.

Stat. 34 Edw. 3. cap. 22. A Hawk taken up shall be delivered to the Sheriff, who after Proclamation made in the Market-towns of the County (if challenged) shall deliver her to the right owner.

II. If the Hawk were taken up by a mean man, and be not challenged within four Moneths, the Sheriff shall detain her, satisfying the party for taking her; but if by a man of Estate, who may conveniently keep an Hawk, the Sheriff shall restore her to him again, he answering for the charge of keeping her.

III. If any do take away or conceal a Hawk, he shall answer the value thereof to the owner, and suffer two years imprisonment; and in case he be not able to answer the value, he shall remain in Prison a longer time.

Stat. 37 Edw. 3. cap. 19. He that steals and carries away an Hawk, not observing the Ordinance of 34 Edw. 3. 22. shall be deemed a Felon.

FINIS.

THE
GENTLEMAN'S
Recreation :

Containing
DIRECT RULES
For the famous G A M E of
F O W L I N G:

With Inſtructions for the taking
of all manner of L A N D and
W A T E R - F O W L;

Whether by FOWLING-PIECE, NET,
ENGINE, or otherways.

With a ſhort Account of
Singing-Birds.

To which is added
An Abſtract of all Statute or penal
Laws relating to that curious Art.

The Third P A R T.

L O N D O N; Printed by J. C. for N. C.

OF
FOWLING:

OR,

The compleat Art and Secrets of Fowling, *either by Water or by Land, according to ancient and modern Experience.*

What Fowling *is; with the nature and diver-sity of all manner of* Fowl.

FOWLING is used two manner of ways: either by Enchantment, or Enticement; by winning or wooing the Fowl unto you by Pipe, Whistle, or Call; or else by Engine, which unawares surprizeth them.

Fowl are of divers sorts, which alter in their nature as their Feathers: but by reason of their multiplicity, I shall for brevity sake distinguish them onely into two kindes, Land and Water-Fowl.

The

The Water-fowl are so called from the natural delight they still take in and about the Water, gathering from thence all their food and nutriment.

Here note, that Water-fowl are in their own nature the subtilest and wisest of Birds, and most careful of their own safety : Hence they have been formerly compared to an orderly and well-governed Camp, having Scouts on Land afar off, Courts of Guards, Sentinels, and all sorts of other watchful Officers surrounding the body, to give an alarm on any approach of seeming danger.

For in your observation you may take notice, that there will be ever some straggling Fowl, which lie aloof from the greater number, which still call first. Now it is the nature of Water-fowl to fly in great Flocks, having always a regard to the general safety ; so that if you see a single Fowl, or a couple fly together, you may imagine they have been somewhere affrighted from the rest by some sudden amazement or apprehension of danger : but so naturally are they inclined to society, that they seldom leave wing till they meet together again. And this is occasioned not onely by the neer approach of men, but also by the beating of Haggards on the Rivers, as also by the appearance of the very bold *Buzzard* and *Ring-tail*.

Of Water-fowl there are two sorts ; such as live of the water, and such as live on the water : the one taking their sustenance from the water , without swimming thereon, but wading and diving for it with their long Legs : The other are Web-footed, and swim, as the *Swan, Goose, Mallard,* &c.

Of

Of the Haunts of Fowl.

THe thing of greateft moment for the Fowler to underftand, is the Haunts of Fowl. In order thereunto you are to underftand, that all forts of greater
Fowl, *viz.* thofe who divide the foot, have their refidence by the edge of Rivers that are fhallow, Brooks,
and Plafhes of water: and thefe appear not in Flocks,
but you fhall fee here one fingle, there a couple, and the
like ; which makes them difficult to be taken by Engine or Device ; but they are the beft flights for *Hawks*
that can be imagined.

Likewife thefe Fowl delight in low and boggy places ; and the more fedgie, marifh and rotten fuch
grounds are, the fitter they are for the haunting of
thefe Fowl.

They love alfo the dry parts of drowned Fens, which
are overgrown with tall and long Rufhes, Reeds, and
Sedges.

Laftly, they delight in half-drowned Moors, or the
hollow vales of Downs, Heaths, or Plains, where there
is fhelter either of Hedges, Hills, Tufts of Bufhes or
Trees, where they may lurk obfcurely.

Now the leffer Fowl, which are Web footed, haunt
continually drowned Fens, where they may have
continually plenty of water, and may fwim un-
difturbed by man or beaft: Their Haunt is likewife
in the main Streams of Rivers, where the Current
is fwifteft and leaft fubject to freez ; and the broader
and deeper fuch Rivers are, the greater delight thefe
Fowl take therein, the *Wild-goofe* and *Barnacle* excepted, who abide no waters above their founding ;
for when they cannot reach the Ouze, they inftantly remove thence, feeking out more fhallow places.

Thefe

These two laſt named are infinitely delighted with green Winter-Corn, and therefore you ſhall ſee them evermore where ſuch Grain is ſown, eſpecially if the ends of the Lands have much water about them.

Likewiſe theſe ſmaller Fowl do very much frequent ſmall Brooks, Rivers, Ponds, drowned Meadows, Paſtures, Moors, Plaſhes, Meres, Loughs and Lakes, eſpecially if well ſtored with Iſlands unfrequented, and well furniſhed with Shrubs, Buſhes, Reeds, &c. and then they will breed there, and frequent ſuch places both Summer and Winter.

The readieſt way of taking great Fowl with NETS.

THe firſt thing your are to conſider, is the making of your Nets, which muſt be of the beſt Packthread, with great and large Meſhes, at leaſt two Inches from point to point : for the larger the Meſhes are, (ſo that the Fowl cannot creep through them) the better it is; for they more certainly intangle them.

Let not your Nets be above two fathom deep, and ſix in length, which is the greateſt proportion that a man is able to overthrow. Verge your Net on each ſide with very ſtrong Cord, and extend it at each end upon long Poles made for that purpoſe.

Having thus your Nets in readineſs, let the Fowler obſerve the Haunts of Fowl, that is to ſay, their Morning and Evening feedings, coming at leaſt two hours before thoſe ſeaſons; then ſpreading his Net ſmooth and flat upon the ground, ſtaking the two lower ends firm thereon, let the upper ends ſtand extended upon the long Cord, the farther end thereof being ſtaked

faſt

faſt down to the Earth two or three fathom from the Net; and let the Stake which ſtaketh down the Cord ſtand in a direct and even line with the lower verge of the Net, the diſtance ſtill obſerved: then the other end of the Cord, which muſt be at leaſt ten or twelve fathom long, the Fowler ſhall hold in his hand at the uttermoſt diſtance aforeſaid, where he ſhall make ſome artificial ſhelter either of Graſs, Sods, Earth, or ſuch like matter, whereby he may lie out of the ſight of the Fowl.

Obſerve to let the Net lie ſo ready for the Game, that upon the leaſt pull it may riſe from the Earth and fly over.

Strew over all your Net, as it lies upon the ground, ſome Graſs, that you may hide it from the Fowl. It will not be amiſs (but altogether requiſite) to ſtake down near your Net a live *Hern*, or ſome other Fowl formerly taken, for a Stale. When you obſerve a competent number of Fowl come within the verge of your Net, then draw your Cord ſuddenly, and ſo caſt the Net over them: Continue thus doing till the Sun be near an hour high, and no longer, for then their feeding is over for that time; and ſo do at E-vening from about Sun-ſet till Twi-light. By this means you may not onely take great quantities of larger Wild-fowl, but alſo *Plover*, which takes his food as much from Land as Water.

How to take ſmall Water-fowl with Nets.

LEt your Nets be made of the ſmalleſt and ſtrongeſt Packthread, and the Meſhes nothing near ſo big as thoſe for the greater Fowl, about two foot and a half or three foot deep; line theſe Nets on both ſides with falſe Nets, every Meſh being about a foot and a half fquare each way, that as the Fowl ftriketh either through them or againft them, fo the fmaller Net may pafs through the great Mefhes, and fo ftreighten and entangle the Fowl.

Thefe Nets you muft pitch for the Evening-flight of Fowl before Sun-fet, ftaking them down on each fide of the River about half a foot within the water, the lower fide of the Net being fo plumb'd that it may fink fo far and no farther : Let the upper fide of the Net be placed flantwife, fhoaling againft the Water, yet not touching the Water by near two foot ; and let the Strings which fupport this upper fide of the Net be faftned to fmall yielding Sticks prickt in the Bank, which as the Fowl ftrikes may give liberty to the Net to run and entangle them. Thus place feveral of thefe Nets over divers parts of the River, about twelve-fcore one from another, or as the River or Brook fhall give leave ; and be confident, if any Fowl come on the River that night, you fhall have your fhare.

And that you may the fooner obtain your defire, take your Gun and go to all the Fens and Plafhes that are a good diftance from your Nets, and fire it three or four times ; which will fo affright the Fowl, that they will inftantly poft to the Rivers ; then plant your Nets upon thefe Fens and Plafhes.

In the Mòrning go firft to the River and fee what Fowl are there furprifed ; and having taken them up with your Nets , if you efpy any Fowl on the River, difcharge your Gun, which will make them fly to the Fens and Plafhes, and then go and fee what you have taken : Thus you fhall be fure to be furnifhed with fome, though there be never fo few abroad.

How

How to take all manner of small Birds with Bird-Lime.

IN cold weather, that is to say, in Frost or Snow, all sorts of small Birds do congregate in Flocks , as *Larks, Chaffinches, Lennets, Gold-finches, Yellowhammers, Buntings, Sparrows,* &c. all these but the Lark do perch on Trees or Bushes, as well as feed on the ground : if you perceive they resort about your House or Fields adjacent, then use your Bird-lime that is well prepared, and not over-old ; order it after this manner : Take an Earthen dish and put the Bird-lime into it, and adde thereunto some fresh Lard, or *Capons*-grease, putting an ounce of either to a quarter of a pound of Bird-lime : then setting it over the fire, let it melt gently together ; but let it not boil by any means, for if you do, you will take away the strength of the Bird-lime, and so spoil it. Having thus prepared it, get a quantity of Wheat-ears, as many as you think you shall conveniently use, and cut the Straw about a foot long besides the Ears; then from the bottom of the Ears to the middle of the Straw lime it about six Inches : the Lime must be warm when you lime the straw, that so it may run thin upon the Straw, and therefore the less discernable, and consequently not suspected by the Birds.

Having thus got your Lim'd Straws in this manner ready, go into the field adjacent to your house, and carry a bag of Chaff and thresht Ears, and scatter these together twenty yards wide, (it is best in a Snow) then take the lim'd Ears & stick them up and down with the ears leaning, or at the end touching the ground ; then retire from the place, and traverse the grounds all round about ; the Birds hereupon being disturbed in their other haunts fly hither, and pecking at the ears of Corn , finding that they stick unto them, they straightways mount up

from

from the Earth, and in their flight the Bird-limb'd ſtraws lap under their Wings, and falling are not able to diſengage themſelves from the Straw, and ſo are certainly taken.

By the way take this Caution; do not go and take up five or ſix you ſee entangled, for that may hinder you it may be from taking three or four dozen at one time. If they be *Larks* that fall where your Bird-lim'd Straws do lie, go not a neer them till they ſpontaneouſly riſe of themſelves; and flying in great Flocks, I can aſſure you I have caught five dozen at one lift.

You may lay ſome nearer home to take *Finches*, *Sparrows*, *Yellowhammers*, &c. who reſort neer to Houſes, and frequent Barn-doors, where you may eaſily take them after the ſame manner as aforeſaid. The taking of *Sparrows* is a very great benefit to the Huſbandman, for they are his and the Farmer's principal Enemies, of all ſmall Birds; inſomuch as I dare aſſure them, that every dozen of *Sparrows* taken by them in the Winter, ſhall ſave them a Quarter of Wheat before Harveſt be ended. In the taking of them, you may ſtick the top of your Houſe if thatcht; and though you never have the Birds, yet the deſtruction of them will be a great advantage. Before a Barn-door if you lay your Twigs, or Limed ſtraws, you may there take them, with abundance of other ſmall Birds. The *Sparrow* is excellent food, and a great reſtorer of decayed Nature. You may alſo take them at Rooſt in the Eaves of Thatcht houſes, by coming in the night with a Clap-net; and rubbing the Net againſt the hole where they are flying out, you clap the Net together, and ſo take them: the darkeſt night with a Lanthorn and Candle is the chiefeſt time to take them.

Having performed your Morning Birding-Recreation, go bait the ſame place where you were before, and bait it with freſh Chaff and Ears of Corn, and
let

let them reſt till next Morning ; then take ſome freſh Wheat-ears again, and ſtick them as aforeſaid : and when you bait in the Afternoon, take away all your Limed ears, that ſo the Birds may feed boldly, and not be frighted or diſturbed againſt next Morning.

How to take great Fowl with
LIME-TWIGS.

YOu muſt ſupply your ſelf with good ſtore of Rods, which are long, ſmall, and ſtraight-grown Twigs, being light, and apt to play to and fro.

Lime the upper part of theſe Twigs, holding the Bird-lime before the fire, ſo that it may melt, for the better beſmearing them.

Having firſt well acquainted your ſelf where theſe Fowl do frequent Morning and Evening, you muſt then obſerve before Sun-ſet for the Eveng-flight, and before day for the Morning, that you plant your Lime-twigs where theſe Fowl haunt, pinning down for a Stale one of the ſame Fowl alive (which you have formerly taken for that purpoſe) which you intend to catch with your Bird-lime. Round about the Stale (giving the Fowl liberty to flutter to and fro) prick your Twigs in rows a foot diſtant one from the other, till you have covered all the place ſo haunted, that there ſhall be no room left, but that they muſt certainly fall foul with the Lime-twigs.

Prick the Rods ſloaping with their heads bending into the Wind about a foot or ſomewhat more above ground : If you pleaſe (and I think it the beſt way) you may croſs-prick your Rods, that is, one point in-to the Wind, and another againſt the Wind ; by which

means

means you may take the Fowl which way foever they come.

Place alfo a Stale fome diftance from your Lime-twigs, and faften fmall ftrings to it, which upon the fight of any Fowl you muft pull, then will your Stale flutter, which will allure them down.

If you fee any taken, do not run inftantly and take them up if you fee any Fowl in the Air; for by their fluttering others will be induced to fwoop in among them. It will not be amifs to have a well-taught Spaniel with you for the retaking of fuch Fowl (as it is common) which will flutter away with the Lime-twigs about them.

If you intend to ufe thefe Twigs for fmaller Wild-fowl, and fuch as frequent the water onely, then muft you fit them in length according to the depth of the River; and your Lime muft be very ftrong Water-lime, fuch as no wet or froft can injure. Prick thefe Rods in the water, as you did the others on the Land, as much of the Rod as is limed being above water ; and here and there among your Rods you muft ftake down a live Stale, as a *Mallard*, a *Widgeon* or *Teal* : and thus you may do in any fhallow Plafh or Fen.

You need not wait continually on your Rods, but come thrice a day, and fee what is taken, *viz.* early in the Morning, at high Noon, and late in the Evening; but come not unattended with your Water-fpaniel : for if you perceive any of your Rods miffing, you may conclude fome Fowl are faftned to them which are crept into fome Hole, bufh, or Sedge by the River-fide, and then will your Dog be very neceffary for the dif-covery.

Do not beat one Haunt too much, but when you finde their number fail, remove and finde out another, and in three weeks time your firft will be as good as ever.

Of

Of the great and lesser SPRINGES.

HAving noted the Morning and Evening feeding of divided-footed-Fowl, observing the Furrows and Water-tracts where they usually stalk and paddle to finde Worms, Flote grass-roots , and the like, you must mark where many Furrows meet in one, and break out as it were into one narrow passage, which so descending afterwards divides it self into other parts and branches ; then mark how every Furrow breaketh and cometh into this Center or little Pit, which is most paddled with the Fowl , or which is easiest for Fowl to wade in : This being done , take small and short Sticks , and prick them cross-wise a-thwart over all the other passages , one Stick within half an Inch of the other , making as it were a kinde of Fence to guard every way but one which you would have the Fowl to pass: if they stand but somewhat more than a handful above the Water , such is the nature of the Fowl , that they will not press over them, but stray about till that they finde the open way.

Having thus hemmed in all ways but one, take a stiff Stick cut flat on the one side , and prick both ends down into the Water, and make the upper part of the flat side of the Stick to touch the water, and no more : then make a Bow of small Hazel or Willow made in the fashion of a Pear, broad and round at one end, and narrow at the other , at least a foot long, and five or six Inches broad, and at the narrow end make a small nick : then take a good stiff-grown Plant of Hazel , clean without knot , three or four Inches about at the bottom , and an Inch at the top,

and

and having made the bottom-end sharp, at the top you must fasten a very strong Loop of about an hundred Horse-hairs plaited very fast together with strong Packthread, and made so smooth that it will run and slip at pleasure: let the Loop be of the just quantity of the Hoop, made Pear-wise as aforesaid: then hard by this Loop you must fasten a little broad thin Tricker within an Inch and half of the end of the Plant, which must be made equally sharp at both ends: thrust the bigger sharp end of the Plant into the ground close by the edge of the water, the smaller end with the Hoop and the Tricker must be brought down to the first Bridge, and then the Hoop made Pear-wise being laid on the Bridge, one end of the Tricker must be set upon the nick of the Hoop, and the other end against a nick made on the small end of the Plant, which by the violence and bend of the Plant shall make them stick and hold together until the Hoop be moved. This done, lay the Swickle on the Hoop in such fashon as the Hoop is proportioned; then from each side of the Hoop prick little Sticks, making an impaled path to the Hoop; and as you go farther and farther from the Hoop or Springe, so make the way wider and wider, that the Fowl may enter a good way before it shall perceive the Fence. By this means the Fowl will be enticed to wade up to the Springe, which shall be no sooner toucht, but that part of the Bird so touching will be instantly ensnared: And thus according to the strength of the Plant you shall take any Fowl of what bigness soever.

The Springe for lesser Fowl, as *Woodcock, Snipe, Plover*, &c. is made after the fashion aforesaid, onely differing in strength according unto the bigness of the Birds you intend to catch.

The main Plant or Sweeper you may make of Willow, Osier, or any stick that will bend and return to its proper straightness.   This

This device is for the Winter onely, when much wet is on the ground, and not when the Furrows are dry. Now if the waters be frozen, you muſt make plaſhes ; and the harder the Froſt, the greater reſort will there be of theſe ſmaller Fowl.

Of the FOWLING-PIECE and the STALKING-HORSE.

THat is ever eſteemed the beſt Fowling-piece which hath the longeſt Barrel, being five foot and a half or ſix foot long, with an indifferent bore, under Harquebuſe.

In ſhooting obſerve always to ſhoot with the wind, if poſſible, and not againſt it ; and rather ſide-ways, or behinde the Fowl, than full in their faces.

Next, obſerve to chuſe the moſt convenient ſhelter you can finde, as either Hedge, Bank, Tree, or any thing elſe which may abſcond you from the view of the Fowl.

Be ſure to have your Dog at your heels under good command, not daring to ſtir till you bid him, having firſt diſcharged your Piece : for ſome ill-taught Dogs will upon the ſnap of the Cock preſently ruſh out, and ſpoil all the ſport.

Now if you have not ſhelter enough, by reaſon of the nakedneſs of the Banks and want of Trees, you muſt creep upon your hands and knees under the Banks, and lying even flat upon your Belly , put the noſe of your Piece over the Bank, and ſo take your level ; for a Fowl is ſo fearful of Man, that though an Hawk were ſoaring over her head, yet at the ſight of a man ſhe would betake herſelf to her wing, and run the riſque of that danger.

But

But sometime it so happeneth that the Fowl are so shie, there is no getting a shoot at them without a Stalking-horse, which must be some old Jade trained up for that purpose, who will gently, and as you will have him, walk up and down in the Water which way you please, flodding and eating on the Grass that grows therein.

You must shelter your self and Gun behinde his fore-shoulder, bending your body down low by his side, and keeping his body still full between you and the Fowl: being within shot, take your level from before the fore-part of the Horse, shooting as it were between the Horse's Neck and the water; which is much better than shooting under his Belly, being more secure, and less perceiveable.

Now to supply the want of a Stalking-horse, which will take up a great deal of time to instruct and make fit for this exercise, you may make one of any pieces of old Canvas, which you must shape into the form of an Horse, with the Head bending downwards as if he grazed. You may stuff it with any light matter; and do not forget to paint it of the colour of an Horse, of which the brown is the best; and in the midst let it be fix'd to a Staff with a sharp Iron at the end, to stick into the ground as you shall see occasion, standing fast whilst you take your level.

It must be made so portable, that you may bear it with ease in one hand, moving it so as it may seem to graze as you go. Let the stature of your artificial Stalking-horse be neither too low nor too high; for the one will not abscond your body, and the other will be apt to frighten the Fowl.

Instead of this Stalking-horse, you may fashion out of Canvas painted an Ox or Cow: and this change is necessary, when you have so beaten the Fowl with your Stalking-horse, that they begin to finde your de-

ceit,

ceft, and will no longer endure it, (as it frequently falls out.) Then you may ftalk with an Ox or Cow, till the Stalking-horfe be forgotten, and by this means make your fport lafting and continual.

Some there are that ftalk with Stags or Red-Deer form'd out of painted Canvas, with the natural Horns of Stags fixt thereon, and the colour fo lively painted, that the Fowl cannot difcern the fallacy ; and thefe are very ufeful in low Fenny grounds, where any fuch Deer do ufually feed ; and are more familiar with the Fowl, and fo feed nearer them than Ox, Horfe, or Cow : by which means you fhall come within afar nearer diftance.

There are other dead Engines to ftalk withal, as an artificial Tree, Shrub, or Bufh, which may be made of fmall Wands, and with painted Canvas made into the fhape of a Willow, Poplar, or fuch Trees as grow by Rivers and Water fides ; for thefe are the beft.

If you ftalk with a Shrub or Bufh, let them not be fo tall as your Tree, but much thicker ; which you may make either of one entire Bufh, or of divers Bufhes interwoven one with another, either with fmall Withy-wands, Cord, or Packthread, that may not be difcerned : and let not your Bufh exceed the height of a man, but be thicker than four or five, with a Spike at the bottom to ftick into the ground whilft you take your level.

How to take all manner of Land-fowl by day or night.

SInce the diffolution and fpoil of Paradife, no man hath either feen, or can give the names of all Land-fowl whatever, there being fuch great variety, every Country producing fome particular forts which are unknown to other Nations.

B   To

To avoid prolixity, I shall rank them under two heads.

The first are such who are either fit for Food or Pleasure, either for eating or singing: for eating, *Pigeons* of all sorts, *Rook*, *Pheasant*, *Partridge*, *Quails*, *Rails*, *Felfares*, &c. and for eating or singing, the *Blackbird*, *Throstle*, *Nightingale*, *Linnet*, *Lark*, and *Bull-finch*.

Secondly, such as are for Pleasure onely, and they are all manner of birds of Prey, as *Castrels*, *Ring-tails*, *Buzzards*, &c.

The general way of taking these Land-fowl of several sorts together, is either by day or by night. If by day, it is done with the great Net, commonly called the *Crow-net*, and not at all differs in length, depth, bigness of Mesh, manner of laying, &c. from the *Plover-net*; onely it will not be amiss if the Cords be longer.

This Net you may lay before Barn-doors, or where Corn hath been winnowed, also in Stubble-fields, so concealing the Net that the Fowl may not discern the Snare. When you perceive a quantity within the Net scraping for food, and you lie concealed afar off, with your Cord in your hand suddenly pull the Net over upon them.

You may do well to take notice of their Morning and Evening Haunts to worm and feed upon the Greensward; and here lay your Net, and it will prove as effectual as in other places, so that you observe to abscond your self in some Covert so as not to be descried: in the next place, pull not too hastily, but wait for a good number of Fowl within the Net, and then pull freely and quickly; for the least deliberation after the Net is raised, is the ruine of your designe.

Thus much for Day-fowling with the Net: now if you will prosecute your Sport by Night, you must do

it

it according to the nature and manner of the Country, or situation or fashion of the ground, whether Woody, Mountainous, or Champain.

In plain and Champain Countries you must use the *Low-bell*, from the end of *October* until the end of *March* ; and this method you must follow.

The day being shut in, the Air milde without Moon-shine, take a *Low-bell*, (which must have a deep and hollow sound, for if it be shrill it is stark naught) and with it a Net whose Mesh is twenty yards deep, and so broad, that it may cover five or six Lands or more, according to the company you have to carry it. With these Instruments go into any Stubble Corn-field, but Wheat is the best. He that carries the Bell must go foremost, toling the Bell as he goes very mournfully, letting it but now & then knock on both sides : after him must follow the Net, born up at each corner and on each side by several persons ; then another must carry some Iron or Stony Vessel which may contain burning, but not blazing Coals, and at these you must light bundles of Straw : or you may carry Links with you. And having pitcht your Nets where you think the Game lies, beat the ground and make a noise, and as the Fowl rise they will be entangled in the Net. Thus you may take good store of *Partridge, Rails, Larks, Quails,* &c.

Having so done, extinguish your Lights, and proceed laying your Net in some other place as before mentioned.

Here note, that the sound of the *Low-bell* makes the Birds lie close, so as they dare not stir whilst you are pitching the Net, for the sound thereof is dreadful to them ; but the sight of the Fire much more terrible, which makes them instantly to fly up, and so they become entangled in the Net.

Furthermore, if you intend to have the full fruition of your Sport, you must be very silent, and nothing

B 2 must

must be heard but the sound of the *Low-bell* till the Net is placed and the Lights blazing ; but as soon as they are extinguish'd, a general silence must be again.

The Trammel is much like this Net for the *Low-bell*, and may be necessarily used on the same grounds ; onely it ought to be longer, though not much broader.

When you come to a place fit for your purpose where Birds lodge on the Earth, you shall then spread your Trammel on the ground ; and let the farthest end thereof, being plumbed with Lead, lie loose on the ground ; but let the foremost ends be born up by two men, and so trail the Net along, keeping the foremost ends a yard or more distance from the ground.

On each side of the Net carry Wisps of Straw lighted, or Links, and let some beat the ground with long Poles ; and as the Birds rise under the Nets, take them. And thus you may continue doing as long as you please, to your great profit and pleasure.

---

of BAT-FOWLING.

BAT-*FOWLING* is the taking of all manner of Birds, great and small, by night, which roost in Bushes, Shrubs, Hawthorn-trees, &c.

The manner is : you must be very silent till your Lights are blazing, and you may either carry Nets or none : if none, you must then have long Poles with great bushy tops fixt to them ; and having from a *Cresset* or vessel to carry fire in lighted your Straw, or other blazing combustible matter, then must you beat those Bushes where you think Birds are at Roost ; which done,

if

if there be any in thofe Bufhes or Trees, you will inftantly fee them fly about the Flames : for it is their nature, through their amazednefs at the ftrangenefs of
the Light, and extream darknefs round about it, not
to depart from it, but they will even fcorch their
Wings in the fame, fo that thofe who have the bufhy
Poles may beat them down as they pleafe, and take
them up. Thus you may continue your fport as long
as it is very dark, and no longer.

Of the DAY-NET, and how to take Birds therewith.

THe *Day-Net* is generally ufed for the taking of
Larks, *Buntings*, *Merlins*, *Hobbies*, or any Birds
which play in the Air, and will ftoop either to Stale,
Prey, Gig, Glafs, or the like.

The feafon for thefe Nets is from *Auguft* to *November :* the time you muft plant thefe Nets muft be before Sun-rifing. Where note, the milder the Air, the
brighter the Sun, and the pleafanter the Morning is,
the better will your Sport be, and of longer continuance.

Let the place you elect for this purpofe be plain and
Champain, either on Barley-ftubbles, green Lays, or
level and flat Meadows; and thefe places muft be remote from any Villages, but near adjacent to Corn-
fields.

The fafhion of a Day-net is this : you muft make
them of fine Packthread, the Mefh fmall, and not a-
bove half an Inch fquare each way; let the length be
about three fathom, the breadth one fathom and no
more : the fhape is like the Crow-net, and it muft be
verg'd about in the fame manner with a ftrong fmall
Cord, and the two ends extended upon two fmall

long

long Poles suitable to the breadth of the Net, with four Stakes, Tail-strings, and Drawing-lines, as afore mentioned : onely whereas that was but one single Net, here must be two of one length, breadth and fashion. These Nets must be laid opposite to each other, yet so close and even together, that when they are drawn and pull'd over, the sides and edges may meet and touch one the other.

These Nets being staked down with strong Stakes very stifly on their Lines, so as with any nimble twitch you may cast them to and fro at your pleasure ; you shall then to the upper ends of the foremost Staves fasten your Hand-lines or drawing Cords, which must be at the least a dozen, a fathom long ; and so extend them of such a reasonable streightness, as with little strength they may raise up the Nets and cast them over.

When your Nets are laid, some twenty or thirty paces beyond them place your Stales, Decoys, or playing Wantons, upon some pearching Boughs, which will not onely entice Birds of their own Feather to stoop, but also *Hawks* and Birds of Prey to swoop into your Nets.

Remember to keep the first half dozen you take alive for Stales, and to that end have a Cage or Linnen-bag to put them in : The rest squeez in the hinder part of the Head, and so kill them. And thus do every day.

Of taking small Birds which use Hedges and Bushes with Lime-twigs.

THe great Lime-bush is best for this use, which you must make after this manner : Cut down the main Arm or chief Bough of any bushy Tree, whose
branches

Branches or Twigs are long, thick, smooth and straight, without either pricks or knots; of which the Willow or Birch-tree are the best: when you have pickt it and trimm'd it from all superfluity, making the Twigs neat and clean; take then of the best Bird-lime, well mixed and wrought together with Goose-greace or Capon's-greace, which being warmed, lime every Twig therewith within four fingers of the bottom. The body, from whence the branches have their rise, must be untouch'd with Lime.

Be sure you do not dawb your Twigs with too much Lime, for that will give distaste to the birds; yet let none want its proportion, or have any part left bare which ought to be toucht: for, as too much will deter them from coming, so too little will not hold them when they are there.

Having so done, place your Bush on some Quick-set or dead Hedge neer unto Towns-ends, back-yards, old houses, or the like; for these are the resort of small Birds in the Spring-time: in the Summer and Harvest in Groves, Bushes, White-thorn-trees, Quick-set-hedges neer Corn-fields, Fruit-trees, Flax and Hemp-lands; and in the Winter about Houses, Hovels, Barns, Stacks, or those places where stand Ricks of Corn, or scattered Chaff, &c.

As neer as you can to any of these Haunts plant your Lime-bush, and plant your self also at a convenient distance undiscovered, imitating with your Mouth the several Notes of Birds, which you must learn by frequent practice, walking the Fields for that very purpose often, observing the variety of several birds sounds, especially such as they call one another by. I have known some so expert herein, that they could imitate the Notes of twenty several sorts of birds at least, by which they have caught ten birds to another's one that was ignorant therein.

But

But if you cannot attain to it by your industry, you must then buy a *Bird-call*, of which there are several sorts, and easie to be framed, some of Wood, some of Horn, some of Cane, and the like.

Having first learned how to use this Call, you shall sit and call the Birds unto you ; and as any of them light on your Bush, step not to them till you see them sufficiently entangled : neither is it requisite to run for every single Bird, but let them alone till more come, for their fluttering is as good as a Stale to entice more.

This Exercise you may use from Sun-rising till ten a clock in the Morning, and from one till almost Sun-set.

You may take these small Birds with Lime-twigs onely, without the Bush. When I was a boy, I have taken two or three hundred small Twigs about the bigness of Rushes, and about three Inches long, and have gone with them into a field where were Hemp-cocks,; upon the tops of half a score, lying all round together, I have stuck my Twigs, and then have gone and beat that field, or the next to it, where I saw any Birds ; and commonly in such fields there are infinite numbers of *Linnets* and *Green-birds* which are great lovers of Hemp-seed. I say, they fly in such vast flocks, I have caught at one fall of them upon the Cocks eight dozen at a time.

But to return, there is a pretty way of taking Birds with Lime-twigs, by placing near them a Stale or two made of living *Night-bats*, placing them aloft, that they may be visible to the Birds thereabouts ; which will no sooner be perceived, but every bird will come and gaze, wondering at the strangeness of the sight : then they having no other convenient lighting-place but where the Lime-twigs are, you may take what number you list of them.

But the *Owl* is a far better Stale than the *Bat*, being
bigger

bigger, and more eafily to be perceived ; befides, he is never feen abroad, but he is followed and perfecuted by all the birds near adjacent.

If you have not a living *Bat* or *Owl*, their Skins will ferve as well being ftuffed, and will laft you twenty years. There are fome have ufed an *Owl* cut in Wood , and naturally painted, with wonderful fuccefs.

It is ftrange to me that this bird above all others fhould be fo perfecuted by all birds whatfoever, efpecially by the *Goofe* ; and therefore fome arch Cracks in *Lincoln-fhire* and other places where are great quantities of *Geefe*, obferving their tempers, have made great advantage of them ; for by onely throwing a live *Owl* among a flock of *Geefe*, they got as many Quills as they knew what to do with ; for the *Geefe* endeavouring to beat the *Owl* with their Wings, never left till they did beat the Quills out of their Wings, and commonly the beft, which are Seconds.

How to make the beft fort of Bird-lime, and how to ufe it.

TAke at Midfummer the bark of Holly, and pill it from the Tree, fo much as will fill a reafonable big Veffel ; then put to it running water, and fet it over the fire, and boil it till the grey and white bark rife from the green, which will take up fixteen hours in the boiling : then take it from the fire, and feparate the barks after the water is very well drain'd away : then take all the green bark, and lay it on the ground in a clofe place and moift floor, and cover it over with all manner of green Weeds, as Hemlock, Docks , Thiftles, and the like ; thus let it lie ten or twelve daies, in which time it will rot, & turn to a filthy flimy matter:

then

Then take it and put it into a Mortar, and there beat it till it become univerfally thick and tough, without the difcerning of any part of the Bark or other fub-ftance; then take it out of the Mortar, and carry it to a running Stream, and there wafh it exceedingly, not leaving any mote or foulnefs within it; then put it up in a very clofe Earthen Pot, and let it ftand and purge for divers days together, fcumming it as often as any foulnefs arifes for four or five daies: when you perceive no more Scum, you fhall then take it out of that Pot, and put it into another clean Earthen Vef-fel, cover it clofe, and keep it for your ufe.

When you are about to ufe your Lime, take what quantity you think fit and put it into a Pipkin, adding thereto a third part of Goofe-greafe or Capons-greafe finely clarified, and fet them over a gentle fire, and there let them melt together, and ftir them continually till they are well incorporated: then take it from the fire, and ftir it till it be cold.

When your Lime is cold, take your Rods and warm them a little over the fire; then take your Lime and wind it about the tops of your Rods, then draw your Rods afunder one from the other and clofe them a-gain, continually plying and working them together, till by fmearing one upon another you have equally beftowed on each Rod a fufficient proportion of Lime.

If you lime any Strings, do it when the Lime is ve-ry hot and at the thinneft, befmearing the Strings on all fides, by folding them together and unfolding them again.

If you lime Straws, it muft be done likewife when the Lime is very hot, doing a great quantity together, as many as you can well grafp in your hand, toffing and working them before the fire till they are all befmear'd, every Straw having his due proportion of Lime: having fo done, put them up in cafes of Lea-ther till you have occafion to ufe them.   Now

Now to prevent the freezing of your Lime either as it is on Twigs, Bushes, or Straws, you must adde a quarter as much of the Oil called *Petroleum* as of your Capons-greafe, mix them well together, and then work it on your Rods, *&c.* and fo it will ever keep fupple, tough and gentle, and will not be prejudiced fhould it freeze never fo hard.

The beft and moft Experienced way of making Water-Bird-lime.

Buy what quantity you think fit of the ftrongeft Bird-lime you can procure, and wafh it as long in a clear Spring-water till you finde it very pliable, and the hardnefs thereof removed; then beat out the water extraordinary well, till you cannot perceive a drop to appear, then dry it well; after this put it into a Pot made of Earth, and mingle therewith Capons-greafe unfalted, fo much as will make it run; then adde thereto two fpoonfuls of ftrong Vinegar, a fpoonful of the beft Sallet-Oil, and a fmall quantity of *Venice-Turpentine* : This is the allowance of thefe ingredients, which muft be added to every pound of ftrong Bird-lime as aforefaid. Having thus mingled them, boil them all gently together over a fmall fire, ftirring it continually; then take it from the fire and let it cool : when at any time you have occafion to ufe it, warm it, and then anoint your Twigs or Straws, or any other fmall things, and no Water will take away the ftrength thereof. This fort of Bird-lime is the beft, efpecially for *Snipes* and *Felfares.*

In

In what manner a man may take Snipes *with this* Bird-lime.

TAke what number you shall think most expedient for your purpose, of Birch-twigs, and lime fifty or sixty of them very well together. After this, go and seek out those places where *Snipes* do usually frequent, which you may know by their Dung.

In very hard frosty or snowy Weather, where the Water lies open, they will lie very thick : Having observed the place where they most feed, set two hundred of your Twigs, more or less as you please, at a yard distance one from the other, and let them stand sloaping some one way and some another ; then retire a convenient distance from the place, and you shall finde there shall not one *Snipe* in ten miss your Twigs, by reason they spread their Wings, and fetch a round close to the ground before they light. When you see any taken, stir not at first, for he will feed with the Twigs under his Wings ; and as others come over the place, he will be a means to entice them down to him. When you see the Coast clear, and but few that are not taken, you may then take up your birds, fastning one or two of them, that the other flying over may light at the same place. If there be any other open place neer to that where your Twigs are planted, you must beat them up : The reason why they delight to haunt open places, and where Springs do gently run, is because they cannot feed, by reason of their Bills, in places that are hard and stony ; and about these Plashes in snowy Weather they very much resort.

The

The manner of taking Felfares by Water-bird-lime.

ABout *Michaelmas*, or when the cold weather begins to come in, take your Gun and kill some *Felfares*; then take a couple of them, or one may serve, and fasten them to the top of a Tree, in such manner that they may seem to be alive: having so done, prepare two or three hundred Twigs, take a great Birchen-bough, and therein place your Twigs, having first cut off all the small Twigs; then set a *Felfare* upon the top of the bough, making of him fast, and let this bough be planted where the *Falfares* do resort in a Morning to feed; for they keep a constant place to feed in, till there is no more food left. By this means others flying but neer, will quickly espie the top-bird, and fall in whole flocks to him. I have seen at one fall three dozen taken.

How to take Pigeons with Lime-twigs.

PIgeons are great devourers and destroyers of Corn; wherefore when you finde any ground much frequented by them, get a couple of *Pigeons*, either dead or alive, if dead; put them in such a stiff posture as if they were living and feeding; then at Sun-rising take a quantity of Twigs, as many as you think fit, let them be small, (but I judge Wheaten-straws are better for this purpose) and lay them up and down where your *Pigeons* are placed, and you shall finde such sport at every fall that is made, that you may quickly be rid of them without offending the Statute:

if

If there come good flights, you may easily take four or five dozen of them in a Morning.

How to take Mag-pies, Crows, and Gleads with Lime-twigs.

WHen you have found any Carrion on which *Crows*, *Pies*, *Kites*, &c. are preying upon, over night set your Lime-twigs every where about the Carrion; but let them be small, and not set too thick; if otherwise, being subtile Birds, they will suspect some danger or mischief designed against them. When you perceive one to be fast, advance not to him presently; for most commonly when they are surely caught, they are not sensible thereof.

You may take them another way, and that is by joyning to a Packthread several Nooses of Hair up and down the Packthread, and peg it down about a yard from the Carrion: for many times when they have gotten a piece of Flesh, they will be apt to run away to feed by themselves; and if your Nooses be thick, it is two to one but some of the Nooses catch him by the Legs.

How to take Rooks when they pull up the Corn by the Roots.

TAke some thick Brown-Paper, and divide a sheet into eight parts, and make them up like Sugarloaves; then lime the inside of the Paper a very little; (let them be limed three or four daies before you set them) then put some Corn in them, and lay threescore or more of them up and down the ground; lay them as near as you can under some clod of Earth, and

and early in the Morning before they come to feed; and then ſtand at a diſtance, and you will ſee moſt excellent ſport; for as ſoon as *Rooks, Crows*, or *Pigeons* come to peck out any of the Corn, it will hang upon his head, and he will immediately fly bolt upright ſo high, that he ſhall ſoar almoſt out of ſight; and when he is ſpent, come tumbling down as if he had been ſhot in the Air. You may take them at Ploughing time when the *Rooks* and *Crows* follow the Plough; but then you muſt put in Worms and Maggots of the largeſt ſize.

How to take Birds with BAITS, either Land or Water-fowl.

IF you have a deſire to take *Houſe-doves, Stock-doves, Rooks, Choughs*, or any other-like Birds, then take Wheat, Barley, Fetches, Tares, or other Grain, and boil them very well with good ſtore of *Nux vomica* in ordinary running water: when they are almoſt boil'd, dry and ready to burſt, take them off the fire, and ſet them by till they be throughly cold. Having ſo done, ſcatter this Grain in the Haunts of thoſe Birds you have a minde to take; and as ſoon as they have taſted hereof, they will fall down into a dead ſwound, and ſhall not be able to recover themſelves in a good while.

And as you take theſe great Land-fowl with this drunken device, ſo you may take the middle and ſmaller ſort of Birds, if you obſerve to boil with what food they delight in a quantity of this *Nux vomica*.

Some inſtead of *Nux vomica* uſe the Lees of Wine, the ſharper and quicker they are the better, boiling their Grains in theſe Lees, alſo Seeds or any other food, and ſtrewing them in the Haunts of thoſe Birds

you

you would furprize. Thefe do as effectually as *Nux vomica* ; and it's the cleanlier and neater way, there being not that poifonous quality in them.

You may chufe whether you will boil your Grain or Seed in the aforefaid Lees ; for they will be every whit as effectual if onely fteeped a confiderable while therein, giving them leave to drink in the Lees till they are ready to burft before you ufe them.

Others, having neither *Nux vomica* nor Wine-lees, take the juice of Hemlock, and fteep their Grains therein, adding thereto fome Henbane-feed or Poppy-feed, caufing them to be infufed therein four or five daies ; then draining the Grain or Seed from the Liquor, ftrew them as aforefaid. The Birds having tafted hereof are immediately taken with a dizzinefs, which will continue fome hours, fo that they cannot fly ; but they will recover again if you kill them not. If you intend them for food, let them be firft recovered.

Thus much for the Land ; now let us fpeak of the Water-fowl.

The ready way by Bait to take fuch Fowl as receive part of their food by land and part by water, as *Wilde-geefe, Barnacle, Grey-plover, Mallard, Curlew, Shoveler, Bitter, Buftard,* with many more, I fay, the beft way my experience hath found out is, to take Bellenge-leaves, Roots and all, and having cleanfed them very well, put them into a Veffel of clear running Water, and there let them lie in fteep twenty four hours ; then never fhift them from the Water, but boil them together till the Water be almoft confumed : then take it off, and fet it a cooling. Then take a quantity hereof, and go to the Haunts of any of the aforefaid Fowl, and there fpread of this Bait in fundry and divers places ; and thofe that fhall tafte hereof will be taken with the like drunken dizzinefs as the former. To make this Confection the more effectual, it will be

requi-

requilite to adde a quantity of Brimſtone thereunto in its boiling.

How to recover Fowl thus entranced.

If you would reſtore any of theſe entranced Fowl to their former health, take a little quantity of Sallet-oil, according to the ſtrength and bigneſs of the Fowl, and drop it down the Throat of the Fowl ; then chafe the head with a little ſtrong White-wine-vinegar, and the Fowl will preſently recover, and be as well as ever.

And thus much for taking Fowl of all ſorts by Baits.

A moſt excellent and approved way how to take the HERN.

A Hern is as great a devourer of Fiſh as any is ; nay ſome dare affirm, ten-times as much as an Otter, and ſhall do more miſchief in one Week than an Otter ſhall do in three moneths : for I have been told by one that hath ſeen a Hern that hath been ſhot at a Pond to have had ſeventeen Carps at once in his Belly , which he will digeſt in ſix or ſeven hours, and then betake himſelf to fiſhing again. I have been informed by another, that he ſaw a Carp taken out of an Hern's Belly which was nine Inches and an half long.

Several Gentlemen that have kept Herns tame, have put fiſh in a Tub, and tried the Hern how many ſmall Roaches and Dace he would eat in a day, and they have found him to eat about fifty in a day one day with a-nother.

One Hern that haunts a Pond , in a Twelve-moneths time, shall destroy a thousand Store-*Carps*; and when Gentlemen sue their Ponds, they think their Neighbours have robbed them, not in the least considering an *Hern* is able to devour them in half a years time, if he put in half as many more.

Now since this ravenous Fowl is so destructive to Ponds and fish of the River, it will be very necessary to finde out a way to destroy that that destroys so many; which may be done in this manner.

Having found out his haunt, get three or four small *Roaches* or *Dace*; and have a strong Hook with Wyre to it, draw the Wyre just within the skin of the said Fish, beginning without side of the Gills, running of it to the Tail, and then the Fish will live five or six daies. Now if the Fish be dead, the *Hern* will not meddle with him. Let not your Hook be too rank; then having a strong Line with Silk and Wyre about two yards and a half long, (if you twist not Wyre with your Silk, the sharpness of his Bill will bite it in two immediately) and tie a round Stone about a pound-weight to the Line, and lay three or four Hooks, and in two or three nights you shall not fail to have him if he comes to your Pond. Lay not your Hooks in the water so deep that the *Hern* cannot wade unto them. Colour your Line of a dark green, for an *Hern* is a subtile bird. There are several other Fowl devourers of Fish, as *Kings-fisher*, *More-hens*, *Balcoots*, *Cormorant*, &c. but none like the *Hern* for Ponds and small Rivers.

How

How *to take* PHEASANTS *several ways.*

THe taking of *Pheasants* is to be performed three several ways, by Nets, by Lime-bush, or else by other particular Engines, which shall be discours'd of hereafter.

The taking of *Pheasants* with Nets, is done either generally, or particularly : generally, when the whole Eye of *Pheasants* is taken, that is, the old Cock and old Hen with all their Powts, as they run together in the obscure Woods ; or particularly, when you take none but the old *Pheasants*, or the young, being of an age fit to couple or pair.

For the greater facility of taking *Pheasants*, you must first understand their Haunts, which are never in open Fields, but in thick young Copses well grown, and not in old high Woods.

Having thus found out their Coverts, which must be solitary and untraced by Men or Cattle, the next thing will be how to finde out the Eye or Brood of *Pheasants*.

The first way, is by going into these young Copses, and carefully viewing the same, searching every where ; and by that means at last finding where they run together, as Chickens after a Hen. Or, secondly, you must rise early in a Morning, or come late in the Evening ; and observe how and when the old Cock and Hen call their young ones to them, and how the young ones answer back unto them again ; and so from that sound direct your Path as near as you can to the place where they are, lying there down so close you may not

C 2 be

be difcerned ; by which means you will know where they meet, and how accordingly you may pitch your Nets.

But the moft certain way of finding them out, is to have a natural *Pheafant* call, which you muft learn how to ufe, underftanding all their Notes, and how to apply them : For they have feveral Notes, and all different ; one to cluck them together when the Hen would brood them, another to chide them when they ftraggle too far , a third to call them to meat when fhe hath found it , a fourth to make them look out for food themfelves , and a fifth to call them about her to fport withal. You muft ufe your Call in the morning early, at which time they ftraggle abroad to finde Provender ; or elfe in the Evening juft about Sun-fetting, which is their time likewife for feeding.

Now although thefe are the beft times to ufe your Call, yet you may call them at any other time of the day, onely altering your Note. Juft at, or before Sunrifing, your Note muft be to call them to feed, and fo at Sun fet : but in the Forenoon and Afternoon your Notes muft be to cluck them together to brood, or to chide them for ftraggling, or to give them notice of fome approaching danger.

Knowing your Notes, and how to apply them, with the places where *Pheafants* haunt, which you fhall know by the ftrength of the under-growth, obfcurenefs, darknefs, and folitarinefs of the place , you muft then lodge your felf as clofe as poffible, and then call at firft very foftly, left the *Pheafants* being lodg'd very near you, fhould be affrighted at a loud Note ; but if nothing reply, raife your Note higher and higher, till you extend it to the utmoft compafs : and if there be a *Pheafant* within hearing, fhe will anfwer in a Note as loud as your own, provided it be not untunable, for that will fpoil all.

As

As soon as you hear this answer, if it be from afar, and from one single Fowl, creep nearer and nearer unto it, still calling, but not so loud ; and as you approach nearer to it, so will the *Pheasant* to you ; and as you alter your Note, so will she : and in all points you must endeavour to imitate her, and in fine you will get sight of her, either on the Ground or Pearch : Then cease your calling, and spread your Net between the *Pheasant* and your self, in the most convenient place you can finde, with all secrecy and silence, making one end of the Net fast to the ground, and holding the other end by a long Line in your hand; by which, when any thing straineth it, you may pull the Net close together : which done, call again, and as soon as you perceive the *Pheasant* come underneath your Net, then rise up and shew your self, that by giving the *Pheasant* an affright he may offer to mount, and so be entangled within the Net.

Now if it so fall out that you hear many answers, and from divers corners of the Wood, then stir not at all, but keep your place; and as you hear them by their sounds to come nearer and nearer unto you, so shall you in the mean time prepare your Nets ready, and spread them conveniently about you, one pair of Nets on the one side, and another on the other side; then lie close, and apply your self to the Call till such time as you have allured them under your Nets; then stand up and shew your self, which will affright them and make them mount, whereby they will be entangled.

The fashion of Pheasant-*nets.*

You must make these Nets of double-twined brown Thread dyed blue or green; let the Mesh be reasonably

nably large and fquare, almoft an Inch between Knot and Knot ; let the length of it be about three fathom, and the breadth about feven foot, and verge it on each fide with ftrong fmall Cord, and let the ends be alfo fo, that it may lie compafs-wife and hollow.

Some make thefe Nets of a much larger fize ; but then they are too cumberfome, and hardly to be ruled with one hand : but the others are readier to pitch, and better to take, alfo more nimble for any purpofe you fhall employ them to.

Of Driving of Pheafant-powts.

The driving and taking young *Pheafants* in Nets is done after this manner. Having either by your eye or Call found out an Eye of *Pheafants*, you muft then (taking the wind with you, for they will naturally run down the wind) place your Nets crofs the little Pads and ways which you fee they have made, (for they will make little Paths like Sheep-tracks) and as near as you can, come to fome fpecial Haunts of theirs, which you fhall know by the barenefs of the ground, Mutings, and loofe Feathers which you fhall finde there : and thefe Nets muft be placed hollow, loofe, and circular-wife, the nether part thereof being faftned to the ground, and the upper fide lying hollow, loofe and bending, fo that when any thing rufheth into it, it may fall and entangle it : which done, you muft go before where you found the Haunt, and there with your Call (if you finde the Eye is fcattered and feparated one from the other) you muft call them together.

Then take your Inftrument called a *Driver*, which is made of ftrong white Wands or Ofiers fet faft in a handle, and in two or three places twifted about and bound with other Wands, bearing the fhape of thofe
                                                                                    things

things Cloath-dreffers ufually drefs their Cloath withal:
I fay, with this Driver you muft make a gentle noife,
raking upon the Boughs and Bufhes round about you;
which as foon as Powts do hear, they will inftantly
run from it a little way, and then ftand and liften, keeping all clofe together: then give another rake, at
which they will run again as before: And by thus raking you will drive them like fo many Sheep before
you which way or whither you pleafe, and confequently at laft into your Nets.

In ufing your Driver there are two things to be obferved. The firft is Secrecy, in concealing your felf
from the fight of the *Pheafants*; for if they chance to
fee you, they will inftantly hide themfelves in Holes
and bottoms of Bufhes, and will not ftir from thence
by any means whatever as long as any day endu-
reth.

The other thing to be obferved, is Time and Leifure
in the work; for there is nothing obftructs this Paftime
more than too much hafte: For they are very fearful
Creatures, and are foon ftartled; and when once a-
larm'd, their fears will not fuffer them to argue or dif-
pute with the affrighting object; but the very firft ap-
prehenfion is fufficient to make them all fly at an in-
ftant, without ftaying to behold what they are fo much
affraid of.

Of taking Pheafants *with a Lime-bufh.*

Having obferved their Haunts as aforefaid, take a
Bufh, or fingle Rods, and trim them with the beft and
ftrongeft Lime that can be got: let your Rods be
twelve Inches; your Lime-bufh muft not contain a-
bove eight Twigs, being the Top-branch of fome Wil-
low-tree, with an indifferent long Handle, made fharp

C 4 either

either to ſtick into the ground, or into Shrubs and Buſhes. You may plant your Buſh neer that Branch of ſome little Tree which the *Pheaſant* uſually pearch-eth on.

When you have placed your Buſh or Rods, take out your Call, but remove not from your place, lying cloſe without diſcovery. If your Call be good, and you have skill to uſe it, you will quickly have all the *Pheaſants* within hearing about you; and if one hap-pen to be entangled, ſhe will go near to entangle all the reſt, either by her extraordinary fluttering, or their own amazement and confuſion. And as they are ta-ken by the Rods on the ground, ſo you will ſurprize them with your Buſhes; for being ſcared from be-low, they will mount to the Pearch or Buſhes, to ſee what becomes of their fellows, and be there taken themſelves.

Here note, that it is very requiſite to count all your Rods, and when you have gathered up your *Pheaſants*, ſee what Rods you have miſſing, and then conclude from the miſs of them that ſome *Pheaſants* are run with them into the Buſhes; and therefore it will be neceſſary to have a Spaniel which will fetch and carry, and one that will not break nor bruiſe either Fleſh or Feather.

The ſeaſons for the uſe of Nets or Lime.

The Lime is onely for the Winter-ſeaſon, beginning from *November*, when the Trees have ſhed their Leaves, (and then Lime-buſhes and Branches of Trees are a-like naked and of the ſame complexion) and ending at *May*, at which time the Trees begin to be furniſhed with Leaves.

The true uſe of the Nets is from the beginning of *May* till the latter end of *October*.

So

So that there is no time of the year but their Bree-
ding-time, which may not be exercifed in this pleafure;
whence what profit may arife, I fhall leave to the judgment of thofe who keep good houfes, and fuch as have
good Stomacks.

How to take PARTRIDGES *feveral
ways, either by* Net, Engine, Driving,
or Setting.

P*Artridges* are naturally cowardly, fearful, fimple,
and foolifh, and therefore moft eafily to be deceived or beguiled with any Train, Bait, Engine, or o-
ther Device whatever, whether by Enticement, Call,
or Stale.

It will be neceffary in the firft place to confider their
Haunts, which are not (like the *Pheafants*) certain,
but various; any covert will ferve their turn, and
fometimes none at all.

The places they moft delight in are the Corn-fields,
efpecially whilft the Corn grows; for under that covert they fhelter, ingender and breed. Neither are
thefe places unfrequented by them when the Corn is
cut down, by reafon of the Grain they finde therein,
efpecially in Wheat-ftubble; and the height thereof
they delight in, being to them as a covert or a fhelter. Now when the Wheat-ftubble is much troden
by Men or Beafts, then they betake themfelves to
the Barley-ftubble, provided it be frefh and un-
troden; and they will in the Furrows amongft
the Clots, Brambles, and long Grafs, hide both
themfelves and Covies, which are fometimes twenty in
number,

number, sometimes five and twenty : nay I have heard of thirty in a Covie.

Now after the Winter-season is come, and that these Stubble-fields are plough'd up, or over-soiled with Cattle, then do these *Partridges* resort into the up-land Meadows, and do lodge in the dead Grass or Fog under Hedges, amongst Mole-hills, or under the Roots of Trees : Sometimes they resort to Copses and Underwoods, especially if any Corn-fields are near adjacent, or where grows Broom, Brakes, Fern, or any Covert whatsoever.

In the Harvest-time, when every field is full of men and Cattle, then you shall finde them in the day-time in the Fallow-fields which are next adjoyning to the Corn-fields, where they lie lurking till the Evening, and then they feed among the Shocks or Sheaves of Corn ; and so they do likewise early in the Morning.

When you know their Haunts according to the scituation of the Country and season of the year, your next care must be to finde them out in their Haunts ; which is done several ways. Some do it by the Eye onely ; and this art can never be taught, but learned by frequent experience, distinguishing thereby the colour of the *Partridge* from that of the Earth, and how and in what manner they lodge and couch together : for which purpose you may come near enough to them, for they are a very lazy Bird, and so unwilling to take the Wing, that you may even set your foot upon them before they will stir, provided you do not stand and gaze on them, but be in continual motion ; otherwise they will spring up and be gone.

There is another way to discover them, and that is by going to their Haunts very early in the Morning, or at the close of the evening, which is called the *Jucking-time*, and there listening for the calling of the

Cock-*Partridge*, which will be very loud and earneſt; and after ſome few Calls the Hen will anſwer, and by this means they meet together; which you ſhall know by their rejoycing and chattering one with another: upon the hearing of which, take your range about them, drawing nearer and nearer to the place you heard them *juck* in; then caſt your eye towards the Furrows of the Lands, and there you will ſoon finde where the Covie lies, and ſo take them as your fancie ſhall lead you.

The beſt, ſafeſt, and eaſieſt way for finding of *Partridges* is by the Call, having firſt learn'd the true and natural Notes of the *Partridge*, knowing how to tune every Note in its proper key, applying them to their due times and ſeaſons.

Being perfect herein, either Mornings or Evenings (all other times being improper) go to their Haunts, and having convey'd your ſelf into ſome ſecret place where you may ſee and not be ſeen, liſten a while if you can hear the *Partridges* call; if you do, anſwer them again in the ſame Note, and as they change or double their Notes, ſo muſt you in like manner: thus continue doing till they draw nearer and nearer unto you. Having them in your view, lay your ſelf on your back, and lie as if you were dead without motion, by which means you may count their whole number.

Having attained to the knowledge of diſcovering them where they lie, the next thing will be a ready way how to catch them.

Of taking Partridges with Nets.

The Nets wherewith you enſnare *Partridges* muſt be every way like your *Pheaſant*-nets, both for length and breadth; onely the Meſh muſt be ſmaller, being made of the ſame Thread, and dyed of the ſame colour.

Having

Having found out the Covie, draw forth your Nets, and taking a large circumference walk a good round pace with a carelefs eye, rather from than towards the *Partridges*, till you have trimmed your Nets, and made them ready for the purpofe : which done, you muft draw in your circumference lefs and lefs, till you come within the length of your Net : then pricking down a Stick about three foot in length, faften one end of the Line of your Net, and make it faft in the Earth as you walk about ; (for you muft make no ftop nor ftay ;) then, letting the Net flip out of your hands, fpread it open as you go, and fo carry and lay it all over the *Partridges*.

But if they fhould lie ftraggling, fo that you cannot cover them all with one Net, then you muft draw forth another, and do with that as you did with the former ; doing fo with a third, if occafion require : having fo done, rufh in upon them, who, affrighted, will fly up, and fo be entangled in the Nets.

How to take Partridges with Bird-lime.

Take of the faireft and largeft Wheat-ftraws you can get, and cut them off between Knot and Knot, and lime them with the ftrongeft Lime. Then go to the Haunts of *Partridges*, and call : if you are anfwered, then prick at fome diftance from you your limed Straws in many crofs rows and ranks crofs the Lands and Furrows, taking in two or three Lands at leaft : then lie clofe and call again, not ceafing till you have drawn them towards you, fo that they be intercepted by the way by your limed Straws, which they fhall no fooner touch but they will be enfnared ; and by reafon they all run together like a brood of Chickens, they will fo befmear and daub one another, that very few of them will efcape.

This

This way of taking *Partridges* is onely to be ufed in Stubble-fields from *Auguft* till *Chriftmas.* But if you will take them in Woods, Paftures, or Meadows, then you muft lime Rods, as was afore expreffed for the *Pheafant*, and ftick them in the ground after the fame manner.

How to drive Partridges.

The Driving of *Partridges* is more delightful than any other way of taking them: The manner of it is thus.

Make an Engine in the form and fafhion of a Horfe, cut out of Canvas, and ftuff it with Straw, or fuch light matter: with this artificial Horfe and your Nets you muft go to the Haunts of *Partridges*, and having found out the Covie, and pitcht your Nets below, you muft go above, and taking the advantage of the Wind, you muft drive downward: Let your Nets be pitcht flope-wife and hovering. Then, having your Face covered with fomething that is green, or of a dark blue, you muft, putting the Engine before you, ftalk towards the *Partridges* with a flow pace, raifing them on their Feet, but not their Wings, and then will they run naturally before you.

If they chance to run a by-way or contrary to your purpofe, then crofs them with your Engine, and by fo facing them they will run into that track you would have them: thus by a gentle flow pace you may make them run and go which way you will, and at laft drive them into your Net, and fo difpofe of them at your pleafure.

How

How to take Partridges *with a Setting-dog.*

There is no art of taking *Partridges* so excellent and pleasant as by the help of a Setting-dog: wherefore, before we proceed to the Sport, we shall give you an account what this Setting-dog is.

You are to understand then, that a Setting-dog is a certain lusty Land-spaniel, taught by nature to hunt the *Partridge* more than any chace whatever, running the fields over with such alacrity and nimbleness, as if there was no limit to his fury and desire, and yet by art under such excellent command, that in the very height of his career by a Hem or sound of his Master's voice he shall stand, gaze about him, look in his Masters face, and observe his directions, whether to proceed, stand still, or retire: nay, when he is even just upon his Prey, that he may even take it up in his mouth, yet his obedience is so framed by art, that presently he shall either stand still, or fall down flat on his Belly, without daring either to make any noise or motion till his Master come to him, and then he will proceed in all things to follow his directions.

Having a Dog thus qualified by art and nature, take him with you where *Partridges* do haunt, there cast off your Dog, and by some word of encouragement which he is acquainted with, engage him to range, but never too far from you; and see that he beat his ground justly and even, without casting about, or flying now here now there, which the mettle of some will do, if not corrected and reproved. And therefore when you perceive this fault, you must presently call him in with a Hem, and so check him that he dare not do the like again for that day; so will he range afterwards with more temperance, ever and anon looking in his Master's

ster's face, as if he would gather from thence whether he did well or ill.

If in your Dog's ranging you perceive him to stop on the sudden, or stand still, you must then make in to him, (for without doubt he hath set the *Partridge*) and as soon as you come to him, command him to go nearer : but if he goes not, but either lies still, or stands shaking of his Tail, as who would say, Here they are under my nose, and withal now and then looks back ; then cease from urging him further, and take your circumference, walking fast with a careless eye, looking straight before the Nose of the Dog, and thereby see how the Covy lie, whether close or straggling.

Then commanding the Dog to lie still, draw forth your Net, and prick one end to the ground, and spread your Net all open, and so cover as many of the *Partridges* as you can ; which done, make in with a noise, and spring up the *Partridges* ; which shall no sooner rise, but they will be intangled in the Net. And if you shall let go the old Cock and Hen, it will not onely be an act like a Gentleman, but a means to increase your Pastime.

How to take RAILS, QUAILS, MOREPOOTS, *&c.*

FRom what is contain'd in the foregoing Chapters, you may collect a method how to take other Fowl, as *Rails*, *Quails*, *Morepoots*, &c. all which are very good flights for *Hawks*.

Their Haunts are much alike with those of the *Partridge* ; onely the *Quail* loves most the Wheat-fields, the

the *Morepoot* moſt the Heath and Foreſt-grounds, and the *Rails* love the long high Graſs where they may lie obſcure.

The way of finding them is like that of the *Partridge*, by the Eye, the Ear, and Haunt : but the chief way of all to finde them out is the Call or Pipe, to which they liſten with ſuch earneſtneſs, that you can no ſooner imitate their Notes, but they will anſwer them, and will purſue the Call with ſuch greedineſs, that they will play and skip about you, nay run over you, eſpecially the *Quail*.

The Notes of the Male and Female differ very much, and therefore you muſt have them both at your command ; and when you hear the Male call, you muſt anſwer in the Female's Note ; and when the Female calls, you muſt anſwer in the Male's Note : and thus you will not fail to have them both come to you, who will gaze and liſten till the Net is caſt over them.

The way of taking theſe Birds is the ſame with that of the *Partridge*, and they may be taken with Nets or Lime, either Buſh or Rod, or Engine, which you muſt ſtalk with ; or by the Setting-dog, which I ſhall treat of in the next Chapter.

How to elect and train a SETTING-DOG *from a Whelp till he come to perfection.*

THe Dog which you elect for Setting muſt have a perfect and good Sent, and be naturally addicted to the hunting of Feathers. And this Dog may be either Land-ſpaniel, Water-ſpaniel, or Mungrel of them both ; either the Shallow-flewed Hound, Tumbler, Lurcher,

Lurcher, or fmall baftard Maftiff. But there is none better than the Land-fpaniel, being of a good and nimble fize, rather fmall than grofs, and of a courageous mettle ; which though you cannot difcern being young, yet you may very well know from a right breed, which have been known to be ftrong, lufty and nimble Rangers, of active Feet, wanton Tails, and bufie Noftrils; whofe Tail was without wearinefs, their Search without changeablenefs, and whom no delight did tranfport beyond fear or obedience.

When you have made choice of your Dog, begin to inftruct him about four moneths old, or fix moneths at the uttermoft.

The firft thing that you fhall teach your Dog, is to make him loving and familiar with you, knowing you from any other perfon, and following you where-ever you go. To effect this the better, let him receive his food as near as you can from no other hand but your own ; and when you correct him to keep him in awe, do it rather with words than blows.

When you have fo inftructed your Dog that he will follow none but your felf, and can diftinguifh your frown from your fmile, and fmooth words from rough, you muft then teach him to couch and lie down clofe to the ground ; firft, by laying him often on the ground, and crying, *Lie clofe.* When he hath done any thing to your minde and pleafure, you muft then reward him with a piece of Bread : if otherwife, cha-ftife him with words, but few blows.

After this, you muft teach him to come creeping un-to you with his Belly and Head clofe upon the ground, as far or as little way as you fhall think fit : and this you may do by faying, *Come nearer, come nearer,* or the like ; and at firft, till he underftand your meaning, by fhewing him a piece of Bread or fome other

food

food to entice him to you. And this obferve in his creeping to you, if he offer to raife his Body or Head, you muft not onely thruft the rifing part down, but threaten him with your angry voice; which if he feem to flight, then adde a fharp jerk or two with a Whip-cord-lafh.

You muft often renew his Leffons till he be very perfect, ftill encouraging him when he does well.

If you walk abroad with him, and he take a fancy to range, even when he is moft bufie fpeak to him, and in the height of his paftime make him fall upon his Belly and lie clofe, and after that make him come creeping to you.

After this teach him to lead in a String or Line, and to follow you clofe at your heels without trouble or ftraining of his Collar.

By that time he hath learned thefe things aforefaid, I conceive the Dog may be a twelvemonth old ; at which time, the feafon of the year being fit, take him into the field and permit him to range, but ftill in obedience to your command. But if through wantonnefs he chance to babble or open without caufe, you muft then correct him fharply, either with a Whipcord-lafh , or biting him hard at the Roots of his Ears.

Having brought him to a good temper and juft obedience , then, as foon as you fee him come upon the Haunt of any *Partridge*, (which you fhall know by his greater eagernefs in hunting, as alfo by a kinde of whimpering and whining in his voice, being very defirous to open, but not daring)you fhall fpeak to him, bidding him take heed, or the like : but if notwithftanding he either rufh in and fpring the *Partridge*, or opens, and fo the *Partridge* efcapeth , you muft then correct him feverely, and caft him off again, and let him hunt in fome Haunt where you know a Covie lies,

ard

and fee whether he hath mended his fault : And if you catch any with your Nets, give him the Heads, Necks, and Pinions for his future encouragement.

Many more obfervations there are, which are too numerous here to recite; wherefore I fhall defift, and give you an account of a Water-dog, and fo finifh this prefent Difcourfe.

How to train a W A T E R - D O G, and the ufe thereof.

I Shall begin with the beft proportion of a *Water-dog*, and firft of his Colour. Although fome do attribute much to the colour, yet experience lets us know they are uncertain Obfervations.

To proceed then, your Dog may be any colour and yet excellent; but chufe him of Hair long and curled, not loofe and fhagged : his Head muft be round and curled, his Ears broad and hanging, his Eye full, lively and quick, his Nofe very fhort, his Lip Hound-like, his Chaps with a full fet of ftrong Teeth , his Neck thick and fhort, his Breaft fharp, his Shoulders broad, his Fore-legs ftraight, his Chine fquare, his Buttocks round, his Belly gaunt, his Thighs brawny, &c.

For the Training this Dog, you cannot begin too foon with him ; and therefore as foon as he can lap you muft teach him to couch and lie down, not daring to ftir from that pofture without leave. Obferve in his firft teaching to let him eat nothing till he deferve it; and let him have no more Teachers, Feeders, Cherifhers, or Correctors but one; and do not alter that word you firft ufe in his information, for the Dog takes notice of the found, not the language.

When

When you have acquainted him with the word fuitable to his Leſſon, you muſt then teach him to know the word of Reprehenſion, which at firſt ſhould not be uſed without a Jerk. You muſt alſo uſe words of Cheriſhing, to give him encouragement when he does well : and in all theſe words you muſt be conſtant, and let them be attended with ſpitting in his mouth, or cheriſhing of the hand. There is alſo a word of Advice, inſtructing him when he does amiſs.

Having made him underſtand theſe ſeveral words, you muſt next teach him to lead in a String or Collar orderly, not running too forward, nor hanging backward. After this you muſt teach him to come cloſe at your heels without leading ; for he muſt not range by any means, unleſs it be to beat Fowl from their Covert, or to fetch the wounded.

In the next place you muſt teach him to fetch and carry any thing you throw out of your hands. And firſt try him with the Glove, ſhaking it over his Head, and making him ſnap at it ; and ſometimes let him hold it in his Mouth, and ſtrive to pull it from him ; and at laſt throw it a little way, and let him worry it on the ground : and ſo by degrees make him bring it you where-ever you throw it. From the Glove you may teach him to fetch Cudgels, Bags, Nets, *&c.*

If you uſe him to carry dead Fowl, it will not be amiſs ; for by that means he will not tear or bruiſe what Fowl you ſhoot.

Having perfected this Leſſon, drop ſomething behinde you which the Dog doth not ſee ; and being gone a little way from it, ſend him back to ſeek it, by ſaying, *Back, I have loſt.* If he ſeem amazed, point with your Finger, urging him to ſeek out, and leave him not till he hath done it. Then drop ſomething

at

at a greater diftance, and make him finde out that too, till you have brought him to go back a mile.

Now may you train him up for your Gun, making him ftalk after you ftep by ftep, or elfe couch and lie clofe till you have fhot.

Many more neceffary Rules there are, which for brevity fake I muft omit.

The laft ufe of the Water-dog is in moulting-time, when Wild-fowl caft their Feathers and are unable to fly, which is between Summer and Autumn : at this time bring your Dog to their Coverts, and hunt them out into the Stream, and there with your Nets fur-prize them, driving them into them ; for at this time Sheep will not drive more eafily. And though fome may object, that this fickly time is unfeafonable ; yet if they confider what excellent food thefe Fowl will prove when cramm'd, the taking of them may be very excufable. I have eaten of them after they have been fed a while with Livers of Beafts, Whey, Curds, Bar-ley, pafte, fcalded Bran, and fuchlike ; they have pro-ved exceeding fat, and have tafted not fo fifhy as they do by their natural feeding, but exceeding fweet, and deferve to be preferred before any Fowl whatever.

How

How to take, preserve, and keep all sorts of Singing-birds that are commonly known in England. *Giving also an account of their Nature, Breeding, Feeding, Diseases of the same, with their Remedies.*

IN the preceding Difcourfe I have given you a Summary account of the feveral ways and artifices which are ufed to take either Land-fowl, or Fowl properly belonging to the Water. Upon fecond thoughts I look upon this Third Part of the *Gentleman's Recreation*, called a *Treatife of Fowling*, imperfect, if I adde not now what I omitted before ; a fmall Effay as to the Taking, Preferving, and Keeping all forts of Singing-Birds commonly known in thefe his Majefties three Kingdoms. They are thus called.

The *Nightingal.*	The *Starling.*	The *Gold-finch.*
The *Black-bird.*	The *Tit-lark.*	The *Green-finch.*
The *Wood-lark.*	The *Bull-finch.*	The *Wren.*
The *Linnet.*	The *Canary-bird*	The *Red ftart.*
The *Chaff-finch.*	The *Throftle.*	The *Hedgefparrow.*
The *Rob. Red-breaft*	The *Skie-lark.*	

Laftly, their Difeafes and Cures.

Of

Of the NIGHTINGAL.

ACcording to the judgement of moſt men the *Nightingale* carries the Bell from all other Singing-birds, opening her charming Mouth not onely ſweetly, but with much variety of pleaſant Notes : It is but a ſmall Bird, yet hath a loud voice ; which made the Poet call her——*Vox, & præterea nihil.* They are ſo well known, a deſcription of them would be needleſs ; and are not onely eſteemed of here, but in *Italy* and other parts.

They appear to us at the latter end of *March*, or beginning of *April*, and very few know where they inhabit all the Winter ; ſome think they ſleep all that ſeaſon.

She makes her Neſt commonly about two foot above ground, either in thick Quick-ſet-hedges, or in Beds of Nettles where old Quick-ſet hath been thrown together. She hatcheth her young ones about the beginning of *May*, and naturally delights to frequent cool places, where ſmall Brooks are garniſhed with pleaſant Groves, and Quick-ſet-hedges are not far diſtant.

That *Nightingale* which in my opinion is the beſt to keep, is he that is the earlieſt Bird of the Spring ; for he will ſing the better, having more time to hear the old one ſing than thoſe that are hatched later.

The young *Nightingales* muſt be taken out of their Neſts when they are indifferently well fledg'd in a mediocrity : for if well feathered, they will become ſullen ; and if too little, they are ſo tender the cold will kill them.

For

For their meat give them lean Beef, Sheeps-heart, or Bullocks-heart, taking away firſt the fat Skin that covereth it, and take away the Sinews; after this ſoak the like quantity of white Bread in water, and ſqueeze out ſome of the Water; then mince it ſmall; then feed them with a Stick, taking upon the point thereof the quantity of a Grey Pea, and give every one of them three or four ſuch gobbets in an hour, as long as they ſhall endure to be in the Neſt: when they are able to fly out of the Neſt, then put them into a Cage with ſeveral Pearches for them to ſit upon, and line them with ſome green Bays, for they are very ſubject to the Cramp at firſt; and at the bottom of the Cage put in ſome Moſs or Hay, as well for other Birds as the *Nightingale* : it is ſafe to line their Cages againſt Winter, or keep them in ſome warm place. When they are firſt Caged, continue for a while to put ſome of their meat by them mingled with Ants, which will induce them to feed themſelves.

In the Summer you muſt feed them every day with freſh meat, otherwiſe it will quickly grow ſtale or ſtink. When they begin to moult, give them half Egg hard boiled, and half Sheeps-heart mingled with Saffron and Water. Here note, Duck-eggs will kill them : you may give them ſometimes red-Worms, Caterpillars, and Hog-lice; Meal-worms make them familiar, ſuffering them to take them out of your hand.

The way of taking Old and Young is thus : For the Young, obſerve where the Cock ſings; and if he ſings long the Hen is not far from that place, who oftentimes betrays her Offspring by being too careful; for when you come near her Neſt ſhe will *Sweet* and *Cur*: if notwithſtanding this you cannot finde her Neſt, ſtick a Meal-worm or two upon a Thorn, and

and then lying down or ſtanding, obſerve which way it is carried by the Old one, and drawing near you will hear the young ones when ſhe feeds them. When you have found out the Neſt, touch not the young ; for if you do, they will not tarry in the Neſt.

The way to take *Branchers*, by others called *Puſhers*, (becauſe when throughly fledg'd the Old ones puſh them out of the Neſt) I ſay, you muſt take them after this manner : When you have found where they are, which you ſhall know by their *Curring* and *Sweeting* ; (for if you call true, they will anſwer you immediately) having your Tackle all ready, ſcrape, in the Ditch or Bank-ſide, the Earth about three quarters of a yard ſquare, that it may look freſh ; then take a Bird-trap or Net-trap, which you muſt make after this faſhion.

How to make a Net-trap for Nightingales.

Take a Net made of green Silk or Thread, about the compaſs of a yard , made after the faſhion of a Shove-net for Fiſhes ; then get ſome large Wyre, and bending it round, joyn both ends, which you muſt put into a ſhort Stick about an Inch and an half long ; then you muſt have a piece of Iron with two Cheeks and a hole on each ſide, through which you muſt put ſome fine Whip-cord three or four times double, that ſo it may hold the piece of Wood the better unto which the ends of the Wyre are put, and with a Button on each ſide the Iron twiſt the Whip-cord, that ſo the Net may play the quicker : you muſt faſten the Net to the Wyre as you do a Shove-net to the Hoop ; then get a Board of the compaſs of your Wyre , and joyn your two cheeks of Iron at the handle of your Board ; then make a hole in the middle of your Board ; and put a piece of Stick of about two Inches long, and a Hole at the Top of your Stick, which you muſt

have

have a Peg to put in with two Wyres, an Inch and half long, to ſtick your Meal-worm upon; then tie a String in the middle of the top of your Net, drawing the Net up, having an eye at the end of the handle to put your Thread through, pull it till it ſtands upright, then pull it through the hole of the Stick that ſtands in the middle of your Board, and put your Peg in the hole, and that will hold the String that the Net cannot fall down : you muſt put two Worms upon the Wyres, before you put it into the hole , and ſet it as gently as you can, that it may fall with the firſt touch of the *Nightingale* : When you have your Net and Worm ready, having firſt ſcraped the place, then put ſome Ants in your Trap-cage, and upon your Board put ſome Worms upon Thorns, and ſet them at the bottom of your Trap-cage, little holes being made for the ſame purpoſe to ſtick in the ends of your Thorns : Then plant your Trap near to the place where you heard them call, either in the Ditch, or by the Bank-ſide, or corner of a Hedge, and then walk away; you may ſet what number of Trap-cages you think convenient. Do what is here propoſed, and you need not doubt the having of your deſires ſatisfied.

Having taken your *Nightingales*, (the time is in *July* or *Auguſt*) tie the ends of their Wings with ſome brown Thread, that ſo they may be diſenabled to hurt themſelves by beating their tender bodies againſt the top and Wyres of the Cage.

Let the Cage be covered above half with green Bays, and for four or five daies let him be very little diſturbed by company; but withal forget not to feed them half a dozen times every day with Sheeps-heart and Egg ſhred very fine, and mingle red Ants therewith, and a few Red Earth-worms would not do amiſs.

Here note, that no *Nightingale* at firſt taking will eat any other food than what is living, as Worms, Ants,

Ants, Flies, or Caterpillars ; which through fullenneſs if he will not eat, then take him out, and upon the point of a Stick (firſt opening his Bill) give him four or five gobbets one after another ; then turn him into the Cage, ſtrowing the bottom thereof with Egg and minced Sheeps-heart mingled with ſome Piſmires. Theſe *Nightingales* that are taken at this time of the year will not ſing till the middle of *October*, and then they will hold in ſong till the middle of *June* : But the *Nightingales* that are taken from the firſt of *April* to the twentieth, are the beſt Birds for Song in the whole Univerſe ; and theſe are taken with Trap-cages or Trap-nets, as the Branchers aforeſaid, in *June*, *July*, and *Auguſt*. Here obſerve, that Neſtlings nor Branchers (except they have an old Bird to ſing over them) have not the true Song for the firſt twelve moneths. When you have ſo tamed them that they begin to *Cur* and *Sweet* with chearfulneſs, and record ſoftly to themſelves, it is a certain ſigne that they eat , and then you need not trouble your ſelf with feeding them ; but if they ſing before they feed , they commonly prove moſt excellent Birds : Thoſe Birds that are long a feeding, and make no *Curring* nor *Sweeting*, are not worth the keeping. If you have a Bird that will flutter and bolt up his head in the night againſt the top of the Cage, keep him not , for he is not onely good for nothing, but his bad example will teach the beſt of your Birds to do the like.

Now to the intent you may not keep Hens inſtead of Cocks, and ſo not onely be at uſeleſs charge, but be fruſtrated of your expectation, you ſhall diſtinguiſh their Sexes by theſe obſervations. The Cock in the judgement of ſome is both longer and bigger : others ſay the Cock hath a greater Eye, a longer Bill, and a Tail more reddiſh : others pretend to know them by the Pinion of the Wing, and Feathers on the Head. Theſe

These Rules I look not upon as infallible , having found them contrary to truth by my own experience : Now to undeceive you, take thefe true Experimental Obfervations. Firft , take notice that if any of your Neftlings (before they can feed themfelves) do Record a little to themfelves, and in their Recording you perceive their Throats to wag, you need not doubt that they are Cocks; but when they come to feed themfelves, the Hen will Record as well as the Cock; therefore mark them when young, for it is very difficult to diftinguifh afterwards.

Branchers, whether Cocks or Hens (when taken and do feed themfelves) will Record; but the Cock does it much longer, louder, and oftner.

The beft fort of *Nightingales* frequent High-ways, Orchards, and fing clofe by houfes : thefe when taken will feed fooneft, being more acquainted with the company of people; and after their feeding will grow familiar, and fing fpeedily. Obferve, not to untie too foon the Wings of your *Nightingale*; for if he be not very familiar and tame when he is untied, he will be apt to beat himfelf againft the Cage, and fo fpoil himfelf.

Now as to their Difeafes and Cures, obferve this, that at the latter end of *Auguft* they grow very fat either abroad or in a Cage : when it begins to abate when they do not fing, it is a dangerous figne; wherefore to remedy this, keep them very warm, giving them Saffron in their meat or water : when you perceive the growth of their fat, purge them thrice a Week for a Moneth, either with a Worm which is found in *Pigeon*-houfes, or with a fpeckled Spider, which you may finde plentifully about Vines, Currans, or Goofe-berry-bufhes in *Auguft*, and at no time elfe. If they are melancholy, put into their drinking-pot fome Liquorifh with a little white Sugar-candy, giving them to feed

on

on Sheeps-heart shred small, some Meal-worms, and Eggs mingled with Pismires. It is strange that some of these Birds when fat will fast three weeks, which I have known; but it is better when they eat.

Nightingales kept in a Cage two or three years, are subject to the Gout; for their Cure, take fresh Butter and anoint their Feet four or five daies, and they will be well again. Here note, that for want of keeping them clean, their Feet are clog'd, and then their Claws will rot off, and are subject to Gout and Cramp, and will take no delight in themselves; to prevent these mischiefs, put dry Sand into the bottom of their Cages.

They are likewise troubled with Apostumes and breaking out about their Eyes and Neb; for which, use Capons-grease. And thus much of the Diseases of the *Nightingale*.

Of the CANARY-BIRD.

THough many of these Birds are lately brought from *Germany,* and therefore are called by the name of that Country, yet undoubtedly their Original proceeded from the *Canary*-Islands. They are in colour much like our *Green-birds*, but differ much in their Song and Nature; and in this they differ from all Birds: For as others are subject to be fat, the Cocks of these never are, by reason of the greatness of their mettle, and their lavish singing; either of these will not suffer him to keep hardly flesh upon his back.

The best of them are shaped long, standing straight and boldly.

Before you buy either these *German* or *Canary-birds,* hear them sing, and then you will know how to please your

your Ear or fancy, either with Sweet-song, Lavish-note, or Long-song, which is best, having most variety of Notes. Some like those that *whisk* and *chew* like unto a *Tit-lark*; others are for those that begin like a *Skie-lark*, and so continue their Song with a long, yet sweet Note; a third sort are for those that begin their Song with the *Skie-lark*, and then run upon the Notes of the *Nightingale*, which is very pleasant if he does it well: The last is for a loud Note and lavish, regarding no more in it than a noise.

If you would know whether your *Canary-bird* be in health before you purchase him, take him out of the Store-cage, and put him into a clean Cage alone; where if he stand boldly without crouching, without shrinking Feathers, and his Eyes looking brisk and chearfully; these are good signes of a healthy Bird: But now observe, if he bolts his Tail like a *Nightingale* after he hath dunged, it shews he is not well; though he seem lively for the present, there is some distemper near attending: likewise if he either dung very thin and watry, or of a slimy white and no blackness in it; these are dangerous signes of death approaching.

These Birds are subject to many Diseases, as Impostumes which afflict their head, and are of a yellow colour, causing a great heaviness, and withal a falling from the Pearch, and death ensuing if this malady be not speedily cured. The most approved cure is to make an Ointment of fresh Butter and Capons-greace melted together, and anoint therewith the Bird's Impostume three or four daies together: if it become soft, open it gently and let out the matter; then anoint the place with some of the same Ointment, and this will immediately cure him: during the cure give him Figs, and Liquorish, and white Sugar-candy in his Water.

Canary-birds above three years old are called *Runts*;

at

at two years old they are called *Eriffs* ; and thofe of the firft year are called *Branchers* ; when they are new flown and cannot feed themfelves, they are called *Pufhers* ; and thofe that are brought up by hand, *Neftlings*. Now fince there are but few *Canary-birds* which breed in *England*, it being fo great a trouble to look after them, I fhall here infert nothing concerning the ordering when they intend or begin to build ; what things are neceffary for them when they begin to breed ; how to order them when they have young ones ; or how to breed the young ones when taken out of the Neft : Thofe who intend to be informed of every thing hereunto belonging, may eafily be inftructed by applying themfelves to feveral *Germans* in and about the City, who make it their bufinefs to breed *Canary-birds* after the beft *(German)* fafhion.

Of the BLACK-BIRD.

AS fome do efteem the *Nightingale* to be the beft Singing-bird in the World, fo in my opinion the *Black-bird* is the worft ; yet they are as frequently kept as their betters, and are in great eftimation amongft the Vulgar ; for no other reafon that I know, than for the loudnefs and coarfnefs of his Song, as they are Borifh in their Speech, and have little but rufticity in their Conditions. To be fhort, he is better to be eaten than kept, and is much fweeter to the palate when dead, than to the ear when living.

She builds her Neft upon old Stumps of Trees by Ditch-fides, or in thick Hedges. As they begin betimes, that is, in the beginning of *March*, (when many times the Woods are full of Snow) fo they breed

often

often, that is, three or four times a year, according as they loose their Nest.

The young *Black-birds* are brought up almost with any meat whatsoever; but above all, they love Ground-worms, Sheeps-heart, hard Eggs, and white Bread and Milk mixt together.

This Bird sings somewhat more than three moneths in the year; his Note as I said is harsh, therefore to adde a value to him, let him be taught to whistle; yet put Song and whistle together, in my judgement it is fitter for a large Inne than a Lady's Chamber.

Of the THROSTLE.

OF *Throstles* there be five kinds; the *Mistle-throstle*, the *Northern-throstle* or *Felfare*, the *Wind-throstle*, the *Wood-song-throstle*, and the *Heath-throstle*.

The first is the largest of all the five, and the most beautiful; it feeds for the most part on the Berries of Mistletoe: and since that they are so good against the Falling-sickness and Convulsions, these *Throstles* when dried and pulverized and drank in the water of Mistletoe, or Black-cherry-water, are much more effectual against those two distempers. He sings but little, and therefore though the young ones are easie to be brought up being hardy, yet he is not worth the keeping; for his Notes are rambling and confused, yet not lavish neither.

The second is the *Felfare*, who comes into *England* before *Michaelmas*, and goes away about the beginning of *March*. In hard weather they feed on Hips and Haws; but when it is indifferently warm, there being neither Frost nor Snow on the ground, they feed on young Grass and Worms.   They

They breed upon certain Rocks near the Scotiſh Shore three or four times a year, and are there in very great numbers : They are not ſo fit for the Cage as the Spit, having a moſt lamentable untun'd chattering tone : in Froſt and Snow they are very fat, and then are moſt delicate food ; but being killed in open weather, they are ſo bitter that they are not worth the eating.

Thirdly, the *Wind-throſtle*, (or *Whindle*) which travels with the *Felfare* out of the North, is a ſmaller bird, with a dark red under his Wing. He breeds in Woods and Shaws as *Song-throſtles* uſe to do, and hath an indifferent Song, exceeding the two former; but yet they are fitter for the Pot or Spit than for a Cage or Avery.

The fourth is the *Wood-ſong-throſtle*, and ſings moſt incomparably, both laviſhly, and with variety of Notes : To adde to his eſtimation, he ſings at leaſt nine of the twelve moneths in the year.

They build about the ſame time, place, and manner as the *Black-bird* does : her policy in the building of her Neſt is much to be admired, ſince the compoſure cannot be mended by the art of Man - beſides the curious building, ſhe leaves a little hole in the bottom of her Neſt, as I conceive to let out the Water if a violent ſhower ſhould come, that ſo her Eggs or young ones may not be drowned.

They go very ſoon to Neſt if the Weather favour them, and breed three times a year, that is, in *March* or *April*, *May* and *June*; but the firſt Birds uſually prove the beſt.

Take them in the Neſt when they are fourteen daies old, and keep them warm and clean, not ſuffering them to ſit on their Dung, but ſo contrive it that they dung over the Neſt. Feed them with raw meat and ſome Bread chopped together

E   with

with bruised Hemp-feed, wetting your Bread before you mingle it with the meat.

Being throughly fledg'd, put them into a Cage where they may have room enough, with two or three Pearches, and some Mofs at the bottom of the Cage, to keep them clean; for otherwise they will be troubled with the Cramp, and for want of delighting in themselves, the finging will be spoil'd.

Bread and Hemp-feed is as good food for them as can be given; and be mindful of turnifhing them at leaft twice a week with frefh water, that they may bathe and prune themfelves therein, otherwife they will not thrive.

The fifth and laft is the *Heath throftle*, which is the leaft we have in *England*, having a dark breaft. Some are of opinion that this Bird exceeds the *Song-throftle*, having better Notes, and neater plume.

The Hen builds by the Heath-fide in a Furz-bufh, or Stump of an old Haw-thorn, and makes not Shaws and Woods her haunt as other *Throftles* do. She begins not to breed till the middle of *April*, and breeds but twice in a year; and if kept clean and well fed, will fing three parts in four of the whole year. Their manner of breeding is in like-fort as the former.

To know the Cock from the Hen, according to old Country-judgement, is to chufe the top-bird of the Neft, which commonly is moft fledg'd. Others think that to be the Cock which hath the largeft Eye, and moft fpeckles on his breaft. Others chufe the Cock by the pinion of his Wing, if it hath a very dark black that goes acrofs it; but above all, chufe him thus: If his Gullet be white with black ftreaks on each fide, his fpots on his Breaft large and black, having his head of a light fhining brown, with black ftreaks under each Eye and upon the pinion of the Wing; thefe are the beft marks that ever I obferved.

Of

Of the ROBIN-RED-BREAST.

IT is the opinion of some, that this little King of Birds for sweetness of Note comes not much short of the *Nightingale.* It is a very tender Bird, and therefore must have its Cage lined. They breed very early in the Spring, and commonly thrice a year.

When the young are about ten daies old, take them from the Old ones, and keep them in a little Bower-basket: if they tarry long in the Nest, they will be sullen, and therefore more difficultly brought up: you must feed them as you feed the *Nightingale* in all respects: finding them grow strong, put them into a Cage, put Moss in the bottom thereof, and let them stand warm.

The way of taking a *Robin-red-breast* is so easie and common, that every Boy knows how to take him in a Pit-fall; but with a Trap-cage and a Meal-worm you may take half a score in a day: hearing them sing, keep those Birds which most delight you. If you take any without hearing them sing, thus you shall know whether he be Cock or Hen; if a Cock, his breast will be of a darker red, and his red will go farther up upon the Head than the Hens.

Of the WREN.

THis Bird in my opinion is a pretty sweet dapper Songster, being of a nature cheerful; as he is pleasant to the Ear, so he is to the Eye; and when he

sings

sings cocks up his Tail, and throws out his Notes with so much alacrity and pleasure, that I know not any bird of its bigness more delights the sense of hearing.

This bird builds twice a year, about the latter end of *April*, in Shrubs where Ivy grows thick, and sometimes in old Hovels and Barns. They lay a numerous quantity of Eggs; and I can assure you I have seen a Nest containing two and twenty: herein are two things greatly to be wondred at: first, that so small a bird should cover such a great quantity of Eggs; secondly, when they have hatched, to feed them all, and not to miss one bird, and in the dark also.

Their second time of breeding is in the middle of *June:* of either breed, what you intend to keep must be taken out of the Nest at thirteen or fourteen daies old. Let their food be Sheeps-heart and Egg minced very small, or Calves or Heifers-heart; but be sure to clear them of the Fat and Sinews, which must be a general rule to be observed for all Meat-birds. Feed them in the Nest every day very often, but a little at a time; let the Instrument you feed them with be a Stick; and when you observe them to pick it off of their own accord, then cage them, and putting meat to them in a little Pan, and about the sides of the Cage, to entice them to eat; however, have a care to feed them too, lest they neglect themselves and die. When they can feed themselves very well, give them once in three daies a Spider or two. You may teach them to whistle tunes if you so desire it; for they are easily taught, being a bird that's very docible. Here note, if they be fed with Paste, they will live longer than if they fed upon Hearts. The brownest and largest of the young *Wrens* are the Cocks.

Of the WOOD-LARK.

SOme prefer the *Wood-lark* before the *Nightingale*; but it is of this bird as all others, some are more excellent in length and sweetness of Song.

This bird breeds the soonest of any we have, by reason of his extraordinary mettlesomeness: and therefore if they are not taken in the beginning of *February* at least, they grow so rank, that they will prove good for nothing.

The places this Bird most delights in are gravelly grounds, and Hills lying towards the Orient, and in Oat-stubs. Their building is in your Laiers grounds, where the Grass is rank and russet, making their Nests of Bennet-grass, or dead Grass of the field under some large Tuffet, to shelter them from the injury of the Weather.

This Bird hath very excellent pleasant Notes, with great variety, insomuch that I have observed some have had almost thirty several Notes; which if they sing lavish, is a most ravishing melody or harmony, if the *Nightingale* joyn in consort.

These Birds are never bred from the Nests as ever I could hear: I have several times attempted it, but to no purpose; for notwithstanding my greatest care, they died in a Week, either of the Cramp or Scowring.

The times of the year to take them are *June*, *July*, *August*; and then they are called young *Branchers*, having not yet moulted. They are taken likewise at the latter end of *September*; but having then moulted, the young and old are not distinguishable.

Lastly

Lastly, they are taken from the beginning of *January* to the latter end of *February*, at which time they are all coupled and returned to their Breeding-places.

The way to take them in *June, July*, and *August*, is with an Hobby, after this manner: get out in a dewy Morning, and go to the sides of some Hills which lie to the rising of the Sun, where they most usually frequent; and having sprung them, observe where they fall; then surround them twice or thrice with your Hobby on your Fist, causing him to hover when you draw near, by which means they will lie still till you clap a Net over them, which you carry on the point of a Stick.

If three or four go together, take a Net like one made for *Partridges*: when you go with a Setting-dog onely, the Mesh must be smaller, that is, a *Lark*-mesh; and then your Hobby to the *Lark* is like a Setting-dog to *Partridges*, and with your Net at one draught you may take the whole flock.

The *Wood lark* that is taken in *June, July*, and *August* will sing presently, but will not last long, by reason of their moulting. That which is taken in *January* and *February* will sing in five or six daies, or sooner; and these are the best, being taken in full stomack, and are more perfect in their Song than those taken at other seasons.

If in the Cage you finde him grow poor at the beginning of the Spring, give him every two or three daies a turff of Three-leav'd-grafs, (as is used to the *Skie-lark*) and boil him a Sheeps-heart and mince it small, mingling it among his Bread, Egg, and Hemp-seed, which will cause him to thrive extraordinarily.

If he be troubled with Lice, (a Distemper he is commonly afflicted withal) take him out of the Cage, and

smoak

fmoak him with Tobacco ; give him frefh Gravel, and fet him in a hot place where the Sun fhines , and this will cure him if he have ftrength to bask in the Sand.

If you would have him fing lavifh, feed him with Sheeps-heart, Egg, Bread and Hemp-feed mixt together, and put into his Water a little Liquorifh, white Sugar-candy, and Saffron : let this be done once a week.

Upon the firft taking of your *Wood-lark* thus muft you do : you muft put into your Cage two Pans, one for minc'd Meat, and another for Oat-meal and whole Hemp-feed. Then, having boiled an Egg hard, take the crums of white Bread, the like quantity of Hemp-feed pounded in a Mortar, and mingle your Bread and it with your Egg minced very fmall, and give it him. Let there be at the bottom of the Cage fine red Gravel, and let it be fhifted every week at fartheft ; for he delights to bask in the Sand, which will not be convenient if foul'd with his Dung. Let the Pearch of the Cage be lined with green Bays, or which is better, make a Pearch of a Mat : and left they fhould not finde the Pan fo foon as they fhould do, to prevent Famine, ftrew upon the Sand fome Oat-meal and Hemp-feed.

How to know the Cock, is thus : firft, the largenefs and length of his Call : Secondly, his tall walking : Thirdly, at Evenings the doubling of his Note, which Artifts call *Cuddling* ; but if you hear him fing ftrong, you cannot be deceived.

Here note, that if a Bird fings not that is taken in *February* and *January* within one moneth after, you may conclude him not worth the keeping, or elfe is an Hen infallibly.

The *Wood-lark* as it is naturally endewed with incomparable Notes, fo it is a tender Bird, and difficult to be kept ; but if rightly ordered, and well look'd to,

E 4   will

will be a most delightful Songster to its Master, growing better and better every year even to the very last.

These Birds are very subject to the Cramp, Giddiness in the Head, and to Louziness. The best remedy to prevent the Cramp, is to shift the Cage often with fresh Gravel, otherwise the Dung will clog to their Feet, which causeth the Cramp. The Giddiness of the Head proceedeth from feeding upon much Hemp-seed: perceiving this distemper, give him some Gentles, (the common Bait for Fisher-men) Hoglice, Emmets and their Eggs, with Liquorish, all put into water, will serve in their stead, and will cure immediately. Louziness (which causeth leanness in this bird) is cured as I said before by smoaking Tobacco.

Of the SKIE-LARK: The several ways to take them; and when taken, how to order them.

THere is a great difference between one *Skie-lark* and another; for one may not be worth two pence, when another shall be worth two pounds.

This Bird is very hardy, and will live upon any food in a manner, so that he have but once a week a Turff of Three-leav'd-grass. As the *Wood lark* hath young ones in *March*, the *Skie-lark* hath rarely any till the middle of *May*. They commonly build in Corn, or thick high Grass Meadows, and seldom have more than four: take them at a fortnight old, and at first give them minced Sheeps-heart with a chopt hard Egg mingled: when they can feed alone, give them Bread, Hemp-seed, and Oat-meal; let the Bread be mingled

gled with Egg, and the Hemp-feed bruifed: Let
them have Sand in the bottom of their Cage; Pearches
therein are to no purpofe.

As the *Wood-lark* is taken with Net and Hobby,
fo may the *Skie-lark* be taken alfo. They are taken
likewife in dark nights with a Trammel; this Net
is about fix and thirty yards long, and fix yards over,
run through with fix ribs of Pack-thread; which ribs
at the ends are put upon two Poles fixteen foot long,
made taper at each end, and fo is carried between two
men half a yard from the ground; every fix fteps
touching the ground, to caufe the Birds to fly up,
otherwife you may carry the Net over them without
difturbing them: hearing them fly againft the Net,
clap it down, and they are fafe under it. This is a
very murdering Net, taking all forts of Birds that
it comes near, as *Partridges, Quails, Woodcocks, Snipes,
Felfares,* and what not, almoft in every dark night.

The next way of taking them is with a pair of
Day-nets and a Glafs, which is incomparable paftime
in a frofty morning. Thefe Nets are commonly feven foot deep, and fifteen long, knit with your
French-Mefh, and very fine Thread. Thefe Nets
take all forts of fmall Birds that come within their
compafs, as *Bunting-larks,* and *Linnets* in abundance.

Thefe *Larks* are alfo taken by a Low-bell, with a
great light carried in a Tub both by one man, and the
Net by another; this Bell and Light fo amazeth them,
that they lie as dead, and ftir not till the Net overcaft
them. By this Bell are all forts of Fowls and Birds
taken, as *Partridge* and *Pheafant;* and if the Bell be
lowd, or very deep, *Duck, Mallard, Wood-cock,* and
Snipe may be taken.

The laft way of taking *Larks* is in a great
Snow, by taking an hundred or two hundred yards

of

of Pack-thread, faftning at every fix Inches a Noofe made with Horfe-hair ; two hairs are fufficient. Now fince I have already defcribed this way of taking *Larks*, I fhall defift, and onely inform you that thofe *Larks* you intend to preferve for finging, muft be taken in *October* or *November* : chufe the ftraighteft, largeft, and loftieft Bird, and he that hath moft white on his Tail, for thefe are the marks of the Cock. Obferve in this Bird , as in all others, that you give no falt-meat, nor Bread feafon'd with Salt.

Of the LINNET.

THeir Nefts are ufually in Thorn-bufhes and Furz-bufhes; and fome of the hotter fort of them will breed four times a year. The young ones may be taken at four daies old, if you intend to teach them to whiftle, or learn the Song of other Birds : for being fo young, they know not the tune of the old Bird. Being fo young, keep them very warm, and feed them often, and a little at a time : there muft be bruifed foaked Rape-feeds, with the like quantity of white bread, of which there muft be frefh made every day to prevent fowring, which will make them fcowr to death : let not their meat be too dry, for fear of being Vent-burnt. If you intend they fhall whiftle, do you whiftle to them in the time of Feeding , being more apt to learn before they can crack hard feeds. Whatever bird you intend your *Linnet* fhall learn his Notes of, hang him under it, and he will perfectly imitate him : nay fo docible this bird is, as I have been credibly infor-med, that fome of them have been taught to fpeak. To know the Cock from the Hen, muft not always

be

be difcovered by their Breafts; but the Cock is beft known by the brownnefs of his Back and the white in his Wing, that is to fay, take your young *Linnet* when the Wing-feathers are grown, and ftretch out his Wing, holding his body faft with the other hand; and then obferve the white upon the fourth, fifth, and fixth Feather; if it caft a gliftering white, and the white goes clofe to the Quill, this is a fure figne of a Cock.

Many are the Difeafes of this Bird, as the Ptifick, known by his panting, ftaring Feathers, lean Breaft, and fpilling his Seeds up and down the Cage; and this Difeafe happens for want of Water, or for want of green meat in the Spring: He is troubled alfo with Streins or Convulfions of the Breaft: Sometimes he is afflicted with hoarfnefs in his voice, being over-ftrein'd in finging: he is fometimes melancholy, at other times afflicted with fcowring, of which there are three forts; the firft is thin, and with a black or white fubftance in the middle, not very dangerous; the fecond is between a black and white, clammy and fticking, this is bad; but the third and laft is moft mortal, which is the white clammy fcowring: the feveral Cures I fhall not here fet down for brevity fake, but refer you to the care of the Bird-merchant.

Of the GOLD-FINCH, or CHRIST-MAS-FOOL, *fo called in* Norfolk.

THey are taken in great plenty about *Michaelmas*, and will foon become tame. The beauty of this Birds feverally-colour'd Feathers is not much taken notice of, becaufe they are fo common among us; but

they

they have been so noted and valued beyond Sea, that they have been transported in great quantities for great rarities.

They breed commonly in Apple-trees and Plum-trees thrice a year. You must take the young ones with the Nest at ten daies old, and feed them after this manner: take some of the best Hemp-seed, pound it, sift it, and mix it with the like quantity of white bread, with some flower of Canary-seeds; and taking up the quantity of a white Pea upon a small Stick, feed them therewith three or four bits at a time, making fresh every day: You must keep these Birds very warm till they can feed themselves, for their nature is very tender.

For the purgation of this Bird, as well as all others which feed on Hemp-seed, take the seeds of Mellons, Succory, and Mercury, which is a principal herb for the *Linnet*; but the best for the *Gold finch* are Lettice and Plantain; and nothing can be more wholesome for him than Wall or Loom-earth, and some fine Sand, and a lump or two of Sugar put always into his Cage.

Of the TIT-LARK.

THis Bird is very short in his Song, and no variety in it; yet some fancy him for his *Whisking*, *Turring*, and *Chewing*: He commonly appears at that time of the year that the *Nightingale* does, which is the beginning of *April*, and leaves us at the beginning of *September*: They are fed when taken as the *Nightingale*; you must cram him at first, for he will not feed himself, by reason he always feeds on live
meat

meat in the field, for which cause he is unacquainted with the meat we offer him: when he comes to feed of himself, he will eat what the *Wood-lark* eats, or almost any other meat.

This Bird breeds about the latter end of *April*, or beginning of *May*, and builds her Nest on the ground by some Pond-side or Ditch-side, and feeds her young with Caterpillars or Flies. They are easily brought up being hardy, and are not subject to Colds or Cramps as other birds are, but live long if preserved with care. If you breed up this bird young and cleanly, you may please your self with his Song; all that I can say of it is, *Short and sweet.*

Of the CHAFF-FINCH.

THere is no scarcity of this bird, and in my minde fitter for the Spit than a Cage, having but one short plain Song, yet for that he is admired by some, and kept very charily.

They build their Nests in Hedges and Trees of all sorts, and have young ones twice or thrice a year; they are seldom bred up from the Nest, because they are not apt to take another birds Song, nor to whistle. The *Essex-finch* is best both for length of Song and variety, concluding it with several Notes very prettily. He is very little subject to any Disease, onely he is inclinable to be very lousie, if he be not sprinkled with a little Wine twice or thrice a moneth.

Of

Of the STARLING.

THis Bird is generally kept by all forts of people above any other bird for whiftling; but their greateft fault is, they have them too fledg'd out of the Neft, and that makes them retain commonly fo much of their own harfh Notes: therefore thofe who do intend to have them excellent, and avoid their own fqueaking Notes, muft take them from the old ones at the end of three or four daies; and thus you muft do to all birds you would learn to whiftle, or fpeak, or learn another Birds Song by hanging under him.

Of the RED-START.

THis Bird is a Fore-runner of the *Nightingale*, and is of a very fullen dogged temper in a Cage; but abroad is very chearful, and hath a very pleafant kinde of whiftling Song.

The Cock is fair and beautifully coloured, and is delightful to the eye. They breed thrice a year; the latter end of *April*, in *May*, and towards the latter end of *June*.

They build ufually in holes of hollow Trees, or under houfe-eaves: She is the fhieft bird I know, of her building; for when fhe is about her Neft, if fhe perceive any look on, fhe forfakes it; and if you touch an Egg fhe never comes more to the Neft; and if fhe have young ones and you do the like, fhe will either ftarve them, or break their Necks over the Neft.

Now

Now though the old ones are thus dogged, yet if you bring up their young, their nature will alter, and become very tame.

You must take them out of the Nest about ten daies old; if they stay longer, they will learn somewhat of the old one's sullen temper. You must feed them with Sheeps-heart and Eggs chopped and mixt together, about the quantity of three white Peas, upon the end of a Stick, when they open their mouths: when they will thus feed, put them into a Cage with meat about it, and a Pan of meat therein; and though he feed himself, yet it will be very sparingly for four or five daies, wherefore you must now and then feed him your self. Keep him warm in the Winter, and he will sing as well in the night as the day.

Of the BUL-FINCH.

THe *Bull-finch* hath no Song of his own, nor whistle neither, but is very apt to learn any thing almost, if taught by the mouth.

Of the GREEN-FINCH.

THis Bird is not worth a keeping for his Song, but for his colour, and being a hardy heavy Bird to ring the Bells.

They breed very sillily by the High-way-side, and early before the Hedges have Leaves upon them; which causes every one to see their Nests at first, so that seldom their first Nests come to any thing. They breed three

times

times a year, and the young ones are very hardy birds to be brought up. You may feed them with white Bread and Rape bruised and soaked together: He is apter to take the Whistle than another Bird's Song. All that can be said of him, he is a very dull Bird, and will never kill himself either by singing or whistling.

Of the HEDGE-SPARROW.

THis is not so despicable a bird as some would have it; for if you will minde its Song, you will finde very delightful Notes, and sings early in the Spring with great variety. Old or young become tame very quickly, and will sing in a short time after they are taken; so that you take them at the latter end of *January* or beginning of *February*: they will feed almost on any thing you give them.

They commonly build in a White-thorn or private Hedge, laying Eggs much different from other Birds, being of a very fine blue colour. This Bird is very tractable, and will take any bird's Song almost, if taken young out of the Nest. I shall onely speak a few Experiments of others, and deliver some Observations of my own concerning the length of Birds lives, and which are most proper for whistling, and so shall end this Treatise.

First, As to the length of Birds Lives: Among *Nightingales* some live but one year, some three, some five, some eight, and some twelve; singing better and better for the first seven or eight years, and after that decline by little and little: They must have careful Keepers that can preserve their lives to the fifth year;

experience

experience informs us, where one lives to that age, an hundred die.

The *Wood-lark* feldom lives in a Cage above fix years, and hardly five.

The *Robin-red breaft* rarely lives above feven years; for he is a tender Bird, and much fubject to the Falling Sicknefs, Cramp, and oppreffion of the Stomack.

The *Skie-lark* as he is a hardy bird, fo he is long liv'd alfo. All forts of Seed-birds live longer than any foft-Beak'd birds, efpecially the *Canary* and *Linnet*. I have known a *Canary-bird* live and fing within a year of twenty; in like manner the *Linnet*.

So much as to the Lives of Singing Birds; let us now confider which are moft fit for Whiftling:

In the firft place I look upon the *Starling* to be the beft; and never heard better than at the *Grey-Hound* in St. *Mary Ax*, taught and fold by the ingenious Mafter of that Houfe. But fince I have fpoken of the *Starling* and *Bull-finch* already, I fhall infift no farther.

The *Black-bird* hath a kinde of rude Whiftle; and if young taken out of the Neft, is very apt to learn.

The *Robin-red-breaft* is a moft incomparable bird for the Whiftle, and to Speak alfo. A *Robin* is a hot-mettled Bird, and therefore he muft not be in the hearing of another; wherefore if you breed two, let them be feparated into two feveral Rooms, that they may not hear, and fo confequently fpoil each other.

The *Canary-bird* will learn to Whiftle any thing almoft if taken young out of the Neft, otherwife not; for being a very hot-mettled Bird, he will run upon his own Song do what you can.

The *Linnet* will learn any Tune almoft, if not too

long, and too full of variety. Learn him one tune firſt, then another, keeping him dark and ſtill, out of the noiſe of other Birds.

Take this for a general rule for all Birds, that the younger they be, the better they will prove, and anſwer your expectation for all your trouble and pains in bringing up and keeping them.

An

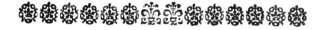

An Abſtract of ſuch
STATUTE-LAWS
As concern
FOWLING.

Stat. 11 Hen. 7. cap. 17.

NOne ſhall take Pheaſants or Partridges with Engines in another's ground without Licenſe, in pain of 10 l. to be divided betwixt the Owner of the Ground and Proſecutor.

Stat. 25 Hen. 8. cap. 11.

None ſhall deſtroy or take away the Eggs of any Wild-Fowl, in pain to forfeit for every Egg of a Crane or Buſtard ſo taken or deſtroyed 20 d. Of a Bittern, Hern, or Shoveland 8 d. And of a Mallard, Teal, or other Wild-Fowl 1 d. to be divided betwixt the King and the Proſecutor.

F 2 Stat.

Stat. 23 Eliz. cap. 10.

None shall Kill or Take any Pheasants or Partridges with any Net or Engine in the night-time, in pain to forfeit for every Pheasant 20s. And for every Partridge 10s. which if the Offender pay not within ten days, he shall suffer one moneths Imprisonment without Bail, and enter into Bond (for two years) with good Sureties before some Justices of Peace, not to offend in the like kinde.

II. None shall Hawk or Hunt with his Spaniels in standing Grain, or before it is Stocked (except in his own Ground, or with the Owner's consent) in pain to forfeit 40s. to the Owner of the said Ground, to be recovered as aforesaid.

This Act shall not restrain Fowlers who unwillingly take Pheasants or Partridges, and forthwith let them go at large.

Stat. 1 Jacob. cap. 27.

Every person convicted by his own Confession, or by two Witnesses upon Oath, before two or more Justices of Peace, to have Killed or Taken any Pheasant, Partridge, Pigeon, or other Game; or to have taken or destroyed the Eggs of Pheasants, Partridges, or Swans, shall by the said Justices be committed to prison without Bail, unless he immediately pay to the use of the Poor where the Offence was committed

ted, or he apprehended, 20 s. for every Fowl or
Egg so killed, taken or destroyed; and after
one Moneths Commitment shall before two
or more Justices of Peace be bound with two
sufficient Sureties in 20 l. apiece, with condition never to offend in the like kinde again.

II. Every person convicted as abovesaid,
to keep a Grey-hound, Dog, or Net to kill
or take Deer, Hare, Pheasant or Partridge (unless he have Inheritance of 10 l.
per Annum, a Lease for life of 30 l. per Annum,
or be worth 200 l. in Goods, or otherwise be
the Son of a Baron or Knight, or Heir
apparent of an Esquire) shall suffer Imprisonment as aforesaid, unless he pay 40 s.
to the use abovesaid.

III. None shall sell, or buy to sell again
any Pheasant or Partridge, (except by
them reared up or brought from beyond
Sea) in pain to forfeit for every Pheasant
20 s. and every Partridge 10 s. to be divided
betwixt the Prosecutor and the Poor of the
parish where such Offence is committed.

Stat. 7 Jacob. cap. 11.

Every person convicted by his own Confession, or by two Witnesses upon Oath, before two or more Justices of Peace, to have
Hawked, or destroyed any Pheasant or Partridge, betwixt the first of July and the last
of August, shall suffer one Moneths Imprisonment without Bail, unless he pay to the
use of the Poor where the Offence was committed

mitted, or he apprehended 40 s. for every time so Hawking, and 20 s. for every Pheaſant or Partridge ſo taken or deſtroyed : But this Offence ſhall be proſecuted within ſix moneths after it ſhall be committed.

II. It ſhall be lawful for the Lord of a Mannor, or any having free Warren, Inheritance of 40 l. per Annum, Free-hold of 80 l. per Annum, or Goods worth 400 l. or their Servants (Licenſed by them) to take Pheaſants or Partridges within their own Grounds or Precinct, ſo they do it in the day-time, and oneIy betwixt Michaelmaſs and Chriſtmaſs.

III. If any perſon of a mean condition ſhall be convicted by his own Confeſſion, or by one Witneſs upon Oath before two or more Juſtices of the Peace, to have killed or Taken any Pheaſant or Partridge with Dogs, Nets, or Engines, he ſhall by the ſaid Juſtices be Committed to Priſon without Bail, unleſs he pay to the uſe of the Poor where the Offence was committed 20 s. for every Pheaſant or Partridge ſo killed or taken: And alſo become bound before one or more Juſtice of Peace in a Recognizance of 20 l. never to offend in the like kinde again.

IV. Every Conſtable or Headborough (upon Warrant under the hand of two Juſtices of Peace) hath power to ſearch the Houſes of perſons ſuſpected to have
any

any Setting-Dogs or Nets for the taking of Pheasants, or Partridges; and the Dogs or Nets there found to kill and cut in pieces at pleasure, as things forfeited unto the said Officers.

v. He that shall be punished by vertue of this Act, shall not be punished again by vertue of any other Law for the same Offence.

The

THE
GENTLEMAN'S
Recreation :

Containing

DIRECT RULES

FOR THAT

NOBLE & DELIGHTFUL

ART OF

ANGLING:

Whereunto is annexed
An Abſtract of all ſuch Statute
or penal Laws relating to that Curious Art.

The Fourth PART.

LONDON:
Printed by *J. C.* for *N. C.*

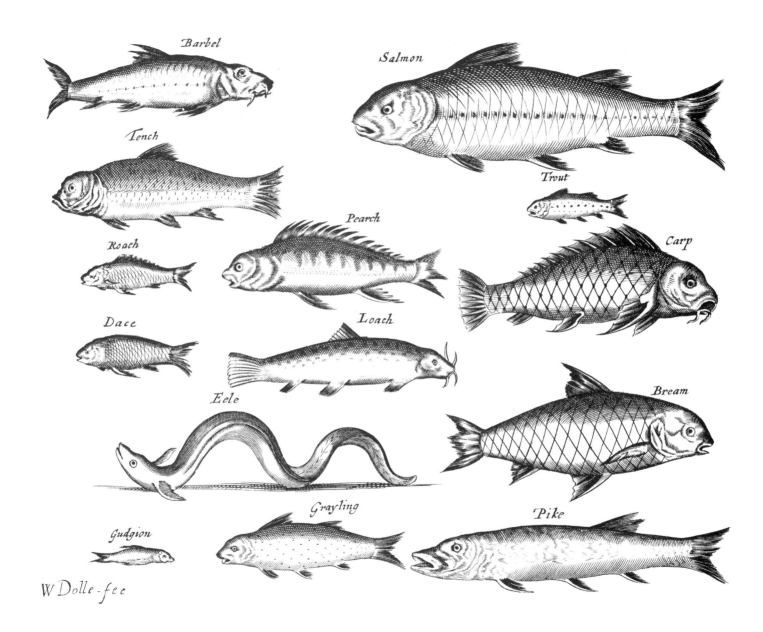

Barbel

Salmon

Tench

Trout

Pearch

Carp

Roach

Dace

Loach

Bream

Eele

Gudgion

Grayling

Pike

W Dolle · fec

O F
FISHING.

The Introduction.

NGLING is an excellent Art, which as it pleads great Antiquity, so the knowledge thereof is with much difficulty to be obtained: and indeed it bears some similitude to Poetry in this, that as it is said, *Poeta nascitur, non fit,* so ought the Piscator or Fisher-man to have a natural inclination unto the Art of Angling, or his knowledge therein will be always dull and imperfect; not but that it may be much heightned by practice and experience.

Now he that intends to be his Crafts-master in this harmless Pastime or Recreation, must not onely diligently search and enquire into the Mysteries and depths of this Art, but must also be furnished, as aforesaid, with a natural propensity thereunto, attended with hope and Patience: And having gotten by observation and practice a competent knowledge, or having

conquer-

conquer'd the difficulties of Angling, it will then not onely prove pleasant, but profitable, and be like Vertue, a Reward to it self.

Now that I may farther commend this ingenious profession, be pleased to take notice of the Antiquity thereof; some saying it is as ancient as *Deucalion*'s Flood. Some attribute it to the invention of one *Belus*, the first Author of vertuous Recreations. Others say that *Seth* left the knowledge of Angling to his posterity ingraven on brazen Pillars with the first Rudiments of the Mathematicks, and other useful Arts; by which means they were preserved from perishing in the universal Deluge.

Divers are the opinions of men concerning the Antiquity of this Art : let it suffice, that certainly it is older than Christ's Incarnation; for both *Job* and the Prophet *Amos* make mention of Fish-hooks, and consequently there must be Anglers then in those days.

The next thing that offers it self in the commendation of this Art, is the benefit of Contemplation, which is acquired hereby; which is a thing (according to the opinion of some learned Cloister'd men) to be preferred before Action, because (say they) it makes us mortals the nearer to come to the Creator by way of imitation; for he is all Contemplation of his own infinite Power, Goodness, &c.

But waving this, I cannot let slip the expression of an ingenious Forreiner, who said, *That Rivers and the Inhabitants of the watry Element were made for wife men to contemplate, and fools to pass by without consideration.* Modesty will not permit me to rank my self in the number of the first; and I shall endeavour to clear my self from the scandal of the last, by giving you a short account of Rivers and their watry Inhabitants.

I shall first discourse of Rivers: one whereof I have read

read of, fcituate in *Epirus*, which hath a ftrange double
and contrary property; the one is, that it will extin-
guifh any Torch that is lighted : and the other is, to
light a Torch never lighted before.

The River *Silarus* in a few hours will (as report
faith) convert a Rod into Stone. And I my felf
know a Lough in *Ireland*, that in fome years will
convert Wood into Stone, of which are made the beft
Hones. *Cambden* makes mention of a Well near
Kerby in *Cumberland*, that ebbs and flows feveral times
every day.

The fame Author makes mention of the River
Mole in *Surrey*, which, running feveral miles under
ground, being oppofed by Hills, at laft breaks out again
fo far off, that the Inhabitants thereabout boaft (as
the *Spaniards* of the River *Ama*) that they feed feveral Flocks of Sheep on a green Bridge. There is fuch
another green Bridge in *Wales*, the River running a
great way under ground, and there difemboguing it
felf into the Sea. Some thereabout report, that they
have put a living Goofe into the Hole where the Water falls, and fhe hath fwam out at the other end ; but
with no Feathers on her back.

Mr. *Thomas May* in his Hiftory of *The Raign of King*
Henry the fecond, relates two ftrange things from *Gri-*
caldus Cambrenfis, of certain Wells in *Ireland*. His
Words are thefe :

> A Well there is in Munfter *to be feen*,
> *Within whofe Waters whofoe're hath been*
> *Once drench'd, his Hair ftreight takes an hoary dye.*
> 　*Another Fountain of quite contrary*
> *Effeci to that in* Ulfter *fprings*; *for there*
> *Thofe that have wafhed once, how old foe're,*
> *Shall never after have an hoary Hair.*

　　　　　　　　Another

Another thing, though against Nature, yet for the strangeness of it I cannot choose but relate, and that is of a certain River neer *Harwood* in *Bedford-shire*, which in the year of our Lord 1399, (a little before the Civil Wars between the Houses of *York* and *Lancaster* burst forth) of a sudden stood still, and divided it self asunder , so that men might pass three miles together on foot down the midst of the Channel, leaving the Waters like a Wall behinde them. *Speed* in his descript. *Bedford.*

I shall conclude with two of the strangest Rivers that ever were heard of. The first is a River called *Eleusina*, which is so merrily disposed, (if you will believe a man of no less Authority than *Aristotle*) that it will dance to a Fiddle, bubling at the noise of Musick, and will grow very muddy ; but as soon as the Musick ceaseth, it ceaseth its motion, returning to its former calmness and clearness. The other is as wonderful, and (if you will believe *Josephus* that learned *Jew*) it is a River in *Judæa*, which runs very swiftly all the six days of the Week, but resteth on the seventh, which is the Jewish Sabbath.

And now a word or two concerning Fish : *Pliny* saith, That Nature's great and wonderful power is more demonstrated in the Sea than on the Land : and this may appear by those numerous and various Creatures which inhabit in and about that Element; which will appear more at large, if you will read their History written either by *Rondeletius*, *Gesner*, *Johnstonus*, or *Aldrovandus*. The number and the various shapes of these Fishes are not more strange, than their different Natures, Inclinations and Actions. Give me leave to speak a little hereof.

There is a Fish called the *Cuttle-fish* , which will cast a long Gut out of her Throat, with which she angles : For lying obscurely in the Mud , she permits

small

small fish to nibble at it, and by that means draws them near her by little and little, till coming within her reach, she leaps upon them and devours them: hence she is called the *Sea-Angler*.

The *Hermit* is a Fish that when she grows old will seek out a dead Fish's shell, fit for her purpose, and there dwell secluded from all company, studying nothing more than how to defend her self against the injuries of Wind and Weather.

The *Sargus* is a Fish so lascivious, (as *Du-Bartas* expresseth it rarely well) that when he cannot finde change of Mates enough in the Sea, he will get ashore and Cuckold a Goat.

Goes courting She Goats on the grassie Shore,
Horning their Husbands that had Horns before.

Whereas it is reported that the *Mullet* is so chaste, that when she is deprived of her Mate, she will follow him to the shore and die.

The *Torpedo*, or *Cramp-fish*, is a Fish of so baneful and poysonous a nature, that all other Fish that come within her reach are immediately stupified and without motion, so that they easily become her prey; nay, she will so suddenly convey her Poyson up the Rod and Line of the Angler, when she feels her self entangled, that his Hands and Arms immediately losing their strength, become nummed and senseless.

The *Scolopendra* hath as rare and strange a way of defending her self from the Anglers subtilty, as any Fish whatever, if we may credit the relation of *Du-Bartas*, whose words are these :

But if the Scolopendra *have suckt in*
The sowre-sweet morsel with the barbed pin,
She hath as rare a Trick to rid her from it ;
For instantly she all her Guts will vomit ;
And having clear'd them from the danger, then
She fair and softly sups them in again,
So that not one of them within her Womb
Changeth his Office or his wonted room.

The *Remora* is a Fish of so strange and secret a property (and for that reason is often used for a Metaphor) that as the same *Du Bartas* saith,

Let all the Winds in one Wind gather them,
And (seconded with Neptune's *strongest stream)*
Let all at once blow all their stiffest gales,
Astern a Galley under all her sails ;
Let her be holpen with an hundred Oars,
Each lively handled by five lusty Rowers ;
The Remora *fixing her feeble Horn*
Into the Tempest-beaten Vessels Stern,
Stays her stone-still.

In the year of our Lord 1180, near *Orford* in *Suffolk*, there was a Fish taken in the perfect shape of a Man; he was kept by *Bartholomew de Glanvile* in the Castle of *Orford* above half a year; but at length, not being carefully looked to, he stole to the Sea, and was never seen after. He never spake, but would eat any Meat that was given him, especially raw Fish, when he had squeezed out the juice : He was often had to Church, but never shewed any signe of Adoration.

Let what is already spoken of Fish suffice, since it will not onely be impertinent to enlarge farther, but
impos-

impoffible here to give an account of the natures of all Fifh : I fhall therefore refer you to fuch Authors who have made it their bufinefs thereof to write great Volumes.

Before I put an end to this Introduction, permit me to infert fomething in praife of *Fifhermen* and *Fifhing.*

A fhort Encomium, or fomewhat in praife of Fifher-men *and* Fifhing.

IT is very remarkable, that amongft the twelve Holy Apoftles there were four of them Fifher-men, whom our Saviour elected and infpired to preach the Gofpel. And the reafon that fome give for this choice is, that he knew and found the hearts of fuch men naturally more fitted for Contemplation and quietnefs, having Spirits milde, fweet, and peaceable.

Befides, our Saviour feems to have a more than common refpect for their Occupation, for two reafons. Firft, He never reproved thefe for their Profeffion, as he did others, *viz.* the Scribes and Money-changers. Next, He dignified thefe poor Fifher-men with the priority of Nomination in the Catalogue of his twelve Apoftles. Nay, that which is more obfervable is this, that our Saviour took onely three of thefe Fifher-men with him when he afcended the Mount to bear him company at his Transfiguration.

Now as to the lawfulnefs of Fifhing, I think none can fpeak againft it, fince our Saviour himfelf commanded St. *Peter* to fifh to pay *Cæfar* his Tribute.

And as the Ancients have highly applauded and approved
proved

proved of this ingenious Exercife, feveral of the He-
ro's of old, in the height of their glory, having excr-
cifed themfelves herein: fo feveral of our eminent
late Divines have done the like ; as Dr. *Whitaker*, learned *Perkins*, Dr. *Nowel* Dean of St. *Pauls London*,
and the incomparable Sir *Henry Wotton* Provoft of
Eaton-Colledge, who was a great lover of Angling,
and would frequently fay thereof, That it was after
his Study a Reft to his minde, a Chearer to his Spirits,
a Diverter of fadnefs, a Calmer of unquiet thoughts,
a Moderator of Paffions, a procurer of Contentednefs ;
and that it begot habits of Peace and Patience in thofe
that profefs and practice it. And thus I conclude the
praife of *Angling*, though much more might be fpoke
thereof.

How to improve Fifh-ponds, and the Fifh therein contained.

BEfore I fhall lay down fuch Obfervations and Inftructions, which with much pains and coft I have
collected, to render a Fifher-man compleat in that delightful Exercife of taking Fifh: I fhall give an account of Ponds, and how they may in the beft manner
be improved.

Imprimis. Confider the fcituation of your Pond,
and the nature of thofe Currents which run into it.
In the next place, obferve whether it be a Breeder or
not: If it be a Breeder, Experience will inftruct you
never to expect any large *Carps* from fuch Ponds ; for
the greatnefs of the number of the Spawn will over-
ftock the Pond ; therefore for large *Carps* a Store-
pond is ever accounted beft.

Now

Now to make a Breeding-pond become a Store-pond, when you cannot make a Store-pond become a Breeding-pond, thus you muſt do. When you ſue your pond, conſider what quantity of *Carps* it will maintain; then put in all Milters, or all Spawners, by which means in a little time you will have Carps that are both large and fat beyond your expectation. By putting in but one ſex of them, there is an impoſſibility of encreaſing of them; but of the *Roach* it will notwithſtanding multiply abundantly: Therefore it is needful, and altogether neceſſary for ſuch who keep Breeding-ponds, to ſue them once in three years, for fear of the encreaſe of *Roaches*, though none were ever put in; which may ſeem very ſtrange, if the truth thereof could not be made manifeſt; as thus: there are ſeveral ponds frequented by Wilde-ducks, which uſually come at nights to feed with the Tame ones there abiding: Now thoſe Wilde-ducks bring theſe *Roaches* with them, for their feeding amongſt Weeds in Rivers.

Beſides, the Spawn of *Roaches* will hang about their Feet and Feathers, which is waſhed off by the Water of thoſe ponds they are accuſtomed to haunt; by which means in a few years they become ſo numerous, though you your ſelf did not put one into the Breeding-pond; for which cauſe you finde your *Carps* ſo lean, and almoſt hunger-ſtarved.

By the way, give me leave to inſert this true ſtory. A Gentleman, not far from the City of *London*, had a large pond of about four Acres of ground; a Gentleman ſtanding by at the ſuing thereof, and ſeeing not only a great quantity of Fiſh, but the beſt grown that ever he ſaw, he adviſed him to put in two or three hundred of ſtores of *Carp*, about three or four years growth, out of a pond that was over-ſtocked, and to put ſixty of thoſe he had taken out; which

accor-

accordingly he saw done, fancying to see stately *Carps* at the next suing.

After the expiration of four years, this Gentleman was advised to sue his pond, to see what Monsters four years addition to their growth would produce; for those sixty *Carps* were from Eye to Fork from fifteen Inches to eighteen Inches when he put them in: now having sued his pond, he found almost the whole number of his *Carps*; but they were in such a lean condition, that he did not know them; for they were Monsters in Nature, their Heads being bigger than their whole Bodies, and almost as heavy: and this happen'd it seems by his own folly, by putting in but twenty *Roaches*; and when the Pond was sued there were bushels of small *Roaches*, and these *Roaches* eat up all the sweet feed from the *Carps*; for *Roaches* are like Sheep to great Cattle, which eat up and devour all the sweet feed, and what affords the greatest nutriment. This Gentleman was very much frustrated of his expectation; and the Fishmonger which came from *London* to buy a penny-worth, as soon as he perceived the Monsters, he mounted his Horse and rid as if the Devil drove him, not so much as bidding the Gentleman farewel. Here is to be noted, that Ponds which will not breed one *Carp*, *Roaches* in one year will multiply by thousands; therefore you must be careful every year to view your Pond, and observe if any such fry appears, lest when you come to sue your pond, you be deceived in your expectation.

How to make Carps grow to an extrodinary bigness in a Pond.

PErceiving about the month of *April* that your pond begins to grow low in Water, then with an Iron-

Rake

Rake, rake all the sides of your pond where the Water is fallen away ; then fow fome Hay-feeds, and rake it well; by this means at the latter end of Summer there will be a great growth of Grafs; which when Winter comes, and the pond being raifed by Rain to the Top, will overflow all that Grafs; and then the *Carps* having Water to carry them to the feed, will fill themfelves, and in a fhort time become as fat as Hogs that are kept up for that purpofe : Do this every Summer till you fue your pond, and you will finde no River-*Carp* to furpafs them either in fatnefs or fweetnefs.

General Obfervations to be underftood by all fuch who defire to attain to the compleat and perfect art of Angling.

BY no means fifh in light and dazling Apparel, but let your Cloathing be of a dark dusky colour.

Wherefoever you ufe to angle (for the Angler hath his peculiar Haunts) caft in once in four or five daies Corn boiled foft; if for *Carp* and *Tench* , oftner : alfo you may caft in Garbage , Livers of Beafts, Worms chopt in pieces, or Grains fteep'd in Bloud and dried. This will attract the Fifh unto the place : and to keep them together as you fifh, throw in half a handful of Grains of ground Malt. This muft be done in ftill Water ; but in a Stream you muft caft your Grain above your Hook, and not about it ; for as they float from your Hook, fo will they draw the Fifh after them.

If

If you will bait a Stream, get some Tin-boxes made full of holes, no bigger than just fit for a Worm to creep through; then fill these Boxes with them, and having fastned a Plummet to sink them, cast them into the Stream with a String tied thereto, that you may draw them forth when you lift. By the smalness of the Holes aforesaid, the Worms can crawl out but very leasurely, and as they crawl the Fish will resort about them.

If you would bait for *Salmon*, *Trout*, *Umber*, and the like, in a Stream, then take some Bloud, and therewith incorporate fine Clay, Barley, and Malt ground, adding thereto some Water; make all into a Paste with Gum of Ivy; then form it into Cakes, and cast them into the stream. Some will knead or stick Worms therein fast by the head. If you finde your Bait take no effect in the attracting of the Fish, you may then conclude some *Pike* or *Pearch* lurketh thereabout to seize his Prey, for fear of which the Fish dare not venture thereabout: you must therefore remove these obstructions of your sport, by taking your Trowl; and let your Bait be either Brandlings or Lob-worms; or you may use Gentles or Minows, which they will greedily snap at.

Keep your Rod neither too dry nor too moist, lest the one make it brittle, and the other rotten. If it be very soultry dry Weather, wet your Rod a little before you Angle: and having struck a good Fish, keep your Rod bent, and that will hinder him from running to the end of the Line, by which means he will either break his hold or the Hook.

If you would know what Bait the Fish loves best at the time of your fishing, having taken one, slit his Gill, and take out his Stomach, and open it without bruising, and there you will finde what he last fed on and had a fancy to; by which means you may bait your Hook accordingly.   When

When you fish, shelter your self under some Bush or Tree, or stand so far from the brink of the River that you can onely discern your Float: for Fish are timorous, and are affrighted at the least sight or motion. The best way of Angling with the Fly is down the River, and not up, as you will finde by experience.

You never need make above half a dozen trials in one place, either with Fly or Ground-bait, when you angle for *Trout*; for by that time he will either offer to take, or refuse the Bait, and not stir at all.

If you will have Fish bite eagerly and freely, and without suspition, you must present them with such Baits as naturally they are inclined to, and in such manner as they are accustomed to receive them.

If you use Pastes for Baits, you must adde Flax or Wooll, otherwise the Paste will wash off the Hook.

The Eyes of such Fishes as you kill, are most excellent Baits on the Hook for almost any sort of Fish.

Lastly, make not this or any other Recreation your dayly practice, lest your immoderate Exercise therein bring a Plague upon you rather than a pleasure.

Astrological Elections for Angling in general.

IF as the Wise man saith, (and I think there is none that dare question his Authority) that *There is a proper time and season for every action under the Sun*, I hope it will not be offensive nor impertinent to show what times and seasons the intelligent Angler ought to make choice of, that may answer his expectation. For my own part, I have so often experimented the truth of these Rules, that by my good will I would

never

never Angle but at an elected time: the ingenious
will not despise them, and for others they were not intended: And they are these;

If you would Neptune's *scaly Subjects get,*
Nights horned Queen in the Midheaven set: ☽
Thence let her on the Paphian *Goddess shine* ♀
I'th' West, and greet her with a friendly Trine.
Be sure you always fortifie the East,
And let the Maiden-Star possess the West: ♍
However let some Aquatick Signe ascend, ♋.♏.♓
And let all power his happy Lord attend.
Then see the setting Constellation be
Afflicted by some hateful Enemy, ♂
At least his Lord: the sixth with strength defend;
Let active power his Radiant Lord attend.
Then may you boldly venture to the Flood,
And take from thence what Fishes you see good.

What provision is to be made for Ang-
ling-Tools.

THe time of providing Stocks is in the Winter-
Solstice, when the Trees have shed their Leaves,
and the Sap is in the Roots: For after *January* it
ascends again into the Trunk and Branches, at which
time it is improper to gather Stocks or Tops.

Let your Stocks be taper-grown, and your Tops the
best Rush-ground-shoots you can get, not knotty, but
proportionable and slender; otherwise they will neither cast nor strike well, and by reason of their un-
pliableness your Line will be much endanger'd.

Having gathered your Stocks and Tops all in one season,

as ſtraight as you can, bathe them, ſaving the Tops, over a gentle fire, and uſe them not till fully ſeaſoned, till about a year and four months : they are better if kept two years.

Now to preſerve theſe Stocks or Tops from rotting, or worm-eating, rub them over thrice a year with Sallet or Linſeed-oyl ; ſweet Butter will ſerve, if never ſalted ; and with any of theſe you muſt chafe well your Rods : if bored, pour in either of the Oyls, and let them bathe therein twenty four hours , then pour it out again; and this will preſerve your Tops and Stocks from injury.

How to joyn the Stock or Top together, or how to make all ſorts of Rods for Fly, Ground, or otherwiſe, with what lengths are beſt for ſeveral ſorts of Fiſhing, I need not here relate ; ſince without putting your ſelf to the trouble, you may purchaſe them of ſuch as ſell them at no dear rates.

How to make a Line after the beſt manner.

Et your Hair be round, and twiſt it even, for that ſtrengthens the Line ; and let your Hair, as near as you can, be of an equal bigneſs : then lay them in Water for a quarter of an hour, by which means you will finde which of the Hairs do ſhrink ; then twiſt them over again.

Some intermingle ſilk in the twiſting, but I cannot approve of it ; but a Line of all ſilk is not amiſs ; alſo a Line made of the ſmalleſt Lute-ſtring is very good, but that it will ſoon rot by the Water.

The beſt colour for Lines is the ſorrel, white, and grey ; the two laſt for clear waters, and the grey for muddy Rivers : neither is the pale watry green to be contemned, which colour you may make after this manner :   H   Take

Take a pint of strong Ale, half a pound of Soot, a small quantity of the juice of Walnut-leaves, with the like quantity of Alume; put these into a Pipkin, and boil them together about half an hour: Having so done, take it off the fire, and when it is cold put in your Hair. Or thus:

Take a pottle of Alume-water, somewhat more than a handful of Marigold-flowers, boil them till a yellow scum arise; then take half a pound of green Copperas, with as much Verdegrecce, and beat them together to a fine powder: put these with the Hair into the Alume-water, and let it lie ten hours or more; then take the Hair out, and let it dry.

In the making your Line leave a *Bought* at both ends, the one to put it to and take it from your Rod, the other to hang your lowest link upon to which your Hook is fastned; and so you may change your Hook as often as you please.

Of the Hook, Flote, and other things worth the Observation.

YOur Hook ought to be long in the shank, somewhat round in its circumference, the point standing even and straight; and let the bending be in the shank.

Use strong, but small silk, in the setting on of your Hook, laying the Hair on the inside of your Hook: for if it be on the outside, the silk will fret and cut it asunder.

As for the Flotes, there are divers ways of making them: Some use your *Muscovy*-Duck-quills, which are the best for still Waters; but for strong streams take good sound Cork without flaws or holes, and bore it through with a hot Iron; then put into it a

Quill

Quill of a fit proportion; then pare your Cork into a Pyramidal form of what bigness you think fit; after this grinde it smooth.

To plum your Ground, you must carry with you a Musquet-bullet with a hole made through it, tying this to a strong twist, hang it on your Rod, and so you will finde the depth of the Water.

And that you may not incommode your Tackle, it will be very requisite to make several partitions in pieces of Parchment sowed together, by which each Utensil may have a place by it self.

In any wise forget not to carry a little Whetstone with you, to sharpen your Hooks if you finde them blunt and dull.

I need not advise you how to carry your B O B and P A L M E R, or put you in minde of having several Boxes of divers sizes for your Hooks, Corks, Silk, Thread, Lead, Flies, &c. or admonish you not to forget your Linnen and Woollen Bags for all sorts of Baits; but let me forewarn you not to have a P A U N-D E R that is heavy, for it can never be light enough: those which are made of Osiers I think are the best.

Lastly, forget not to carry with you a small Pole with a Loop at the end thereof, to which you may fasten a small Net to land great Fish withal.

There is another way much better, and that is by the Landing-hook, which hath a Screw at the end of it to screw it into the Socket of a Pole: to which Socket may be fitted also two other Hooks, the one to pull out Wood, and the other sharp to cut away Weeds.

Of Flies *Natural and Artificial, and how to use them.*

Natural *Flies* are innumerable, there being as many kinds as there are different sorts of Fruits : to avoid prolixity, I shall onely name some of them, *viz.* the *Dun-fly*, the *Stone* or *May-fly*, the *Red Fly*, the *Moor-fly*, the *Tawny-fly*, the *Shell-fly*, the *Cloudy* or *Blackish-fly*, the *Flag-fly*, the *Vine-fly*; also *Caterpillers*, *Canker-flies*, and *Bear-flies*, with thousands more which frequent Meadows and Rivers, for the contemplation of all, but particularly the recreation of Anglers.

These come in sooner or later, according to the season of the year, that is, sooner or later according to the forwardness or backwardness of the Spring; for Flies being bred of putrefaction, commence their being according as the Heat doth further the seminal vertue unto animation.

I cannot prescribe you Rules to know when each Fly cometh in, and is most grateful to every sort of Fish; and therefore I shall leave the knowledge hereof to your own observation.

Moreover, there are several sorts of Flies according to the several natures of divers Soils and Rivers, or diversity of Plants; yet some there are common to all, although but few.

All Flies are very good in their seasons for such Fish as rise at the Fly; but some more peculiarly good, as being better beloved by some sort of fish.

Fish generally rise at these Flies most eagerly when most sorts of Flies resort to the Water-side, hanging in a manner in clusters on Trees and Bushes, delighting themselves to skip thence to play upon
the

the water ; and then do the fish shew their craft in catching them.

To the intent you may the better know what kinde of Fly the fish then most covet, observe thus to do; coming in the Morning to the River-side, beat the Bushes with your Rod, and take up what variety you may of all sorts of Flies, and try them all; by which means you will quickly know which are in greatest estimation among them. Not but that they will change their Fly sometimes , but then it is when they have glutted themselves therewith for five or six days together, which is commonly upon the going out of that Fly: for Fish never covet that Fly more than when there is greatest plenty, contemning them at their first coming in.

There are two ways to fish with these natural Flies; either on the surface of the water, or a little underneath it. Now when you angle for *Chevin, Roach,* or *Dace* with the natural Fly, move it not swiftly when you see the Fish make at it, but rather let it glide spontaneously towards it with the Stream : If it be in a still and slow water, draw the Fly slowly sideways by him, that will make him eager in the pursuit of it; whereas if you should move it swiftly, they will not follow it, being a lazy fish and slow of motion. These fish delight to shew themselves in a Sun-shiny-day almost on the very surface of the Water, by which means you may pick and choose.

The *Artificial Fly* is seldome used but in blustering weather, when by the Winds the Waters are so troubled, that the Natural Fly cannot be seen, nor rest upon them.

There are (according to the opinion of Mr. *Walton,* a very ingenious man, and an excellent Angler) twelve sorts of Artificial Flies to angle with on the top of the Water, of which these are the principal.

The

The firſt is (to uſe his own words) the *Dun-fly*, in *March*, made of dun Wooll, and the Feathers of a Partridge's Wing.

The ſecond is a *Dun-fly* too, and made of black Wooll, and the Feathers of a black Drake ; the Body made of the firſt, and the Wings of the latter.

The third is the *Stone-fly*, in *April* ; the Body is made of black Wooll made yellow under the Wings and Tail.

The fourth is the *Ruddy-fly*, in the beginning of *May* ; the Body being made of red Wooll, and bound about with black Silk, with the Feathers of a red Capon, which hang dangling on his ſides next his Tail.

The fifth is the *Yellow* or *Greeniſh Fly*, in *June* ; the Body is made of black Wooll, with a yellow Liſt on either ſide, and the Wings taken off the Wings of a Buzzard, bound with black braked Hemp.

The ſixth is the *Mooriſh-fly* ; the Body made of duſkiſh Wooll, and the Wings made of the blackiſh Mail of the Drake.

The ſeventh is the *Tawny-fly*, good until the middle of *June* ; the Body made of tawny Wooll, the Wings made contrary one againſt another, of the whitiſh Mail of the white Drake.

The eighth is the *Waſp-fly*, in *July* ; the Body made of black Wooll lapt about with yellow Silk, the Wings made of Drake-feathers.

The ninth is the *Shell-fly*, good in the middle of *July* ; the Body made of greeniſh Wooll lapt about with the Herle of a Peacock's Tail, and the Wings made of Buzzards Wings.

The tenth and laſt is the *Drake-fly*, good in *Auguſt* ; the Body made of black Wooll lapt about with black Silk, his Wings of the Mail of the black Drake with a black head.

And then having named two more, he concludes wittily,

tily, *Thus have you a Jury of Flies, likely to betray and condemn all the* Trouts *in the River.*

This in my opinion seems a tedious and difficult way. I should rather think it better to finde the Fly proper for every season, and that which the Fish at that time most eagerly covet, and make one as like it as possibly you may, in colour, shape, and proportion; and for your better imitation lay the natural Fly before you.

There are several ways of making these artificial Flies, which I shall forbear here to relate, thinking it more proper to leave it to the ingenuity of every particular person, which will be very much help'd by seeing and observing the Artist's method in their composition.

The best Observations I can collect for artificial Fly-fishing, are these:

First, Observe to fish in a River somewhat disturbed by Rain, or in a clowdy day when the Waters are moved by a gentle breez: the South-wind is best, the West indifferent, but the East stark naught. But as to this I give not much credit; for let the Skie be cloudy, and the Season not too cold, I'le bid defiance to any Wind that blows not too hard. If it blow high, yet not so high but that you may conveniently guide your Tackle, they will rise in plain Deeps, where you shall kill the best Fish: but if the Wind be small, then is the best angling in swift Streams; and be sure to keep your Fly in continual motion.

Secondly, Keep as far from the Water-side as you can, whether you fish with a Fly or Worm; and fish down the Stream, having the Sun on your back, not suffering your Line to touch the Water, but your Fly onely. Here note, that the light Fly makes most sport in a dark night, and the darkest or least Fly in a clear day.

Thirdly,

Thirdly, In clear Rivers ever angle with a fmall
Fly with flender Wings; but in fuch as are muddied by
Rain, ufe a Fly that is larger bodied than ordinary.

Fourthly, When the water beginneth to clear after
Rain, and becomes brownifh, then ufe a Red or O-
range Fly; if the day be clear, a light-coloured fly,
and a dark fly for dark Waters; if the Water be of a
wheyifh complexion, then ufe a black or brown fly.
I will not fay thefe Directions or Rules are without
exceptions.

Fifthly, Let your Line for Fly-fifhing be twice as
long as your Rod, unlefs the River be cumbred with
Wood.

Sixthly, For every fort of fly, have feveral of the
fame differing in colour, to fute with the different complexions of feveral waters and weathers.

Seventhly, You muft have a nimble eye, and an a-
ctive hand to ftrike prefently with the rifing of the fifh,
or elfe he will be apt to fpew out the Hook, finding
his miftake.

Eighthly, Let your fly fall firft into the Water; for
if your Line fall firft, it fcares the fifh, and therefore
you muft draw again and caft.

Ninthly, When you angle in flow Rivers or ftill
places with your Artificial fly, caft it over crofs the River, and let it fink a little in the water, and draw it
gently back again, fo as you raife no Circles, nor break
the Water; and let the fly float gently with the Current, and hereby you will finde excellent fport.

Laftly, Take notice that your Salmon-flies muft be
made with their Wings ftanding one behinde the o-
ther, whether two or four. He delights in the fineft
gaudieft colours you can chufe, in the wings chiefly,
which muft be long, and fo muft the Tail.

Of

Of Ground Angling.

IF you fish under the Water for a *Trout*, it must be without a Float, onely with a Plumb of Lead, or a Bullet, which is better, because it will rowl on the ground. And this way of fishing is very good in cold weather, when the Fish swim very low: you must place this Bullet about nine Inches from the baited Hook; your Top must be very gentle, that the fish may more easily run away with the Bait, and not be scared with the stifness of the Rod. You must not strike as soon as you feel the fish bite, but slack your Line a little, that he may the better swallow the Bait and Hook. When you strike do it gently, for the least matter does it.

Let your Tackle be fine and slender, for that is better than your big and strong Lines, which serve onely to fright the Fish.

You will finde it a better way of Angling to do it without Float or Lead, onely making use of a Garden-worm, drawing it up and down the Stream; by which you will take more *Trouts* than any other way, especially if it be in a clear day. The Morning and Evening are the chiefest seasons for the Ground-Line for *Trout*: but if the day prove Cloudy, or the Water muddy, you may Angle at Ground all the day.

Of Night-Angling.

GReat Fish (especially *Trouts*) are like Bucks, wary and circumspect in their self-preservation, and know the seasons most fit for them to feed without danger ; and that is the Night , as they suppose, thinking then they may most securely range abroad.

In your Night-angling take two great Garden-worms of an equal length, and place them on your Hook ; then cast them a good distance, and draw them to you again upon the superficies of the Water, not suffering them to sink ; to which end you must not use a Plummet. You may easily hear the Fish rise, and therefore give him some time to swallow your Bait, then strike him gently. If he will not take it at the top, sink your Bait by adding some Lead, and order your self as at Day-angling on the Ground.

I have frequently experienced it, that the best *Trouts* bite in the Night, rising most commonly in the still Deeps, but unusually in the Streams.

Instead of these Garden-worms you may use a black Snail, or a piece of Velvet in its likeness : this is a most excellent Night-bait for a *Trout*, and nothing like the black Snail for a *Chub* in the Morning early.

You may bait your Hook with a *Minnow* for a *Trout* thus : put your Hook through the point of his lower Chap, and draw it quite through ; then put your Hook in at his Mouth, and bring the point to his Tail ; then draw your Line straight, and it will bring him into a round compass : But be sure you so order his Mouth that the water get not in.

What

What times are seasonable, and what unsea-
sonable to Angle in.

CAlm and clear weather is very good to angle in ;
but cool cloudy weather in Summer is best ; but
it must not be so boisterously windy as that you cannot guide your Tackle.   The cooler the weather is in
hottest Moneths, the better it is : and if a sudden violent shour hath disturbed and muddied the River, then
is your time to angle in the Stream at the ground with
a red Worm.

Likewise a little before the Fish spawn is a very good
time for Angling ; for then their Bellies being full,
they come into sandy Fords, and there rub their Bellies to loosen them, at which time they will bite very
freely.

If you intend to. fish for *Carp* and *Tench*, you must
commence your sport early in the Morning, fishing
from Sun-rising till eight of the Clock, and from four
in the Afternoon till Night ; and in hot Moneths till
it be very late.

In the heat of Summer *Carps* will shew themselves
on the very rim of the water ; at which time, if you
fish with a Lob-worm as you do with a Fly natural,
you will have excellent sport, especially if it be among
Reeds.

In *March, April, September*, and all the Winter, (in
which season Fish swim deep very neer the Ground)
I say, in those Moneths it is best fishing in a clear serene
warm day, for then they bite fastest : But all the Summer-time Mornings, Evenings, and cool cloudy weather are the best times for Angling.

Here note, that by experience you will finde that
Fish rise best at the Fly after a shour of Rain that hath
                                                        onely

onely beaten the Gnats and flies into the River without muddying them. The proper Moneths and times of the day for the Fly, are *March*, *April*, *May*, and the beginning of *June* ; in which Moneths let your times be in the Morning about nine , and between three and four in the Afternoon. A warm Evening is very seasonable, if the Gnats play much.

After a clear Moon-shiny-night, if the day succeeding prove cloudy, it is a very good time for Angling ; for, having abstained from food all the night, (for they will not stir for fear in bright nights) the next day they become hungry and eager, and the gloominess of the day makes them bite boldly.

At the opening of Sluces or Mill-dams go along with the course of the water, and you will finde *Trouts* and other fish will then come out to seek for what food the water brings down with it.

Having shewn you what seasons are most proper and profitable to Angle in, I will demonstrate to you such as are not.

And *First*, In the extremity of Heat, when the Earth is parched with Drought, there is little sport to be obtained, especially in muddy or clear shallow Rivers.

Secondly , In the Winter or Spring-time , when there happeneth any hoary Frost, then will not the fish bite kindly all that day, unless it be in the Evening, and if that prove serene and pleasant : but it is not convenient to fish at any time when the Wind bloweth so high that you cannot manage your Tools to advantage.

Thirdly, Sheep-shearing-time is an Enemy to the Angler, for then the Fish glut themselves with what is washt off the Sheep, and will scarcely bite till that season be over. Likewise sharp East and North nipping-winds do very much prejudice the Anglers Recreation : neither is it good to fish immediately after

Spawning-

Spawning-time ; for at that time their appetite is much abated.

It is a very ſtrange thing to conſider the natural inſtinct in Fiſh in foreknowing the approach of a ſhowr of Rain ; for I have tried , that upon the riſe of a Cloud that threatned a ſudden Showr, they would not bite ; from which obſervation I have often ſav'd my ſelf from being wet to the Skin.

Laſtly , If the preceding night prove dark and cloudy, the ſucceeding day will prove ineffectual for fiſhing, unleſs for ſmall fiſh ; for at ſuch times the great ones prey abroad for the leſſer,who,by inſtinct knowing the danger, hide themſelves till the Morning ; and having faſted all night become then very hungry, whilſt the great ones having gorg'd themſelves lie abſconded all the day long.

The next thing we ſhall inſiſt on, is the way of taking ſeveral ſorts of fiſh (as they are here alphabetically ſet down) with ſeveral proper Baits according to the beſt of experiences.

Of the BARBEL.

THE *Barbel* is ſo called by reaſon of the Barb which is under his Noſe or Chaps.   He is a leather-mouth'd-fiſh, that is, ſuch a one as will not break his hold when hook'd ; but will frequently break, if big, both Rod and Line.

They ſwim together in great Shoals,and are at worſt in *April*, though not very good at any time.

The places where he loves moſt to reſort, are where Weeds grow, or in a gravelly riſing ground, wherein he will dig and root like a Hog with his Noſe : not

but

but that he frequents the strongest swifts of water sometimes, as deep Bridges or Wears, where he will so settle himself among the Piles and hollow places, or amongst Moss or Weeds, that let the water be never so swift, he will remain immoveable. This is his custome in the Summer-time; after which time he retires into deep waters, and there helps the Female to dig a hole in the Sand for her to hide her Spawn from being devoured by other Fish.

This Fish is of a delicate Cast and handsome shape, with small Scales placed after a most curious manner; and as his shape is curious, so is his palate, for he will not eat any thing but what is clean; and therefore if you intend to make any sport with him your Bait must be very well scowred. The best for him is a Lob-worm, at which he will bite boldly, if you bait your ground the night before with big Worms cut in pieces. For him you can never bait the Ground too much, nor can you fish for him too early or too late.

Gentles also are a very good bait for him, if green; and so is Cheese made tough by keeping it in a wet Linnen Bag a day or two: This Cheese steeped in clarified Honey, and the Ground where you intend to fish baited therewith, will give you an opportunity to catch store enough of *Barbels*, if there be any thereabout. You may do well to bait your Hook with Cheese that is soft, and Sheeps-tallow wrought into a Paste: but there is no bait like the well-scowred Lob-worm, or Cheese steeped in Honey an hour or two.

When you fish for this *Barbel*, let your Rod and Line be both long and strong; for as he is very subtile, so is he extraordinary strong and dogged to be dealt withal, and will so struggle, that if you manage him not dextrously, he will break your Line.

His best time of biting is about nine of the Clock,
and

and the chiefest time of fishing for him is at the latter end of *May*, *June*, *July*, and the beginning of *August*.

Of the BREAM.

THere are two sorts of *Breams*, the one a fresh and the other a salt-water-Fish, yet neither differ much in shape, nature, or taste.

I shall onely speak of the fresh-water-*Bream*, which at full growth is a large and stately Fish, and breeds either in Ponds or Rivers; but chiefly delights in the former, which if he likes, he will not onely grow exceeding fat, but will fill the Pond with his issue, even to the starving of the other Fish.

As for his shape, it is very broad, and thick scaled very excellently, with a forked Tail; his Eyes are large, but he hath a very little sucking Mouth, disproportionate to his Body.

The flesh of this Fish is accounted more pleasant than wholsome by some : but as for my part, I am of the judgement of the *French*, who have a great estimaton for it; and if you will but taste his Belly or Head, you will say it is most excellent food.

The *Bream* spawneth in *June*, or the beginning of *July*, and is easily taken; for after one or two gentle turns he will fall upon his side, and so you may draw him to Land with ease. The best time of Angling for him, is from St. *James-tide* till *Bartholomew-tide*; for having had all the Summers food, they are exceeding fat.

The *Bream* is a great lover of red Worms, especially such as are to be found at the root of a great Dock, and lie wrapt up in a round clue; also he loves Paste, Flag-worms, Wasps, green Flies, Butter-flies, and a Grashopper with his Legs cut off.   The

The way of taking *Breams* is thus : Firſt bait the ground(where you know they reſort)with a convenienʳ quantity of ſweet groſs-ground Barley-malt , boyled but a little while, and ſtrained when it is cold : go with it to the place-about nine a clock at night, then take your Malt, and ſqueezing it between your Hands, throw it into the River, and it will ſink : If the ſtream run hard, caſt in your ſqueezed Balls a little above the place you intend to angle in. Having thus baited your ground, in the Morning bait your Hook with the greateſt red Worm you can get ; you may finde them in Gardens or Chalky Commons after a ſhowre of Rain ; of which you muſt ſtore your ſelf beforehand, keeping them a Moneth at leaſt in dry Moſs, changing the Moſs every three daies. Having baited your hook ſo that the worm may crawl to and fro, for the better inticing of the Fiſh to bite without ſuſpition, obſerve where your fiſh play moſt and ſtay longeſt, which commonly is in the broadeſt and deepeſt part of the River : then plumb your ground, and fiſh within half an Inch of it ; for although you ſhall ſee ſome *Breams* play on the top of the Water, yet theſe are but the Sentinels for them beneath.

You may have three or four Rods out at a time ſtuck in the Bank-ſide, and let them be long, the Floats Swan or Grooſe-quills , which muſt be ſunk with Lead , the tops bearing above water about half an Inch. Let your Rods be caſt in one above the other about a yard and a half diſtant, and then withdraw your ſelf from the Bank ſo far that you can perceive nothing but the top of the Float ; and when you perceive it to ſink, then creep to the Water-ſide, and give it as much Line as you can : if it be a *Carp* or *Bream*, they will run to the other ſide ; then ſtrike gently, and hold your Rod at a bent a little while, but do not pull, for then you ſpoil all ; but you muſt firſt tire

them

them before you can land them, being very shie. Of the two, the *Carp* is the worst, being more brisk and strong.

Here take notice by the way, if *Pike* or *Pearch* be thereabout, it will be but a folly to think of killing *Carp* or *Bream* ; and therefore you must remove those obstacles, by fishing them out first. And to the intent you may know whether there be those Fish of Prey thereabout, take a small *Bleak* or *Gudgeon*, and bait it, setting it alive among your Rods, two foot deep from your Float, with a little red Worm at the point of your Hook : if a *Pike* be there, he will certainly snap at it.

Of the BLEAK.

THE *Bleak* is an eager fish, and is caught with all sorts of Worms bred on Trees or Plants, also with Flies, Paste, Sheeps-bloud, &c. You may angle for them with half a score Hooks at once, if you can fasten them all on. Also in an Evening the *Bleak* will take the natural or artificial Fly.

If it be a warm clear day, there is no Bait so good for the *Bleak* as a small Fly at the top of the water, which they will take at any time of the day, but especially in the evening : there is no fish that yields better sport for a young Angler than this, for they are so eager that they will leap out of the water at the Bait.

If the day be cold and cloudy, Gentles or Cadice are best about two foot under water.

This same *Bleak* by some is called a Fresh-water-sprat, or River-swallow, by reason of his continual motion.

Some would have him called *Bleak* from his whitish colour, and that is onely under his Belly, for his Back is of a pleasant Sea-green. I   There

There is another way of taking *Bleaks*, by whipping them in a Boat or on a Bank-side in swift Water in a Summers evening, with a Hazel-top about five or six foot long, and a Line twice the length of the Rod; but the best way is to tie eight or ten small Hooks along a Line two Inches above one another, and bait them with Gentles or Flies, by which means you may take half a dozen or more at one time.

Of the B U L L-H E A D, *or* M I L-LER'S-T H U M B.

THE *Bull-head* is a fish which hath a broad Head and wide Mouth, with two broad Fins neer his Eyes, and two Fins under his Belly: instead of his Teeth his rough Lips assist him in nibbling at the bait. He hath Fins also on his Back, and one below the Vent; and his Tail is round, his Body being all over covered with whitish, blackish, and brownish spots.

They begin to spawn about *April*, and are full of Spawn all the Summer-season. The *Bull-head*'s common habitation is in Holes, or among Stones in clear Water in Summer; but in the Winter he takes up his quarters with the *Eel* in the Mud: So doth the *Loach* and *Minnow*; or we cannot guess otherwise where their Winter-abode should be.

He is easily taken in the Summer, for he is lazie and simple. You may see him in hot weather lie Sunning himself on a flat Stone or gravelly Ground, at which time you may put your Hook (which must be baited with a small Worm) very neer his Mouth, at which he seldom refuseth to bite, so that the veriest bungling Angler may take him.

He is an excellent fish for taste, but of so ill a shape, that many women care not for dressing him, he so much resembles a Toad.

Of

Of the CHEVIN.

THE *Chevin* fpawneth in *March*, and is a very ftrong (yet unactive) fish, yielding in a very little time after he is ftruck. The larger he is, the quieter he is taken.

As for his food, he loveth all forts of Worms and Flies, also Cheefe, Grain, black Worms, flitting their Bellies that the white may appear: he loveth to have his Bait large, and variety of Baits at one Hook. He delights very much in the Pith that grows in the bone of an Ox-back, of which you muft be careful in taking off the tough outward Skin, without breaking the tender inward Skin.

Early in the Morning angle for your *Chevin* with Snails; but choofe fome other bait for him in the heat of the day, for then he will not bite at them. In the Afternoon fish for him at Ground or Flie. There is no Fly he loveth better than a great Moth with a great head, whofe Body is yellow, with whitish Wings; which is to be found commonly in Gardens about the Evening. He will not ftick fometimes to fnap at a Lamprey.

Of the CHAR.

I Could never read nor hear that the *Char* was taken any where but in a Mere in *Lancafhire*, called *Winander-mere*, the largeft, according to report, that is in the Kingdom of *England*, being ten miles in length, and as fmooth as a Bowling-green at the bottom.

This *Char* is fpotted like a *Trout*, and its dimenfion feldome exceeds feventeen Inches or a foot and half. This Fifh is delicate food, having fcarce a Bone but what is on the Back. Now since the place is so remote from *London* where these *Chars* are taken, I shall forbear to trouble our City-Angler with Rules and Directions how to angle for him, and pass to such Fish as are frequently found in every River here neer adjacent.

Of the C H U B.

THis Fish hath several appellations; for he is called a *Chub*, a *Chavender* by the *French*, by some a *Villain*, by others a *Cheven*. As for my part, call him what you please, I like him not for these reasons: first, he is full of small forked Bones disperst every where throughout his Body; next, he eats very waterish; and lastly, this Fish is unfirm, and (in my opinion) in a manner tasteless.

Of all fish he is the best to enter a young Angler, for he is very easily taken: however give me leave to prescribe you some more Rules than what I have already shewn in the Angling for the *Cheven*, which is the same with the *Chub* or *Chavender*.

You must finde out some hole, where you shall have twenty or more of them together in a hot day floating almost on the very surface of the water: then bait your Hook with a Grashopper; but so abscond your self that you may not be seen, for he is a very fearful fish, and therefore the least shadow will make him sink to the bottom of the water, yet he will rise again suddainly.

Having baited your Hook, drop it gently some two foot before that *Chub* you have elected by your eye to be the best and fairest, and he will instantly bite greedily thereat, and be held so fast by reason of his Leather-mouth, that he can seldom break his hold:

and

and therefore you may do well to give him play e-
nough, and ſo tire him; otherwiſe you may endanger
your Line.

If you cannot finde a Graſhopper, then bait your
Hook with any kinde of Fly or Worm, as I ſaid before,
as Dors, Beetles, Bobs, Cod or Caſe-worms.

When you fiſh for the *Chub* with a Fly, Graſhopper,
or Beetle, it muſt be at the top of the water, if with
other baits, underneath.

In *March* and *April* angle for your *Chub* with
Worms; in *May*, *June*, and *July*, with Flies, Snails,
or Cherries. Where note, he will rarely refuſe a Graſhopper on the top of a ſwift Stream, nor at the bottom
the young humble-bee. In *Auguſt*, *September*, &c.
make uſe of a Paſte made of Parmiſan, or *Holland*-cheeſe
pounded with Saffron in a Mortar, adding thereunto
a little Butter. Others make a Paſte of Cheeſe and
Turpentine for the Winter-ſeaſon, at which time the
Chub is in his prime; for then his forked Bones are either loſt, or converted into a Griſtle; and he is excellent meat baked.

In hot weather angle for him in the middle of the
water, neer the top thereof; but in cold weather fiſh
for him neer the bottom.

To finiſh all other diſcourſe of this *Chub*, *Cheven*, or
Chavender, I ſhall only ſay that his Spawn is excellent;
and if he be large, the Head, when the Throat is well
waſht, is the beſt part of the fiſh.

Of the CARP.

IT is confeſs'd by all, that the *Carp* is the Queen of all
Freſh-water-fiſh, being not only a good, but ſubtile
fiſh, and living longeſt of all fiſh (excepting the *Eel*)
out of his proper Element. Thoſe that die ſooneſt are
Herrings, for ſalt-water; and for freſh-water, *Trouts*.

Carps are observed to breed several Moneths in one year; and for this reason you shall hardly ever take either Male or Female without Melt or Spawn. They breed ever more naturally in Ponds than in running water: in the latter very seldom or never; and where they breed, they breed innumerably.

He that intends to Angle for a *Carp*, must arm himself with a world of Patience, by reason of the extraordinary subtlety and policy of that fish. Next, you are to observe that the *Carp* will seldom bite in cold weather; and in hot weather you cannot be too early or too late at your sport: and if he bite, you need not fear his hold, for he is one of those leather-mouth'd-fish, who have their Teeth in their Throat.

When you angle for the *Carp*, your Rod and Line must be strong; and because he is so very wary, it is good to entice him by baiting the Ground with course Paste: In *March* he seldom refuseth the red Worm, the Cadice in *June*; nor the Grashopper in *July*, *August*, and *September*.

The *Carp* takes delight in Worms or sweet Pastes, of which there are great variety: the best are made up of Honey and Sugar, and ought to be thrown into your Water some hours before you intend to angle; or if you throw in your Paste made into small Pellets two or three daies before, it will not be the worse, especially if you throw in also Chickens-guts, Garbage, or Bloud incorporated with Bran or Cow-dung.

You may make your Paste in this manner: Take a convenient quantity of Bean-flour, or any other Flour, and mingle it with the flesh of a Cat cut small; make up this Composition with Honey, and then beat them all together in a Morter so long, till they are so tough as to hang upon a Hook without washing off. For the better effecting thereof, mingle therewith some whitish Wooll; and if you would keep it all the

year,

year, adde thereunto some Virgins-wax and clarified Honey.

If you fish with Gentles, anoint them with Honey, and put them on your Hook with a piece of Scarlet dipt in the like. This is the most approved way to deceive and captivate the subtile *Carp*. Honey and crums of White-bread mixt together is a very good Paste for a *Carp*.

An approved way how to take Carp *in a muddy Pond*, Vide *Chap. Of the Tench.*

Of the DACE and DARE.

THE *Dace,Dare,* and *Roach,* are much of a kinde, both in manner of feeding, cunning, goodness, and commonly in size.

The *Dace* or *Dare* will bite at any Fly, but especially at Ant-flies, of which the blackish are the best ; which are found in Mole-hills about the Moneths of *June, July, August,* and *September.* The way of preserving them for your use is, to put them alive into a Glass-bottle , having first laid therein some of the moist Earth from whence you gathered them, with some of the Roots of the Grass of the said Hillock: having laid your Ant-flies in gently without prejudicing their Wings, lay a clod of Earth over it: thus you may keep them a Moneth, if you bruise them not. If you would keep them longer, put them into a large Rundlet, having first wash'd the inside with Water and Honey : having thus kept them three Moneths, they are an incomparable Bait in any Stream and clear Water, either for *Dace, Dare,* or *Roach,* and are good also for a *Chavender,* fishing within a handful from the bottom.

The

The beſt time for making uſe of the Ant-flie , is when they ſwarm, and that is generally about the latter end of *July*, and beginning of *Auguſt* : they will cover a Tree or Buſh with their multitude, and then if you make uſe of them, you may load your ſelf with *Roach* and *Dace* in a ſmall time.

In a warm day he rarely refuſeth a Fly at the top of the water; but remember that when you fiſh under water for him, it is beſt to be within an handful or ſomething more of the ground.

If you would fiſh for *Dace* or *Dare* in Winter, then about *Alhallontide*, where ever you ſee Heath or Sandy grounds ploughing up, follow the Plough, and you will finde a white Worm with a read head, as big as the end of a man's little finger. You may know where the moſt of them are, by the number of Crows and Rooks which ſit on the plow'd-land. The worm is very ſoft, and is by ſome termed a *Grub*, which is nothing but the ſpawn of a Beetle. Gather what quantity you think fit, and put them into a Veſſel with ſome of the Earth from whence they were taken, and you may keep them all the Winter.

Laſtly, the young brood of Waſps and Bees, having their heads dipt in Bloud, are an excellent bait for *Dace* and *Dare*.

Of the E E L.

I Shall not trouble you with variety of diſcourſes concerning the being of an *Eel*, whether they breed by ſome Generation, or Corruption as Worms; or by certain glutinous Dew-drops, which falling in *May* and *June* on the Banks of ſome Ponds or Rivers, are by the heat of the Sun turned into *Eels* : and theſe are by ſome called *Yelvers*, of which I have ſeen Cakes made, and have eaten thereof when fried, with

with much satisfaction. I say, waving all Discourses of this nature, I shall onely tell you that some have differenced *Eels* into four sorts chiefly: namely, the Silver-*Eel*; a Greenish *Eel*, (which is called a *Greg*;) a blackish *Eel*, with a broad flat head; and, lastly, an *Eel* with reddish Fins.

I shall onely speak of the first, which is the Silver-*Eel*. This *Eel* is generally believed to have its being from Generation, but not by Spawning, but the young coming from the Female alive, and no bigger than a small Needle.

This *Eel* may be caught with several sorts of Baits, but principally with powder'd Beef. A Garden-worm or Lob, or a *Minnow*, or Hen's-gut, or Garbage of Fish, is a very good bait: but some prefer a *Pride*, which others call a *Lamprey*, beyond any yet named.

As *Eels* abscond themselves in Winter, taking up their constant residence in the Mud, without stirring out for six Moneths; so in the Summer they take no delight to be abroad in the day, and therefore the most proper time to take them is in the night, with any of those baits aforesaid, fastning your Line to the Bank-side with your Laying-hooks in the water. Or you may throw in a Line with good store of Hooks baited, and plumb'd with a Float to discover where the Line lieth, that in the Morning you may take it up with your Drag-hook.

There is another way of taking *Eels*, and that is by *Sniggling*. This Sniggling is nothing else but taking in the day-time a strong Line and Hook baited with a Lob or Garden-worm, and marking such Holes and places where the *Eels* use to abscond themselves in the day-time neer Wears, Mills, or Floud-gates, and gently by the help of a Stick putting your bait into such holes where you imagine *Eels* are:

and

and if there be any, you shall be sure to have a bite; but then have a care you pull not too hard, left you spoil all. Here note, that the Top of your Stick must be cleft, wherein you must put in a strong Hook, but of a narrow compass; which Stick must guide the Bait into the Hole where the *Eel* is, by which means, if your Tackling hold, you may get as large *Eels* as any are in the River, Mill-pond, or Floud-gate, *&c.* And as this way of fishing is called *Sniggling,* so it is called *Broggling* for *Eels.*

Bobbing for Eels is done after another manner : that is, Take very large Lobs, scowr them well, and with a Needle run some strong-twisted Silk through them from end to end; take so many as that you may wrap them about a board a dozen times at least; then tie them fast with the two ends of the Silk, that they may hang in so many Hanks; then fasten all to a strong Cord, and about a handful and a half above the Worms fasten a Plumb of three quarters of a pound in weight, and fasten your Cord to a strong Pole : having so done, fish in muddy Water, and you will feel the *Eels* tug lustily at them. When you think they have swallowed them as far as they can, gently draw up your Line, till you have brought your *Eels* to the top of the water, and then bring them ashore as fast as you can. The Gentleman (and an experienced Angler) from whom I received this Instruction, told me, he hath taken six or seven large *Eels* at a time this very way.

There is another way also for taking of *Eels* (though it be somewhat laborious, and for that reason is best to be made use of in cold weather) and that is by an Instrument called an *Eel-spear* : it is made for the most part with three Forks or Teeth, jagged on the sides; but those are better that have four. This you are to strike into the Mud at the bottom of the

River,

River; and if you chance to light where they lie, you need not fear taking them if your Instrument be good.

If you would take very large *Eels* indeed, bait your Night-hooks with small *Roaches*, and let the Hooks lie in the Mouth of the Fish.

Of the FLOUNDER.

I Shall not go about to tell you the nature of a *Flounder*, or give you his defcription, fince he is a Fish fo well known to every one.

In *April*, *May*, *June*, and *July*, you may fish for the *Flounder* all day long, either in a fwift Stream or in the ftill Deep, but beft in the Stream. Your moft proper Baits are all forts of red Worms, Wafps, and Gentles.

Of the GRAILING.

WHen you angle for the *Grailing*, you muft head your Hook upon the Shank with a very flender narrow plate of Lead, and let it be flendereft at the bent of the Hook, that the Bait, which muft be a large Grafhopper, may with more facility come over it: At the point let there be a Cad-bait, and keep your Bait in continual motion; and forget not to pull off the Grafhopper's Wings which are uppermoft.

In the Moneths of *March* and *April*, there is an excellent Bait for the *Grailing*, which is called a *Tag-tail*: This Worm is of a pale Flesh-colour, with a yellow Tag on his Tail, fomewhat lefs than half an Inch long; which is to be found in

Marled

Marled Grounds and Meadows in fair weather, but
not to be seen in cold weather, or after a showre of
Rain.

Of the GUDGEON

THe *Gudgeon*, though small, is a fish of so pleasant
a taste, that in my opinion it is very little inferiour to the *Smelt.* I need not describe him, he is so
well known.

He spawns three or four times in the Summer-season. His feeding is much like the *Barbel*'s, in sharp
Streams and on Gravel, slighting all manner of Flies.
He is easily taken with a small red Worm, fishing near
the ground.

This fish is Leather-mouth'd, and will not easily be
lost off the Hook when struck. You may fish for him
with a Float, your Hook being on the ground; or by
hand with a running Line on the ground, without either Cork or Float.

Wasps, Gentles, and Cad-baits are good baits for
the *Gudgeon.* When you angle for a *Gudgeon*, stir up
the Sand or Gravel with a long Pole, which will make
them gather to that place, and bite faster and with
more eagerness.

Of the GUINIAD.

I Cannot say much of this Fish, only that it is excellent food; and therefore I shall conclude my dif-
course of the *Guiniad* with a very strange observation;
and that is, This Fish is not found any where but in a
large Water called *Pemble-Mere*: but that which is most
remarkable is this, That the River which runs by *Che-*
ster

ster hath its Head or Fountain in *Merionith-shire*, and in its course runs through this *Pemble-mere*, which abounds as much with *Guiniads*, as the River *Dee* doth with *Salmon*, of each both affording great plenty; and yet it was never known that any *Salmon* was ever caught in the Mere, nor ever any *Guiniad* taken in the River.

When Dee that in his course fain in her lap would lie,
Commixtion with her store, his stream she doth deny,
By his complexion prov'd, as he through her doth glide,
Her Wealth again from his she likewise doth divide:
Those white fish that in her do wonderously abound,
Are never seen in him ; nor are his Salmons *found*
At any time in her ; but as she him disdains,
So he again from her as wilfully abstains.

Drayton's Polyolb. Song 9.

Of the LOACH.

THe *Loach*, though a small, is yet a dainty fish : his breeding and feeding is in little and clear swift Brooks or Rivulets ; here and in sharp Streams Gravel is his usual food.   He is small and slender, seldom exceeding three Inches in length : he is bearded like a *Barbel*, having two Fins at his sides, four at his Belly, and onely one at his Tail, and is freckled with many black or brown spots.

This *Loach* is commonly full of Spawn, which is, with the fish, a very grateful food to weak Stomachs, affording great nourishment.   He is to be taken with a very small Worm neer the ground ; for he delights to be neer the Gravel, and therefore is seldom seen on the top of the water.

Of

Of the MINNOW.

THE *Minnow* is a fish without Scales, and one of the least of the watry Inhabitants; but for excellency of meat he may (in my opinion) be compared to any fish of greatest value and largest size; and little things should not be despised. The Spawners are usually full of Spawn all the Summer long, for they breed often, as it is but necessary, being both Prey and Baits to other fish. They come into the Rivers generally about *March* and *April*, and there continue till the cold weather drive them into their Winter-quarters again.

Of colour this Fish is greenish , or wavy sky-coloured; his Belly is very white, but his Back is blackish. This fish will bite sharply at a small Worm; and if you will trouble your self to catch enough of them, you may make an excellent Tansie of them, cutting off their Heads and Tails, and frying them in Eggs, saucing them with Butter, Sugar, and Verjuice.

Anglers use to finde him oftner than they would : Deep places he seldome frequents. It is a Fish no way curious of his feeding, for any Bait pleaseth him if he can but swallow it , and he will strain hard for what he cannot gorge. The chiefest food he loveth is a small red Worm, Wasps, or Cad-baits.

Of the POPE, or RUFF.

THis Fish with a double name is small, and seldome grows bigger than a *Gudgeon*; in shape he is not unlike a *Pearch*, but esteemed better food, being of taste as pleasant and delightful as any fish whatever.   The

The *Ruff* makes excellent fport with an unexpe-
rienced Angler, for he is a greedy biter; and they are
in great Shoals together where the Water is deep,
fmooth, and calm. If you would catch a good round
quantity, bait your ground with Earth, and angle for
them with a fmall red Worm.

Of the PIKE.

THE *Pike* is a very long-liv'd creature, and if
we may credit Sir *Francis Bacon*, or *Gefner* that
famous Brutologift, he outlives all other Fifh; which
is pitty, he being as abfolute a Tyrant of the Frefh-
waters, as the *Salmon* is, the King thereof.

The larger the *Pike*, the courfer the food, the fmaller being ever beft; contrary to the nature of *Eels*,
which improve their goodnefs by their bulk and age.

He is a melancholick Fifh, becaufe he never fwims
in Shoals, but refts himfelf alone; and he is as bold
as any fifh whatever, if we may believe Report, which
informs us a *Pike* hath been known to fight with an
Otter for a *Carp* he had taken, and was carrying out of
the Water. Another bit a Mule by the Lip as he was
drinking, and ftuck thereunto fo faft, that by that
means the Owner of the Mule took him. Another
bit a Maid by the Foot as fhe was wafhing. He will
frequently devour his own kinde unnaturally; from
whence I fuppofe he may obtain the name of a *Frefh-
water-wolf.*

As the *Pike* is in nature like the Hawk, a Bird of
Prey, fo is he like her in generation, neither of them
breeding but once a year: and when the *Pike* fpawns
it is between *February* and *March*. The beft *Pikes* are
found in Rivers, the worft in Meres or Ponds.

His common Food is either Pickerel-weed, Frogs,
or

or what fish he can procure. This Pickerel-weed some say, both feeds and breeds them.

There are two ways of fishing for the *Pike* ; first by the Ledger, secondly by the Walking bait.

The Ledger-bait is fix'd in one certain place, whilst the Angler may be absent ; and this must be a living bait, either Fish or Frog. Of Fish the best are a *Dace*, *Roach*, or *Pearch* : for Frogs , the yellowest are the best. How to keep them alive on your Hook, your own ingenuity will inform you.

When you intend to use the Ledger-bait, if it be a Fish, stick your Hook through his upper Lip ; and then fastning it to a strong Line of at least twelve or fourteen yards in length, tie the other end of the Line either to some Stake in the ground, or to some bough of a Tree neer the *Pike*'s usual haunt, or where you think 'tis like he may come. Then winde your Line on a forked stick, (big enough to keep the bait from drawing it under water) all except about half a yard or somewhat more ; and your Stick having a small cleft at the end , fasten your Line therein ; but so, that when the *Pike* comes, he may easily draw it forth, and have Line enough to go to his hold and pouch.

If your bait be a Frog, put the Arming-wyre in at his Mouth, and out at his Gills ; and then with a fine Needle and Silk sow the upper part of his Leg with one stitch onely to your Arming-wyre, or tie his Leg above the upper joynt to the Wyre ; but as gently as you can, left you hurt him.

I have seen excellent sport with the living baits tied about the Bodies of two or three couple of Ducks, driven over a place where store of *Pikes* have frequented. I have observed the *Pike* to strike so violently at the living Bait, that being hung, he hath drawn the Duck clear under water. The like may be done with such baits tied to Bladders, suffering them to float down

the

the River, whilst you minde your sport walking on
its Banks.

The next way of Angling for a *Pike* is with a *Trowl*
with a Winch to wind it up withal. As this fish is
very strong, so must your Tackle; and your Rod must
not be very slender at top, where must be placed a Ring
for your Line to run through. Your Line must be
Silk two yards and a quarter next the Hook, which
must be double, and strongly armed with Wyre a-
bout seven Inches: the rest of your Line may be
strong Shoemakers-thread. Upon the shank of the
Hook fasten some smooth Lead; and having placed
your Hook in the Mouth of a *Minnow*, *Dace*, or
Roach; with your Lead sink your Bait with his
Head downward. Having so done, cast your bait
up and down: if you feel him at the Hook, give
him length enough to run away with the bait and
pouch it; which when you think he hath done, strike
him with a smart jerk, and so continue your sport
with him as long as you shall think fit. Take likewise this next Direction from a friend who speaks not
much different.

When you intend to Trowl, you may make choice
either of *Roach*, *Dace*, *Bleak*, or *Gudgeon* to bait
withal, (but for my own part I always prefer the
Gudgeon) which you must do thus: put your Arming-wyre in at the Mouth, and thrusting it along by
the Back, bring it out again at the Tail, and there fasten it with a Thread. Having your Reel in your hand,
and your Line fastned to your hook through a Ring at
the top of your Rod, cast your bait into some likely
place, and move it up and down in the water as you
walk gently by the River-side: when you have a bite
(which you may easily feel, for he will give a good
tug) be sure to give him Line enough. You
may let him lie almost a quarter of an hour

K before

before you strike ; and then have a care you do it not too fiercely, left you endanger your Tackle, and lose the Fish to boot.

If you fish at Snap, you must give him leave to run a little, then strike, striking the contrary way to which he runneth. For this way of Angling, a Spring-hook is best ; and your Tackle must be much stronger than that for the Trowl, because you must strike with greater force.

Here note, that a large Bait more invites the *Pike* to bite, but the lesser takes him more infallibly, either at Snap or Trowl.

If you fish with a dead bait for a *Pike*, this is a most excellent bait : Take a *Minnow*, Frog that is yellow, *Dace*, or *Roach*, and having dissolved Gum of Ivy in Oil of Spike, anoint your bait therewith, and cast it where *Pikes* frequent. Having lain a little while at bottom, draw it to the top, and so up the Stream, and you will quickly perceive a *Pike* follow it with much eagerness.

A *Pike* will bite at all baits, excepting the Fly, and bites best about three in the afternoon in clear water with a gentle gale, from the middle of Summer to the latter end of Autumn ; he then bites best in still places or a gentle Stream : but in Winter he bites all the day long. In the latter end, and beginning of the Spring, he bites most eagerly early in the morning, and late in the evening.

Of the PEARCH.

THe *Pearch* is a fish that is hook-backt, somewhat bow'd like a Hog, and armed with stiff Gristles, and his sides with dry thick Scales. He is a bold biter, which appears by his daring to adventure on one

of

of his own kinde with more courage than the *Pike* by much.

Some say there are two sorts of *Pearches*, the one salt-water, and the other fresh : the first hath but one Fin on his Back, the latter two, which is more than most Fishes have.

He spawns but once a year, and that is in *February* or *March*, and seldom grows longer than two foot. His best time of biting is when the Spring is far spent, at which time you may take at one standing all that are in one hole, be they never so many.

His baits are a *Minnow*, or little Frog ; but a Worm called a *Brandling* is best, if well scoured. When he bites give him time enough, and that can hardly be too much.

The *Pearch* biteth well all the day long in cool cloudy weather ; but chiefly from eight in the Morning till ten, and from three till almost six.

You may angle for him with Lob-worms well scoured, Bobs, Oak-worms , Gentles, Colewort-worms, *Minnows*, Dors, Wasps, and Cad-baits.

He will not bite at all the seasons of the year, especially in Winter, for then he is very abstemious ; yet if it be warm he will bite then in the midst of the day ; for in Winter all fish bite best about the heat of the day.

If you rove for a *Pearch* with a *Minnow*, (which of all baits yields the most delightful recreation to the Angler) it must be alive, sticking your Hook through his upper Lip or back Fin, and letting him swim about mid-water, or somewhat lower ; for which purpose you must have an indifferent large Cork with a Quill on your Line.

I always make use of a good strong Silk-Line, and a good Hook arm'd with Wyre, so that if a *Pike* do come I may be provided for him ; and have by this

means

means taken feveral. I ufe alfo to carry a Tin-pot of about two quarts or three pints, in which to keep my *Minnows* or *Gudgeons* alive: the Lid of the Pot is full of little holes, fo that I can give them frefh Water without opening it; which ought to be about every quarter of an hour, left they die.

If you take a fmall Cafting-net with you, you may at a caft or two take baits enough to ferve you all day without farther trouble.

When you fifh with a Frog, you muft faften the Hook through the skin of his Leg towards the upper part thereof.

The *Pearch* is none of the Leather-mouth'd fort of fifhes; and therefore when he bites give him time enough to pouch his bait, left when you think all fure, his hold break out, and vou lofe your fifh and your patience too.

Of the RUD.

THe *Rud* hath a forked Tail, and is fmall of fize: fome fay he is bred of the *Roach* and *Bream*, and is found in Ponds; in fome they are in a manner innumerable.

There is little lefs difference between the *Rud* and *Roach*, than there is between the *Herring* and *Pilchard*, their fhape being much alike, onely differing in bulk or bignefs. Since the *Rud* is but a Baftard-*Roach*, I fhall fpeak no more of him, but difcourfe of the genuine *Roach* onely.

Of the R O A C H.

THE *Roach* is not looked on as any delicate Fish at all ; if there be any thing prizable, it is his Spawn.

The *Roach* is a very silly fish, being every whit as simple as the *Carp* is crafty. They are more to be esteemed which are found in Rivers than in Ponds, although those that breed in the latter are of a much larger size ; yet the *Thames* below Bridge abounds with very large fat *Roach*, such as I may confidently affirm exceed in magnitude all others either in Ponds or Rivers.

The *Roach* is a Leather-mouth'd-fish, having his Teeth (as I said before) in his Throat, as all Leather-mouth'd Fish have.

In *April* the Cads or Worms are proper Baits to angle for *Roaches*; in Summer fish for them with small white Snails or Flies: but note, they must be under water, for he will not bite at the top. Or, take a *May*-fly, and with a Plumb sink it where you imagine *Roaches* lie, whether in deep water, or neer the Posts and Piles either of Bridge or Wear: having so done, do not hastily, but gently pull your Fly up, and you will see the *Roach* (if any there) pursue and take it neer the rim of the water, lest by flight it should escape.

In Autumn you may fish for them with Paste onely made of the crums of fine White-bread, moulded with a little water and the labour of your hands into a tough Paste, with which you must fish with much circumspection, or you lose your bait. In like manner in Winter you may angle for *Roach* with Paste ; but Gentles are then the better bait.

Take

Take these next Observations experimentally tried by some of us, *viz.* There is another excellent bait either for Winter or Summer, and that is this: Take an handful of well-dried Malt, and put it into a Dish of Water, and then having grubbed and washed it betwixt your hands till it be clean and free from Husks, put that water from it; and having put it into a little fresh water, set it over a gentle Fire, and let it boil till it be pretty soft; then pour the Water from it, and with a sharp Knife, turning the sprout-end of the Corn upward, take off the back-part of the Husk with the point of your Knife, leaving a kinde of inward Husk on the Corn, or else you spoil all: then cut off a little of the sprout-end, that the white may appear, and also a very little of the other end for the Hook to enter. When you make use of this bait, cast now and then a little of it into the water; and then, if your Hook be small and good, you will finde it an excellent bait either for *Roach* or *Dace*.

Another good bait is the young brood of Wasps or Bees, if you dip their Heads in Blood. So is the thick blood of Sheep being half dried on a Trencher, and then cut into such small pieces as will best fit your Hook: a little Salt will keep it from turning black, and make it the better.

Or you may take an handful or two of the largest and best Wheat you can get, boil it in a little Milk till it be soft, then fry it gently with Honey and a little beaten Saffron dissolved in Milk.

The *Roach* spawns about the middle of *May*; and the general baits by which he is caught are these: small white Snails, Bobs, Cad-baits, Sheeps-bloud, all sorts of Worms, Gnats, Wasps, Paste, and Cherries.

The way of fishing for *Roach* at *London*-bridge is after this manner: In the Moneths of *June*, and *July*, there is great resort of those Fish to that place, where

where those that make a trade of it take a strong Cord,
at the end whereof is fastned a three-pound-weight; a
foot above the Lead they fasten a Packthread of twelve
foot long to the Cord, and unto the Packthread at
convenient distances they adde a dozen strong Links
of Hair with *Roach*-hooks at them, baited with a
white Snail or Periwinkle; then holding the Cord in
their Hands, the biting of the Fish draweth the Packthread, and the Packthread the Cord, which admo-
nisheth them what to do: whereby sometimes they
draw up half a dozen, sometimes less, but commonly
two or three at one draught.

Of the STICKLEBAG.

THis Fish is small, prickly, and without Scales, and
not worth the consideration, but that he is an
excellent bait for *Trouts*, especially if his Tail on the
Hook be turned round, at which a *Trout* will bite
more eagerly than at *Penk*, *Roach*, or *Minnow*. The
Loach is every whit as good a bait as the *Sticklebag*,
provided you place either aright on the Hook. To
the intent you may do it, take this observation: the
nimble turning of the *Penk*, *Minnow*, *Loach*, or *Sticklebag*, is the perfection of that sort of fishing. That
you may attain thereunto, note, that you must put
your Hook into the Mouth of any the aforesaid Baits,
and out at his Tail, tying him fast with white Thread
a little above it, in such manner that he may turn: after this sow up his Mouth, and your designe is accom-
plished. This way of baiting is very tempting for
large *Trouts*, and seldom fails the Angler's expectation.
This fish in some places is called a *Banstickle*.

Of the SALMON.

THe *Salmons* evermore breed in Rivers that are not brackish, yet difcharge themfelves into the Sea, and fpawn commonly in *Auguft*, which become *Samlets* in the Spring following. The Melter and Spawner having both performed their natural duty, they then betake themfelves to the Sea. I have known that when they have been obftructed in their paffage, they have grown fo impatient, that, clapping their Tails to their Mouthts, with a fudden fpring they have leapt clear over Wear, or any other obftacle which ftood in their way: Some having leapt fhort, have been taken by that means. If they are fo obftructed that they cannot finde their way to the Sea, they become fick, lean, and pine away, and die in two years. If they fpawn in the mean time, from thence proceeds a fmall *Salmon* called a *Skegger*, which will never grow great. It is the Sea that makes them grow big; but it is the frefh Rivers that makes them grow fat; and fo much the farther they are from the Sea up in the Rivers, the fatter they grow, and the better their food.

From a *Samlet* (which is but little bigger than a *Minnow*) he grows to be a *Salmon* in as fhort time as a Goflin will grow to be a Goofe.

A *Salmon* biteth beft at three of the clock in the Afternoon, in the Moneths of *May*, *June*, *July*, and *Auguft*, if the water be clear, and fome little breeze of Wind ftirring, efpecially if the Wind bloweth againft the Stream, and neer the Sea.

Where note, that he hath not his conftant refidence, like a *Trout*, but removes often, coveting to be as neer the Spring-head as he may, fwimming

general-

generally in the deepest and broadest parts of the River neer the ground; and he is caught like a *Trout*, with Worm, Fly, or *Minnow*. The Garden-worm is an Excellent bait for the *Salmon*, if it be well scoured, and kept in Moss about twenty daies, after which time those Worms will be very clear, tough and lively.

There is a way of fishing for *Salmon* with a Ring of Wyre on the top of the Rod, through which the Line may run to what length is thought convenient, having a Wheel also neer the hand.

I have been told that there is no bait more attractive of and eagerly pursued by the *Salmon* and most other fish, than Lob-worms sented with the Oil of Ivy-berries, or the Oil of Polypodie of the Oak mixt with Turpentine; nay, *Assa Fœtida* they say is incomparably good.

The Artificial Fly is a good bait for a *Salmon*; but you must then use a Trowl as for the *Pike*, he being a strong fish. As the *Salmon* is a large fish, so must your Flies be larger than for any other, with Wings and Tails very long.

You shall observe, when you strike him, that he will plunge and bounce, but doth not usually endeavour to run to the length of the Line, as the *Trout* will do; and therefore there is less danger of breaking your Line.

If you will angle for *Salmon* at ground, then take three or four Garden-worms well scoured, and put them on your Hook at once, and fish with them in the same manner as you do for *Trouts*.

Be sure to give the *Salmon* (as well as all other fish) time to go gorge the bait, and be not over-hasty, unless your bait be so tender it will not endure nibbling at. Much more may be said of *Salmon*-fishing, which I shall pass by, leaving the rest to your own practice and observation.

Of

Of the TENCH.

I Shall now discover an approved way how to take *Tench* and *Carp* in a muddy Pond : but know, I do not make publick this following Secret, to teach Knaves how to rob Gentlemens Ponds , but that the proper Owners may be able upon cases of necessity to supply themselves with Fish, without being put to so much trouble and charge as to sue their Ponds. But to the purpose. In the first place you must provide your self with a very good large Casting-net , well leaded ; let not the Meshes from the Crown to a full yard and a half be too small ; for then if the Pond be any thing of a depth, the fish will strike away before the Net comes to ground : the whole Net ought to have a very large Mesh, well leaded, and deep tucked.

The second thing to be done is, to make the place clean from Stakes and Bushes, and try with the Net before you intend for the sport : if your Net happen to hang, then all your pains will prove ineffectual ; therefore you must be sure before you cast in your Net that you clear and cleanse the place very well twice or thrice with a Rake. Then take a quarter of a peck of Wheat, baking it well in an Oven, putting in near three quarts of Water ; when it is well baked, take five pints of Blood, and incorporate the Wheat and Blood together, adding thereto as much Bran as is sufficient to make a Paste thereof : and that it may the better hold together, put some Clay to it ; after this, knead it well together with a quart of Lob-worms chopt in pieces, and worked into a Paste as aforesaid : then roll it into balls as big as a Goose-egg, and throw it into the Pond within the circumference of your
Casting-

Casting-net; and between whiles throw in some Grains; and when you think the fish have found out the Bainting-place, then come in the close of the Evening (having baited very early in the Morning) and cast your Net over the baited place : then take a long pole with a large Fork made for the purpose, and stir all about the Net; for the *Carps* and *Tench* are struck up beyond their Eyes in Mud, and stand exactly upon their Heads : let the Net lie neer an half hour, still stirring with your Pole, if the place be not too deep: when you have covered the Fish, you may go into the Pond, and take them out with your hands; but if the water be deep, when you finde the *Carps* begin to stir, (for they cannot stand long on their heads in the Mud) then lift up the Crown of your Net bolt upright with a long Staff, that so the fish may play into the Tuck of the Net.

Here note, that should you draw up your Net suddenly after you have cast it in, it is an hundred pound to a penny whether you should take one *Carp* or *Tench*; but letting the Net lie, the Mud will choak them if they remove not out of it.

Now here I cannot omit a very pleasant story in my opinion : A Gentleman having especial *Carps* in his pond, but not knowing how to take one of them, unless it were by chance with Hook and Line; I desired him that we might taste of his *Carps*, and modestly told him, a brace of them would serve our turns : He answered me, I might freely have them, if I knew how to catch them. Hereupon I prepared some ingredients, and having baited a convenient place very early in the Morning, at the dusk of the Evening we came with a Casting-net, and at the first throw covered a great quantity of fish, as hereafter will appear; but not one seem'd to stir a jot under the Net, being all struck into the Mud. Hereupon the Gentleman

fell

fell a laughing heartily, saying, *Sir, If I had no other provision to trust to but what fish you shall catch this night, I believe I shall go supperless to Bed.* Hearing him say so, I desired that he would have a little patience, for the fish were asleep, and I was as yet loath to disturb them ; but half an hour hence, if he would stay so long, I should make bold to awake them with a witness : So the Gentleman having smoaked a pipe of Tobacco, a *Carp* began to play in the Net ; and after this in a very little time a great many more began to dance and skip : whereupon I lifted up the Crown, that they might play in the Tuck ; and when I thought they were all got out of the Mud I began to draw, and at one draught drew up in the Net seventy odde *Carps*, great and small, to the admiration and great satisfaction of the Owner and the rest of the company, having in all their life-time not seen the like before.

The *Tench* hath but small Scales, (and they smooth) yet very large Fins, with a red Circle about his Eyes, and a little Barb hanging at each corner of his Mouth.

The Slime of a *Tench* is very medicinal to wounded Fishes ; and therefore he is commonly called the *Fishes Physician.*

The *Pike* is so sensible of his vertue, that he will not injure the *Tench*, though he will seize on any other fish of his size that comes in his way : And when the *Pike* is sick or hurt, he applies himself to the *Tench*, and findes cure by rubbing himself against him.

The *Tench* hath a greater love for Ponds than clear Rivers, and delights himself amongst Weeds, and loves to feed in very foul Water ; and yet his food is nourishing and pleasant.

The time of Angling for him is early and late, both morning and eveing, in the moneths of *June, July* and *August* ; or all night in the still parts of the River.

He

He is a great lover of large red Worms, and will
bite most eagerly at them, if you first dip them
in Tar. The *Tench* loves also all sorts of Paste
made up with strong-sented Oils, or with Tar, or a
Paste made of brown Bread and Honey. He will
bite also at a Cad-worm, a Lob-worm, a Flag-worm,
green Gentle, Cad-bait, Marsh-worm, or soft boil'd
Bread-grain.

Of the TORCOTH.

THe *Torcoth* is a fish having a red Belly, but of what
estimation I know not; for that, let the Welshmen
speak, who best know him: for as I have heard he is
only to be found in the pool *Lin-peris* in *Carnarvan-shire.*
I only name him, that you may know there is such a fish.

Of the TROUT.

IT is observed that the *Trout* comes in and goes out
of season with the Stag and Buck, and spawns a-
bout *October* or *November:* which is the more to be
wondred at, because most other fish spawn in warm
weather, when the Sun by his heat hath adapted
the Earth and Water, making them fit for generation.

All the Winter the *Trout* is Sick, Lean and
unwholsome, and you shall frequently then finde
him Louzy. These Trout-lice are a small Worm
with a big Head sticking close to his sides, and sucking moisture from him that gave them being: and he
is not freed from them till the Spring or the beginning
of Summer, at which time his strength increaseth; and
then he deserteth the still deep waters, and betakes
him

himself to gravelly ground, against which he never leaves rubbing till he hath cleansed himself of his Louziness; and then he delights to be in the sharp Streams, and such as are swift, where he will lie in wait for *Minnows* and *May-flies*; at the latter end of which Moneth he is in his prime, being better and fatter in that Moneth, especially at the latter end thereof, than in any other throughout the whole year.

There are several sorts of *Trouts* highly prizable; as the *Fordidge-Trout*, the *Amerly-Trout*, a *Bull-Trout* in *Northumberland*, with many more which I shall forbear to mention, but onely tell you what is generally observed; and that is, that the red and yellow *Trouts* are the best; and as to the sex, the Female is the best, having a less Head and a deeper Body than the Male. By their Hog-back you shall know that they are in season, with the like note for all other fish.

The *Trout* is usually caught with a Worm, *Minnow*, or Fly natural or artificial. There are several sorts of Worms which are Baits for the Angler; the Earthworm, the Dug-worm, the Maggot or Gentle; but for the *Trout*, the Lob-worm and Brandling are the best, or Squirrel-tail, having a red Head, streakt down the Back, and a broad Tail. The Brandling is found commonly in an old Dung-hill, Cow-dung, Hogsdung, or Tanners-bark. Here note, that whatever Worms you fish withal are the better for keeping; which must be in an Earthen pot with Moss, which you must change often in Summer, that is, once in three or four daies, and in twice as long time in Winter.

When you fish for a *Trout* by hand on the ground, take a Lob-worm and clap your Hook into him a little above the middle, and out again a little below the same; then draw your Worm above the arming of your Hook, making your first entrance at the Tail end, that the point of the Hook may come out at the Head-end.

When you fish with a *Minnow*, take the whiteft and middle-fized, for thofe are the beft, and place him fo on your Hook, that he may turn round when he is drawn againft the Stream.

The beft Inftructions (for putting the *Minnow* on the Hook) which I can lay down are thefe: Put your Hook in at his Mouth and out at his Gill, drawing it through about three Inches; then put the Hook again into his Mouth, and let the point and beard come out at his Tail; then the Hook and his Tail you muft tie about with a fine white Thread, and let the body of the *Minnow* be almoft ftraight on the Hook: then try againft the Stream whether it will turn; where note, it cannot turn too faft. If you want a *Minnow*, a fmall *Loach* or *Sticklebag* will ferve the turn: if none of thefe can be gotten, you may in their feafon have an Artificial one made of Cloath by one that is living, which I have found to be every whit as good a Bait as what are natural.

If you fifh with a Natural or Artificial Fly, then follow fuch directions as I have already prefcribed in a foregoing Chapter, which particularly difcourfes of Flies Natural and Artificial.

Of the UMBER.

IT is the opinion of fome, that the *Umber* and *Grailing* differ onely in Names, and are of a *Trout*-kind, but feldom grow to the bignefs of a *Trout*, I having never feen nor heard any exceed the length of eighteen Inches.

He frequents fuch Rivers as the *Trouts* do, and is taken with the fame Baits, efpecially the Fly;

and,

and, being a simple Fish, is more bold than the *Trout* is.

In the Winter he absconds himself, but after *April* he appears abroad, and is very gamesome and pleasant. He is very tender-mouth'd, and therefore quickly lost after he is struck. For what more may be said, I refer you to the Chapter of the *Grailing*.

THus have I given you an Alphabetical and summary account of the Nature of Fish, and the several ways to take them, according to ancient and modern experience: I shall onely give you more a short discovery of their Haunts; and so I shall conclude this Treatise.

Next to the Art of taking Fish, the knowledge of their Haunts and proper places to finde them in according to their kinds is rightly to be considered: for not knowing what Rivers or what parts of them are fittest for your Baits, or what Baits best sute with each River and the fish therein contained, you onely angle at adventure, and, instead of reaping satisfaction, you onely lose your pains and your labour.

Wherefore in the first place you are to understand, that fishes change places with the season. Some in the Summer keep always neer the top or rim of the Water; others are continually at the bottom. For the first, you may angle with a Float, or Fly; the latter are to be found at the Arches of Bridges, Mill-ponds, Wears, Floud-gates, &c. In Winter all fish in general fly into deep Waters.

The *Barbel, Roach, Dace,* and *Ruff* delight in sandy gravelly ground. The deepest part of the River and the Shadows of Trees are equally grateful.

The *Bream, Pike,* and *Chub* choose a Clay and Ouzie ground. The *Bream* delights most in the midst of a
                                        River

River whose Stream is not too rapid, but gently gliding: the *Pike* is for still Waters full of Fry; and that he may the better and securer seize his Prey, he frequently absconds himself amongst Water-docks, under Bushes or Bull-rushes.

Carp, *Tench*, and *Eel* frequent still Waters, and what are foul and muddy. *Eels* lie lurking under Roots or Stones: The *Carp* is for the deepest place of the Water; and where there are green Weeds the *Carp* and *Tench* delight most of all.

Pearch delight in gentle Streams not too deep, yet they must not be shallow; and a hollow Bank is their chiefest refuge.

Gudgeons love sandy ground in gentle Streams, they affect small Rivers above the large, or small Brooks, and bite best in the Spring till they spawn.

The *Salmon* delights most in Rivers which ebb and flow, are large, and have a swift current; in such Rivers are the greatest plenty. If the Rivers are rocky or weedy, so much the better.

Shad, *Thwait*, *Plaice*, and *Flounder* have the greatest love for salt or brackish Waters which ebb and flow.

The *Umber* affects Marly Clay grounds, clear and swift Streams; but they must then be far from the Sea, for they seldom come near it.

There are many more Rules to be observed, which generally hold good, but I will not conclude them infallible, since I have found some of them (well credited) very false; wherefore let every man's experience be his guide in the knowledge of the nature of Rivers, and the Fish their Inhabitants. And therefore it will be very requisite for him that would be compleat in the Art of Angling, diligently to observe whatever River or water he fisheth in, whether it be

muddy,

muddy, slimy, stony, gravelly, swift, or of a slow motion.
And as he must have a competent knowledge in Rivers,
Ponds, or all fishable waters he is acquainted with;
so must he know the nature of each Fish, and what
Baits are most proper for every kinde, or he shall never
attain to the reputation of a good experienced A N G-
L E R.

I shall conclude this Treatise with the experimental observations of an ingenious Gentleman, who hath
practiced the Art of Fishing many years, and therefore the more fit to give Directions for the right use
of the Angle.

Experi-

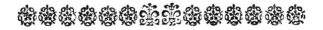

Experimental Observations and useful Directions for the right use of the Angle ; and is a true and brief Epitome of the whole Art and Mystery of the Fishing Recreation.

NOne certainly is so ignorant to address himself to the River for Recreation, but he will be mindful to carry necessary Tackle with him : being compleatly furnished therewith, let him in the first place consult Sun, Wind, Moon, Stars, and change of Air ; for without observing Times and Seasons, his Tackle, though never so good, will prove ineffectual.

Wherefore observe, if the Sun be obscured with Clouds, and his Face hidden from your Eyes, then set forth your Ground-baits, and use your brightest Flies. If the Sun shine out gloriously, then use the darkest of your Flies. Here note,

> *If that the Wind be in the South,*
> *It blows the Fly in the* Trout's *Mouth.*

If the weather be warm, it is no matter in what point of the Compass the Wind lieth, so that it blow not too high; the same observation holds good at Night as well as Day. If the Sun shine bright, the Moon prove clear, or the Stars glitter, there is but little sport to be expected.

Gentlemen, I write to you that have more than common experience in the Art of Angling, and therefore I hope you will not expect that I should here inform you how to prosecute the little recreation of the *Thames*, how to catch *Bleak*, *Dace*, &c. since there is hardly any young beginner that is ignorant thereof: Wherefore, omitting such trifling discourse, I shall fall upon that which is somewhat more material, and first, how to take *Eels*. When the Angler stays a night or two, let him take five or six Lines, (or what number he thinks fit) each of them about sixteen yards long, and at every two yards long make a Noose to hang an Hook armed either to double Thread, or Silk-twist, for it is better than Wyre. His Hooks must be baited with *Millers-thumbs*, *Loaches*, *Minnows*, or *Gudgeons* : to every Noose there must be a Line baited, and all the Lines must lie cross the River in the deepest place, either with Stones, or pegged lying in the bottom. He must bait his Hooks with a small Needle, and must make two Flies; the Palmer rubbed with Silver or Gold, and the *May-fly*, both which are the ground of all Flies.

In the making of the Palmer-Fly he must arm his Line on the inside of the Hook; then with a pair of Sizers let him cut so much of the brown of a Mallard's Feathers as he shall think sufficient to make the Wings; then let him lay the outermost part of the Feather next the Hook, and the point of the Feather towards the Shank of the Hook ; let him whip it three or four times about the Hook with the same Silk he armed the Hook; then make his Silk fast : Then let him take the Hackle of the

Neck

Neck of a Cock or Capon , (but a Plovers Top is
best) and let him take off the one side of the Feather; then he must take the Hackle-silk , or Gold
or Silver-Thread; and let him make all these fast
at the bent of the Hook , working them up to the
Wings; every bout shifting his Fingers, and making
a stop, then the Gold will fall right , and let him
make it fast : Then work up the Hackle to the same
place, and make it fast: after this let him take the
Hook betwixt his Finger and Thumb in the left hand
with Needle or Pin, and part the Wings in twain;
then with the Arming-silk (having fastned all hi-
therto) let him whip it about as it falleth cross between the Wings, and with his Thumb he must
turn the point of the Feather towards the bent of
the Hook : then let him work it three or four times
about the Shank, so fasten it , and view the proportion for other Flies.

If he make the grounds of Hogs-wooll , sandy,
black, or white, or Bears-wooll, or of a red Bullock
two years old , he must work these grounds on a wax-
ed Silk , and must arm and set on the Wings as a-
foresaid.

The body of the *May-fly* must be wrought with some
of these grounds , which will do admirably well,
when ribbed with black Hair. The *Oak-fly* he must
make with Orange-Tawny and Black, for the body,
and the brown of the *Mallard*'s Feather for the Wings.

He that will take a *Pearch* must first take notice that
this fish feeds well, and bites freely. Let the Angler o-
ver-night bait his ground with Lobworms chopt in
pieces; and in the morning let him come to the place,
where he must first plumb his ground , then gage
his Line and bait his hook with a red knotted worm, or
a *Minnow*,which is better in my opinion : the hook must
be put in at the back of the *Minnow* betwixt the fish and

L 3
th:

the skin, that the *Minnow* may swim up and down alive, being buoyed up with a Cork or Quill, that the *Minnow* may have liberty to swim a foot off the ground. Let these directions be carefully observed and followed, and the Angler need not fear the frustration of his expectations.

The next thing to be considered, is the Floating for Scale-fish in Pond or River: First, take notice that the Feed brings the fish together, as the Sheep to the Pen; and there is no better in all Angling for Feed, than Bloud and Grains; though Paste is good, yet inferiour to these.

Next, let him observe to plumb his ground, Angling with fine Tackles, as single hair for half the Line next the Hook, round and small plumb'd according to his Float. There is a small red worm with a yellow tip on his Tail, which is an excellent bait for this sort of fish or any other. Other special baits are these: Brandlings, Gentles, Paste or Cadice (otherwise called Cock-bait.) They lie in a gravelly husk under the stones in the River.

There is a way of Trowling for *Pike* with an Hazle-rod of twelve foot long, with a Ring of wyre on the top of the Rod for the Line to run thorough: within two foot of the bottom of the Rod there is a hole made to put in a Winde to turn with a Barrel, to gather up the Line and loose it at pleasure: This is the best manner of Trowling.

There is another way to take more *Pikes* either in Mere, Pond, or River, than any Trowler with his Rod can do; which is done after this manner:

Take a forked stick with a Line of twelve yards long wound upon it; at the upper end leave about a yard, either to tie a bunch of Sags or a Bladder to buoy up the fish, and to carry it from the ground. The Bait must be a live fish, either *Dace*, *Gudgeon*, *Roach*, or small *Trout*: The forked stick must have a slit in

the

the one fide of the Fork to put in the Line, that he may fet his live fifh to fwim at a gage, that when a *Pike* taketh the Bait, he may have the full liberty of the Line for his feed.   He may turn thefe loofe either in Pond or River : in the Pond with the Wind all day long, the more the better : At night let him fet fome fmall weight that may ftay the Buoy till the fifh taketh it.

For the River he muft turn all loofe with the Stream ; the Hooks muft be double, the Shanks muft be fomewhat fhorter than ordinary ; for the fhorter the Hook is off the Shank, without doubt it will lefs hurt the fifh : and it muft be armed with fmall Wyre well foftned ; but certainly a Hook armed with twifted Silk is better.

If you arm your Hook with Wyre, the Needle muft be made with an eye ; then muft he take one of thofe living baits, and with one of his Needles enter within a Straws breadth of the Gill of the fifh, fo pull the Needle betwixt the Skin and the Fifh ; then pull the Needle out at the hindmoft Fin, and draw the Arming thorough the fifh, until the Hook come to lie clofe to the Fifh's Body : having fo done, let him put off in Mere or Pond with the Wind ; in the River with the Stream : The more that he pulls off in Mere or Pond, he is the likelier to have the greater paftime.

There is a time when *Pikes* go a Frogging in Ditches, and in the River to Sun them, as in *May*, *June*, and *July* ; at thefe times you fhall hardly mifs one in twenty ; and thus muft the Angler deal with them. Let him take a Line of feven or eight foot, and let him arm a large Hook of the largeft fize that is made, and arm it to his Line ; let him lead the fhank of his Hook neatly, of fuch a weight that he may guide the Hook at his pleafure.   He may ftrike the *Pike* that he fees with the bare Hook where he pleafes.   This Line and Hook doth far exceed Snaring.   L 4   In

In the taking of a *Carp* either in Pond or River, if the Angler intends to adde profit to his pleasure, he must take a peck of Ale-Grains and a good quantity of any Blood, and mix the Grains together, with which let him bait the Ground wherein he intends to Angle. This feed will wonderfully attract the Scale-fish, as *Carp*, *Tench*, *Roach*, *Dace*, and *Bream*. In the Morning early let him prosecute his pastime, plumming his ground, and Angling for a *Carp* with a strong Line: the Bait must be either Paste, or a knotted red Worm; by this means he shall finde sport enough.

In the taking of a *Trout* with Ground-baits thus must the Angler do: In the first place he must have a neat taper Rod, light before, with a tender Hazle top. He may angle with a single hair of five lengths, one tied to the other for the bottom of the Line, and a Line of three hair'd links for the upper part; and so if he have room enough he may take the largest *Trout* that swims. He that angles with a Line made of three hair'd links at the bottom, and more at the top, may take *Trouts*; but he that angles with one Hair, shall take five *Trouts* to the other's one: For this Fish is very quick-sighted; therefore the Angler both Day and Night must keep out of sight. He must angle with the point of his Rod down the Stream.

He must begin to angle in *March* with the Ground-baits all day long: but if it prove clear and bright, he must take the Morning and Evening, or else his labour will be in vain.

He that angles with Ground-baits, must set his Tackles to his Rod, and begin at the upper end of the Stream, carrying his Line with an upright hand, feeling the Plummet running on the ground some ten Inches from the Hook, plumming his Line according to the

swift-

swiftness of the Stream that he angles in ; for one Plummet will not serve for all streams.

For his Bait let him take the red knotted Worm, which is very good where Brandlings are not to be had. The *Minnow* (or as some call it a *Penk*) is a singular Bait for a *Trout* ; for he will come as boldly at it as a Mastiff-dog at a Bear. It will be advantageous to him in his angling to use a Line made of three Silks and three Hairs twisted for the uppermost part of the Line, and two Silks and two Hairs twisted for the bottom next the Hook, with a Swivel nigh to the middle of his Line, with an indifferent large hook. Let him bait his hook with a *Minnow*, putting the hook through the lowermost part of his mouth, so draw the Hook through ; then put the hook in at the mouth again, and let the point of the hook come out at the hindmost Fin ; then let him draw his Line, and the *Minnows* mouth will close, that no Water will get into his Belly. As I said before, he must angle with the point of his Rod down the Stream, drawing the *Minnow* up the Stream by little and little nigh the top of the Water : the *Trout* seeing the bait will come most fiercely at it ; but the Angler must not then presently strike : this is a true way without Lead ; for many times they will come to the Lead, and forsake the *Minnow*.

The next direction is how to angle with a Flie. In the first place let the Angler fit himself with a Hazle of one piece or two set conveniently together, light and pliable. The lower part of his Line next the Fly must be of three or four hair'd Links ; but if he can attain (as aforesaid) to angle with a single Hair, he shall meet with more profit and pleasure.

Before he begin to angle, having the wind on his back , let him trie how far he can cast his Line, or at what length his Fly , and let him be careful
that

that the Fly fall firſt on the Water ; for if any of the Line light upon the Water, he had better to have ſtood ſtill than to have thrown at all. He muſt always caſt down the Stream, with the Wind behinde and the Sun before him ; it is a great advantage to have either Sun or Moon before him.

March is the moneth for him to begin to angle with the Flie ; but if the Weather prove windy or cloudy, there are ſeveral ſorts of Palmers that are good at that time : The firſt is a black Palmer ribbed with Silver : The ſecond a black Palmer with an Orange-tawny Body : Thirdly, a Palmer whoſe body is all black : Laſtly, there is a red Palmer ribbed with Gold , and a red Huckle mixed with Orange Cruel. Theſe Flies ſerve all the year long Morning and Evening , whether Windy or Cloudy Weather. But if the Air prove ſerene, he may then imitate the Hawthorn-fly, which is all black and very ſmall, and the ſmaller the better.

In *May* let him take the *May*-fly and imitate that, which is made ſeveral ways : Some make them with a ſhammy Body, 'tis beſt with black Hair : Others make them with ſandy Hogs-wooll, ribbed with black Silk., and winged with a *Mallards* Feather ſeveral ways, according to the humour of the Angler. Another called the *Oak-fly* , is made of Orange-coloured Cruel, and black, with a brown Wing. Laſtly, there is another Fly , the Body whereof is made of the ſtrain of a Peacock's Feather , which is very good in a bright day. Theſe ſeveral ſorts of Flies will ſerve the whole year, obſerving the times and ſeaſons.

Here note, that the lighteſt Flies are for cloudy and dark Weather, the darkeſt for bright and light, and the reſt for indifferent ſeaſons, for which his own Judgement , Diſcretion , and Experience muſt guide him.

Of

Of late days the Hogs-wooll of several colours, the Wooll of a red Heifer and Bears-wooll are made use of, which make good grounds, and excellent pastime.

The *Natural-fly* is a sure way of Angling to augment the Anglers Recreation. Now how to find them take notice that the *May-fly* is to be found playing at the River-side, especially against the Rain.

The *Oak-fly* is to be found on the But of an Oak, or an Ash, from the beginning of *May* to the end of *August* : It is a brownish Flie, and stands always with his head towards the Root of the Tree, very easie to be found.

The *Black-fly* is to be found on every Hawthornbush, after the Buds are come forth.

Now with these Flies he must use such a Rod as to angle with the Ground-bait : the Line must not be as long as the Rod.

Let the Angler withdraw his Flie as he shall finde it most convenient and advantageous in his Angling. When he comes to deep Water (whose motion is but slow) let him make his Line about two yards long, and dop his Fly behinde a Bush, and he shall finde incomparable sport.

The way to make the best Paste, is to take a convenient quantity of fresh Butter, as much Sheeps-suet that is fresh, a sufficient quantity of the strongest Cheese can be gotten, with the pith of an old stale white Loaf : Let all these be beaten in a Mortar till they come to a perfect Paste ; and when the Angler intends to spend some time in Angling, let him put hereof the quantity of a green Pea upon his Hook, and let him observe what pleasant effects it will produce.

An

An Angling SONG.

COme lay by your cares, and hang up all sorrow,
   Let's Angle to day, and ne're think of to morrow ;
And by the Brook-side as we Angle along,
Wee'l cheer up our selves with our sport and a Song.

Sometimes on the Grass our selves we will lay,
And see how the watery Citizens play ;
Sometimes with a Fly stand under a Tree,
And chuse out what Fish our Captives shall be:

Thus void of all care we're more happy than they
That sit upon Thrones and Kingdoms do sway ;
For Scepters and Crowns disquiet still bring,
But the Man that's content is more blest than a King.

An

An Abstract of such penal

STATUTES

As relate to

F.ISHING.

13. **E** Dw. 1. cap. 47. No Salmons shall be taken from the Nativity of our Lady unto St. Martin's Day. Young Salmons may not be destroy'd nor taken by Nets nor other Engines, at Mill-pools from the midst of April until St. John Baptist. The Penalties you may see in the said Statute at large.

I. Eliz. cap. 17. None shall take and kill any young Brood, Spawn, or Fry of Eels, Salmon, Pike, or any other Fish, in any Flood-gate, Pipe at the tail of a Mill, Wear, or in any Straights, Streams, Brooks, Rivers fresh or salt. Nor take or kill any Salmons, or Trouts not being in season, being Kipper Salmons, or Kipper Trouts, Shedder Salmons, or Shedder Trouts.

II. None shall take and kill any Pike or Pickeril not being in length ten inches Fish, nor Salmon not being in length sirteen inches Fish, nor Trout under eight inches, nor Barbel under twelve inches.

III. None shall take Fish with any manner of Trammel, &c. in any River or other places,

places, but onely with Net or Trammel, whereof every Mesh or Mask shall be two inches and ½ broad. Angling excepted.

IV. Nevertheless this Statute allows Smelts, Loaches, Minnows, Gudgeons, Eeles, &c. to be taken by Net, &c. in such places, and such ways as heretofore they have been.

V. The penalty for every offence is 20 s. and the Fish so taken, as also the Engine or device whatsoever whereby the offence was committed.

5 Eliz. cap. 21. None may by day or night break down, cut out, or destroy any Head or Dam of any Ponds, Pools, Motes, &c. where any Fish shall be put in or stored with-al by the owners thereof. Nor shall Take, Kill, or Steal away any of the said Fish in the said Ponds, &c. against the will of the Owner.

22 & 23 Car. 2. cap. 25. It is not lawful for any person to use any Casting-net, Thief-net, Trammel, Shove-net, or other Net; nor to use any Angle, Hair, Noose, Spear, or Trowl: Nor to lay any Nets, Wears, Pots, Fish-hooks, or other Engines; Or to take any Fish by any other means or device whatsoever, in any River, Sew, Pond, Mote, or other Water; Nor be aiding or assisting thereunto, without the License or consent of the Lord or Owner of the said Water. And in case any person be convict of any of these Offences, by his own confes-sion, or by Oath of one sufficient Witness, within

within one Moneth after the Offence be committed, before any Justice of the Peace of such County, Riding, Division, or Place, wherein such be committed; every such person in Taking, Stealing, or Killing Fish, shall for every such Offence give to the party or parties grieved or injured such recompence for his or their Damages, and within such time as the said Justice shall appoint, not exceeding treble Damages: And over and above pay down presently unto the Overseers for the Poor where such Offence is committed, such sum of Money, not exceeding 10 s. as the said Justice shall think meet. And in default of payment, as aforesaid, the same to be levied by distress and sale of the Offenders Goods, by Warrant under the Hand and Seal of such Justice before whom the Offender shall be convicted, rendring the overplus, if any be: And for want of Distress the Offender or Offenders shall be committed to the House of Correction, for such time as the Justice shall think fit, not exceeding one Moneth, unless the party offending shall enter into Bond with one competent Surety or Sureties to the party injured, not exceeding ten pounds, never to offend in like manner.

II. And every Justice of Peace, before whom such Offender shall be convict, may take, cut in pieces, and destroy all such Angles, Spears, Hairs, Noses, Trowls, Wears, Pots, Fish-hooks, Nets, or other Engines whatsoever, wherewith such Offender as aforesaid shall be taken or apprehended.

III.

III. Nevertheless, any person aggrieved may appeal to the Justices of Peace in their next quarter Sessions; who may give relief, and make such Order therein as shall be agreable to the Tenor of this Act: whose Order therein shall be final, if no title of Land, Royalty, or Fishery be therein concerned.

FINIS.

THE
TABLE
FOR
HUNTING:
Being the First PART.

L   Of

The TABLE.

Of

The TABLE.

M 2   The

THE
TABLE
FOR
HAWKING:
Being the Second PART.

The TABLE.

wea-

Of

The T A B L E.

The

THE
TABLE
FOR
FOWLING:

Being the Third PART.

In

The TABLE.

The TABLE.

THE

THE
TABLE
FOR
FISHING:

Being the Fourth and Laſt PART.

Of

The TABLE.

F I N I S.